Industrial
Model Building

Industrial
Model Building

LOUIS GARY LAMIT

and

ENGINEERING MODEL ASSOCIATES, INC.

PRENTICE-HALL, INC., *Englewood Cliffs, New Jersey 07632*

Library of Congress Cataloging in Publication Data

Lamit, Louis Gary
    Industrial model building.

    Includes index.
      1. Engineering models. 2. Design, Industrial.
I. Engineering Model Associates. II. Title.
TA177.L35   624′.0228   80-23671
ISBN 0-13-461566-2

Editorial/Production supervision and interior design
    by Barbara A. Cassel
Cover design by Jayne Conte
Page makeup by Diane Koromhas
Manufacturing buyer: Anthony Caruso

Printed in the United States of America

10 9 8 7 6 5 4 3 2 1

Prentice-Hall International, Inc., *London*
Prentice-Hall of Australia Pty. Limited, *Sydney*
Prentice-Hall of Canada, Ltd., *Toronto*
Prentice-Hall of India Private Limited, *New Delhi*
Prentice-Hall of Japan, Inc., *Tokyo*
Prentice-Hall of Southeast Asia Pte. Ltd., *Singapore*
Whitehall Books Limited, *Wellington, New Zealand*

For Margie, Angie, Corina, and Jamie

Contents

1
Engineering Process Models and Design Modeling

2
Model Descriptions

3
Information Flow and Model Chronology

4
Industrial Design (Drafting and Modeling)

5
Academic Modeling Programs

6
Model Facility Requirements and Considerations (Industry and Schools)

7
Modeling Tools

Preface

Industrial Model Building is based on the author's experience teaching piping drafting and industrial modeling at the college level. This text is primarily a synthesis of Engineering Model Associates' two books, *The Model Procedure Manual* and the *Design Model Training Manual*. These two books appear in their entirety within this book. Also, various parts of the author's text, *Piping Systems Drafting and Design*, appear throughout the book. Almost all information that is available on modeling at the present date is provided herein. In general, piping drafting and design information in theory have been elimi-

nated because of its appearance in *Piping Systems Drafting and Design*.

Sections 1 to 24 cover modeling information, including the types of industrial models, the how-to-do aspects of modeling, background information, tools, components, construction methods, tagging, photography, crating, job availability, and so on—all the information that is necessary for the education of a model technician or a piping designer wishing to emphasize modeling. Sections 25 to 32 provide the student with a series of projects, including EMA's design training model in Section 25. Section 26 simply refers to

Engineering Model Associates' new *Introduction to Design Modeling* and does not include the drawings. A series of drawings and instructions are provided in EMA's kit.

Sections 27 to 32 provide a wide variety of modeling projects, including petrochemical, fossil-fuel power generation, nuclear power, geothermal power, and solar power installations. These projects are designed for individuals or groups, depending on the complexity of the project and the time allotted for the student to complete the project. Sections 33 to 35 give background information, such as a model glossary, abbreviations, piping drafting symbols, and essential piping information. Besides being a combination and synthesis of Engineering Model Associates' two books and the author's previous text, other materials and procedures have been included. This book has been designed basically as a companion text to *Piping Systems Drafting and Design*, which covers all forms of piping drafting for industrial installations, including drafting and design, pipe supports, isometrics, layout and development of views of petrochemical, power plants, and other types of industrial installations. It would benefit students to have a copy of *Piping Systems Drafting and Design* so as to acquaint themselves with overall theory and specifications.

Industrial modeling is being presented here as one of the newest innovations available to industry. Consider this comparison. To study the routing of a single piping system or structural configuration, it may be necessary to consult any number of drawings and views, then arrange them mentally to visualize image. In the process, any number of misconceptions can occur—but not so with a model. The system or configuration under study is totally visible from any angle or view, leaving nothing to the imagination. The image is instant and clear and can readily be photographed for distribution. Thousands of drawings may be required for industrial projects, whereas a series of models can easily convey the necessary information. Modeling has shown itself to be one of the most efficient, time-saving, and cost-saving devices available to the modern industrial firm. The need for modelers, piping designers, and model technicians grows daily with the increasing use of modeling as a design tool. Upon the completion of this text, the student should be sufficiently trained to take a position in industry that will provide a lucrative career for a serious-minded person. The goal of this text is to train individuals in the use of models as a design medium, including training in the model shop and in piping design, covering everything from essential knowledge of materials and tools, bases, and tables to the intricate piping of the model associated with the design level. Instruction in the use of tools, of course, cannot come through a book but must be provided by the instructor. All aspects of safety, materials, tools, and components have been presented as thoroughly as possible, together with the essential nature of modeling, such as the construction of components, fabrication of vessels, piping installation, and tagging. Because of the rapid increase in the number and size of our power-generation systems, and the continual demand for petrochemical products, the need for trained technicians, drafters, and modelers has become more urgent. With modeling taking over many of the drafting and design areas in these heavy industries, the possibilities are becoming unlimited for a person trained in this field.

A sincere appreciation is hereby conveyed to all who have helped in compiling this book. Hopefully, students and instructors who utilize the text will forward corrections or constructive comments for future publications or revisions.

Louis Gary Lamit
Engineering Model Associates, Inc.

Acknowledgements

The author is extremely grateful for the photographs provided by various industrial sources. An appropriate credit line identifies contributors to the text.

Special thanks is due to Herbert A. Wanderman of Engineering Model Associates, Inc., who granted full permission to include in their entirety *The Model Procedure Manual* and *Design Model Training Manual*. In reality, this text is a cooperative effort between EMA and myself.

Art McCoy and Charles Bliss, both representatives of EMA during production of this book, were extremely helpful in gathering materials and providing industrial contacts.

I thank the following students for providing drawings used throughout the book: Steve Dung, Pak Kelly, Ray Mariano, George Pompakais, Mark Russel, Pat Scheetz, David Ugalde, and Jeff Wise.

Sincere appreciation is here conveyed to my typist, Sherran Boll.

The author is also grateful to Nils C. Neklason, Head of Mission College's model program.

Industrial
Model Building

Introduction

WHEN?

A model is justified, and indeed necessary, when complexity, high investment due to exotic materials, language differences, limited space, or hazardous conditions are a factor, or if there exists the possibility of misunderstanding or misinterpretation. There is no "rule of thumb" dictating when or if a model is justified. The judgment is purely a matter of evaluation based on experience. Frequently, the reversal of the decision not to model a "simple tank farm" has proven wise when interference problems, bad design, or bad planning are revealed. Perhaps it would be more correct if the approach were: When is a model not justified?

WHO?

Companies that operate, plan, design, engineer, construct, or maintain a complex plant all share the requirement for an economical means of achieving optimum design, safety, and meeting "on-stream" target dates. A "complex plant" can be an oil refinery, chemical plant, fossil-fuel or nuclear power plant, or any of the dozens of others in the fields of pulp and paper, food processing, metallurgy, pharmaceuticals, shipbuilding, plastics, and so on.

Each company is unique and tailors its model program to its own functions, management philosophies, and customer requirements. Each varies,

1

too, in the degree of its commitment to relatively new design concepts. There is enough history and experience now, however, to permit standardization of many of the methods and materials of this engineering medium, which in turn makes it easier for new firms to decide to follow suit.

WHERE?

Model programs have been adapted by virtually every major engineering company in the world. Languages and systems of measurement are of no consideration. In Europe it is not uncommon to see a design model in a drafting room with designers conversing in six different languages and working with ASA standards to metric dimensions.

HOW?

That is what this book is all about!

ENGINEERING SCALE MODELS

Many of us, when we hear the term "scale model," think back to the days of our youth when we were building airplanes or model railroads. Many people still think of all scale models as being toys, or perhaps a sales gimmick, rather than an actual engineering tool. Today, virtually every major engineering and construction company in the world has some involvement with engineering scale models.

Many engineering/construction companies build models to demonstrate to their clients the complicated intricacies of the project they are proposing. Some companies build models simply because their customers (aware of the benefits of modeling) demand them. Most companies building models, however, are doing so because they realize that they can achieve optimal design and construction by using a model as a design tool. They save both time and money. Today, every scientific or engineering discipline uses models to evaluate a given design or to prove out a design before the actual end product is built.

Many engineering companies have adopted the policy of building models on all projects regardless of size. Some, particularly those providing both engineering and construction, have largely reduced their drawing requirements and charge additional fees if the client, for whatever reason, demands the full complement of drawings. Some companies have developed model photography

procedures which adequately compensate for those drawings not provided.

Regardless of the involvement or the degree of sophistication of a company's model program, one highly significant fact is indisputable: an engineering model provides an instant three-dimensional view of the current design status. The benefits of that visibility are obvious and explain why the model is so frequently referred to as a "communications tool." The ultimate benefit of improved communication is far less misunderstanding, fewer omissions, and a far-greater awareness of what has been done and what remains to be done.

Engineering scale models can serve many different purposes. Following are some of the basic functions:

- Hasten plot plan approval
- Improve project design
- Minimize arrangement drawings
- Coordinate design groups
- Facilitate communications
- Expedite decisions
- Shorten design time
- Eliminate interferences
- Arrest costly errors
- Level out drafting peaks
- Speed client approval
- Reduce contingencies in bids
- Train operators
- Schedule erection sequence
- Save fittings and pipe runs
- Valuable sales tool
- Settle labor disputes
- Train designers
- Simplify progress reports
- Assist material take-off

We will narrow the discussion of engineering models in this book to that of equipment and piping arrangement models as used in heavy industrial, refinery, petrochemical, and nuclear and fossil-fuel power facilities. Throughout the remainder of the book we will refer to equipment arrangement and/or piping arrangement models simply as models or engineering models.

The purpose of the book is to instruct engineering students in the effective uses and limitations of models as an engineering tool. It is intended that designers and drafters be trained sufficiently to enable them to present their designs in three dimensions. The emphasis is on developing a working knowledge of the tools and materials used in model construction, as well as developing the ability to think through the model by blending, assembling, and installing pipe, using rough design sketches, which are prepared and used only as necessary to develop design concepts. This will be accomplished through careful study of and work with the uses of preliminary and design models, model base equipment layout, and construction of all components needed to pipe typical process models. This includes heat exchangers, columns, horizontal vessels, pumps, structures, and pipeways. Instruction in all tagging procedures needed for piping design models, pipe bending procedures, various methods used for cutting plastic pipe, familiarization with model components, and working in three dimensions. The ultimate goal of this text will be to help students of design modeling to:

- Become familiar with the uses of design models.
- Think and work in three dimensions.
- Fulfill industry requirements.
- Broaden their piping background.
- Meet the requirements for the A.A. degree in piping design/model building.

What is usually referred to as a design model is actually an engineering model. It is used as a design tool and also as an engineering tool throughout a project by all engineering groups and construction. Through this medium engineers and designers develop their ideas and designs in three dimensions rather than with two-dimensional drawings.

The model is a scale representation of the plant to be constructed and shows equipment, structures, piping, valves and fittings, instrumentation, lighting, and other features necessary for clarifying design. It provides considerable assistance to the construction forces at the job site, and is later used by the client as an operator's training device.

ADVANTAGES OF MODELS

- Communications among individuals, design groups, contractor, and client, and between different nationalities, are improved by the model's aid to visualization.
- Better visualization results in better design as greater use of talent and experience is made.
- Better coordination results from improved communications and leads to quicker deci-

sions and approvals, resulting in a shorter elapsed time required to design and construct plants.

All facets of a project benefit from the use of the model:

- The demonstration of a well-planned equipment arrangement results in a reduction in plant material costs; for example, the optimum routing of piping systems can be readily determined, resulting in a saving in pipe and fittings.
- Construction planning can be worked out in detail, thus facilitating solutions to rigging and erection problems.
- Jurisdictional matters can be foreseen, discussed, and resolved more easily at the model level.
- From the model, subcontractors can see exactly what their assignments are and will often submit lower bids than if they were bidding from drawings alone.
- Startup teams find the model helpful in planning their operations.
- Overall job progress, material requirements, and budget forecasts are more easily determined by use of the model.
- The client can make advantageous use of the model for operator training.

It must be emphasized that engineering models do not provide solutions to all engineering problems, nor are they an end in themselves. They should be appropriately applied to meet the principal engineering objects of designing and constructing a project at the lowest cost consistent with sound engineering practices and overall project requirements and conditions.

PERSONNEL CLASSIFICATION

There are two general classifications for personnel who prepare design models. Those who build the basic model and work largely in the model shop are model technicians. Those who design and install the piping on the model are piping designers. Because the model is an ideal training medium, the normal progression is for the model technician to advance into the piping design group.

Often, models are constructed as after-the-fact or check models from finished piping drawings. Projects of this type are accomplished by model technicians.

Model Technician—
Description of Capabilities

- Knowledge of blueprint reading and sketching
- Familiar with the operations of shop power tools and machinery
- Capable of fabricating bases, structures, and full range of vessels and equipment
- Trained in requirements of detail to be shown
- Capable of reading a variety of discipline drawings, i.e., piping, HVAC, electrical, civil, etc.

Piping Designer—Description of Capabilities

- Knowledge of piping fittings and hardware
- Familiar with piping and instrument diagrams
- Knowledge of piping specifications
- Familiar with vessel and equipment functions
- Capable of designing and installing pipe on models
- Knowledge of considerations for expansion, insulating, and supporting pipe

With the exception of brief descriptions of problems in Sections 25 to 32, piping theory, background, and design projects have been left out of this book. Abbreviations, pipe symbols, and other essential data are provided in the final sections.

Piping Systems Drafting and Design (Prentice-Hall, Inc.) contains a comprehensive treatment of piping background, theory, and so on, and this information is not repeated here. The student should procure a copy of this text for ready reference at school or on the job.

Other modeling and piping information can be obtained from the American Engineering Model Society (AEMS). The brief description of the society that follows has been paraphrased from the *AEMS Model Handbook.*

AMERICAN ENGINEERING MODEL SOCIETY—BACKGROUND AND PURPOSE

The need for an organization capable of bringing together and utilizing the talents of all its members to achieve recognition and understanding of the many uses of engineering models has long been known. It was felt that a society comprised of individual members who shared a common interest in the use of engineering models would become

a major factor in accelerating the acceptance of models as a technical tool. It is the society's objective to promote this technology to the highest degree.

The design model or three-dimensional prototype is perhaps the earliest form of engineering. Primitive man, knowing nothing of the tools available to the engineers and scientists of today, having no written language or numbering system, could still whittle a canoe or prop two sticks together to test their strength. In doing this, primitive man was designing with a model. The impetus of this approach has vastly accelerated since the late 1940s. Because of the rapid development of the design model, the need for an organization such as the American Engineering Model Society became important. Its goals of organizing, standardizing, and publicizing are necessary to attain proper recognition for persons working in this field.

Objectives

The objectives of the organization are:

- To develop and provide practical and technical data, facts, and standards fundamental to the building and use of engineering models
- To promote the interchange of ideas among its members and to arrange for the collection and dissemination of information related to the building and use of engineering models
- To educate the general public regarding the various uses and applications of engineering models in industry, science, and government
- To promote the social and economic welfare and the ethical responsibilities of engineering modelers

ENGINEERING PROCESS MODELS— HISTORY

American industry began to give serious consideration to modeling in the late 1940s and early 1950s. Early models were built primarily to check out designs. In other words, they were used as a check against paper designs. It soon became apparent that models were very useful to discover and prevent interference problems from getting past the early design stage. It is easy to imagine how piping and equipment interference develops on the drawing board when one considers the maze of drawings that one has to comprehend and retain in one's head when laying out a given line. Management quickly observed the benefits that could be derived from the use of models. From the single standpoint of reducing the cost of field changes, modeling was considered worth the expenditure. Modeling virtually eliminated all interference problems at the design level. It has been said that a picture is worth ten thousand words. If this is true, it must also be true that a three-dimensional model is worth at least ten thousand pictures.

The value of these early models for use as a training tool soon became apparent in addition to their value as a design check. Managers then detected that they were putting out unneeded effort by creating extensive plot plans and piping arrangement drawings and then building a model after all the design was complete. These first models were "after-the-fact models" (also referred to as "check models").

In 1951, the first design model was fabricated. A design model is defined as one in which the equipment and structures are placed on the model base and the actual arrangement of the equipment and piping design is carried out directly on the model. This opened up a whole new field of design using the model as an engineering design tool. Working from flow sheets, the appropriate engineering personnel installed the piping and equipment directly on the model base. Vessels and equipment were constructed primarily from wood, while the piping was represented by 1/16″ brass wire with fiber discs threaded over the brass wire to simulate the appropriate pipe diameters. These early models were very time consuming to build compared to the models that we build today as a result of the hand-forming of the brass wire and hand-making of the individual vessels and equipment.

Today it is possible to buy virtually any type of valve, pipe fitting, structure, vessel, and many of the equipment items directly off the shelf. These model components are precision-injection molded plastic parts that can very quickly be solvent-welded to a plastic model base or fastened with nuts and bolts.

The early model designers and fabricators had to be highly skilled, in that brass wire had to be soldered at all the connections and an assortment of nails and tacks were used to simulate various valves and instruments. Although today's model technician or model designer also needs to be skillful, he or she need not be deft in so many areas. Model fabrication techniques consist basically of cutting plastic and of solvent welding. Most of today's piping designers can be trained to be model builder/designers in a relatively short period of time.

Engineering Process Models and Design Modeling

FIGURE 1-1   Design model of fossil-fuel power plant.

Besides being a complete degree program in itself, model building is an engineering design tool that, when possible, should be taught within every piping drafting course so as to introduce the prospective drafter to a field with which he or she will have much contact throughout a career as a draftsperson. Even the smallest drafting room will have sufficient space to enable the construction of a model project by an individual student or group.

Although this book deals with model building as a profession and the wide variety of tools that are useful in a model room, most tools are not absolutely necessary. Any drafting class can set up an inexpensive model area for under $300 with a few basic tools, which will make possible the hand construction of many of the projects that are provided throughout this text. Only the more complicated and larger models will need more sophisticated equipment.

Models are used throughout the industrial piping field as scale representations of various projects that will be constructed. A model shows a piping installation, including valves, fittings, and other components; structural aspects of the complex; equipment; instrumentation; architectural aspects; pipe supports; and so on. A model provides a better understanding of the basic design of any piping installation, and the advantages of a model as a tool for design and checking will become fully apparent as one reads the text.

Because they are three-dimensional representations of an actual piping installation completed to an accurate scale, models eliminate many of the problems encountered in the use of piping drawing. Models provide an opportunity to design piping systems that are better suited for the needs of the particular situation and offer the designer/checker the ability to examine critically all the aspects of the design and construction necessities for the industrial complex in question, thereby eliminating the majority of problems that may be encountered at the material procurement, construction, and installation phases of the job.

Models are not necessary or justified in every piping system design. Their cost, which may be high, is fully justified when the complexity and intricacy of a large industrial complex would cause a problem if only drawings were used. Models enable the transfer of engineering and construction data, transcending language differences and eliminating the majority of interference problems.

The construction of some of the smaller projects provided herein will not, of course, represent what might be encountered in industry as to complexity, but will, nevertheless, provide the student with valuable experience in the use of modeling.

Engineering models are truly a design tool that can eliminate unnecessary problems, bad design, inefficient planning, and other expensive, time-loss situations. They are used throughout the petrochemical, nuclear, and conventional power-generation industries, as well as in food and beverage processing, pulp and paper manufacture, pharmaceutical processing, and other fields.

Traditionally, drawings have been used to convey the necessary design information to the construction crew, but in this age of complex piping systems, the exclusive use of drawings is diminishing rapidly because of the special skills necessary to read and interpret the complex, often-overdetailed drawings. Drawings are a two-dimensional medium, and the obvious advantages of the third dimension will become apparent after the construction of just one model.

Models were first used after-the-fact for checking a design that was already completed by the use of the traditional plan, elevation, and section method of design. Their use enabled the designer to iron out many of the errors commonly associated with the use of orthographic projection in pipe design. Everything from water pollution control plants to bridges have been modeled, enabling the users to convey before construction all the necessary information to buyers or government agencies that are purchasing a particular system.

The benefits of models vary, depending upon the complexity of the prospective project, whether or not the model is used in the design stages, the

FIGURE 1-2 Petrochemical design model.

amount of substitution for drafting the modeling will do, and the amount of accuracy and complexity to which it will be built.

In general, 3/8″ to 1′ to 3/4″ to 1′ are the most commonly used scales; 3/8″ = 1′ is used throughout the petrochemical industry and 1/2″ = 1′ is more common in the power-generation field. Larger scales are sometimes used for subsections in problem areas encountered, and full-scale models may be constructed in the case of extremely important problem areas. Industrial models include the use of model tables, model bases and frames, floors, and walls, with representations of all structural elements, piping instrumentation and components, electrical trays, HVAC (heating, ventilation, and air conditioning), and a variety of other equipment and machinery that may be involved in a particular project, such as fossil-fuel power-generation boilers, turbines, economizers, feedwater pumps, and so on. Each individual industry has its own variations of equipment and components that will make up its typical industrial model. Any person involved in the drawing of piping systems will be likely to encounter the use of models sometime during his or her career. In some cases, companies turn to the experienced designer/drafter to lay and run the pipe and other equipment directly onto the model from their drawings. This has been the case in the petrochemical industry, especially where design changes to existing installations have been made directly on models in the drafting room. Model building offers a wide variety of excellent job opportunities throughout the world.

Models offer acurate, three-dimensional drawings that allow for advantages unavailable in two dimensions. Every complex piping installation has a maze of piping, structural, mechanical, and electrical equipment and components. When using drawings, it may be impossible to locate the interference problems that may occur, because of the inability to correlate the mass of drawings, views, and sections that are necessary for the use of orthographic projection in piping systems. Two dimensions can only show a cross section. Even with isometrics one cannot represent all layers on the same drawing, and if there are several drawings, the points of correspondence must be kept in mind three-dimensionally. Add to this the fact that several departments, such as structural, electrical, HVAC, and pipe supports, will have systems occupying the same physical volume of space, and the number of correlations needed becomes enormous.

Drafters/designers in each department show on their drawings their own set of standards and design situations, which may not always be included on the piping system drawing. Therefore, interference problems and misconceptions in design can occur much more readily when using only drawings. These problems cannot occur with a model, where all systems are accurately placed to scale as they will appear on the future project. The model enables all the groups that are concerned with the project to visually study it from a variety of angles, views, and so on, for all the necessary information that may be required for accurate placement and design of their particular systems.

When working in three dimensions, the designer is able to visualize the design sequences and operations that are necessary for the project, which may not be possible when using such a large quantity and assortment of drawings. In some cases, the construction company will actually use the model to design the total system without recording the design on drawings. Models are most advantageous when used as a working tool from the beginning stages of a project through the entire design phase. The beginning or preliminary models may look nothing like the final designed model. Many stages may be needed in between to provide the designer with the necessary three-dimensional medium to iron out any difficulties that may be encountered. Besides being a tool for interdepartmental communication, the model offers a three-dimensional view for recording on film the actual construction sequence that may be required for the production of the system. Where only the model is used, it becomes the only channel of communications between the designers and the field construction crew. Utilizing photographs and the model itself, the design model then becomes an extremely valuable tool that is treated with great secrecy and protection. As much as three to four years of design work could go down the drain if the model were destroyed. When recently touring a large power-generation construction company, students were asked to be careful not to touch any portion of the model because it was the *only* record that existed of the nuclear project being constructed. This shows the seriousness with which some companies take their model building. They have created an essential design service parallel to the drafting fields within their company. On the construction site, the model provides the fabricator, erectors, construction crews, and so on, with an actual scale representation of what is to be constructed and can also be used to develop construction and labor schedules, and to help determine the sequence and priorities of installation. Field forces utilize the model constantly during the construction period and again for training personnel at startup time.

In general, the engineer will develop the basic plant arrangement by use of the preliminary model, enabling the designers to achieve all job specifications and maintain design uniformity throughout the project, and helping to improve supervision in the actual design stage. In many cases, this will include elimination of a number of piping, plan, elevation, and section drawings. This may also extend into the HVAC, instrumentation, and electrical groups, where the model will help eliminate a variety of formerly necessary drawings. During the construction stage, a great amount of time will be saved, which is usually lost in the interpretation of drawings. Models will also help to determine whether or not sufficient space has been provided for the routing of small piping and smaller electrical items.

After the construction of the project has been completed, the model serves as an excellent tool for reference in the training of maintenance and plant operators. The economic advantages of the use of models vary throughout the different engineering fields that use them. Some companies have claimed a variety of benefits, such as the ability to tie down subcontractors with lower and firmer bids on components, cutting down the total engineering and construction time as much as 10 to 20 percent, elimination of 10 to 40 percent of the drafting requirements, and saving large amounts of money by the elimination of piping footage and fittings, among others.

Although the petrochemical field has found that model construction and use in the design stage may cost about the same as the required number of orthographically projected engineering drawings, the savings came in the ability of the model to provide more accurate, quicker designs and correspondingly lower engineering costs. The elimination of some drawings has facilitated quicker, more efficient designs, drawings being especially hard to read and understand without an extensive background in experience when they involve intricate, complex systems.

PRESENT AND FUTURE MODEL USES AND PROCEDURES

One of the newly developed procedures in modeling has been the use of photography. Although still in its formative stage, a majority of companies that do highly complex, industrial piping models utilize photography, enabling the project to exhibit a variety of views similar to those available when using the drafting procedure of multiple drawings. Color photos have been found most useful because the model itself is constructed of multicolored, color-coded materials. Photos of the model assist in project orientation and can establish a detailed sequence of construction and determine pipe installation schedules. Also, when models are used as one of the only available sources of design recording, photographs can be sent to the field prior to the completion of the model so that portions of the project can be started before the model reaches the job site. A flat-field camera can sometimes be utilized to photograph models, thereby permitting enlargement to drawing size. These photographs can be used in place of drawings, especially with the use of photographic drafting, in which the dimensioning can be done on vellum transparencies of the photograph.

Another newly developed procedure in the modeling field is the use of computer-drawn isometrics instead of hand-drawn ones. The model is completely labeled to locate the positions of all components, elevations, pipe runs, and so on. This information is then fed into a computer, which will construct an isometric view of any line in question. Material specifications, bills of materials, and so on, can all be drawn up by the computer. Computer isometrics, although they have their disadvantages, are still being developed into a viable tool for large industrial complexes. In smaller projects, after tagging, the model is sent directly to the pipe fabrication unit, which will then work directly from the model in sketching the isometric or orthographic spools necessary for the erection and construction of the particular portions of the pipeline.

The majority of the items used in construction models have been standardized to some extent by Engineering Model Associates, Inc., enabling valves, fittings, pipes, and other components to be interchangeable with a high degree of accuracy. EMA provides a wealth of research and development activities available to the piping industry, and they have developed 6000 different components that are available for piping models. Both the AEMS and EMA provide numerous publications, newsletters, and standards that should be a part of any model-building course, enabling the student to have access to a variety of reference materials.

FIGURE 1-3 Engineering Model Associates' *Reporter,* **news-letter on model building.**

ADVANTAGES OF THE USE OF MODELS

The following is a list of advantages that have been documented by model users throughout the piping industry.

- Provides essential three-dimension visualization.
- As a communication tool, enables various design groups, individuals, contractors, clients, and so on, who may speak different languages, to communicate through the medium of the model.
- As a design tool, provides an extremely adaptable medium for the engineer and piping designer.
- Provides for quicker decision making and approvals, thereby eliminating time-consuming evaluation of drawings.
- Eliminates costly drafting procedures.
- Provides an excellent engineering design checking system.
- Can be used for construction checking.
- Has been found excellent when used for contractor bidding.
- Provides for excellent scheduling of the actual construction work.
- It is a perfect example of an as-built record.
- Provides for a variety of operator and maintenance training opportunities.
- Can be used for public relations for nontechnical graphic display.
- It is a colorful, attractive sales tool.
- Can be used for modifications before construction.

- Allows for rearrangement of components and design without costly drafting changes.
- Allows for more accurate planning in the preliminary stages of the project, with regard to civil engineering aspects and land use.
- Color-coded piping provides excellent identification for the various pipeline uses and clearances.
- Shows access to components, valves, and other operator situations, such as instrumentation.
- Can be used for insurance examination, painting and insulation contractors, and so on.
- Cuts down on the total time of the construction project.
- Can be used for construction planning, including the sequence of building operations.
- Provides for jurisdiction decisions.
- Helps cut engineering and drafting time.
- When used as a checking device, eliminates extremely costly errors that may be encountered in the use of drawings.
- The use of preliminary models allows for the construction of alternative arrangements for a variety of piping, plot plans, and installations.
- Almost completely eliminates all major interference problems encountered in a complex piping installation.

Models as Communication Tools

The area in which models provide the greatest asset to the design process for piping installations is that of communication. This includes communication between various design groups; portions of the company in regard to outside vendors and planners; between engineers, designers, and construction personnel; and between the purchaser of the project and the engineering firm—to name some of the principal areas. Compared to drawings, models are a much more reliable source of communication. Because of their two-dimensional aspect and their complexity, drawings present communication problems within all the groups in a design engineering firm. Models, on the other hand, when constructed to accurate, complete, professional standards, facilitate communication by showing clearly the various aspects of the design project in three-dimensional form. Because many subfields and groups within an engineering firm must make use of the same drawing and design data, the model is an excellent means

FIGURE 1-4 Design model.

whereby all these subfields, such as electrical, piping, instrumentation, civil, pipe supports, and so on, can come together in common understanding of a project as a whole, working out the problems of interference and priorities that will be a natural part of any highly complex, industrial plant. Models offer subfields the opportunity to rearrange, redesign, and reach compromises regarding problems at the design stage instead of having these problems show up in the field during construction or even near the end of the construction stage, when such problems can create extremely expensive, time-consuming changes.

As a means of communication, the model offers a needed opportunity to create a design that incorporates better operating techniques, alternative design options, and more efficient, less complicated overall plants. Models, after they are used in the construction stage, are utilized as a communication tool in the writing of operating man-

uals and the training of operators and maintenance crews, and they offer long-range design capabilities that can be tested for problems (on the model) before they are implemented in the plant.

In the beginning stages, all models offer communication variables that are not present in preliminary drawings, enabling nontechnical personnel, such as government agencies, business leaders, financial contributors, and the public at large to view the prospective project. In the earlier stages, models offer the ability to reduce the total engineering and development process because preliminary errors can be eliminated entirely.

The time required to study complicated drawings may result in large numbers of designers and construction people being held up on the job. Models, on the other hand, can be considered as devices of instant communication, helping individuals concerned with the project cut through aspects of the project not needed by them so that

11

they can concentrate on their specialty item while maintaining an overall perspective of the surrounding area. This, of course, increases the ability of the engineer and designers to make quick modifications, which then can be communicated to the various subgroups of the company. Process and instrument engineers, electrical engineers, HVAC engineers, and others can all be assured that their particular aspects of the project are functioning properly and that the standards and specifications are being met.

Models also offer the extremely valuable ability to create a visual sequence of construction procedures, thus eliminating the trial-and-error method sometimes associated with the use of complicated, orthographically projected piping drawings. The construction crew can plan for their work and establish the sequence of construction well in advance of the actual startup time. Models, in conjunction with preliminary drawings, such as the process flow diagram, can offer an excellent capability for the checking of the projects systems. Design considerations, such as accessibility, economy, structure, pipe runs, placement of instruments and equipment, and maintenance space and requirements, can all be visualized and checked for adequate location directly on the model.

Models as Design Tools

In general, the use of models in design involves two definite stages: the **preliminary equipment arrangement** or **plot plan model**, and the **final piping design model**. Both stages are necessary for the most efficient use of modeling. Preliminary

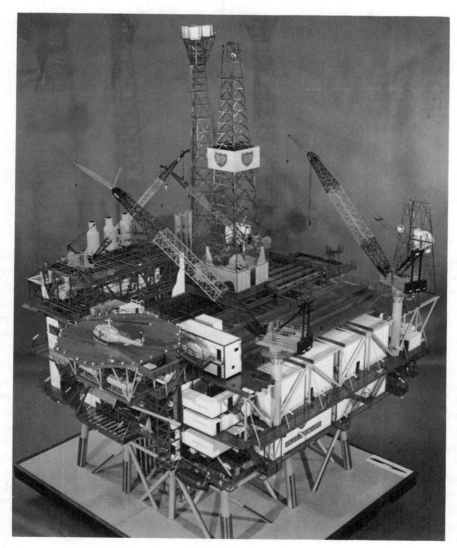

FIGURE 1-5 Offshore drilling and production rig model.

or plot plan and equipment layout models offer engineers and designers and representatives of other interested groups an excellent opportunity to review the status of the project. Design concepts can be developed and examined for feasibility before drawing begins. This preliminary stage offers an opportunity for rearrangement and optional equipment placement and location. Although preliminary models are usually block models utilizing only simple shapes and structural elements, they do offer an excellent three-dimensional overview. The preliminary model is not intended to resemble the final completed project. It is simply an aid to engineers, designers, and drafters in establishing the original layout and arrangement of the project.

In the early history of model building, a check model was used and constructed "after the fact," after the drawings and other necessary items of design had been completed. This, of course, reduced the effectiveness of the model, although it did help eliminate costly interference errors. Check modeling is limited to checking, operator training, and construction planning.

To realize its full value, the model should be started at the earliest state after the process flow diagrams and other necessary drawings have been completed. As the design model moves through its various stages of completion, the piping designer will gradually "pipe" the model. In other words, the designer will run the pipe, do the small-scale piping, and place components, pipe supports, and valves on the model. The design model offers the ability to revise and change the proposed location of much of the equipment, such as moving pipe or a piece of equipment to allow more access, relocating a nozzle, moving a valve, and so on.

FIGURE 1-6 Scale models of trailer rigs. (Courtesy of The Scale Model Makers, Cleveland, Tennessee.)

Elimination of Many Drawings

In some cases, design drawings are still utilized and checked with regard to the three-dimensional aspects involved in the model. This cross-checking, although offering an opportunity to catch any problems that may occur, is a more costly procedure. For the piping design of modern chemical, petrochemical, refinery, food-processing, and power-generation plants, even small jobs require extremely large numbers of complicated orthographic piping drawings. These drawings, of course, need to correlate and accommodate all the various subgroups within the engineering company, such as HVAC, instrumentation, civil, and so on. Because of this, orthographic piping drawings are one of the most expensive aspects of the design stage and total construction cost of any major industrial project. Any changes that need to be made after the original design has been drawn are extremely expensive, because problems such as interference or incorrect location of the equipment must be changed on all the drawings that have anything to do with the particular problem area. This adds an extra, time-consuming, costly element to the use of drawings in piping design. It is estimated that hundreds of hours of time and effort can be saved for the drafter when utilizing models instead of the exclusive use of orthographically projected drawings. Working drawings can still be made of portions of the model, which can then be shipped to the construction site, but these tend to be less complicated and can be done by less experienced personnel in comparison to the large plan, elevation, and section drawings necessary when using drawings alone. Although drawings are still utilized when the model method is the primary design tool, it is possible to greatly improve the detailing of the drawing by making available portions and sections of the model directly in the drafting room. In general, the rule for the use of models in the design stage is not to draw anything until it is absolutely necessary. Only then can the models be utilized to their fullest potential. This procedure allows for the model to be changed before any drawings are completed, thus making it unnecessary to reorganize on a wide scale and limiting the changes to the model and not drawings.

Some sort of timing balance must be obtained between the drawing of isometrics, pipe supports, and so on, before the model is completed and doing the drafting too early. This balance can only be determined through trial and error and experience in various types of piping projects.

The single most important aspect of the utilization of models in piping projects has been the reduction of the number of interference problems normally associated with the vast complicated piping projects in modern industry. Reducing interferences during the design stage between piping, cable trays, HVAC, ducts, pipe hangers, restraints, structural items, and other equipment makes problem finding and correction easier and quicker, at a great savings in construction cost. Drawings themselves do not highlight the problems as models do. Making changes on the model involves less time and cost in comparison to correcting problems that are not recognized before construction. This virtually guarantees correct resolution of problems before any construction has taken place.

Models as Field Construction Tools

By placing the model in a central location at the construction site, the communication among designers, engineers, and construction personnel can be greatly improved. The model is an actual replica of the project. The former procedure of intense design group and construction crew meetings, taking up countless hours and discussions while reviewing complicated orthographically projected drawings, can be cut to a minimum. Models have been referred to as instant communications be-

cause the visual aspect is maximized. By being available to the field forces during construction, the model serves as a constant reference point and discussion tool, offering the ability to directly plan and control the sequence of work and the job progress as a whole. Models also help in the construction bidding stage, as the contractor can readily view the total intended project, therefore giving firmer estimates of the construction cost and scheduling aspects.

Models as Training Tools

The last stages of model utilization arise from their ability to aid in training plant operators and maintenance crews. Sometimes, plant operators will have different ethnic backgrounds and languages. Models also help facilitate communication between the engineering firm that builds the plant, the purchaser, and those who will eventually operate the plant. Language barriers between trainers and trainees can be largely eliminated by using the model in training, especially in complicated projects. The total instruction time can be cut by many hours. As training tools, models offer those being trained the opportunity to familiarize themselves with the total facility and equipment and interconnections of services *before* completion of the project. The model usually remains at the job site or project many years, enabling new plant

FIGURE 1-7   Architecture model. (Photo courtesy Peter Xiques, Mill Valley, CA.)

operators or maintenance crews to be trained throughout the life of the plant. Using models during operator training at the earliest possible date will facilitate the completion of training, and a production-ready crew can be available for an early startup time.

Cost Advantages in the Use of Models

Already mentioned are the many aspects of design tool applications that invariably lead to cost savings in the total engineering. The use of models in piping design can save a good percentage of the total design cost in some projects. In others the savings occur more in the area of construction, because of the elimination of errors and interferences. Field labor cost of a majority of projects runs about 50 percent for the piping installation, 13 to 20 percent for major equipment, 10 to 20 percent for structural elements such as foundations, and 15 to 20 percent for electrical systems and instrumentation. The actual cost of the total engineering is about 45 percent of the home office cost. Half of that goes for the actual piping design.

In more complicated projects, the use of modeling versus drafting techniques runs approximately the same for both time and cost. The savings occur and are affected more in the reduction of field work and amount of calendar time necessary to construct the actual plant.

The use of models can hasten the approval of the plot plan and improve overall project design; eliminate costly interference errors; offer excellent time savings in operator and maintenance training courses; provide quicker material take-off procedures; simplify field construction problems, such as labor disputes and union allocation of construction areas; can be used to train piping designers; provide a cheaper sales tool than drawings; speed government and client approval of the project; lower overall bids; firm up contractor and vendor bids; and reduce the total amount of piping runs and fittings necessary to complete the project. All of these lead to cost savings, which are more readily available when the model is used from the preliminary stages right through to the actual startup time of the project.

TOTAL MODEL COSTS

Total costs, of course, vary depending on the size, complexity of the project, and the number of government specifications, codes, and procedures that must be considered, such as environmental impact statements, seismic disturbances, and so on. So there is no clear-cut answer to the question of what a particular model will cost for a project. It is far better to look at what the model will do in savings and cost reductions.

It is generally felt that one-half of 1 per-

FIGURE 1-8 Design model of a portion of a refinery.

cent of the total plant construction cost will be attributed to the use of a model on the project. Orthographic drawings run slightly more, but because of the engineering advantages listed previously and cost and time savings, it is unfair to base the use of the model totally on its cost. In general, it can be assumed that better-designed, more economically feasible projects can be produced much more readily with the use of a model than by the traditional method of orthographically projecting drawings. Very seldom has it been the case that the use of the model will increase the engineering costs in comparison to the use of orthographic drawings. One case wherein the model cost may become larger than the use of drawings occurs if certain aspects of the project are modeled to a large scale. In general, however, this procedure is only used in situations where the cost of the model will be totally offset by the efficient reduction of problems that can be obtained with the use of a large-scale model. Also, there is a relationship between the size of the project and the model cost. Modeling tends to be more expensive (a higher percentage of the total engineering cost) when the project is smaller. It must be emphasized that better engineering can offset any increase in engineering or design cost.

Like any new or different concept or tool when it is introduced, modeling has received considerable criticism about its cost. On the other hand, proponents of modeling claim that the modeling cost can easily be offset by the reduction of drawings during the early design stages. Some claim that the model cost is offset as a result of the improved communication during the design project; others claim that the real cost benefit comes during construction, in that there are fewer errors on a modeled project and therefore fewer field changes are required. There are very few published data available as to the overall cost of modeling versus the use of drawings. However, one company has made a rather rigorous study of their design modeling program and compared it to their drafting costs. Because this company prefers to remain anonymous, we shall refer to it as Company XYZ. The subsequent text is a copy of this study.

Company XYZ Cost Study

The cost information presented herein can best be used as a guide or a trend to look at the cost effectiveness that can be evolved by using engineering models. Like any cost information, it is dependent upon the way that a particular company

manages its operations, together with the various overhead factors involved in the drafting and modeling departments. Although this information cannot be applied directly to any other company, it does provide a direct relationship between the cost of designing a given project on the board or designing one on the model.

The best way to apply these data to another organization or company is in terms of percentage decrease in drafting or engineering time rather than decrease in dollars. In other words, when we evaluate these data, we are looking at the overall trend. These same trends or percentages can then be translated to other organizations or companies. The overall dollar savings will in some cases be more and in other cases be less as a result of the overall management and design procedural requirements of the design organization.

Prior to the use of modeling, which was introduced in Company XYZ in 1972, the best index that they had generated was a comparison of the total drafting worker-hours as compared to the overall plant cost in dollars. This procedure was then used to generate a set of cost curves: high, medium, and low. These cost curves were used to check preliminary worker-hour estimates on a given project. They were also used at the end of the project to judge how well the job fit the pattern as compared to past projects. Usually, rational reasons could be established for those jobs that did not fit the pattern. For example, some jobs fell below the cost curves. This could usually be attributed to large equipment installations and minimum pipe runs as compared to other projects with numerous pieces of small equipment and congested piping runs; a smooth-running job versus one that suffered numerous process changes along with slow information flow. Evaluating each job after the fact on these cost curves was difficult at best. If there were improvements in the drafting and engineering groups to economize or cut down the overall worker-hours, it was not necessarily obvious by examination of the curves.

With the incorporation of engineering design models and computer-generated isometrics at Company XYZ, this picture has drastically changed for the better after completing seven engineering design models. The first three jobs plotted close to the median curve. In other words, as far as overall drafting and worker hours were concerned, the first three jobs were pretty close to the previously established standards for the number of worker-hours expended for an all-drafting job. The subsequent four modeling jobs plotted signifi-

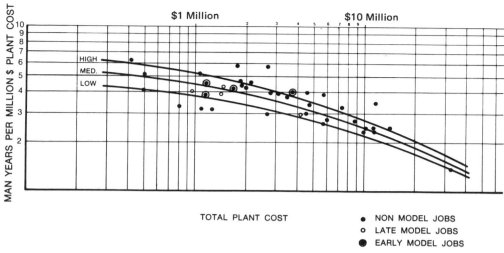

$1 Million $10 Million

MAN YEARS PER MILLION $ PLANT COST

HIGH
MED.
LOW

TOTAL PLANT COST

●   NON MODEL JOBS
○   LATE MODEL JOBS
◉   EARLY MODEL JOBS

Plot of drafting and modeling man years per
Million $ plant cost vs Total plant cost
(Company XYZ Data)

FIGURE 1-9

cantly lower. In fact, these jobs have established a new curve at about the 20 percent lower mark (Fig. 1-9).

The combined modeling and drafting technique has clearly improved worker-hour performance. This improvement has far exceeded the initial desires for such a program. It was anticipated that the combined efforts of modeling and drafting would, at best, be essentially equal to the all-drafting worker-hours. It was visualized that the cost savings would be in the areas of improved communication, construction, coordination, and client satisfaction.

Utilization of models has evolved a very straightforward method to check worker-hour performance on the model. The plant occupies a specific square footage on the model base. The total worker-hours on the job divided by the square footage provides a convenient index in terms of hours per square foot.

The plot plans of Company XYZ are, in general, consistently laid out with about the same amount of density between given projects. Most plant areas are fully occupied with about the same relative amount of piping and equipment. Traffic ways and maintenance clearances are normally uniform between projects. In addition, the vertical stacking of equipment and piping is comparable between one job and the next. This is not necessarily true for many companies, specifically, consulting firms that deal with a variety of industries. When looking at the overall time to design on the model, the size of the piping is a factor. However, it has been determined that areas which have relatively large-diameter pipe runs as compared with

several smaller-diameter pipe runs were not significantly different in the overall worker-hours needed to design and construct the model. Figure 1-10 (a plot of worker-hours per square foot versus job) depicts an almost classic learning curve, but it is not claimed that the total range of improved performance is a direct result of modeling expertise. For example, job 1 was Company XYZ's first

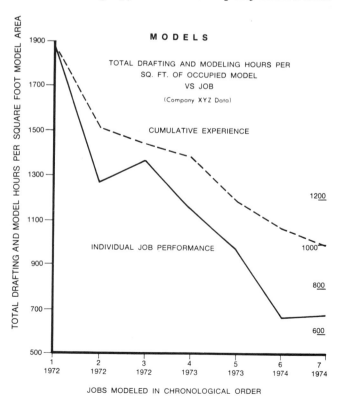

MODELS

TOTAL DRAFTING AND MODELING HOURS PER SQ. FT. OF OCCUPIED MODEL VS JOB
(Company XYZ Data)

CUMULATIVE EXPERIENCE

INDIVIDUAL JOB PERFORMANCE

TOTAL DRAFTING AND MODEL HOURS PER SQUARE FOOT MODEL AREA

JOBS MODELED IN CHRONOLOGICAL ORDER

FIGURE 1-10

model job. It was a very compact and complicated plant. At the other extreme, job 7 was a more normal piping job. Job 7 was also performed under almost ideal circumstances in terms of information flow, timely client reviews, and experienced personnel available. Company XYZ feels that it can do a design model job of average complexity for approximately 16 percent fewer worker-hours than an all-drafting job. Their data reveal that this would translate into approximately 1000 worker-hours total drafting and modeling per 1 square foot of occupied 3/8″ model base. This figure of 1000 worker-hours per square foot includes the fabrication of the model table, the model base, all the equipment, the piping design effort done on the model, and all the drafting associated with completing the job, together with the isometrics. Only 170 hours of the combined effort is that related to the table base, equipment, and model design and construction.

One square foot at 3/8″ scale represents 1024 square feet of plant area. Therefore, we can approximate that 1 square foot of plant area will require 1 hour of drafting design and modeling time when the modeling design method is used. Using 1000 worker-hours per square foot of model base as a parameter, Fig. 1-11 was developed. This

shows the same series of jobs as in Fig. 1-9 but with extrapolated points to show the worker-hour levels at which the seven previous all-drafting jobs could have been performed if they would have been designed using the piping-design-model approach with the present level of model experience. This shows a theoretical savings of 16 percent over the seven previous jobs. Based on this particular company's savings, it resulted in an overall savings of 1.2 percent of the overall plant cost.

Much of this improvement is a result of computer-generated isometrics. Overall time spent on isometrics has been reduced by 33 percent. However, this percentage does not reflect the true potential of the savings. It is clear that if one can delay isometrics input into the computer until the model is complete and subject to client review, the time spent on isometrics is markedly reduced. A current example is job 7 (Fig. 1-9). Isometrics were completed in 2.75 worker-hours per isometric and represented 8.25 percent of the total drafting worker-hours. This number compares with the current average of computer isometrics of 4 worker-hours per isometric and 10.5 percent total drafting hours.

On every model job, reports from the field indicate that models were valuable tools in the

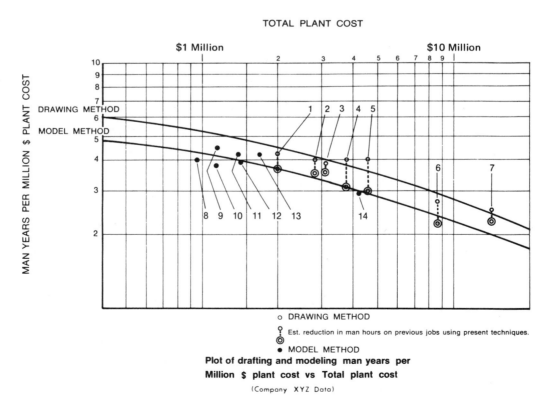

Plot of drafting and modeling man years per
Million $ plant cost vs Total plant cost

(Company XYZ Data)

FIGURE 1-11

field. When personnel reported on two jobs of similar complexity that went to the field at the same time, one with a model and one that was designed on the drawing board, the plant designed with the model had an average of 2.6 percent rework hours of the total piping budget, while the design without the model experienced a 15.6 percent rework rate.

It must be noted again that 1000 worker-hours per square foot of model base may not be comparable to any other design group. For example, a more reasonable estimate for Company ABC may be 1200 hours and Company MNO may experience as little as 350 hours, depending on the type of installation. This information shows a definite trend toward the vast improvement and savings that modeling has to offer.

OTHER CONSIDERATIONS IN MODELING

Many design and construction firms have become involved in modeling as a result of being directed by their client to provide models, while others have taken their own initiative in evaluating and consequently being involved in modeling. Regardless of all the arguments, pro and con, for modeling, it suffices to say that because of the hundreds of companies currently involved in modeling in this age of high costs and very competitive construction and design costs, modeling has proved to be an economical approach. Although the visible cost of any program, innovation, or tool is probably the main consideration when it comes to making the final decision on whether to use it, there are certainly other considerations.

Additional economies are derived basically out of improved communications and coordination. This improved communication and coordination of the project is the heart of design modeling. From this comes cost savings and other benefits. No matter how simple or straightforward a project may appear to be, it can become many times more complex and difficult without good, straightforward communication and coordination.

With the model, communications occur in three dimensions. This is a vast improvement over communication with reams of flat drawings that must be visualized in three dimensions. This improved communication starts at plot plan development on through to equipment arrangement, piping design, checking, bid proposals, bid authorization, construction, plant operator training, and plant operation. The following are additional advantages derived from utilization of a design model:

- Provide superior plot plan development
- Minimize plot plan drawings
- Minimize equipment arrangement drawings
- Improve equipment arrangement
- Eliminate piping plan drawings
- Minimize fittings and pipe runs
- Minimize interference errors
- Assist in material take-off
- Provide better definition for bids
- Reduce contingency in bids
- Schedule erection sequence
- Provide sales tool
- Serve as an instruction tool to train plant operators
- Train maintenance personnel
- Jurisdictional matters can be seen, discussed, and resolved

These accrued advantages are all a direct result of improved communications. They will reduce capital cost, reduce engineering and design time, reduce plant and maintenance cost, increase efficiency in operator training, and result in earlier plant completion. It is often thought that only large engineering and construction companies can afford to be involved with design modeling. However, it is probably more correct to state that the very small companies and medium-sized companies cannot afford to be without design modeling.

FUTURE OF DESIGN MODELING

The techniques of design modeling are continually improving. Probably the biggest single improvement is in the continued research and development of new off-the-shelf model components.

Presently, the state of the art has minimized the need for detailed plot plan drawings, equipment arrangement drawings, piping arrangement drawings, and, in some cases, even isometrics. Some companies take their information directly off the model and feed it into the computer and produce computerized isometric drawings; others have eliminated isometric or spool drawings and send the model directly to the pipe fabrication shop. With the improved use of photography and computerized material take-offs, the strides that can be made in the modeling field are virtually limitless. This book describes design modeling, many of the alternatives that can be utilized to set up a design model program, and the alternatives within a design model program.

Models have been shown to assist greatly in producing and checking the overall design procedure and design implementation of piping projects. The savings in total cost for construction and design far exceeds the total cost of model construction. Models eliminate and minimize interference problems at the design and construction site and can be used in all stages of the project. The major drawback in the use of models in industrial piping engineering firms is the tremendous resistance to the implementation of new techniques, resistance that can only be met by experience and the advantages that have been mentioned, and this experience can only be understood fully if the project is accurately planned and supervised.

QUIZ

1-1. Name four industrial fields in which models are used.

1-2. Describe the difference in using a model versus the drawing method.

1-3. What is an after-the-fact model and when is it utilized?

1-4. What is the most frequently used scale for a petrochemical model and a nuclear power model?

1-5. What are five advantages in using models in industrial installations?

1-6. Describe the difference between the preliminary model and final design model.

1-7. Describe the advantages of models in regard to the cost factor of designing a typical modern piping installation.

1-8. In addition to drafting and modeling, what procedures have helped in the total design effort?

1-9. How can interference problems be eliminated by the use of models?

Model Descriptions

FIGURE 2-1 Petrochemical design model.
(Model photographs courtesy of Badger of
America, Inc., Cambridge, Massachusetts.)

Following is a description of the numerous types of models that may be encountered in industry, of which industrial piping models are only one of the many kinds employed. Engineering models are used in every field, from Defense Department prototypes for missiles (Fig. 2-2) and armories (Fig. 2-3) to highways and architectural models (Fig. 2-13), mass transit systems (Fig. 2-4), and so on. The piping design model for the industrial projects (Fig. 2-1) concept is less than a quarter-century old and is still developing. Models are used for several purposes, such as floor layout models (Fig. 2-6),

models for display and sales (Fig. 2-14), prototype models for public acceptance (Figs. 2-7 and 2-8), education (Fig. 2-9), product development (Fig. 2-10), and so on.

ARCHITECTURAL MODELS

Architectural models (Fig. 2-11) were one of the first uses of models in industry, including study and design models, presentation models of finished projects, sales information models, experi-

FIGURE 2-2 Minuteman silo diorama. This diorama, showing a cutaway of a Minuteman ICBM silo, is part of the Air Force exhibit at the Smithsonian Institution, Washington, D.C. Eight-, 12-, and 20-pound Artfoam was used to produce terrain, components, and some hardware simulation. Foam is both natural and sealed. The diorama was produced with a worker-hour saving of nearly 40 percent. Weight reduction was not critical but greatly facilitated transportation of the exhibit and installation at the Smithsonian. Artfoam (rigid urethane) is a product of The Strux Corporation, Lindenhurst, New York. (U.S. Air Force Photograph.)

mental models, and check models. Often, architectural models end up being purely for show and the appearance of the total facility. Architectural models are also used for environmental impact reports and to present the topographic and geographic features and surrounding areas of the intended structure which are not usually a part of the engineering model. Architectural models offer the opportunity to view the prospective project design in relationship to the surrounding area and construction site. Visual aspects, such as orientation to sun and surrounding existing structures, play an important part in the use of architectural models.

FIGURE 2-4 Model of a mass transit system. (Courtesy of Design Specialties, Pittsburgh, Pennsylvania.)

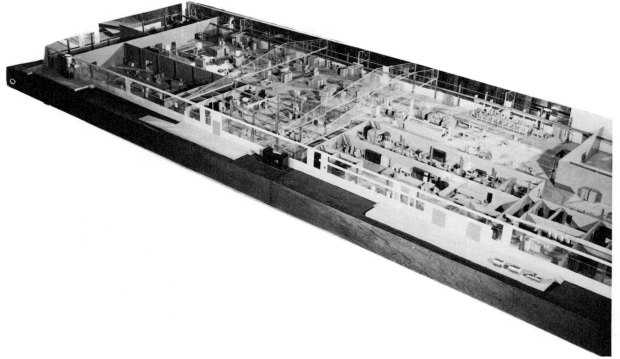

FIGURE 2-3 Edgewood Arsenal model, 22' long (1/4" scale). (Model by Panormic Studies, Philadelphia.)

Architectural models help eliminate problems encountered in business concerning the use of the facility, such as local zoning restrictions on space, utilities, transportation facilities, available government services such as fire and police, and geographical relationship of the architectural structure to the surrounding ecosystem. Architectural models can help provide this environmental analysis. Architectural models are seldom used as design tools in the sense of piping industrial models.

STUDY MODELS

Study models are usually extremely small scale planning tools used by government or industrial groups, enabling the user to gain a large perspective concerning the project. Models may include a whole range of existing and proposed facilities in the relationship to the area as a whole. Study

models are usually constructed of a variety of materials that are quick to use and low in cost.

PRESENTATION MODELS

Presentation models (Figs. 2-5, 2-7, 2-8, and 2-10) are similar to study models, but they involve the definite presentation of a possible project; therefore, the actual model must be complete in detail, showing the design and environmental situations encountered in the project. Presentation models are used throughout government (Fig. 2-18) and the private sector (Fig. 2-5) to gain approval from local communities for a variety of projects. Design elements and overall aspects are shown directly on the presentation model, so that they truly represent the intended project, enabling a thorough, honest decision-making process to take place by those concerned with the implementation of the project.

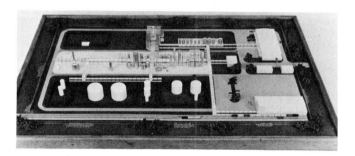

FIGURE 2-5 Presentation model. This type of model shows only main equipment, buildings, and so on. Notice the attention to detail given the landscaping, parking lot, cars, railroad, and the finished wood base. (Model photograph courtesy of Badger of America, Inc., Cambridge, Massachusetts.)

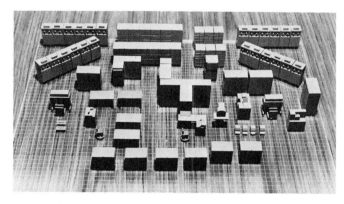

FIGURE 2-6 Three-dimensional office and computer room planning kits are used to present ideas and propose layouts to technical and nontechnical personnel (1/4" scale). (Courtesy of "Visual" Industrial Products, Inc., Indianola, Pennsylvania.)

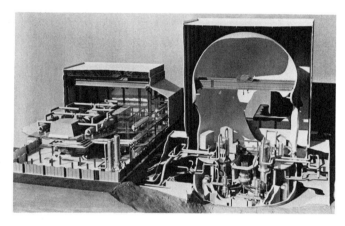

FIGURE 2-7 Nuclear plant sales/display model with animated and lighted areas activated by tape narration for use in airports, lobbies, banks, and the like. (Courtesy of "Visual" Industrial Products, Inc., Indianola, Pennsylvania.)

FIGURE 2-8 Model of nuclear reactor primary containment area. (Courtesy of The Scale Model Makers, Cleveland, Tennessee.)

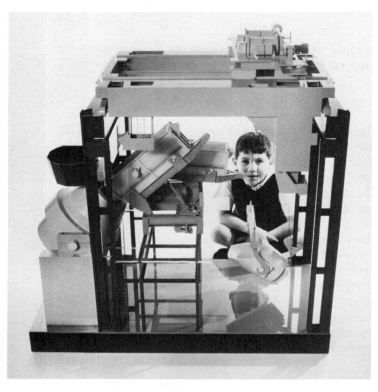

FIGURE 2-9 Working models used for trade shows to demonstrate technical features. (Courtesy of "Visual" Products, Inc., Indianola, Pennsylvania.)

FIGURE 2-10 Offshore drilling platform, scale 3/32"-11'0". Material: wood; purpose: display at launching. (Courtesy of The Scale Model Makers, Cleveland, Tennessee.)

FIGURE 2-11 Architectural model, made of wood. (Photo courtesy Peter Xiques, Mill Valley, CA.)

FIGURE 2-12 Architectural model of a parking facility. (Photo courtesy Peter Xiques, Mill Valley, CA.)

FIGURE 2-13 Architectural model showing a solar powered office building. (Photo courtesy Peter Xiques, Mill Valley, CA.)

PRODUCT MODELS

Product models (Fig. 2-14) are used more often in mechanical engineering fields to help design various aspects of machinery or other mechanical devices, such as components that need to be manufactured. In some cases, these models will be completed to a larger scale than that of the project itself.

TOPOGRAPHIC MODELS

Topographical models are used throughout government and private industry to show geological configurations necessary for such items as mapping, grade, elevation, and terrain of perspective project property. They are primarily used to study the terrain and determine the most effective design use for projects such as highways and for overall

FIGURE 2-14 Girder crane. (Courtesy of The Scale Model Makers, Cleveland, Tennessee.)

FIGURE 2-15 Architectural model of skyscraper. (Photo courtesy Peter Xiques, Mill Valley, CA.)

city and county planning. In general, the topographic map is made to an extremely small scale because of the total amount of area it encompasses.

PROTOTYPE MODELS

Prototype models (Fig. 2-16) are basically similar to product models, but are sometimes actually

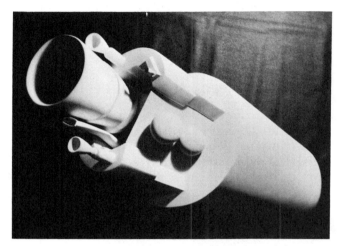

FIGURE 2-16 Model of a space capsule produced by direct carving and fabricating of Artfoam (rigid urethane). (Artfoam is a product of The Strux Corporation, Lindenhurst, New York.)

FIGURE 2-17 Transtage model. This 1/10 scale model of a USAF Transtage space vehicle (actual diameter 12") is one of the exhibits in the Orientation's Group Titan II exhibit. Twenty pounds of Artfoam was used to create the Transtage's fuel tanks (bulletlike shapes on rear bulkhead), resulting in 50 percent weight reduction. A two-part epoxy surface coat was used to seal foam before the final paint was applied. Tanks were lathe-turned. (Courtesy of The Strux Corporation, Lindenhurst, New York; U.S. Air Force photograph.)

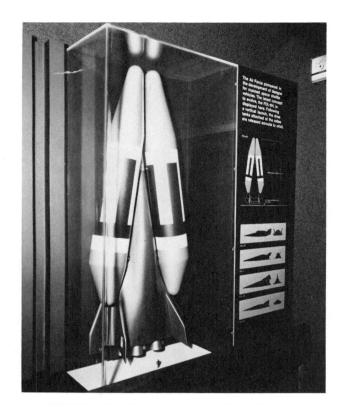

FIGURE 2-18 Spaceship model. This 1/30 scale model of an experimental "lifting body" spaceship concept is one of 19 separate exhibits in the U.S. Air Force Space Exhibit, a Titan missile that has been converted into an air-conditioned space showroom. The nose and tail cones of the two fuel tanks shown were lathe-turned from 12-pound Artfoam and sealed with a two-part epoxy surfacer before final painting. Weight was extremely critical in the creation of this model because of suspension limitations. (Courtesy of The Strux Corporation, Lindenhurst, New York; U.S. Air Force photograph.)

working simulations of the eventual product. In the case of automobiles, the company may build an actual prototype to gain knowledge of its aerodynamic engineering aspects, and also as a "feeler" in estimating public acceptance and sales. Some prototype models are just simplified mock-ups of the eventual product.

PLANT LAYOUT MODELS

Plant layout models (Fig. 2-19) deal primarily with existing or proposed building where the use of existing or eventual space is limited and determined by an architectural structure. The plant layout model will use an assortment of block-type items to represent the diverse types of equipment that will be involved in the project. Plant layout models are often used in architectural areas to divide office space and show other floor-space options.

FIGURE 2-19 Factory planning model (1/4"), including grid boards, columns, and wall materials. (Courtesy of "Visual" Products, Inc., Indianola, Pennsylvania.)

INDUSTRIAL MODELS

Industrial models are what this book is primarily concerned with and deal mainly with petrochemical, refinery, food-processing, power-generation, and manufacturing facilities. These models consist primarily of piping systems and related equipment.

The following describes the type of models that an engineer may choose to utilize in a given design or construction project. These models will be discussed in their order of use on a project. Most projects will require at least one and possibly three different models.

SITE MODELS (PLOT PLAN MODELS)

After the site for a given project has been selected, the site model can be started (Fig. 2-20). In some cases, site models may be used to evaluate or select sites. The site model requires very little actual engineering information for the new facility or

FIGURE 2-20 Site model.

project that is going to be constructed on the site. The main purpose of the site model is to provide a visual concept of the facility to be constructed in relation to the surrounding areas. Site models should include bridges, rail facilities, power right of ways, and utility hookups. In addition to these, any of the major buildings adjacent to the construction site should be shown on the site model. Since site models require very little detail, they should be modeled at a scale of $1'' = 10'$. A smaller scale may be chosen to minimize the size of the site model. For convenience, the model scale should be such that the site model can be constructed on an area no greater than a $4' \times 8'$ sheet of plywood. Site models are used as an engineering tool only in the very early planning stages of a given project. Therefore, the model need only be constructed using temporary materials and in block form rather than utilizing intricate detailed parts. It is recommended that this type of model be constructed of foam and double-sided tape to hold the block forms at their specific location. Colored tape is recommended to outline rails, waterways, bridges, roads, and so on.

The plot plan model offers the ability to create alternative arrangements with regard to the proposed new facility, allowing the designer to take an overall view of the surrounding site in its relationship to its natural features, such as rivers, lakes, and other important features. Site and plot plan models, of course, cannot be made as accurately as models constructed to a larger scale, but they do simulate the available space and design options that are available. Site plan models also offer the opportunity for subengineering groups to discuss the options that are available within the prescribed physical limits. The plot plan may include topographical configurations, thus making its use more effective. Plot plan models are often used as display models to enable governmental and public agencies to have access to the proposed facility's configuration.

SCOPE MODELS

Scope models (Fig. 2-21), like site models, are preliminary planning tools. Both the site model and scope model can be completely eliminated if the project is being constructed in an already existing building or is similar enough to an existing project that has already been constructed. The purposes of the scope model are to evolve the most efficient process, and design the building and/or structures around that process, not to design the process around the structures and/or existing building. The first step in starting on a scope

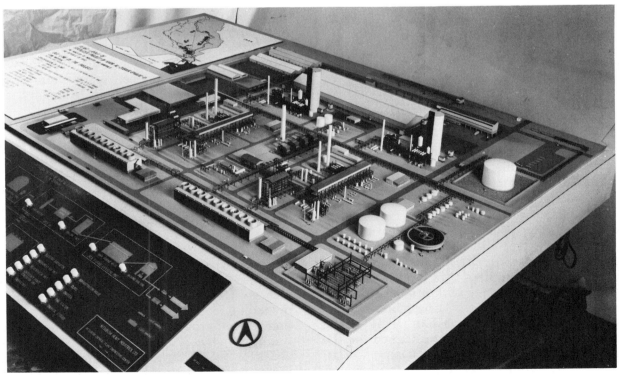

FIGURE 2-21 Scope model.

model is to roughly lay out the location of all major pieces of equipment. Walls, floors, and bays, together with material storage areas, should be laid out around the process equipment. If more than one floor or level is required in the scope model, the floor levels need to be completely flexible so that they can be moved during evolution of the process. A discussion of the types of construction for multi-level structures is presented in a later section. Again, the use of styrofoam is recommended to give the basic shape of all equipment. The scale for scope models should be no larger than $1/4'' = 1'$. Common scales for scope models are $1/8'' = 1'$ and $1'' = 10'$. Before the start of a scope model, the following information must be available:

- List of vessels, towers, exchangers, heaters, compressors, and pumps, together with their approximate sizes
- Process flow diagram
- Special structural requirements

All the major equipment, together with the heating, ventilation, and air-conditioning systems, should be located first. Pipe racks and motor control centers should be shown on the scope model. As mentioned earlier, design modeling permits the ultimate in communication. You can readily see that all disciplines must already be involved to a great degree, even at this very early design stage.

PRELIMINARY MODELS OR STUDY MODELS

The scope model which we just discussed is often considered part of the preliminary model and is not normally considered a separate function. The main purpose of a preliminary model (Fig. 2-22) is to determine the ultimate equipment arrangement and the location of major and/or critical lines.

Preliminary models are also referred to as plot plan models or block-type models. They are used to facilitate quick changes concerning arrangements for plant alternatives, equipment arrangement, or plot plan situations. Review of the preliminary model gathers together all the engineering and design groups within a company for a meeting to determine the best possible arrangement for the project in question. This model therefore takes on extreme significance for the establishment of a variety of important design decisions, including plot plan arrangement,

expenditures for engineering subgroups, operating and maintenance problems, and so on. The preliminary model is usually constructed of block-type materials made from styrofoam or wood that are only temporarily placed on the base of the model, enabling a variety of arrangements to be made quickly. Structural components are also used on the preliminary model and are usually clipped together for easy disassembly. All preliminary models must include the capability to make quick changes by moving the structural elements and block materials which stand for the equipment variations.

The preliminary model's scale is usually kept to a minimum, but it must be large enough so that the reviewing teams can understand the relationships of all the various parts of the equipment and plot plan. This model arrangement is usually sketched by the designer or engineer prior to the assembly of the rough model and after the review board has made its decisions. The preliminary model is then photographed to establish a permanent record. Among the many engineering groups and personnel that will make decisions on the preliminary model are the project engineering manager; the area project engineer; the process engineer; the lead piping draftsperson and designer; the plan design engineer; the construction coordinator; the initial operator; the electrical, civil, instrument, and HVAC designers; the client; and a variety of other personnel who may be necessary on a particular project.

After alternative arrangements are constructed and photographed, the alternatives are reviewed for clearances, maintenance, accessibility, construction problems, economy, design applicability, and so on.

Before the preliminary model can be assembled, a variety of information is necessary for the various subgroups to study before the decisions are made on the alternative arrangements for the project. Among these categories of information, the most important is the process flow diagram, which the process engineer will explain to the other design groups, showing them processes and design capabilities that are indicated on the flow diagram, which must be taken into account. Photographs of possible alternative arrangements are also used at this meeting. After the preliminary model has been established and the arrangement has been approved by several subgroups, the preliminary model is divided into sections, allocating areas for HVAC, pipe runs, columns, electrical and instrumentation needs, aisleways, roads, safety

FIGURE 2-22 Preliminary model.

and construction accessibility areas, storage space, and a variety of other design considerations that must be considered in the early stages of the project. Many of the structural steel and concrete needs can be decided upon at this stage. After this portion of the preliminary model has been completed, the plot plan drawings can be taken from the preliminary model, unless the procedure does not require the use of drawings at this stage, in which case it will go directly into the design modeling stage.

DESIGN MODELS

All of the efforts that go into site models, scope models, and preliminary models culminate in the design model. However, some companies go directly to the design model phase without the benefit of site, scope, or preliminary models. The design model includes all equipment, vessels, piping, valves, fittings, electrical, instrumentation, and HVAC. The main purpose of a design model is to develop the ultimate piping arrangement on the

FIGURE 2-23 Typical design model.

model with a minimum number of drawings. A design model is constructed in two stages: the basic model stage and the final model stage.

Basic Models

The basic model includes all major structures and all equipment with nozzles and tagging in place ready for the piping to be installed. Included in the basic model is the substructure or table with either removable or folding legs (see Section 15).

Final Models

Piping, electrical systems, and instrumentation can be designed directly on the model with only a minimum of sketches and informal drawings. Design models have also been used for study model purposes, although most of the equipment ar-

rangements are finalized by this stage of the job (see Section 16).

The basic model is assembled by the model technician in a modeling room, which includes all types of equipment that are necessary for the model, such as bases, tables, and other structural elements needed to construct the model. Platforms, equipment, vessels, bases, structural steel, concrete and walls, flooring, and so on, are all completed on the basic model.

The piping design (final model) stage is where the basic model is shipped to the drafting and design area and the piping designers are put to work running the pipe connecting the equipment, establishing the instrumentation, electrical, HVAC, and pipe support features. It is from this final design model that the drafting groups work, including the pipe support division and isometric groups.

FIGURE 2-24 Centerline design model.

A design model, when completed, will include all elements of the future plant, including equipment, vessels, structures, piping, and piping components, such as valves, fittings, meters, instrumentation, electrical, HVAC, and lighting. The design model is the completed miniature project. It should be noted that to be efficient the basic model stage of the design model must include the fabrication of all the major equipment and structures that are to be installed on the model base, including structural members, columns, pumps, equipment vessels, and, in general, any nonstandard item that cannot be ordered from a model component company but must be fabricated (including large-diameter piping). This will free the piping designer from the time-consuming task of model fabrication.

AFTER-THE-FACT MODELS OR CHECK MODELS

The after-the-fact model (Fig. 2-25) is fabricated after all the design work has been completed. It is simply a three-dimensional representation of the paper design. In some cases, the after-the-fact model is even constructed after the facility has been built (commonly referred to as an "as-built model"). From an overall cost standpoint, the after-the-fact model is probably the most expensive of all models. Much of the same effort is required on an after-the-fact model and few of the benefits are derived.

Check models in many instances contain all the elements of the design model, but the timing of model construction differs. The check model is made after all the drawings and engineering sketches and design have taken place. They are used only to locate interferences and problems that cannot be readily seen on the orthographic drawings. Therefore, check modeling is an expensive, after-the-fact procedure that does not provide for the most efficient use of modeling.

One drawback for check modeling is that it adds design cost over and above the original engineering expenses incurred by the use of drafting and drafting procedures. In situations where check modeling is used, it can save the company money by eliminating expensive interference problems and enabling the design group to change the plant configuration before the construction crew has discovered the problem of interference.

FIGURE 2-25 Check model.

QUIZ

2-1. What is an architectural model, and what are the more typical materials used to construct it?

2-2. How do presentation models differ from design models?

2-3. Name four industries that utilize prototype models.

2-4. What is another term for site model?

2-5. What is a design model?

2-6. Before starting the scope model, which information must be available?

2-7. What materials are the preliminary models usually made of, and why?

2-8. Before a preliminary model can be assembled, what information is absolutely necessary?

2-9. At what stage in the project are the structural and concrete requirements determined?

2-10. Describe the piping design stage for the final model. Where does this procedure usually take place in a typical engineering firm?

3

Information Flow and Model Chronology

FIGURE 3-1   Chemical plant model. (Model photographs courtesy of Badger America, Inc., Cambridge, Massachusetts.)

This section describes briefly the sequence of events necessary for a smooth design modeling program. Some companies may have slightly different approaches, but what is presented here represents a logical, calculated flow of events and procedures needed to fully utilize modeling in the total design effort for major industrial projects.

The student should fully understand this sequence in order to more easily fit into a company's piping design/model building program, even if traditionally the modeler will only be concerned with a portion of the stages.

INFORMATION FLOW

The key to any successful design effort is good communication. If "good" information cannot be channeled to the right areas in a timely manner, the design effort will fail or at least be adversely affected. Design modeling is no different! "Good" information in a timely manner is essential. Not only does design modeling improve communication, but it serves as a constant, visible, three-dimensional measuring stick of progress. It is much easier to survey a design model and determine the design status than it is to review a stack of incomplete drawings.

Accordingly, engineering procedures require detailed planning for the proper sequence of events during construction in order for a project to be completed with minimum delays. Long-delivery, unusual, or expensive items are generally designed and ordered first. As a result, the design and trade disciplines can schedule their functions without conflict or delay to other groups. Consideration is also given to the size, weight, and bulk of equipment pieces to avoid lifting or interference problems upon installation. The sequence of construction must permit work to be done from the ground (grade) up; and as nearly as possible from the center out.

The characteristics of physical construction and information flow provide the basis for engineering model construction. This sounds reasonable and logical, but it frequently presents problems to an engineering group when forced to change "traditional" procedures. With a model program, a group's work is no longer isolated and independent of other engineering groups. The group's efforts, as well as that of others, become readily apparent in three dimensions. Any omission, error, or delay will be highlighted by the model and thus stand out like the proverbial "sore thumb."

As indicated above, information to design and construct the model must be determined and/ or received in the same order as the natural sequence of project construction. For example, a model must begin from the top of the model base. This point is historically known as the *high point of finished grade*. A real number must be assigned to this "high point." Without this point of reference the model department cannot mount equipment since it has no way of knowing how thick to make the concrete foundations under the equipment. In addition, modelers need to know the actual height of pipe racks which are referenced to this number. Steel sizes can usually be "best-guessed" to within 2″, but racks cannot be built, much less installed, if the relationship between the "top of steel" and "grade" is not known.

Another illustration occurs with equipment. On a drafted project, a person working on the board can "work around" a piece of equipment for days. This usually means a lot of time is wasted waiting for someone to decide what to buy or from whom to buy it; or worse yet, to sit down and decide or design what is needed. On a model, as on the actual project, the designer or modeler can "work around" a piece of equipment only for a very short time. It then becomes obvious to anyone (inevitably the first to notice is the chief engineer) that there is a "hole" in the model.

The point to be made is that the model is basically a communications tool. The model accentuates any "holes," missing information, and causes of delay. It is the focal point of the design effort, and therefore expedites the flow of information and decision making.

MODEL CHRONOLOGY

The purpose here is to discuss the basic flow of information for a successful design modeling project. The obvious things, such as always using the latest issue drawings, will not be dwelt upon. Discussion will lean more toward the "chain of events" (information flow) that must be accomplished for successful design modeling. Figure 3-2 depicts this chain of events in schematic form.

For the purpose of this illustration, a basic assumption is made that a preliminary model is utilized to develop the ultimate equipment arrangement. The following step-by-step chain of events correspond to the activities in Fig. 3-2.

Plot Plan Development on Preliminary Model

Several alternative plot plans are developed by piping and project engineering personnel using preliminary modeling concepts. Inputs from structural, civil, electrical, and instrument groups should be made. Polaroid photographs of these alternative plot plans are made. An aboveground piping plan is developed of the major lines for the best arrangement and the preliminary model is restored to the best arrangement developed.

Preliminary Model Review (Internal)

The project engineer shall conduct the preliminary model design review, meeting with all the discipline engineers and a representative from the construction department. The purpose of this meeting is to secure internal agreement on the best equipment arrangement.

Preliminary Model Review (Client)

The project engineer, together with appropriate management personnel, present the agreed-upon plot plan (preliminary model) to the client. Should major changes be required, the design effort reverts back to the preliminary model development

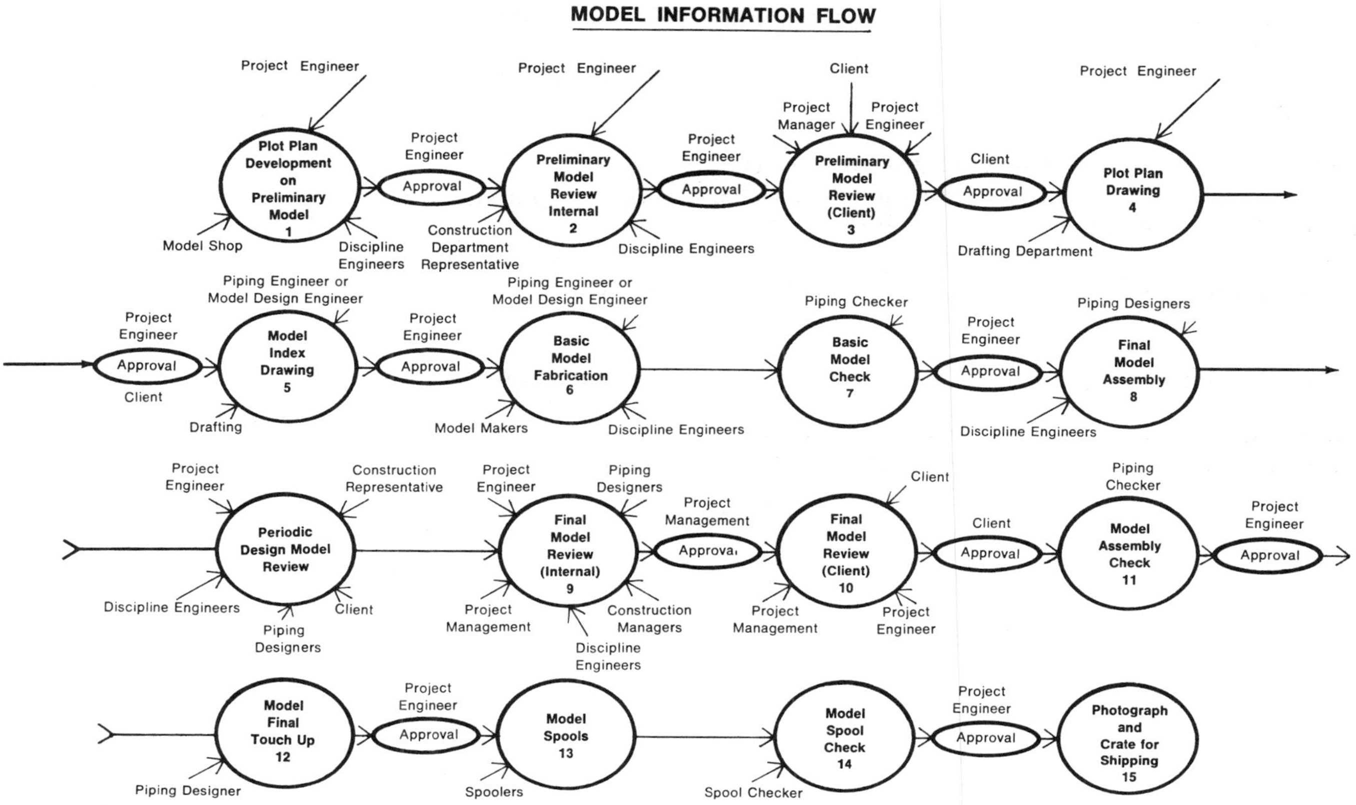

MODEL INFORMATION FLOW

FIGURE 3-2

stage or internal preliminary model review stage as deemed necessary by the project engineer.

Plot Plan (Drafting)

Upon client approval, the plot plan and equipment layout drawings are drafted and issued to the model shop and all disciplines proceed with the design effort.

Model Index (Drafting)

After approval by the client of the plot plan and aboveground piping plan, the model index drawing is created. The main purpose of this effort is to determine the model base perimeters. This is a joint effort by the model design engineer or supervisor and piping project engineer.

Basic Model

Fabrication and coordination of the basic model is a responsibility of the model shop engineer or supervisor. Information and/or suggestions should be solicited from the project engineer and all other design disciplines.

Basic Model Check

After completion of basic model fabrication, all coordinates, elevations, and orientations are checked by a piping checker.

Final Model Assembly

After corrections are made to the basic model, installation of piping commences. Both installation and design are normally performed by piping designers under the direction of the chief piping designer and piping engineers. Several client design reviews are often scheduled during this time period.

Final Model Review (Internal)

After completion of the final model, a review is held by the project engineer with discipline engineers, piping designers, project management, and a construction representative.

Final Model Review (Client)

After any questions and/or changes are resolved

internally, the project engineer and project management hold a final review with the client.

Model Assembly Check

After any questions and/or changes are resolved from the client's comments, the model is then checked by a piping checker. All lines, valves, instruments, and associated tagging are checked against the original design flow diagram and other job specifications.

Model Final Touch-up

All joints and equipment that have not previously been permanently attached are attached.

Model Spools

Drafting spoolers take off all appropriate information from the model and sketch model spools.

Model Spool Check

The spool checker checks spools against the actual model.

Shipping Preparation

The model is then photographed and crated for shipping.

Industrial Design
(Drafting and Modeling)

FIGURE 4-1 Petrochemical complex.

DRAWING AND THE MODEL

Although this section emphasizes the use of models in piping design, by no means is it suggesting that a model will totally eliminate the use of drawings. Many drawings, such as civil, electrical, HVAC, structural, pipe support, isometrics, fabrication, and plot plan, are still required for various types of projects. The model helps to reduce the number of drawings necessary but does not totally eliminate the drafting needs. Even with the use of a model in the design stage, drafting techniques needed to complete fabrication isometrics, spool drawings, pipe support drawings, and so on, still

play an essential part in the total design procedure. In many cases, though, the use of the orthographic, plan, section, and elevation method can be limited, although isometrics and detail views of the project are still extremely necessary. Orthographic drawings then become the exception, not the rule.

When the model has reached a certain stage, isometrics can be taken from lines and an alteration of modeling and drawing can occur. When the model is tagged and labeled, it is easier for the drafter to recognize and construct the isometrics necessary for the completion of the project. Piping arrangement drawings, orthographic drawings, and so on, may be necessary in congested and complicated areas that even models cannot make totally clear.

In some cases, drawings are done from a model as an after-the-fact drafting procedure, for recording all necessary elements of the project. This enables drafters with less experience to work on the drawings, as compared to the use of orthographic, plan, elevations, and section drawings in the design stage, where a high level of competence and engineering experience is an absolute prerequisite. The drafter can depict the work on the background of the model, making sections, elevations, and isometrics, working in conjunction with the model-making procedure. No matter how sophisticated the modern techniques of piping design become, with the use of models, computers, and so on, draftspersons will always find a ready market for their services.

INDUSTRIAL PIPING DRAFTING AND DESIGN

Piping drafting is a specialized area that uses a language of its own to convey the necessary information for the construction of a project. It utilizes symbols, dimensioning systems, specialized notations, and numerous types of lines to convey to the fabricator or construction crew a particular set of calculations and design situations that are peculiar to the piping field. The piping draftsperson has as his or her responsibility the need to conveniently provide accurate and detailed drawings of a particular system.

Drawings are used throughout a company in many capacities, from sales to procurement, including mechanical, electrical, and structural design departments. The information given on the drawings must be concise and readily discernible, enabling the reader to use the drawing for the various areas in which he or she is working.

Drawings are usually completed on paper, Mylar (which is plastic paper), linen, or treated cloth, in either pencil or ink. Ink is used in relatively few areas, with the exception of maps and in some cases plot plans and other drawings which remain somewhat constant and therefore do not need to be erased or changed. All of these media—paper, plastic, and cloth—enable the drawing to be reproduced through the use of a blueprint machine.

The piping draftsperson must use symbols to convey the necessary information and keep to a bare minimum the amount of detail that is shown in order not to confuse the drawing. There is a minimum of pictorial representation used on piping drawings—only where absolutely necessary to show clearances and relationships of equipment size to the surrounding situation.

Besides being able to draw and represent a

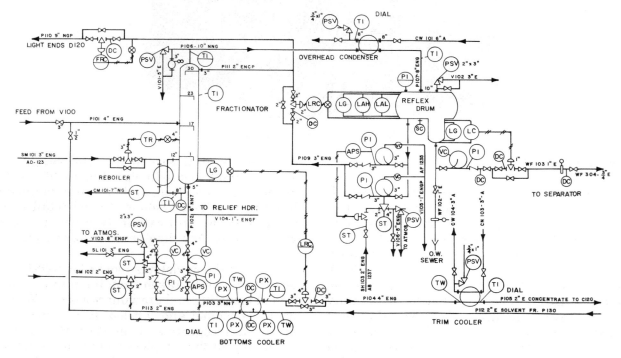

FIGURE 4-2 P&ID for a petrochemical plant.

system, a piping draftsperson must be familiar with component parts that make up a piping system. (See *Piping Systems Drafting and Design*.) One must also be familiar with the use of standards and catalog descriptions of material used on piping drawings. All component parts and standards must be readily available to conveniently display, dimension, and order parts that need to be purchased for a particular project.

Mechanical drafting ability is the most important aspect of any type of drafting. This includes piping drafting. The ability of a person to enter this field is dependent on his or her skill in mechanical drafting and lettering. Mechanical drafting procedures are used throughout all subfields, such as architectural, structural, and piping. The piping draftsperson will come in contact with a vast amount of equipment and machinery that will require adequate detailing through mechanical procedures.

Architectural drafting is also important to the piping draftsperson because many piping problems involve the use of architectural plans for

building complexes. In some cases, the architectural and piping systems are combined as in a power plant. The pipe drafter utilizes architectural, structural, piping, and mechanical drafting besides the use of maps and plot plans. For these reasons, the piping designer/drafter must be familiar with architectural, structural, piping, mechanical, and civil drafting procedures, besides knowing the basic subareas of the piping field, which include isometric drawing, plan, and elevation drawing, model making, and the mathematical calculations needed for pipe sizing, valve selection, fluid flow, stress evaluation, and thermal stresses in a piping system.

USES OF DRAFTING/DRAWINGS

Many companies still use the method where the designer will provide most of the information to the piping drafter, who will in turn lay out the plant with a sufficient number of elevations, plans, and section views so that the particular

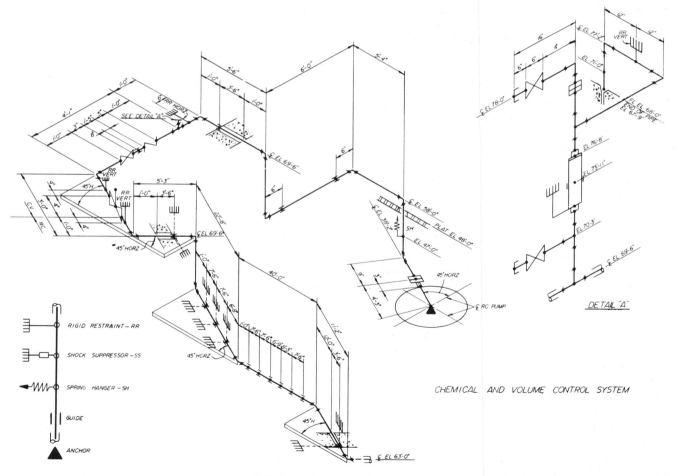

FIGURE 4-3 Nuclear isometric.

system is adequately represented. This method requires a highly qualified drafter who can read architectural, structural, civil, and equipment layout drawings and apply the design information to the laying out of the system. This time-consuming procedure is one of the main reasons for the change in the piping field toward the use of models. Various support plans and drawings are required before the system is put down on paper. These include electrical, structural, architectural, civil, site, mechanical, and HVAC; vendor drawings, the original design flow diagram (P&ID); and the equipment placement drawing.

Electrical drawings will cover the necessary electrical systems to be installed within the building, including separate systems for power, communications and service. It is important to know the location and the electrical design requirements in the beginning stages of any piping job because of the need to run cable trays and electrical conduit, providing adequate room for service, installation, and avoiding interferences between the piping and electrical system. The electrical drawings will include light locations, control panels, conduit runs, junction boxes, and other electrical needs.

The structural information needed for the project is an extremely important aspect of any piping system. The piping system must be attached to, hung from, and supported from the structural system. The structural drawings provide the boundaries in which the particular piping system is to be maintained. Various aspects of structural drawings will include suggested amounts of steel versus concrete construction; size of the actual plant, pads, and floors; building elevations and floor-to-ceiling heights; wall bracing; platforms; column placement; and structural design standards. These are just a few of the considerations that are necessary before starting the physical plant design.

The architectural plans include elevations of the buildings, including a sufficient number of cross-sectional views, indicating foundations, floor penetrations for stair wells and elevators, wall locations, floor elevations, ceilings, windows, ceiling heights, ducts, doors, interior and exterior sectional views, and so on. All of these allow the drafter to work within the limits that have been prescribed, whether the pipe system is to fit in a building or be part of a complex or process plant.

Site plans (site models are also used) provided by the civil engineering department show the location of the plant with regard to the elevation, grade, and the physical (geographic) surroundings

that the plant and/or building is to be located on and in relation to. The site plan will locate the particular boundaries and perimeters on which the building, plant, and/or power station must be laid out. This drawing is usually drawn to a very small scale and will include all natural and man-made boundaries, including ponds, roads, railroad lines, power lines, and waste disposal units.

Plot plans are drawings that depict the actual design situation of the proposed project; this includes north-south orientation and all necessary coordinates. Much of the necessary structural and architectural design information, such as building outlines (existing and proposed), equipment centerlines, and any physical information essential to the construction and design of the piping system, will show on the plot plan.

The equipment placement drawings will be prepared by the design group, or in some cases simplified models will be used to show different equipment placement options. Simplified graphic shapes are used to represent equipment, such as vessels, towers, pumps, storage tanks, and turbines.

HVAC system drawings are as important as electrical system drawings because of the amount of ducting and equipment that is necessary for adequate replacement of air, circulation, air conditioning, and heating, which must meet federal and state standards. All of this requires a considerable amount of space for installation within the project. These requirements must be known well in advance so as not to create interferences with piping and electrical runs. HVAC drawings may also include the location and design of all mechanical equipment, conveyors, cranes, hoists, and so on.

Vendors' drawings include all essential data pertaining to equipment, valves, instrumentation, and so on. Anything that is ordered from a catalog or is not fabricated must have dimensions, sizes, flange types, ratings, and so on, supplied before the system is designed.

Besides drawings of the actual plan, sectional, and elevational views, the draftsperson will be called upon to make small, complicated detailed drawings in which he or she will show standard parts and specialized arrangements, including subdetails of vessels and other fabricated items. These types of drawings require that the drafter know the background information necessary to understand the equipment, valves, fittings, pipes, and other components. This information is available through the catalogs from which he or she

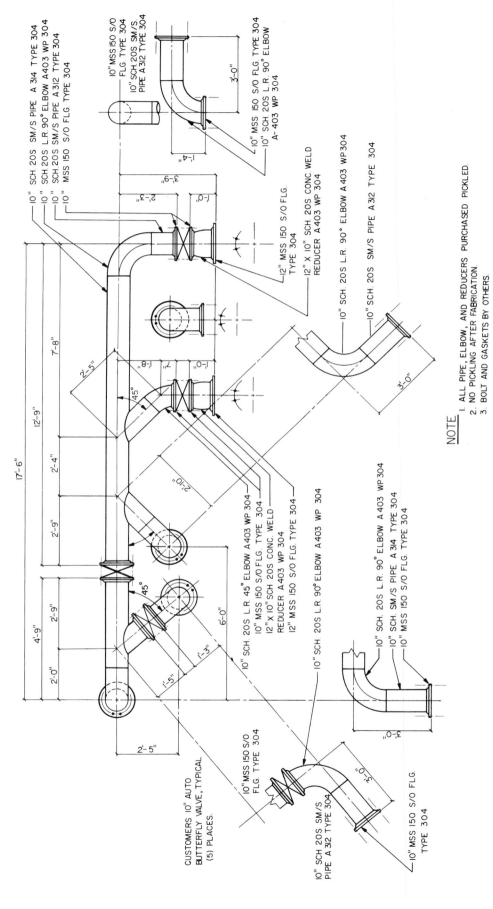

FIGURE 4-4 Pipe fabrication spool.

NOTE
1. ALL PIPE, ELBOW, AND REDUCERS PURCHASED PICKLED.
2. NO PICKLING AFTER FABRICATION.
3. BOLT AND GASKETS BY OTHERS.

43

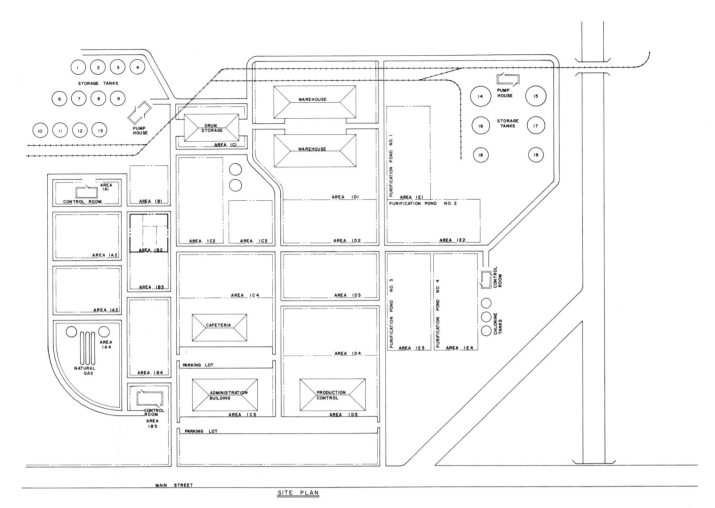

FIGURE 4-5 Site plan.

must order the constituent parts of the piping system.

The piping designer and engineer coordinate the beginning of any project, including the specialized studies and calculations needed to define the requirements that are necessary to produce the product and/or end results, such as production of usable energy or manufacture of a salable commodity.

The first step in this process is the construction of the flow diagram. Flow diagrams (Fig. 4-2) are the most important beginning document necessary for any project. Only after this drawing is completed can the piping designer and drafter start the actual layout of the plant or piping system.

Flow diagrams are the basic blueprint or story of the process, function, and equipment for a particular job, without construction or fabrication details. They provide all the necessary data with which to begin the actual design and layout of the orthographic views or model.

In most cases, flow diagrams can be viewed as pictorial statements of purpose for the whole or part of a project, forming the link between verbal statements or calculations and the designed functional system. Schematic flow diagrams are essential in the early phases of development and process study. After the preliminary calculations and feasibility studies are complete, the more complicated stage of creating a process design with the aid of a flow diagram is instituted, and from this, the mechanical flow diagram (the piping and instrumentation diagram, or P&ID).

The flow diagram is the first drawing to be completed and utilized by almost all design departments in any project involving piping systems. Starting from a sketch, the drafter will lay out the flow diagram according to established standard procedures utilizing symbols and piping line representations. The flow diagrams are the drafter's first responsibility in the sequence of steps toward a completed set of design prints and/or model of the project that will be shipped to the job construction site.

A drafter without much experience will not

readily be able to understand all of the engineering and background information for the particular system. He or she must be able to accurately draw the flow diagram, usually presented in a rough, sketched-out form, with only the minimum essential information from which to start. This sketch is designed and completed by the project or instrument engineer. The drafter, through experience with many types of flow diagrams, will eventually come to understand the function and operating principles behind each individual project, as represented by the flow diagrams.

Flow diagrams are used for all applications of piping systems. The drafter must be able to read the designer's diagram sketch and convert it into a symbolically represented system flow diagram, or if it is an instrumentation sketch, into a P&ID. From this symbolic drawing, the drafter/designer will lay out the complete system in orthographic drawings or the modeler will construct the system directly on the model without the aid of drawings.

In many companies that do petrochemical process work, this procedure of designing, equipment placement, and running the pipelines directly on the model (without the use of orthographic views) from the P&ID has increased the importance of understanding, drawing, and designing the flow diagram in an efficient, accurate manner. Flow diagrams and P&IDs are essential to all projects, whether modeled or drawn.

The following is a description of various design methods used in industry. For examples of these drawings, see Sections 25 to 32.

DESIGN METHODS USED IN INDUSTRY

There are basically three procedures or combinations of these procedures used throughout industry.

Plan, Elevation, and Section Design Method

The first method is the plan and elevation method, where conventional orthographic views are drawn of the system in its totality, using a multitude of views. This type of system can be seen in the drawings provided in Sections 25 to 31.

This method requires a vast quantity of drawings, including a large number of sectional views. All vertical dimensions are called out in elevation designations and all horizontal dimensions are shown in the plan views. Dimensions that cannot show on the major drawings are provided in smaller cutaway sectional views.

This type of system uses and is in need of well qualified and experienced personnel. This is one reason why many companies are moving toward other design methods which require less experienced personnel.

The elevation, plan, and section method has problems that are inherent in the fact that piping systems do not lend themselves to orthographic projection because lines and components that fall below or behind other pipelines and pipe components cannot be shown in relation to the objects that lie in front or on top of them.

Often, this type of drawing method requires that the head or senior drafter complete the major plan and elevation views, leaving for the less experienced draftsperson the cutting of sections and the detailing of the project. This may lead to overdetailing of certain areas, which is hard to avoid, because it is almost impossible to know beforehand, how many views and drawings will be needed. Only after a multitude of sections and details are taken can duplications be seen. When orthographic projection is used, it becomes extremely difficult for the construction group and fabricators to follow the necessary operational sequence needed to construct the project. With this method, isometric drawings (Fig. 4-3) are taken of all lines on a project in order to show the origination to termination of a pipeline, including its component parts. As you can see, this method of representing a piping system is extremely time-consuming, complicated, and expensive.

Isometric Method

The second method is the isometric method (which is not used for large projects because of complexity problems). For heating and plumbing within architectural areas for buildings, schools, houses, this method has proven quite successful and less cumbersome than the orthographic method.

Large drawings are made of whole piping systems and are drawn as isometrics. Also, a particular area of a plant or project may be put in isometric form. This three-dimensional procedure enables the plan and elevation to be combined in one drawing, thereby decreasing the total amount of drawing needed to represent the system.

As in the elevation, plan, and section method, isometric spool sheets are sometimes made of individual lines in order to do material take-off, dimensioning, and pipe support placement unless the system isometric is sufficient to show these aspects clearly.

Design and Check Model Method

The third method, one that is gaining increasing acceptance in the power-generation field, is model making. The petrochemical and process industries have done the essential groundwork for this type of system design.

When utilizing the model method of design, many of the original support drawings, including architectural, civil, electrical, site, mechanical, and flow diagrams, are still required at the onset of each project. The model shop is usually staffed with people who understand only the basics of the

piping design. Therefore, many industries utilize model makers only for the larger construction items, such as bases, architectural construction, walls, elevations, steel, equipment, hanger placement, and other items not within the design realm (the basic model).

The piping designer will usually be called upon to do the actual running of pipe and placement of component parts within the system. Therefore, together with the support drawings and data that are required, the piping designer and draftsperson will requisition the needed model parts, bases, and equipment necessary for the construc-

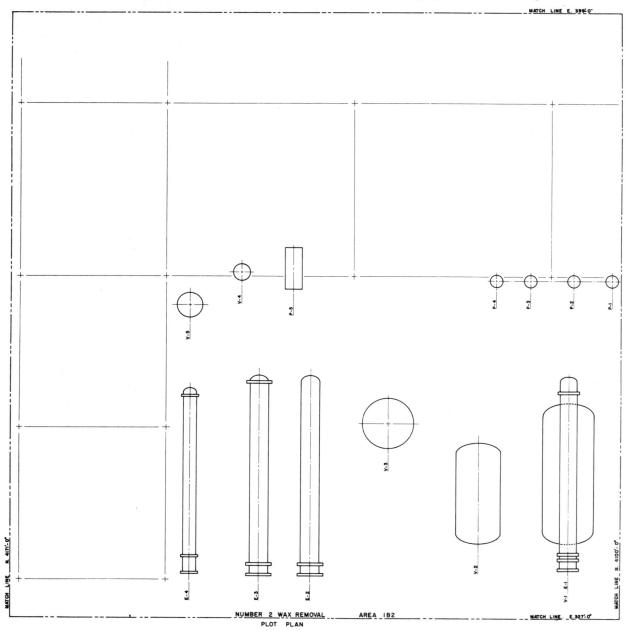

FIGURE 4-6 Plot plan.

tion of the model. Design modeling will often take place within the drafting area of the company.

The model shop will usually provide all support construction necessities for the piping of the model by the pipe designer. This method of pipe design is extremely useful because having physical objects to manipulate, the designer can actually see any clearances or interferences between objects on the model which might not be apparent on drawings. Equipment layout drawings and design sketches are sometimes utilized with this method.

In the petrochemical field, the piping drafter may be put to work on the model running pipe, placing component parts, and so on, under the supervision of a head designer. The head designer can oversee the project much more easily than in the case of the power-generation field, where the systems are so complicated that whole design group may be needed to work on just one portion of a large-scale model.

After equipment requirements have been determined, the placement and construction of equipment on the base of the model is done. This enables the designer to check for sufficient design capabilities that must be met and offers him or her the opportunity to revise and change the layout without resorting to revisions on a large quantity of drawings. Plan and some sectional views may still be used in this method, although to a much lesser extent than when following the elevation, section, and plan method.

The one type of drawing that is used in the model design sequence is the sketched isometric view of each individual line on a model. These sketches are then converted into isometric drawings with dimensions as in the three-dimensional method, or fed into a computer (CAD) graphic system, which will then draw the isometric line and prepare a material take-off.

Checking the model and preparing a material listing and revisions all require a sufficiently reduced degree of labor and experience than do other methods of design. The checkers on the model method must review and systematically check all flow diagrams, equipment placement, isometrics, and any other drawings that have been made to produce the model, but not to such the extent that is required with other methods. The model itself will represent all the other drawings that have been made, therefore making it much easier for the checker to see any problems that may be encountered during the fabrication, installation, and/or functioning stages of the project.

The main drawback of the model-building method is the human element, where resistance within the company and industry comes from seasoned veterans in the piping field who look upon the model method as a waste of money. Many utility companies and other power-generation groups have found it hard to institute model programs because of the built-in resistance to change among designers and drafters. The petrochemical field, because of its competitive nature, has adapted much more rapidly to this advantageous system of piping design.

The model also presents problems in reproduction. Photography of models has become common, enabling the design group to take various photographs of stages and/or the completed views of the model and ship these to the job site along with the model. Still, it is impossible to reach the degree of convenience that blueprinting and photocopying have made available to the drawing method of design.

Upon completion, models are shipped to the job site, where the construction leaders monitor the job through the use of procedural steps that have been laid out for the sequence of construction operations and use the model much more effectively than a set of drawings, which are extremely cumbersome. The model remains at the job site possibly 10 to 20 years after the construction of the plant and becomes part of the project training program for new personnel, enabling the company to train and coordinate services and maintenance of the facility without the need for a large staff. Also, any changes, revisions, or additions of new equipment can be designed on the model before they are tested in the plant.

When comparing the three methods, it is possible to find deficiencies in each case. Seemingly, industry is determined to utilize portions of all three methods of piping design. Modeling, with the use of limited plan and sectional views and isometric take-offs, will be the way of the future for pipe design and drafting.

The three-dimensional or isometric system method will continue to be used for small-system pipe design areas, such as for buildings and plumbing systems where models are not an effective or efficient use of time or money.

DESIGN OF PIPING SYSTEMS

Before the pipe designer can attempt to lay out a piping system or start the construction of a model, it is necessary to have a flow diagram. All manufacturers' drawings or vendors' prints must be accessible to the piping drafter/designer/modeler; this information will establish dimensions and configurations for equipment that are standard items, such as pumps, compressors, heat exchangers, vessels, valves, and other components. These drawings are essential for accurate, economical placement and layout of an industrial plant. The model maker and piping designer must know the configuration and dimensions of the equipment to be used on a particular project. The model maker will construct from plastic or wood the general configuration of the larger pieces of equipment. In some cases, just simple rectangular block shapes are used to represent equipment, such as pumps, generators, and turbines.

Laying out major equipment is one of the earliest steps in the design process. Layout and equipment arrangement of industrial plants will be the first step in the design process. Depending on the type of industrial plant, whether nuclear, conventional, petrochemical, food processing, water treatment, and so on, the specifications and design requirements and layout will be different. In general, most equipment will be located above grade level, although care should be taken not to elevate equipment so that maintenance, repair, and operation procedures are hampered. Many elevations are determined by the process itself and the amount of static head to be developed by the vessel. Using the plot plan, the piping designer can either sketch the general arrangement of equipment or, when using the model method, styrofoam or wood blocks that represent the outer dimensions of the equipment can be used to try out various equipment locations on the plot plan or within the building structure. As we have said, the vertical and horizontal spacing of the equipment is determined primarily by the type of process, and these specifications are different for each subfield unit in the piping.

Layout and Arrangement of Piping

The main job of the pipe designer will be the laying out of equipment and piping, along with the coordinating of the piping group with subfields such as the structural, electrical, and HVAC groups, in order to establish an economical, feasible piping installation which meets all the requirements and other necessities that must be considered in the design phase. The piping designer will also coordinate stress calculations and determine the selection and location of piping components such as valves and pipe supports.

One of the most important duties of the piping designer is the layout and arrangement of the piping runs. The first procedure after equipment location is for the piping designer to sketch on the plot plan all the major pipe requirements. Another method that is used is to sketch on the plot plan the necessary pipelines and then transfer these to the model. By determining the total piping needs in plan view, it is possible to establish pipeways and pipe rack locations. For outdoor facilities, such as petrochemical installations, a majority of the horizontal piping will be run along major pipeways on the pipe racks, or in some cases on sleepers. After the major piping has been determined and located in the plan view, it is then possible to decide upon connections to equipment and other details.

When laying out a piping system, the designer must take into account variables of design requirements; the economics of the system; types of stress under which the system will be placed; accessibility for maintenance, repair, and installation; and the support of the system.

Specifications for piping systems can be found in *Piping Systems Drafting and Design* and are not repeated here.

DRAFTING, LAYOUT, AND ARRANGEMENT OF PIPING SYSTEMS

The following section deals primarily with the initial steps that must be taken to design and lay out a typical industrial installation. Figures 4-5 to 4-8 are a series of drawings which show the general procedures that are necessary for the creation of a piping installation, including the drawing of a site plan, (Fig. 4-5), its corresponding breakdown into a feasible plot plan (Fig. 4-6), and its subsequent division into workable units. Figure 4-7 shows the piping index (model index drawings are also used) and the foundation plan required for such a project (Fig. 4-8).

Figure 4-5 shows a site plan which takes into account all the necessary buildings, piping arrangements, pipeways, storage area, warehouses, shipping facilities, roadways, and personnel needs, such as cafeterias and personnel buildings. This overall site plan is used to determine the logical arrangement of a particular petrochemical installation. This site plan allows for the location and arrangement of all buildings according to specifications, safety requirements, and operation details. It is the first step in the construction and layout of a large-scale refinery. In many cases, the pipe drafter/designer/modeler will come in contact with the construction of an additional unit to an existing facility. In these cases, the original site plan will be necessary in order to establish the general limits from which to create the plot plan for the new unit. Site models are also used. The design and layout of a new unit or total refinery must take into account many elements, including operation, specifications, design requirements, and construction sequences. This site plan, which in some cases is referred to as a master plot plan, shows the general terrain of the total facility, all existing roadways, railroad units, shipping facilities, and in some cases will even show the contours of the site if it is not on flat ground.

In some projects, the facility will only be the construction of one large building, such as power plants (Sections 29 to 31). As can be seen from these projects, all the design and operation requirements are confined to a single structure, which includes areas for equipment, turbines, reactor cores, and so on.

When using a model, the preliminary model stage corresponds to the plot plan, where simple blocks of styrofoam or wood can represent major structures, storage tanks, buildings, and so on, and can be easily rearranged. When using the drawing method, the existing physical traits must be shown on the site plan, and then the area is broken into logical working units, depending on the type of facility and its design needs. In the case of Fig. 4-5, the warehouse and shipping units are established close to the railroad lines, and storage tanks are located well away from the general processing areas. The cafeteria, administration building, and production control buildings are situated close to the main street, which is an existing roadway providing easy access for visiting personnel and employees. There are also roadways which provide access to the general process area.

After the site plan or master plot plan has been developed, or in the case of the model method, the preliminary model finished and approved by all design groups, each unit can be taken separately and designed in greater detail. Figure 4-6 shows a unit plot plan for area 1B2 from Fig. 4-5 of the site plan. On this drawing, area 1B2 has been drawn to a sufficient scale so as to allow for the placement of major equipment. Plot plans will show all major equipment and identify them, such as those shown in Fig. 4-6 of the No. 2 wax removal area. The coordinates are established by north, south, east, west match lines, from which major equipment and pipe rack centerlines are located. E1, E2, E3, and E4 are heat exchange units, V2 is a

horizontal drum, and V3, V4, and V5, are vertical vessels. P1, P2, P4, and P5 are pumping units and their centerlines are located on this particular drawing. The match lines or battery limits look in either a northerly or easterly direction and define the extent of the unit. In this case, match line E327′0″ and match line E399′0″ define the extent of the unit in the east-west direction and match line N4100′0″ and N4171′0″ define the north-south boundaries. These are also referred to as battery limits and will determine the extent of the portion of the facility to be dealt with by the drafter/ designer, although existing local units must, of course, be taken into account since they tie directly into this section of the refinery. Battery limits, match lines, and coordinates are also used on models.

Piping is not shown at this stage. The plot plan or unit plot drawing is one of the first drawings that will be prepared by the pipe designer/ drafter. In some cases, this drawing will be done at a smaller scale than a typical piping installation because of the extent of the unit, such as 1″ = 10′, unless the unit is small, as in Fig. 4-6. Many things determine the logical location of equipment, pipeways, and extent of the battery limits of a new unit, including the design requirements, type of vessels, the materials of construction for pipelines, valving installations, amount of parallel piping runs required, and the general sequence flow between equipment and to other parallel units.

At this stage of plot plan development, the types of equipment, processes, and design needs must be known by the designer in order to establish equipment locations and elevations of equipment and subunits required for a design process. The flow sequence and process requirements, codes, and specifications for equipment must be taken into account by the piping designer/drafter. Also, construction requirements, maintenance, and operation needs must be considered at this point in the design and layout of the plant. The model method offers the easiest and most visible method for establishing a workable plot plan, although the drafting method is still widely used. Besides the design requirements and maintenance and construction details, structural aspects of the plant must be taken into account, such as the extent of the foundation, footings, pier requirements, and so on, including all structural steel, columns, and fireproof structures that may be necessary for the project. The development of a workable plot plan can only be established by an experienced piping designer/drafter; the beginning piping drafter cannot be expected to know all the design specifications and requirements for a particular unit. These are only established through many years of experience on the job, working closely with experienced personnel.

Piping Index Drawing (Model Index Drawing)

Figure 4-7 shows the piping index drawing for the project shown in Fig. 4-5. In this drawing, the plot plan is divided into feasible working units which

then can be drawn at a larger scale, such as $3/8'' = 1'$ or $1/2'' = 1'$. Figure 4-7 shows the plot plan divided at coordinates or match lines into areas A and B for the pipeway pipe racks, and areas C and D for the equipment areas. By breaking the plot plan into smaller indexed units, it is possible for the piping draftsperson to more easily understand and represent a particular portion of a unit, showing piping, components, and equipment in great detail, using the plan, elevation, and section method or, in some cases, the model method.

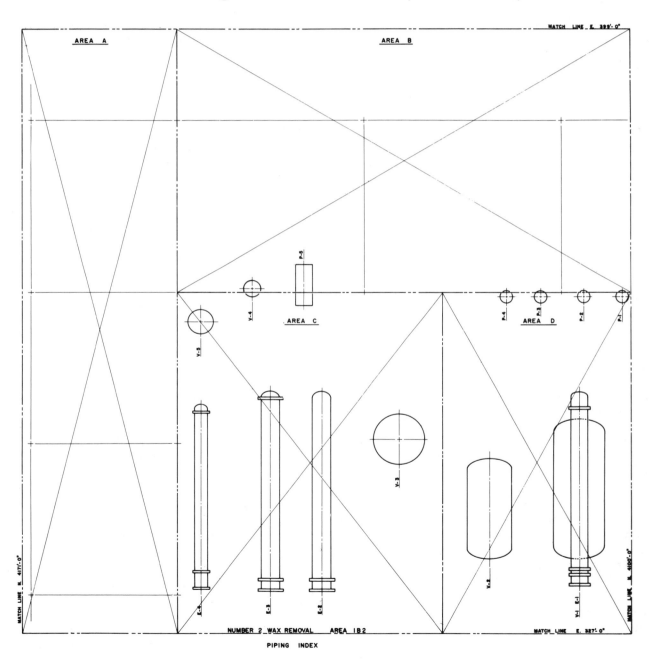

FIGURE 4-7 Piping index drawing.

Related equipment should be kept in the same areas, as in Fig. 4-7, where the horizontal drums or vessels are established in area D together with associated pumping units, and in area C the economizer units and vertical vessels. Areas A and B are allocated to pipeways for multilevel pipe racks. (*Note:* Pipe racks are not usually indexed separately from equipment areas.) The piping index drawing and the plot plan are usually drawn on the same size sheet of paper and to a similar scale, as is the foundation location drawing shown in

Fig. 4-8. This foundation drawing establishes by coordinates the piers, foundations, footings, pedestals, and so on, that are required for a unit. Notice in Fig. 4-8 how the foundations are lined up whenever possible, to provide a logical, neatly arranged installation. (Note that the foundation locations on this drawing, for the economizer units in area C, are not really adequate for the length of the vessels.) By establishing the size of the foundations and footings, possible interferences and structural requirements can be determined at the

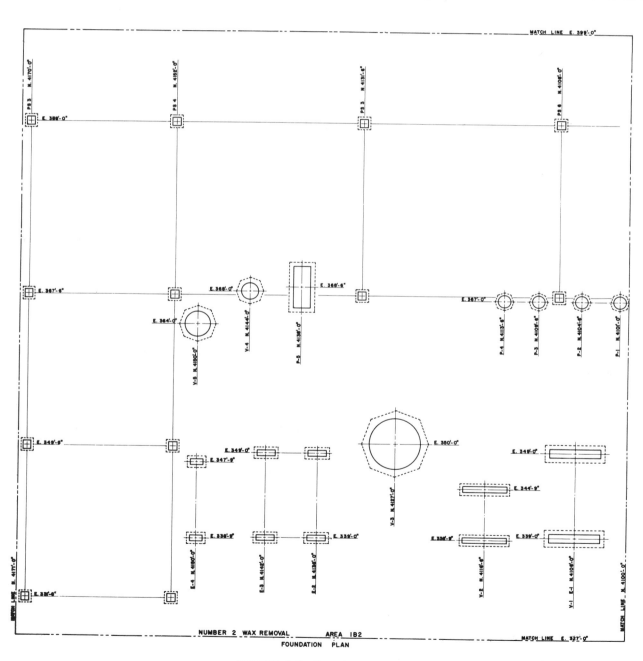

FIGURE 4-8 Foundation plan.

earlier stages of the project. The hidden portions of these foundations, shown in Fig. 4-8, show the extent of the buried footing.

This logical sequence of development proceeds from the site plan to the plot plan to the piping index drawing to the foundation plan and subsequently to each individual indexed area.

PAVING, GRADING, AND DRAINAGE

The paving, grading, and drainage layout and design is usually completed after the plot plan, the unit index, and the foundation plan have been established. Figure 4-9 is an example of a paving, grading, and drainage drawing. In this drawing, the type of drainage systems that are to be used and systems which may be combined should be designated, including the following:

- Storm water
- Storm and oily water
- Corrosive service
- Sanitary service
- Special services, such as acid drainage systems.

It will be necessary to know the size and type of pipe to be used and the minimum and maximum depth of drainage lines for physical protection. The high point of finish grade (HPFG), and any other special requirements that are entailed by the process or types of unit in question, will be provided by the engineer.

FOUNDATION AND CONCRETE DRAWINGS

Foundation and concrete drawings are necessary for all piping system. In some cases, the general foundation drawing, which includes coordinates; boundary limits; battery limits; dimensions; the location, size, extent of rebar, reinforcement steel, and so on, will all be shown on this type of drawing. The piping drafter may be called upon either to draw for or work closely with the structural group, including the engineer and designers who establish the calculations, drains, sewers, grading, and other necessary aspects which involve coordinating the piping and structural/foundation design groups.

All underground equipment, piping, and components must be established prior to the location and determination of foundations. Often, electrical conduit, sewers, and water lines will be placed underground. These must be located and designed, together with the appropriate drains and penetrations that are necessary, before the foundation is established. Underground networks must be one of the first drawings completed after the plot plan has been established.

ISOMETRIC DRAWINGS

Isometric drawings (Figs. 4-10 and 4-11) are a fast and accurate method of representing piping systems. In industries that utilize piping drafters, many people are employed strictly in the area of piping isometrics doing fabrication, pipe support, and stress study isometrics, in some cases using computers for calculations and the actual isometric graphic representations. Power companies, petrochemical firms, and large construction companies all employ a considerable number of draftspersons to do isometric drawing (spools).

Isometric projections are among the most commonly used methods of representing piping. Pipeline isometric drawings provide accurate three-dimensional views of a pipeline and component parts, enabling the fabricator, and construction crew to see complete pipeline views as one would a picture.

In an isometric drawing, the elevation, plan, and side views are presented to the viewer simultaneously. All horizontal and vertical dimensions are shown in one view instead of the normal three views encountered in orthographic projection.

An isometric drawing is usually taken of each individual line within a project to show the details and dimensions required to make up that line; this is referred to as a spool sheet.

Isometric drawings can be used for detailing and dimensioning a particular pipeline, for ordering and specifying component parts, flagging specialized callouts and piping fabrication notes, and for pipe support placement.

Within the more critical industries, such as the nuclear field, piping isometrics are also utilized for seismic and thermal movement studies. By programming the isometric drawing into a computer with the preliminary placement of supports and hangers and doing an analysis of the system's possible negative reaction to seismic and thermal disturbances before installation, the designer can accurately place specialized and standard pipe supports, hangers, and shock suppressors (snubbers).

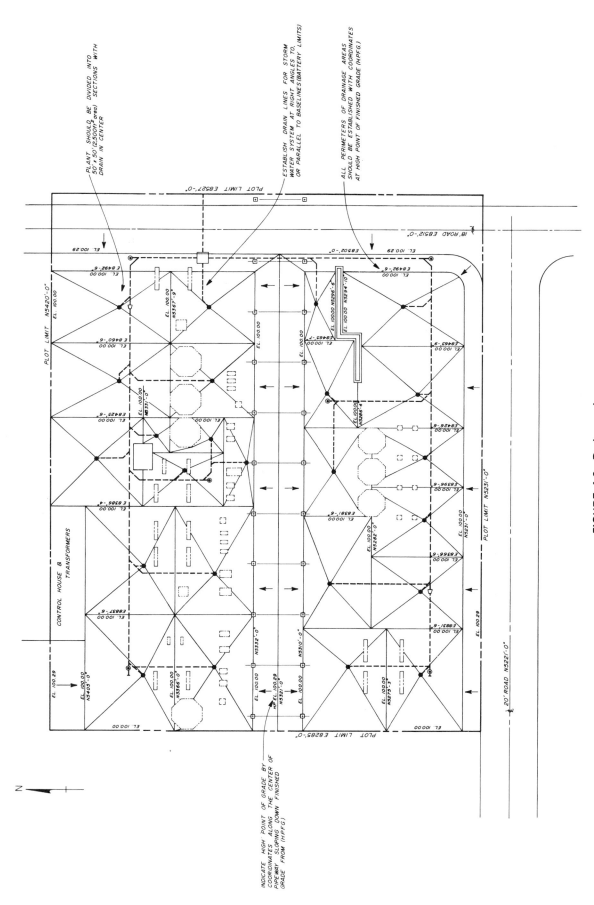

FIGURE 4-9 Drainage plan.

53

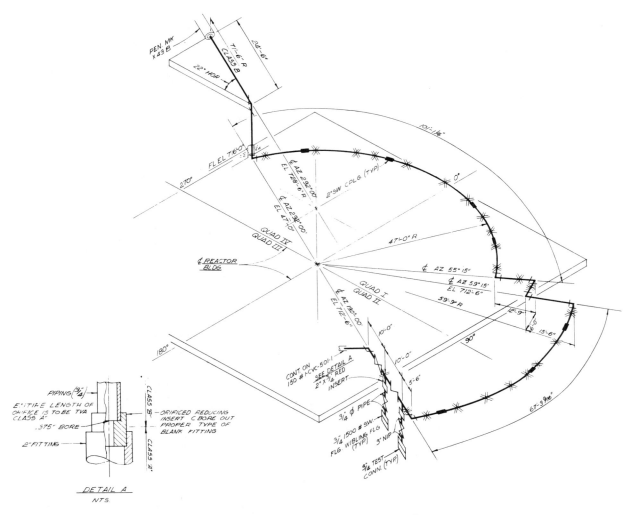

FIGURE 4-10 Isometric in the round.

FIGURE 4-11 Isometric for pipe support placement.

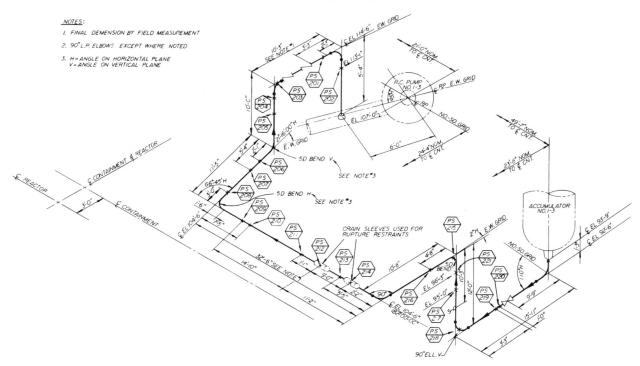

54

Isometric drawings can be divided into four basic types:

1. *System Isometrics:* This type of isometric shows a total or partial system. It is used less than the other types because it is more difficult to draw, exhibiting a complete system instead of a single piping line. System isometrics are also used for pictorially representing a piping system for sales or advertising purposes. The piping system isometric drawing is usually limited to smaller-diameter pipelines, especially where threaded construction is utilized; in this case, many dimensions are left to the fabricator for field placement. System isometrics are usually limited to relatively simple piping systems.

2. *Field Fabrication Isometrics:* This type of drawing will locate only critical aspects of the system, such as major equipment. Dimensions will be given only for overall sizes of the pipeline. Many of the dimensions on the field fabrication isometric drawing are provided and verified at the job site.

3. *Shop Fabrication Isometrics:* All face-to-face dimensions for valves, flanges, and fittings are given, including dimensions for the placement and fabrication of the pipeline. Piping fabrication drawings are meant to be complete in and of themselves because lines on the same project will often be fabricated at different shops. All necessary information must be included on this drawing.

4. *Detail Isometrics:* This type will show particular details and/or special items. Specialized trim and other essential information that may be required for the system is shown on the detail isometric drawing. This type of isometric will sometimes show a small portion of a pipeline or a piece of equipment in order to express the needed dimensions for its fabrication.

Models and Isometrics

Models are employed extensively throughout the piping field. In cases where piping systems are designed directly on the model without the aid of the plan or sectional views, taking the design information from the engineer/mechanical flow diagram, the drafter works from the model dimensions, constructing an isometric drawing of each line that needs to be fabricated. When using this method, the drafter draws or sketches from each line on the model an isometric view of the complete pipeline from its beginning to end, including all valves, fittings, and other equipment related to this specific line.

The sketched piping line isometric will show all the dimensions and components required to "make up" the particular pipeline.

Computers and Isometrics

In some companies, the use of computer graphics for the drawing of line isometrics has become standard practice. After the isometric has been sketched from the model, the dimensions, coordinates, equipment, and calculations such as flow, temperatures, and so on, are fed into a computer. With this data input, the computer is able to produce an isometric drawing and, in some cases, to complete a bill of materials, thus bypassing the need for a perfectly drawn isometric by a drafter.

A computer-aided drafting system (CAD) can do computations and construct the drawing by using sensitized paper and a plotter. The use of a computer is relatively new throughout the industry. This is reflected in the cost and scarcity of the process, which will change drastically within the next few years. In the piping field, computer graphics are used primarily for the construction of isometrics and engineering flow diagrams.

Computers and models will not totally replace the need for hand-drafted plans for a considerable number of years, if ever.

PIPE SUPPORT

Pipe Support Drawings

All piping systems and pipelines require the use of supports and hangers to carry, hold, and sustain the pipeline when under stresses due to thermal expansion, mechanical vibration, and the weight of the piping system (see Figs. 4-12 to 4-14).

In modern terminology, "pipe support" means any type of support, hanger, or mechanism that will allow the system to be suspended from above or supported from below. When breaking this down to more detailed terminology, "pipe supports" refer to mechanical mechanisms which allow the piping to be supported from below, and "pipe hangers" designate mechanical mechanisms which enable the piping system or pipeline to be hung from above.

Many drafters are employed directly and exclusively in this field of piping support, and it is fast becoming one of the most lucrative subfields within the piping industry.

For noncritical uses, the simplest pipe hangers, consisting of split rings, clamps, brackets,

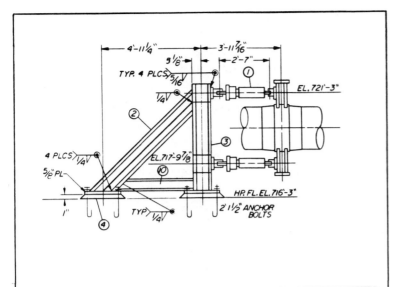

ITEM NO.	NO. REQ'D	FIG. NO.	SIZE DESCIPTION	TW	MAT'L
		H563	3" STD. WT. PIPE STANCHION, TYPE A	8	PIPE
			FOR 8" PIPE, D= , E=		
1	2	306	NO.35 MECHANICAL SHOCK ARRESTOR		
			(OPTION-1) 6" STROKE, C=2'-3"		
			MVT. 1 5/8" (IN), LOAD=13365 NO.		
			LOCKING ACCELERATION = .02 G.		
			MAT'L PER B & PV CODE SECT. 3		
2	2		7'-1 9/16" W10X29 L (CUT TO SUIT)		SA36
3	2		W10 X 29 X 5'-4" LG.	309	SA36
4	4		PL 5/8" X 18 1/2" X 18 1/2 (OR SA515GR65)		SA36
5	2		W10 X 45 X 3'-2" LG.	150	SA36
6	8		ANG. 3 1/2 X 2 1/2 X 3/8 X 8" LG.		SA36
7	2		PL 3/4" X 1 7/8" X 12" (OR SA515GR65)		SA36
8	2		PL 3/4" X 4" X 13 1/2" (OR SA515GR65)		SA36
9	4		PL 3/4" X 12" X 1'-1 1/4" (OR SA515GR65)		SA36

FIGURE 4-12 Pipe support detail.

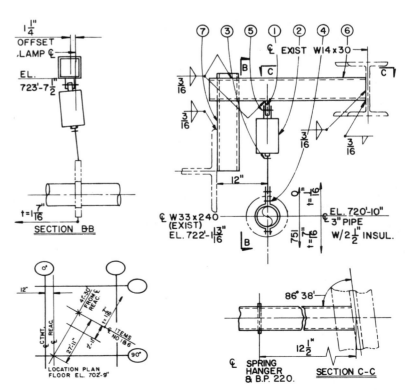

FIGURE 4-13 Pipe support detail.

56

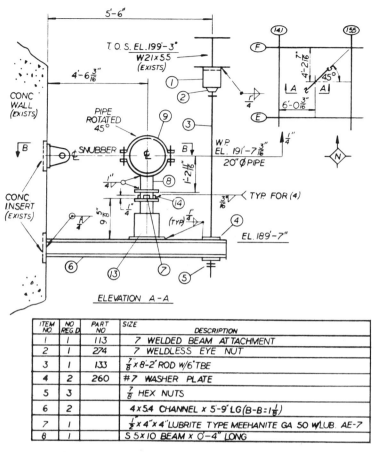

ITEM NO.	NO. REQ'D	PART NO.	SIZE	DESCRIPTION
1	1	113	7	WELDED BEAM ATTACHMENT
2	1	274	7	WELDLESS EYE NUT
3	1	133	$\frac{7}{8}$ x 8-2' ROD W/6'TBE	
4	2	260	#7 WASHER PLATE	
5	3		$\frac{7}{8}$ HEX NUTS	
6	2		4 x 5.4 CHANNEL x 5'-9' LG (B-B = 1$\frac{1}{8}$)	
7	1		$\frac{1}{2}$ x 4" x 4" LUBRITE TYPE MEEHANITE GA 50 W/LUB. AE-7	
8	1		S 5 x 10 BEAM x 0'-4" LONG	

FIGURE 4-14 Pipe support detail.

clips, pipe rolls, pipe stands, and simple hangers, are used by themselves or in combination with other pipe support accessories. These simplified catalog items are used primarily for services and situations such as domestic plumbing and building heating systems, where stresses and strains due to thermal and mechanical vibrations are minimal and the total weight of the piping system is small. In the noncritical area, rods and straps and other simple pipe support mechanisms are usually adequate for small-outside-diameter pipe when suspending the system in horizontal runs. Dummy supports, bottom spring supports, and pipe guides are used for supporting vertical runs, which usually involve heavier weight considerations.

Pipe Support Design and Drafting Group

In the majority of large engineering companies, the pipe support group is a specialist group separate from the other portions of the piping design and drafting areas. It works closely with the stress analysis department and in conjunction with the piping design department. This separation into a subfield of its own has come about because of the importance of pipe support location and design. In areas of less critical importance, such as building heating and plumbing, residential plumbing, and other noncritical areas, the pipe support placement and design is still usually handled by the piping design and layout group and is not differentiated into a subcategory.

The pipe support group is responsible for the design and location of the pipe supports necessary to meet standard specifications and safety requirements. Each project in the pipe support group will have a separate group leader who will coordinate the design and detail drawing of the required pipe supports. The pipe support group will work closely with the stress analysis group, which supplies the necessary information to determine what type of thermal, mechanical, and vibration problems might occur in all portions of the projected pipe system. The stress analysis group, after determining the piping system's movement and problem areas, utilizes a computer to do most of its calculations.

The pipe support group uses data supplied by all other groups, including electrical, HVAC piping, stress analysis, civil, structural, and piping layout groups. The general plan for the design procedure usually proceeds as follows. The pipe support designer, using the calculations provided by the stress group, determines the local placement and location of pipe supports throughout the piping system, with reference to the many different engineering areas, such as the structural configuration of the plant, electrical runs, HVAC, and so on. The designer will then show these locations on the isometrics that are constructed of the individual pipelines. Standard specifications for the project will determine the overall placement and span requirements between pipe supports for straight runs of pipe. After the locations have been determined and shown on the isometrics, they are transferred to all the drawings that are necessary throughout the drafting groups, such as the piping layout drawings, if these are being used in the design procedure. Placement of the supports will depend on the possible interferences with surrounding equipment and other plan piping runs. An attempt should be made to align the supports with existing framing, walls, columns, and structural members.

The designer will then make a rough sketch of the developed pipe support, providing all information needed for the finished detailing of the pipe support by the pipe support drafter. When designing pipe supports, it is important to keep the design simple and functional, attempting to eliminate any elaborate or expensive variations, and utilizing standard supports and equipment whenever possible.

Within the pipe support group, the checker will verify all the various aspects of the pipe support design, such as interferences, welding procedures, structural member size, and adequate load allowances. The pipe support drafter will then receive the rough sketch showing the required pipe support design and from it will be able to complete a final drawing and bill of materials that are necessary for ordering.

Models and Pipe Supports

Models have already been discussed as to their importance and necessity in the piping field. For pipe supports, the designing of the support itself on the model enables the department to use less drawing time and facilitates accurate spotting of the pipe support locations with regard to other equipment. In most cases, the model will totally eliminate the interference problem in the placement of pipe supports and will notably improve the overall planning for placement of pipe supports in

combination with each other. By using a model, the pipe support group will greatly reduce problems between different groups within the company, such as between the electrical and HVAC groups.

Before locating pipe supports on the model, identify the surroundings, important equipment, and objects that may influence the placement of the pipe support, such as surrounding piping runs and piping components, such as valves and fittings; the building structural elements involved; electrical runs and trays; all heating, air conditioning, and ventilation ducts and equipment; and all mechanical equipment and vessels. It is important to establish dimensions with respect to elevations and coordinates for the location of pipe supports, and therefore to eliminate interference problems.

In many cases, the pipe support drafter will be called upon to fabricate the pipe support and place it directly on the model. When spotting pipe supports on a model, it is important to take into account the following information:

- The access and installation space necessary for the construction of pipe support in a particular area.
- Any common supports that may be used to support nearby or parallel pipe runs.
- Beware of any situation on the model where an incomplete structural or concrete area is not shown.
- Be careful to allow sufficient pulling space for equipment when placing pipe supports close to the surrounding vessels and other components. Do not locate pipe supports too close to traps or pipe ends and drains.

Overall, a design model will enable the pipe support group to greatly facilitate design and placement of the pipe support, eliminating a great number of difficulties encountered when using only the drawing method.

PIPE FABRICATION DRAWING

Pipe fabrication is the construction of pipe components or sections that are joined or altered by a variety of procedures, which include shaping, machining, welding, flanging, heat treatment, cleaning, belling, and extruding. All these procedures for the construction of unit fabrications are used throughout the pipe industry.

Pipe fabrications are necessary elements of

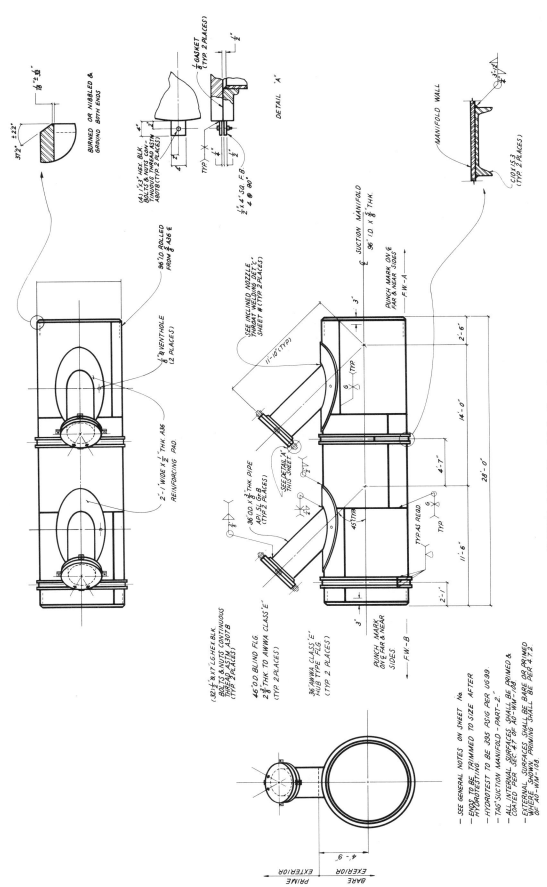

FIGURE 4-15 Pipe fabrication drawing.

59

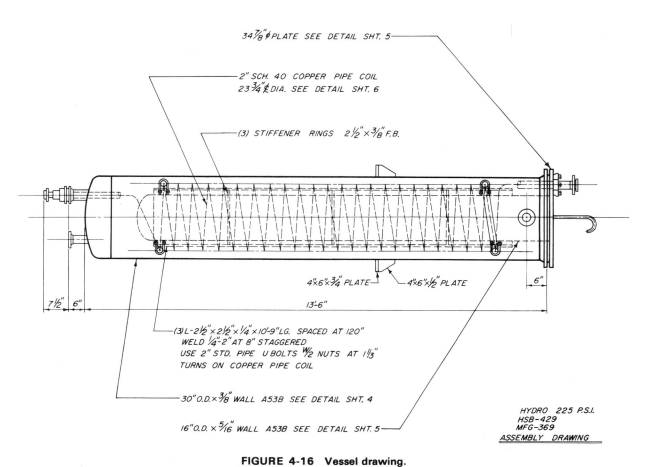

34⅞"⌀ PLATE SEE DETAIL SHT. 5

2" SCH. 40 COPPER PIPE COIL
23¾"℄ DIA. SEE DETAIL SHT. 6

(3) STIFFENER RINGS 2½" × ⅜" F.B.

4"×6"×¾" PLATE

4"×6"×½" PLATE

6"

7½" 6"

13'-6"

(3)L-2½"×2½"×¼"×10'-9"LG. SPACED AT 120"
WELD ¼-2" AT 8" STAGGERED
USE 2" STD. PIPE U BOLTS W/2 NUTS AT 1⅓
TURNS ON COPPER PIPE COIL

30" O.D. × ⅜" WALL A53B SEE DETAIL SHT. 4

16" O.D. × 5/16" WALL A53B SEE DETAIL SHT. 5

HYDRO 225 P.S.I.
HSB-429
MFG-369
ASSEMBLY DRAWING

FIGURE 4-16 Vessel drawing.

FIGURE 4-17 Coil (pipe fabrication detail).

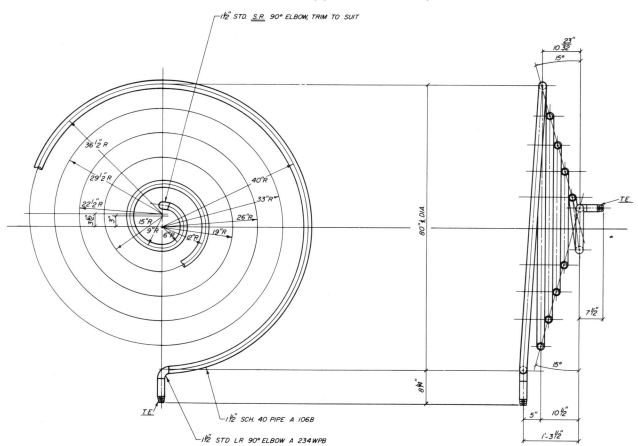

1½" STD. S.R. 90° ELBOW, TRIM TO SUIT

36½" R
29½" R
22½" R
3½"
3"
15" R
9" R
6" R
12" R
19" R
26" R
33" R
40" R

23"
10 32
15°

80"℄ DIA.

7½"

T.E.

15°

5" 10½"
1'-3½"

8¼"

T.E.

1½" SCH. 40 PIPE A 106B

1½" STD LR 90° ELBOW A 234WPB

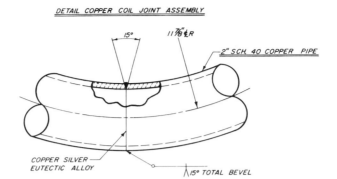

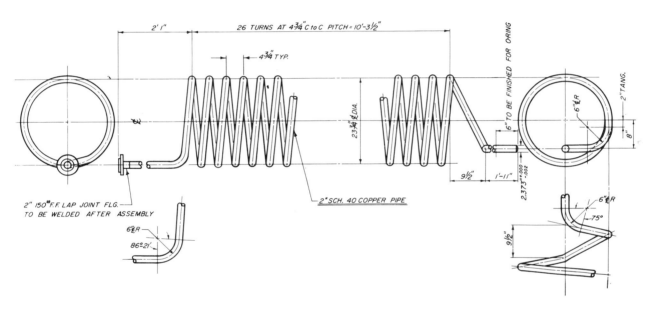

FIGURE 4-18 Pipe coil detail for vessel in Fig. 4-16.

all pipe systems, whether the system is for petrochemical installations, nuclear power plants, process fuel power plants, or building, heating, and plumbing units. Pipe fabrications are sections that make up portions of the total piping system.

The pipe drafter and designer must be quite knowledgeable in this area in order to design and draw the necessary configurations, including such items as headers (Fig. 4-15), exchangers (Fig. 4-16), coils (Figs. 4-17 and 4-18), and a multitude of pipe sections with nonstandard bends. The different type of pipe fabrication procedures convert standard straight pipe into various configurations in conjunction with components, such as valves, fittings, and flanges, which are usually welded or flanged and bolted together to form units that can be shipped to the construction site in one piece and

assembled along with other sections of the piping system.

In the case of pipe fabrications that take place in the field, components are welded and assembled at the job site, based upon drawings or a model of the piping system.

The drafter has as his or her responsibility the drawing of isometric or orthographic spool sheets. The spool sheets will show the portions of the piping system that need to be fabricated, complete with specifications for the fabrication.

The foregoing has been only a general overview of the use of drawings and drafting in relation to models. A more detailed explanation, together with specifications, appears in *Piping Systems Drafting and Design.*

QUIZ

4-1. How can drawings be eliminated by the use of a model?

4-2. What types of drafting procedures are not eliminated by the use of the model?

4-3. Is there any difference between isometric and orthographic spool sheets besides the projection method?

4-4. Is it possible to eliminate the use of the P&ID?

4-5. How would it be possible to eliminate the use of a plot plan or site plan drawings?

4-6. **What is a vendor drawing?**

4-7. Are pipe fabrications necessary when using a model?

4-8. What is the isometric method?

4-9. What does the model shop usually provide as far as the basic structure goes?

4-10. What aspects of the model does the piping designer usually complete?

4-11. To what scale are most piping drawings prepared?

4-12. What is an isometric spool?

4-13. What are piping specifications?

4-14. What is the piping index drawing?

4-15. Why is it necessary to do a paving, grading, and drainage drawing?

4-16. What are pipe support drawings?

5

Academic
Modeling Programs

FIGURE 5-1 Petrochemical model. (Model photographs courtesy of Badger America, Inc., Cambridge, Massachusetts.)

MODEL TRAINING PROGRAMS

Both piping designers and model makers must have sufficient background in piping and piping design to understand what is involved in the modeling procedure. Model technicians spend the majority of their time in the model shop, constructing the larger items, such as the bases, tables, vessels, and large structural elements. Depending on the background and abilities of the model technician, the general procedure is for the modeler to advance into the piping design group. The background necessary for a model technician includes:

- The ability to use power tools and machinery for the construction of items made of a wide variety of materials, including plastics and wood.

- Knowledge of the basics of piping and ability to read piping and other types of engineering drawings, including the ability to sketch.

- The ability to fabricate all items necessary for the construction of a model, such as bases, major equipment, structural items, vessels, and so on. (*Pipe designers or model pipers must have capabilities that are similar to, but go beyond, those of the model technician, in-*

cluding intricate knowledge of piping systems and other components; the ability to read, understand, and draft flow diagrams, isometrics, and other drawings or sketches; and knowledge of piping specifications, codes, and design characteristics that belong exclusively to subfields of piping industrial complexes.)

- Background in engineering capabilities and functions concerning equipment, vessels, and so on.
- Good manual dexterity and a general ability to do intricate designing and pipe installations on the model.

The mastery of the information given throughout this book will provide a firm basis for one to begin to move toward the status of model technician.

In the past, model builders and technicians have been trained on the job by companies that utilize models in their procedure. There are now available technical and vocational schools with model-building programs, which offer an excellent opportunity for a pretraining of model technicians. Companies prefer to consider model technicians a subgroup separate from the pipe design group, which may cause problems in some cases because the technician will not have the varied background that will accompany the person trained in the drafting and design of piping systems.

Other companies use the model-building program as a training tool for a progression of both drafters and model technicians to other subgroups within the corporation, eventually to the status of pipe designer. This enables the worker to understand the subfields and areas of concern involving models and industrial piping projects. A good background in mathematics, science, and engineering, especially electrical engineering, helps the prospective model technician or designer. School programs should create a balanced, employable worker who has the capability to progress from model technician to piping designer. These capabilities are only brought about by education in a program that allows the student to have hands-on experience in model making, in conjunction with drafting, and design.

All piping designers and model technicians should have a basic educational background in materials, power-tool use, hand-tool use, model construction techniques, safety, model piping design, mathematics, and drafting and design. This book covers the background necessary

to understand the aspects of modeling with regard to pipe layout and model technician assignments. Also, the book has been set up to acquaint the student with drawings and piping projects that will be encountered in the field. All drawings and projects provided for in the text have been drawn from industrial sources.

Thus, the student should have the essential background necessary to enter the modeling field. The use of *Piping Systems Drafting and Design* will greatly facilitate the learning of piping design basics which are not a part of this text. The model technician must learn to fabricate bases, tables, large equipment, and so on, and can be trained only with proper equipment in a model shop.

The main emphasis should be on the construction of clear, concise, accurately completed models that represent the original design project in its totality. This does not mean that any project that is drawn must be modeled exactly as the drawing states. The student will find that the book's projects offer ample opportunity for redesigning and relocating various pipelines, equipment, valves, nozzles, and so on. This is an excellent opportunity for the students to utilize their skill in consciously determining alternative positions of equipment, etc. Any project modeled should be at a sufficient scale to enable the student to fully understand the relationship of design to model making and the need to be accurate and concise in model construction.

MODELING AND EDUCATION

Publication of this book will hopefully stimulate interest among educators in the budding new field of industrial model building. The community and junior college areas have made advances in this very promising vocational educational area, but high schools are lagging somewhat in the adoption of this type of program. Model building can operate individually or in conjunction with piping/structural drafting courses. Since the types of machines and shop tools are closely related to other industrial art classes, such as woodworking and metal shop, the modeling of industrial projects using plastics and some wood fits in well with present high school and community college offerings.

The American Engineering Model Society, composed of architects, engineers, model builders, and engineering companies, helps to coordinate and disseminate knowledge concerning models.

FIGURE 5-2 Petrochemical model. (Model photographs courtesy of Badger America, Inc., Cambridge, Massachusetts.)

The society will provide information to schools who wish to investigate the possibility of the initiation of model programs on a small or large basis by directing them to present programs in existence throughout the country and by providing educational materials if possible. The society has already provided assistance to many schools, endeavoring to establish programs involving modeling. In 1977, approximately 25 institutions offered some training in modeling design, and several more were developing courses. Fifty percent of these are in architectural modeling. A number of these schools offer associate degrees. In 1977, the AEMS established a scholarship program and the first scholarship was awarded in the fall of 1979.

Model building as represented here can be supplementary to a drafting course, dealing mainly with piping/structural drafting responsibilities concerning the drawing, piping, and modeling of installations or a full model-making

program. When possible, models should be included within every piping/structural drafting course so as to introduce the prospective drafter to an area with which he or she will have much contact throughout a drafting career. Even the smallest drafting room or school will have sufficient space for the construction of individual or small-group model projects. Any drafting class can set up an inexpensive model area for under $200 with the necessary tools. Primarily, hand tools with an electric hand drill, small electric sander, and a small electric table saw, which can be purchased at many hobby model shops or through the EMA catalog, is all that is needed. These tools will make possible the construction of many small to medium-sized projects. Only the more complicated and very large models need more sophisticated equipment.

The construction of small projects such as those shown in Section 25 will allow the student to have hands-on experience (previous to employment) in modeling, which is increasingly being situated directly in the drafting room alongside the drafting and design group. Although these small models may not totally represent the large complex models that will be encountered in industry, they will nevertheless provide the student with valuable experience in the use of modeling. In situations where a school cannot set up a separate model shop, a small area in the drafting room can be used. Although it is advantageous to have a larger, separate area, it is not an essential. What is important is that the school recognize the amount of emphasis the drafting program wishes to place on modeling and the sophistication and level of equipment that are needed.

Drafting instructors who wish to initiate this program need not be model builders or have any experience in this area. A valid interest in learning and experimenting with the class will greatly stimulate students to explore this new field, and experience has shown that this will greatly increase the enthusiasm of the students for the drafting program by being able to construct in three dimensions actual projects which before were lifelessly exhibited in two dimensions. Teachers can receive valuable help from the AEMS, EMA, and other institutions throughout the country which have already initiated this type of program.

Model building can also be included in a parallel arrangement with architecture, combining new elements of solar energy components and piping with architectural design and modeling (Section 32).

SETTING UP A MODEL SHOP

For a school to initiate a complete model building program, it will, of course, be expensive in the beginning stages because of the purchase of equipment and construction of space necessary to implement the model shop. Any school that wishes to create a model shop would do well to consult the EMA or AEMS in regard to needs, based on the number of students projected for the course. It is possible to do many projects with a minimum of equipment, although it is obviously more advantageous to have certain basic power equipment available. The cost of setting up the model shop depends on the amount of equipment and the sophistication necessary for the shop to be efficient. Power tools, hand tools, furniture, model components, supplies, and so on, all add to the initial cost.

As for material costs for the various types of projects, it has been found that preliminary models, which are usually made of block materials and structural elements that can be reused, are rather inexpensive compared to the design model, with its minute detailing of instrumentation, piping runs, equipment, and so on. The materials used in the preliminary model, such as polyurethane foam, wood, and so on, keep the cost to a minimum. [In industry, the design/check model costs for major components, such as tables, bases, large equipment, and structures, are the expenses usually attributed to the model at the model shop (the basic model stage) prior to being piped by the designer, which usually occurs parallel to or in view of the drafting and design department.] In schools, bases, tables, and the like can be reused; therefore, after the initial investment, only nonreusable components will require further expenditures.

In the design stage, the smaller components, such as valves, fittings, pipe, platforms, stairs, ladders, bracing, and pipe supports, including small equipment such as pumps and vessels, will be completed. Therefore, a majority of the costs involved at the design stage are those associated with labor and small standardized component parts. It is a good idea when doing any of the projects in this book to keep an exact record of the expenses incurred for each of the projects. The EMA project in Section 25 will run close to $80 without a manual (this book covers everything in the manual); Section 26 is considerably less expensive and includes a full set of drawings and instructions, which this book does not cover (consult EMA for up-to-date prices). The projects in Sections 29 to 31 will cost considerably more and should be considered as group projects. Any projects completed from this text can be drawn first, to familiarize the student with the design problems that may be encountered in the modeling of the project. This will eliminate some cost errors and increase understanding among students who complete the project. EMA's design training model, which is presented in Section 25, is a kit and can be partly reused for successive classes/students.

Tools

One way of eliminating many of the initial costs in setting up a model program is to prepare the school for multiple uses of the woodworking and machine shop area, because most of the tools found in these areas are readily adaptable to plastics and light woods (the primary working medium for model building). By instituting a complete model program, the school can supplement its present vocational technical areas in woodworking and machine shop, while still providing training in the use of many of the power tools associated with those areas, together with an introduction to working with model materials, such as plastics, solvents, cements, and other items with which woodworking and machine shop students are usually not familiar.

If a school wishes to set up a small modeling program in conjunction with the piping drafting class, of course, it need only be concerned with tools needed for small projects; but larger machine tools, such as lathes, drill presses, routers, and band and table saws, can greatly facilitate the complexity and level of a model program. Smaller power tools, such as the EMA designer sander and designer table saw, are the only really necessary power tools. These are high-quality portable machines which will assist the accurate construction techniques necessary for the modeler and piping designer. A small electric hand drill will also be necessary.

Model Components

Model components are available through commercial sources. EMA provides most of the precast components, such as those shown in the photographs in this section, and they can be ordered through a catalog. Woods, plastic sheeting, glues, paint, and so on, are usually available locally.

The model industry has been successfully standardized in many areas, thereby eliminating the necessity of creating components from scratch in the model room. Many petrochemical models can be constructed almost entirely from standardized parts. Approximately 6000 items are available from EMA at present, which will make modeling extremely easy, especially in situations where it may be necessary to hold down the amount of model bases, components, and the like to be done in the drafting or model room. The use of standard component parts can in most instances supply 80 to 95 percent of the required component parts for the construction of petrochemical projects. Projects in Sections 25, 26, and 28 require no fabrica-

FIGURE 5-3 Petrochemical model. (Model photographs courtesy of Badger America, Inc., Cambridge, Massachusetts.)

tion of large items that are not made from standard components.

PARALLEL MODEL COURSES

Because in most cases, the model will not totally eliminate the use of drawings in industry, the majority of design disciplines within engineering firms, such as civil, electrical, piping, and HVAC, still require some drawings for most projects. Models will, of course, help eliminate or reduce the total number of drawings, but will not completely eliminate drafting needs. Therefore, all model programs must have drafting as either a prerequisite or as a parallel program (see Section 4). Even with the use of modeling in the design stage, drafting techniques needed to complete fabrication isometrics, spool drawings, pipe support drawings, and so on, all still play an essential role in the total design procedure for most companies, although the use of orthographic projections, plans, elevations, and sections can be reduced. Isometrics can also be taken directly from the model by students, which is a procedure widely used in industry. In this way, the student can develop sketching and drawing skills that can establish a well-rounded educational format, including sketching, modeling, machine shop, and drafting. In some cases, the student should complete the drawings for the project first, then do the modeling, and in the last stages use the model for isometric take-offs.

Elective courses in photography can be developed in conjunction with the model program, since model photography is used throughout industry (see Section 20). Using the students' own cameras to take color photos is probably the best procedure, because of the multicolored coded materials used on models. Photos of the model assist in project orientation and can establish a detailed sequence of construction when used in industry.

ACADEMIC PROGRAMS AVAILABLE

Junior-college-level model programs, such as those presented at West Valley (Mission) College in Santa Clara, California, provide a two-year course in model-building techniques which leads to an associate degree. Other colleges throughout the United States are also experimenting in the use of model building as a technical vocational program. In general, courses in model building, technical drafting, technical math, descriptive geometry, and machine shop, together with electives in photography, technical writing, and other courses, facilitate the students' ability to qualify for jobs in this area.

Schools with modeling programs:

Arizona State University; Tempe, Arizona 85281

Bucks County Community College; Newtown, Pennsylvania 18940

Canton High School; Collinsville, Connecticut 06022

Genesee Community College; Batavia, New York 14020

High Point Regional High School; Sussex, New York 07461

Mankato State University; Mankato, Minnesota 56001

Maury High School; Norfolk, Virginia 23517

Metropolitan State College; Denver, Colorado 80204

Miami–Dade Community College; Miami, Florida 32809

Minneapolis Drafting School; Minneapolis, Minnesota 55407

Ohio College of Applied Science; Cincinnati, Ohio 45210

Pasadena City College; Pasadena, California 91106

St. Augustine Technical Center; St. Augustine, Florida 32084

Stark Technical College; Canton, Ohio 44720

East Tennessee State University; Johnson City, Tennessee 37601

Upson County Area Vocational–Technical School; Thomaston, Georgia 30286

West Valley (Mission) Community College; Santa Clara, California 95070

Whether the school intends to use model building as a supplemental instructional aid to drafting or as a full-fledged offering, the use of models in high school, college, and industry will greatly increase in the near future, whether architectural, study, presentation, product, piping, prototype, or other industrial models. A variety of advantages to the use of models and their introduction at the high school/college level should become apparent, including the ability to use power tools and machinery for construction of models; knowledge of the basics of plastics and other materials; expansion into three dimensions of the basics of structural and piping drafting; increase in general manual dexterity required to do intricate design and piping installations on the model (note that much of modeling resembles the type of commercial hobby-shop models that many students will already have worked on; this is, of course, very advantageous, whether it was building model cars, airplanes or other items); introduction to the background information and design requirements for engineering job offers; stimulating enthusiasm and interest in drafting courses when instituted as a parallel program; and use as a full-scale program, not dependent on the drafting program, and also supplementing or replacing woodworking and machine shop practices for many students, especially women, who may prefer not to engage in those more male-dominated areas.

Women are found throughout the modeling and piping drafting areas. This should be of great interest to schools that wish to include more women in their vocational technical programs, where they have traditionally been relegated to more "female" areas, such as cosmetology and nursing.

Typical Academic Program

The accompanying table is a course outline from West Valley (Mission) College in Santa Clara, California, which offers a two-year A.A. degree in model building technology. The college is a part of the California state system and is fully accredited

Subject	Semester hours	
	Degree	Certificate
Model Building 36A	4	4
Model Building 36B	4	4
Model Building 36C	4	4
Subtotal	12	12
Technical Drafting 51A	3	3
Technical Drafting 51B	3	3
Technical Drafting 52A	3	3
Technical Drafting 52B	4	
Subtotal	14	9
Math A	3	3
Math C	4	
Math D	3	
Subtotal	10	3
Machine Technology 101	3	3
Machine Technology 102	4	4
Subtotal	7	7
Physics 10	4	
Technical Writing 62A	2	2
Descriptive Geometry	2	2
Electives and Other Degree Requirements	12	
Subtotal	20	4
Total	62	35

by the Western Association of Schools and Colleges.

The program was begun in 1970 and included instruction in basic model-making techniques. In 1971, a second course was added, which covered more advanced techniques, machine tool operation, and safety. In 1973, the program became a two-year course, and in 1975 the program was expanded to include a two-year course leading to an Associate degree and a three-semester certificate course.

Electives are selected from all the following subjects: physical education, technical writing, business, data processing, photography, art, management, and architectural drafting. The Associates course also meets the California requirements for general education, including English and history.

Industrial model building

36A   Fundamentals of model building:

Basic knowledge concerning model-making tools and materials, visualization techniques, and the opportunity to study models in various materials. Architectural and engineering models will be studied. Lecture two hours; laboratory six hours; fall and spring.

36B   Advanced model building:

Further development of skills used in the building of scale models as used in the architectural and engineering fields. Shop practice and techniques will be emphasized. Lecture two hours; laboratory six hours; spring.

36C   Advanced model building:

Model building as used in the process piping, power, and related industries. General shop practice and techniques will be followed. Lecture two hours; laboratory six hours; fall.

Mathematics

A   Elementary algebra:

Natural numbers, integers, first-degree equations, products and factors, fractions, simultaneous systems of linear equations, quadratic equations, irrational numbers. Lecture three hours; fall and spring.

C   Intermediate algebra:

Intensive study of the fundamental laws, exponents and radicals, linear and quadratic equations, graphical representations, complex numbers, logarithms, and the binomial theorem. Lecture four hours; fall and spring.

D Trigonometry:

Trigonometry of the real-number system using complex numbers as a vehicle. Emphasis will be placed on applications to analytic geometry and calculus. Trigonometry of right and scalene triangles will also be studied. Lecture three hours; fall and spring.

Other areas

10 Introduction to physics:

Applications of physics to modern life with a minimum of mathematical and technical emphasis. Includes the development of some fundamental concepts of physics, viewed as human activities and part of our culture. Not open to students who have completed high school physics or Physics 2A or 4A. Lecture three hours; laboratory three hours; fall and spring.

22 Descriptive geometry:

Thorough study of orthographic projection techniques. The study of points, lines, and planes in space of their intersections. The graphical solution of space problems. Develops an understanding of visualizing objects in various positions. Lecture one hour; laboratory five hours; spring.

51A Technical drafting—beginning:

Cover the use and care of drafting instruments, lettering, geometric construction, basic orthographic projections, introduction to sections, auxiliaries, drafting practices, dimensioning, freehand sketching. Lecture two hours; laboratory four hours; fall.

51B Technical drafting—intermediate:

Further study of orthographic projection, sections, threads and fasteners, auxiliaries, dimensioning, revolutions, axonometric projection, developments and intersections, and working drawings. Lecture two hours; laboratory four hours; spring.

52A Process piping drafting:

Study of process piping drafting, equipment and terms, flow diagrams, piping plans, piping isometrics and their related mathematical calculations, and a design problem in conjunction with Model Building 36C. Lecture two hours; laboratory four hours; fall.

52B Process piping design:

Design concepts of process piping as found in petroleum, chemical, or food-processing plants. The background and methods of piping various types of vessels, what those vessels do, and how best to utilize them. Designing by use of scale models. Lecture three hours; laboratory five hours.

101 Introduction to machine technology:

Study of fundamental machine tool processes; practice with tools basic to industrial production; concepts of precision metal work; hand tools, and accessories common to mechanical production; metals, their composition and identification.

102 Machine processes:

Theory and practice in the fundamental processes used to machine metals, with emphasis on the lathe, basic shaper, milling machine, and grinder operations; adjustment and care of machines and equipment; cutting speeds and feeds.

62A Fundamental technical writing:

Workshop course for developing technical writing skills. Emphasizes accurate definition, transfer of meaning, and clarity.

6

Model Facility Requirements and Considerations (Industry and Schools)

FIGURE 6-1 Large petrochemical model constructed on multiple bases. (Model photographs courtesy of Badger America, Inc., Cambridge, Massachusetts.)

This section discusses the overall facility requirements for the in-house fabrication of design models and for school programs. The most important consideration in a facility to be used for the fabrication and design of engineering models is that it maintain an engineering design atmosphere. All shop and design areas should include sufficient storage and work space to maintain an orderly work area. As in any shop area, the requirements of all local and national safety standards (e.g., OSHA) must be maintained. Significant use of plastics is required in any model shop or design area; therefore, the temperature must remain rela-

tively stable because of the large thermocoefficients of expansion of plastics. The shop and design areas must also have sufficient heating and air conditioning to maintain comfortable working conditions. A good rule of thumb to use is that the model shop or the design area is simply an arm or extension of the engineering design office.

TYPES OF DESIGN AREAS

There are three basic types of design areas used in a model program (listed below). Some companies

FIGURE 6-2 Petrochemical design model. (Model photographs courtesy of Badger America, Inc., Cambridge, Massachusetts.)

(or schools) may use all three areas, while others will use parts or combinations thereof.

- Table fabrication area (for schools, this may be an existing wood shop)
- Equipment and structure fabrication area (for schools, this would probably be a separate room)
- Piping installation area (design floor) (for schools, this may be done in the drafting room if no separate space is available or it could be combined with the equipment and structures fabrication area)

Table Fabrication Area

The table fabrication area is the least critical of the three areas as regards the effect of dust contamination in the area and table tolerances. This is not to say that table chassis and tops need not meet strict tolerances and the standards for good workmanship. However, the required tolerances can easily be achieved by correct application of the proper tools.

The power tools required to furnish a complete table fabrication area are as follows:

- 10″ table saw
- 3/8″ drill press
- 12″ heavy-duty disc sander
- Portable hand router
- Portable hand drill
- Jointer (or large metal straight edge and hand router)
- Bandsaw
- Paint booth

FIGURE 6-3 Designer at work station, design model behind.

Note: Most of these are available in the typical high school or community college woodworking shop and machine shop. It would therefore be possible to set up multiple uses for these areas instead of a complete new shop.

Along with several glue clamps and assorted hand tools, this equipment will furnish an adequate shop for fabricating wood tables with plexiglass tops. Since wood tables with plexiglass tops are still widely used, this is considered a basic shop. The paint booth is not critical unless spray painting is utilized. A discussion of the various table designs is presented in Section 14.

In the event that commercially available, custom-built tables are used, the jointer, router, and paint booth can be eliminated, together with the floor space required for table fabrication. Thus, an extensive shop should only be considered when there is going to be continuous use of wooden tables on modeling projects. Above all, it is recommended that an intensive study be conducted to determine the most economical approach to setting up a shop. All cost factors should be evaluated in this study: capital equipment costs, labor costs, necessary manpower and utilization, facility space requirements, raw materials supply and maintenance costs, utilities, and safety. For schools with limited budgets and space, precut bases and prefabricated tables could eliminate the need for a table fabrication area.

The most expensive material required on a given table is the plexiglass. Unless one is able to buy sufficient quantities of plexiglass at cast-lot prices, the cost of a top is quite high. The cost of disposal of the scrap plexiglass must also be considered. Unless a very large number of tables (about 30 or 40 per month) are fabricated, there will probably be considerable amounts of scrap plexiglass. One should consider buying the plexiglass cut to your dimensions from a local source rather than setting up an in-house facility to store and cut plexiglass to size for a given table. This also applies to school programs, where cost of the model is an important factor. EMA standard school models in Sections 25 and 26 come with precut bases.

In order to perform an objective evaluation of facility requirements "real" or appropriate numbers must be used. For example, do not use basic labor rates paid to the shop personnel to determine labor costs. In most cases, the basic labor rates should be increased by a factor of 50 percent to include fringe benefits, payroll taxes, and so on, to reflect actual labor costs.

Another consideration in the area of labor is the source of labor. It is recommended skilled designers and model technicians not be used to build tables unless these people have nothing else to do. (This does not apply to school programs.)

There are reliable companies who can furnish tables to your specifications.

Equipment and Structures Fabrication Area

Fabrication and installation of equipment, vessels, and structures is sometimes performed on the design floor. In some cases, this work is performed in a separate shop provided for this activity; in other cases it is done in the area where the chassis and tops are fabricated. It should be noted that the shop floor space required for this particular function is considerably less than that required for table fabrication. This is due entirely to the raw material requirements and the sheer mass and size of the tables. Space requirements for the fabrication of equipment and structures can also be reduced in view of the readily available vessel, equipment, and structural systems which are now available. Standard components should be used by schools wishing to "play down" the fabrication of model items.

The following power tools are required to furnish an equipment and structures fabrication area:

* 3/8″ drill press
* Small table saw
* 12″ disc sander
* Portable hand drill or dremel tool
* Bandsaw (not absolutely necessary)
* Metal lathe (desirable but not mandatory)

Note that these are the only *necessary* power tools for a school modeling program.

Piping Installation Area

In industry, virtually all piping design and installation of piping should be accomplished on the design floor. Figures 6-3 and 6-4 illustrate a model piping design area. The designer's power tool needs include:

* Designer's disc sander
* Designer's saw

These can double for the equipment/structure fabrication area saw and sander. This area can also be directly in the drafting room in schools

FIGURE 6-4 Typical company design area.

with limited space. The construction of a design modeling cart will provide a compact, portable power tool and component storage accessory (Fig. 6-10).

Summary

Although each company and school will have to perform its own evaluation with its unique space and overhead situation, it is recommended that an extensive model shop not be set up simply for the fabrication of table assemblies unless a significant number of tables will be fabricated each month, or the school program is designed to teach every aspect of model building.

It is recommended that a small, separate area in which to fabricate and install equipment, vessels, and structures on the model base be provided. However, some companies and schools have successfully combined the area where they carry out the piping design, equipment fabrication, and equipment installation with the design floor or parallel to the drafting room.

For industry, piping design should never be performed in conjunction with table fabrication. To carry out these functions in the same area is counterproductive to the engineering environment and creates significant dust and noise in the design area.

FIGURE 6-5 Component storage cabinet.

SCHOOL MODEL SHOPS

In situations where a school cannot set up a separate model shop, a small area in the drafting room can be used, although it is advantageous to have access to more space, depending on the amount of emphasis the drafting program wishes to put on modeling and the sophistication level of equipment that may be desired. Industrial model

FIGURE 6-6 College model room consisting of six large layout tables and individual work stations.

FIGURE 6-7 College model machine shop.

FIGURE 6-8 Student laying out a modeling problem.

shops can range from 1100 square feet to entire floors of buildings that stretch out over a city block, depending on the number of model makers that are necessary. Storage space must be provided for equipment, tools, students' supplies, and in some cases, student's models and equipment. For a class of 10 drafters to use a model shop at the same time, it would be necessary to provide a minimum of 2000 to 3000 square feet, although it must be stressed that small, individual models or larger group models can be constructed directly in the drafting room as class or individual projects. All piping drafting classes should construct at least one small project.

FIGURE 6-9 Student using model work station.

The following are guidelines for setting up a model shop.

Workbench Station Layout

In situations where a school or industry has the ability to lay out a model room from scratch, the construction of workbench stations (Fig. 6-9) is an important aspect in an orderly model program. The workbench station should be set up parallel to open areas where major tables can be placed (Fig. 6-6). These island work stations in the center of the room can have work tables next to the major project for open assembly areas. Individual work stations should be approximately 42″ high and consist of a series of two desks or tables and tool drawers. Work station systems are manufactured and sold by various firms throughout the United States for use in schools as laboratory stations for electronics and other uses. In general, these include two work benches 3′ by 6′ placed in an L shape so that the model marker's work station has two tables from which to work. Sets of drawers and cabinets as part of the workbenches are also useful.

Machine Room

Machining spacing and setup for a typical model room will follow that of other types of woodworking or metal shop setup with some modifications if the area is to be used just for modeling, which is not usually the case. Most programs in colleges must share the machine shop area with other classes such as wood shop, power mechanics, and machine shop; therefore, schools usually do not have the choice of using the traditional model-making setup for the machine room (Fig. 6-7).

Storage Areas

The typical model program will require the necessary space for storage of plastics, lumber, components, and combustionable products such as lacquers, paints, sprays, varnish, and glue. A separate room for the storage of all plastics and model components is the most efficient way of setting up a school program. This will allow for the teacher or shop instructor to oversee the distribution of these expensive components. A series of drawers, storage parts, cabinets, and racks for the storage of plastic items are all useful in a typical storage room. In many situations, the model program will not be of sufficient size to require the storage of large amounts of components and plastics, especially where the models and components are ordered individually by the students and are paid for separately.

FIGURE 6-10   Design model cart with a designer saw, sander, component storage compartments, and hand tools.

FIGURE 6-11   Designer model cart.

FIGURE 6-12   Storage drawers.

As for lumber storage, a separate area can be established for that in conjunction with the wood shop lumber, enabling the separation and storage of plywoods, hardboards, fiberboards, in some cases, combining sheet plexiglass storage with these larger 4′ x 8′ sheets.

FIGURE 6-13 Adjustable storage cubicles for student projects.

FIGURE 6-14 Storage cabinets.

FIGURE 6-15 Tool storage cabinet.

Spray Area

The spray booth safety regulations established by OSHA and all local requirements must be strictly adhered to. The location and ventilation of the spray booth are primary considerations. The spray booth should not be too close to areas that are frequented by student groups such as the work station area. There should also be a place set aside close to the spray booth for a paint-drying area. Paint supplies should be stored close to the booth; where a separate room can be set up for spraying, it can be combined with the paint storage area. Storage cabinets for combustionable items can be purchased with approved specifications provided by OSHA. Exhaust filtering and other environmental considerations must be taken into account when setting up a spray booth. (Makeshift spray areas can be set up outside if no adequate room is available in the school.)

FIGURE 6-16 Paint booth and lazy susan.

Tool Storage

Individual tool boxes can be provided per student or model maker and also a central tool storage area where tools can be requisitioned, therefore eliminating the problem of stolen or missing items. Locked, individual tool storage compartments can also be provided at the work station, although this may not be possible if the model room is used for multiple classes. Each student should have access to his or her own small model tool box with typical designer tools, which can be kept in the student's locker when not in use.

Storage of plastics, paints, wood, components, and tools is extremely important when setting up any model program, especially where a clean, safe, efficient environment is to be achieved. As has been stated elsewhere, the model program that wishes to emphasize the piping designer side of modeling and play down fabrication, which is usually associated with a model technician, can order bases and tables to size.

The movement of materials must also be taken into account, especially bulk materials and large tools. Providing easy access to storage rooms for these items and sufficient space in and around machines will help eliminate movement problems.

FIGURE 6-17 Storage room and tool storage cabinet.

QUIZ

6-1. What is a table fabrication area and how is it used in a typical engineering firm?

6-2. Name five power tools required in the machine shop area of a model shop.

6-3. Why is it usually necessary for a school to combine equipment, fabrication, and piping installation areas?

6-4. What procedures and construction methods are employed on a design floor?

6-5. What power tools are necessary for a piping installation area?

7

Modeling Tools

FIGURE 7-1 EMA hot-wire cutter for foamed plastics. Ideal for working on preliminary/study models.

Model-building tools are divided into two separate, but not exclusive, categories: those required for the production of the basic model, and those required by the piping designer or drafter. The first group includes power tools, which are not necessarily large or expensive. The school that wishes to set up a small model program in conjunction with the piping drafting class need only concern itself with tools needed and used by the piping designer. So, the tool requirements can be divided into those necessary for the design room and those required for the model shop, and subdivided into hand tools versus power tools in both areas.

DESIGN AREA TOOLS

Hand Tools

The design area tools include clamps, vises, saws, picks, razors, putty knives, scribers, steel rules, hemostats, pliers, hammers, combination square, toolbox, leather knife, X-Acto knives, hacksaws, small twist drills, solvent applicators, marking pens, pencils, straightedges, metal rules, tapes, metal tapes, scale tapes, protractor, dividers, circle templates, screwdrivers, files, tubing cutters, razor cutters, lightweight hammers, utility knife, pen

FIGURE 7-2 Designer saw.

vises, drill sets, tweezers, needle-nose pliers, cutting pliers, wire cutters, ignition pliers, and a V-block. This list, although not inclusive, offers a variety of possible hand tools that a shop may need.

Among the larger tools for common use in the design area would be bending boards, vises, V-blocks, extension cords, brushes, clamps, hammers, triangles, framing squares, combination square, sets of screwdrivers, hammers, small wrenches, scissors, a variety of file configurations, glue dispensers, calipers, dividers, protractors, utility rules, large metal tapes and scales, hand drill, extension drills, and adjustable wrenches. Safety glasses must be provided for each individual model maker or pipe designer.

The hand tools in the model shop include almost all of the above-mentioned items that are necessary for the piping designer, but also include larger equivalents, such as squares, framing squares, metal rules and tapes, wrenches, and hammers. Other equipment that is not usually present in the design area but is necessary for the model builder are hand saws, large drafting triangles, tap and die sets, hand drills, needle-nose pliers, linesman's pliers, paintbrushes, bench vises, portable vises, large clamps, awls, knives, Allen wrenches, box-end wrenches, crescent wrenches, and screwdrivers of all types. This list, of course, can be greatly expanded. It must be noted that the tools listed for the design and model area are not all necessary and it is possible to construct a model in a drafting room with a very small number of tools. Increasing the number of tools that are available will obviously benefit the accuracy of the model.

Power Tools

Figure 7-3 shows the designer sander and Fig. 7-4 designer table saw. Both are excellent examples of equipment that should be present in the designer's area and in some cases in the model-building room. These are high-quality, portable machines that assist in the accurate construction techniques necessary for the modern model builder and designer. Design area machines include the designer saw, a small disc sander, and a hand-held drill or small drill press. These power tools are all that are really necessary for the piping designer. The designer saw has the ability to cut a variety of angles and shapes on many materials, including wood and plastics. The sander is used for shaping, squaring up, and eliminating rough edges on various components. The hand drill or small drill

FIGURE 7-3 Designer sander.

FIGURE 7-4 Designer table saw.

press, in conjunction with a V-block, can provide quick drilling of holes that are necessary in the construction of vessels and other portions of the model.

MODEL SHOP POWER TOOLS

Model shop power tools include tilting arbor or table saws, precision saws, floor-model drill press, lathe, belt and disc sander, jointer, bandsaw, portable router, portable hand drills, vacuum, spray paint equipment, and radial saw. All this equipment makes the construction of a model more efficient and cost-effective. The disc sander is similar to the designer's sander, but is usually larger and is used for the sanding of many different types of material shapes. The belt sander is used primarily for rectangular objects. The joiner is used for the construction of straight edges on sheet or board stock. The bandsaw is used to cut odd shapes. The radial saw is used for large items that must be cut to a specified length, such as model bases. The drill press can be adapted for drum sanding and drilling and is a necessity when constructing model projects made of plastic. The lathe is primarily for turning nonstandard items, for drilling items that

cannot be drilled on other machines, and for shaping both wood and plastic. Of course, the construction of a complete model shop will run into considerable original cost. Schools may find it prohibitive to provide a model shop with all the equipment that has been listed. The minimum amount of equipment necessary for a model program includes only the design area tools and power tools, which in general can be assembled for approximately $300.

MACHINE AND TOOL LIST AND DESCRIPTIONS

Some of the major machines and special equipment normally found in a model shop are discussed below. The piping designer need only be acquainted with the general use of these machines and the reason model shops require them. The machines that must be mastered by the model technician are discussed in succeeding paragraphs.

Model Shop Machines and Equipment

Tilting arbor or table saw

This is the most used shop machine; it is es-

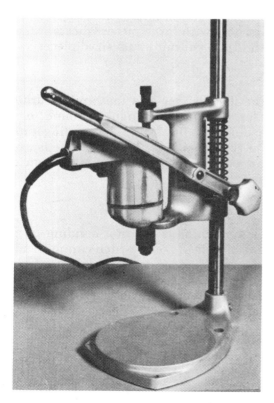

FIGURE 7-5 Small hand drill press.

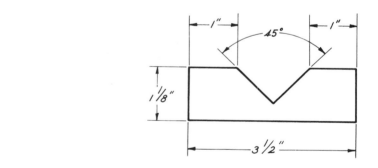

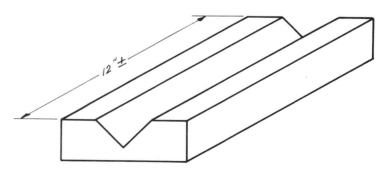

FIGURE 7-6 Typical V-block.

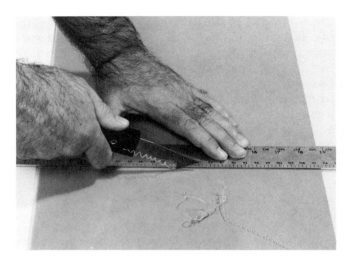

FIGURE 7-7 Modeler cutting plastic sheet.

FIGURE 7-8 Tool box.

FIGURE 7-9 Scales.

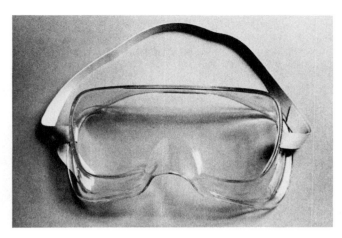

FIGURE 7-10 Safety glasses.

sential for all ripping and most cross-cutting of individual pieces. Points to remember:

- Choice of blades: carbide blade generally used
- Setting fences
- Adjustable height of blades
- Pusher stick
- Spacer block when cutting work to length with miter
- Backup piece on miter
- Get help with large pieces/sheets
- Ability to cut minimum-sized pieces

Disc sander

The disc sander is a fast and accurate machine for bringing rectangular, round, or cone-shaped objects to final size. The sanding is always done on the down side. This machine is used for circular work and for shaping transition pieces and large reducers.

Belt sander

This machine is used for sanding large rectangular objects of a size which cannot readily be shaped on the disc sander, especially for finishing (lighter work is done on this machine rather than on the disc sander), for end work, inside corners, and flat sanding.

Jointer

This machine is used for making straight edges on sheet or board stock. It is the most dangerous machine in the shop. The tasks it performs are edge finishing and cutting 45-degree faces.

FIGURE 7-11 Student using table saw to cut plastic.

FIGURE 7-12 Machine tools in school model shop.

Bandsaw

This machine is used for rough-cutting to virtually any size or shape. A metal cutting blade is generally used.

Radial saw

This machine performs a multiple, repetitive cross-cut operation for cutting material to length and is used for special applications, such as making bases.

Drill press

This machine is used for drilling and drum sanding. A slow rate of cut is used for plastic, and the drills are specially ground for this task.

Metal lathe

The lathe is used for turnings, cones, and accurate drilling and tapping. It may be used for shaping wood, plastic, or metal, and to fabricate pieces not otherwise available.

Spray booth (or room)

Although a separate room for spray painting would be advantageous, it may not be feasible for a school model program. A spray booth is the next best thing. Both must be well ventilated and meet OSHA safety standards.

All painting except touch-up should be confined to the booth or room because of the possibility of fire hazards (see Section 8).

Oven or heating element

Used to mold, shape plastics.

Hot wire cutter

Used for easy, accurate cutting of foamed plastics, this tool is available from EMA and is extremely useful when constructing preliminary models (see Fig. 7-1).

Design Area Machines

The training instructor will demonstrate the safe and proper use of the following machines. Each student should have a working knowledge of these machines and practice each operation.

Designer's saw

A small version of a circular saw for use especially in the design office (see Fig. 7-4). The demonstration stock used will be pipe, rod, and 1/8″ scrap plastic sheet. Factors to be considered in the operation include:

- Location of on-off switch
- Lack of set in milling blades liable to cause jamming
- Use and limitations—accuracy in ripping and adaptability for small pieces
- Use of a pusher stick
- Setting fence and adjusting height of blade
- Multiple cutting setups
- Blade not to be used for cutting wood

Small disc sander

A machine made for use in the design office (see Fig. 7-3). Demonstration stock used will be pipe, acrylic tube (small diameter), rod, and 1/16″ and 1/8″ scrap plastic sheet. The following techniques will be stressed:

- Sanding on the down side only
- Shaping reducers or transitions

- Squaring
- Making dodged pieces

1/4-Inch drill on stand

The operation of this small version of a drill press (see Fig. 7-5) will be used to demonstrate:

- Rate of cut—slow for plastics
- Backup piece
- Holding work—V-block

Personal Designer's Hand Tools and Equipment

The following is a typical list of hand tools and equipment used by designers while working on models:

- Metal tool box
- Combination square, 6″
- Diagonal cutting pliers, 6″
- Long-nose pliers, 6″
- Hemostats, 5-1/2″, straight and curved
- Pin vises (3)
- Stainless steel rule, 6″
- Pocket scriber
- Putty knife
- Film-marking pencil (for plastic)
- Leather worker's knife (shoe knife)
- X-Acto knife with spare blades
- Zona saw, #ZS-500
- Metal scale, 12″ (3/8″ = 1′0″ or applicable scale)
- Metal scale, 6″ (3/8″ = 1′0″ or applicable scale)
- Twist drills for pin vises, #30, #43, and #50
- Solvent applicator
- Tag-marking pen
- Safety glasses (Fig. 7-10)

Instruction should be given in the correct and safe use of the following hand tools:

- Pocket scriber
- 6″ diagonal cutting pliers
- 6″ long-nose pliers
- Hemostats
- X-Acto knives
- Shoe knife
- Zone saws
- Putty knife

The designer's hand tools must be considered as serving the same function as drawing instruments, pencils, and erasers.

Design Area Tools and Equipment

A certain quantity of tools are required in the design area which would not be issued on an individual basis. These would be "community" tools for use by all. The following is a typical list of these tools:

- Double-sided-tape dispenser
- Extension cord
- First-aid kit, small
- C-clamps (assorted sizes)
- Shop mirror (adjustable)
- Tweezers, pointed, flat, and spade
- Set of screwdrivers
- Phillips screwdriver
- Set of files, flat, half-round, round
- Spring calipers, 6″ inside, outside
- Metal protractor
- Metal tape, 8′
- Bending boards (or jig)
- Vise, small
- Bench brush
- Hammer (5 oz)
- Triangles, 6″, 45° and 60°
- Framing square, 24″
- Combination square, 12″
- Scissors, large
- Glue dispenser
- Spring dividers, 6″
- Utility rule, 24″
- Scale tapes, 8′ (3/8″ = 1′0″ or applicable scale)
- Steel scale, 12″ (3/8″ = 1′0″ or applicable scale) (Fig. 7-9)
- Set of high-speed twist drills in holder (1/16″–1/4″)
- Clipboards
- Adjustable wrenches, 4″ and 6″
- 12″ architect's scale
- Diagonal cutting pliers
- Flat-nose pliers
- Shoe knife

- Zona saw, large
- Tap handle
- 8′ metal tape (standard)
- Protractor, plastic
- Adjustable wrench
- Trays, for holding tools
- Flexible-blade putty knives
- Hand drill
- Set of extension drills, 12″ long (1/8″, #30, 3/32, #40, #50, 3/16″, 1/4″)
- Hemostats, straight and curved
- V-block (Fig. 7-6)
- Scriber
- Needle-nose pliers
- X-Acto knives with spare blades
- Box single-edge razor blades
- Zona saw, small
- Model hammer
- Triangles, 45° and 60°
- Shop mirror
- Ice pick
- Safety glasses
- Artist's brushes

Consumable items

- Tagging materials
- Roll masking tape, 1″
- Sandpaper
- Spring clothespins
- 3/4″-wide roll foam double-faced tape
- Roll double-sided tape, 3/4″
- Sandpaper board
- Industrial wipers
- Scrap plastic (1/16″ to 3/8″ thick)
- Pointers

Solvents, spirits, paints, glues, stationery

- Scissors
- Lettering pens
- Marking pens (yellow/red)
- Plastic marking pencils

QUIZ

7-1. What are the two major categories of tools used in model building?

7-2. Name 10 common hand tools used in both the design area and model shop area.

7-3. What are some uses of the drill press in a model shop?

7-4. What are the most necessary design area machine tools?

7-5. Why is a spray booth necessary?

Safety
in the Model Shop

FIGURE 8-1 Preliminary model. (Model photography courtesy of Badger America, Inc., Cambridge, Massachusetts.)

The training for safety in the model shop and design areas will cover hazards in modeling and housekeeping in these areas.

The Occupational Safety and Health Administration's (OSHA) Standards became effective on August 27, 1971, and both employee and employer must comply rigidly with these standards.

In general, employers must comply with the specific Occupational and Health Standards promulgated under the act, and, in addition must furnish each of their employees a place of employment free of recognized hazards that are causing or are likely to cause death or serious physical harm. In turn, employees are required to comply with the standards, rules and orders that have been set up to protect them. Every building or structure shall be so constructed, arranged, equipped, maintained, and operated as to avoid undue danger to the lives and safety of its occupants from fire, smoke, fumes, or resulting panic during the period of time reasonably necessary for escape from the building or structure in case of fire or other emergency.

Design personnel are not normally authorized to operate model shop equipment. This will eliminate exposure to the more dangerous power tools. However, designers will be required to operate the designer's saw and sander.

There are inherent hazards to modeling, and the proper use of tools to work safely is mandatory. It is the individual's responsibility to develop safe working habits.

Safe operation of the designer's saw includes the use of push sticks, backup sticks, blade adjustment, and safety glasses. Push sticks permit the operator's fingers to remain at a safe distance from the saw blade as the material is being cut. Backup sticks give the operator more control of the material so that it does not bind between the fence and the saw blade. Model work does not lend itself to the use of guards on the saw. Since primarily small pieces are cut, a guard would itself present a hazard. It is absolutely necessary, for safety's sake, to adjust the blade to a height of no more than 1/8″ above the material being cut. Safety glasses must be worn to prevent plastic chips and dust from entering the eyes.

Safety glasses must also be worn when operating the sander. Remember: sand on the down side of the disc only. Although sanders have caused no major injuries, they can sand down the tip of the finger if caution is not used.

Hand tools, such as knives, zona saws, dividers, cutting pliers, and scribers, are dangerous to the extent that they are sharp or pointed instruments. Once again, as a reminder, it is the individual's responsibility to develop safe working habits.

There are some other inherent hazards to model building that should be taken into consideration. Most plastics when saw-cut have extremely sharp edges. The model base edges are "scraped" on all four sides, top and bottom, so as not to cut the body or tear a person's clothing. Pipe ends, platforms, edges of structures, and the like can be a hazard to the eyes, face, or hands.

Diagonal cutters used to cut pipe containing wire cores can be a dangerous weapon if the designer fails to exercise caution. The portion of unwanted pipe when cut off becomes a missile soaring through the design area. Prevent injury by directing the unwanted portion toward the floor or into your hand.

Proper housekeeping—keeping the model areas clean—is probably one of the best methods to assure safety on the job. A day-by-day cleanup is necessary to keep items in their proper place. Beware of tripping hazards such as extension cords, or such slipping hazards as small pieces of tubing or pipe as well as dust left carelessly on the floor.

PRIMARY HAZARDS, PRECAUTIONS, AND RULES

Hazards

The following are hazards in the design areas:

- Power tools: saws, sanders, and drills
- Hand tools: cutters, knives, saws, drill bits, scribers
- Sharp edges on plastics

FIGURE 8-2 Table saw with caution instructions.

- Projections on model: pipe ends, platforms, edges of structures
- Trash on floor (especially pieces of tubing and plastic dust)
- Snipped-off ends of pipe (if allowed to fly through the air)
- Extension cords on the floor (can cause tripping)
- Plastic chips and dust

Precautions

It is very important that the following safety precautions be observed:

- Be sure that all moving parts of a machine are clear before starting.
- Be sure of proper footing and balance.
- Do not force a tool or machine.
- Wear safety glasses.
- Where practical, use clamps to hold work.
- Turn a machine off before leaving it.
- Disconnect a machine from the power supply before servicing.
- Prevent snipped-off wires from flying by holding or cupping hand over the end.
- Sand or scrape off exposed sharp edges of plastic.

Housekeeping Rules

While safety in modeling is achieved largely through proper respect for the machines and tools and common sense, good housekeeping also aids in creating a safe working environment. The following rules should be observed.

- Brush off machines after each use.
- Place scrap in bin or trash can; do not leave on machine, tables, or floor.
- Return tools to the storage area.
- Keep extension cords off the floor when not in use.
- Brush off machines and tables and straighten work areas at the end of the day.

OSHA GUIDELINES

Air Contamination

Air within the model shop area must be of such quality that it will not cause harm or discomfort if it is inhaled for extended periods of time. Dust and spray-painting vapors are the most harmful.

The cutting and sanding of wood and plexiglass create harmful dust. A dust-collect system is required so as not to permit dust in quantities capable of passing through the upper respiratory system to the lower lungs. Place dust collectors so that accumulated dust can be removed and emptied while not contaminating other working areas.

Spray painting is the most dangerous operation in a model shop. Lacquers are not only dangerous to the respiratory system but are subject to fire or explosion. Spraying operations should be designed, installed, and maintained to eliminate any hazards. Adequate ventilation will reduce the concentration of air contaminants below the hazard level. Construction of separate spray rooms or booths are essential to proper air quality maintenance.

Hazardous Materials

Lacquers are flammable aerosols and are considered Class 1A liquids. Keep to a minimum the quantity of flammable and combustible liquids in the vicinity of spraying areas. Do not exceed a 1-day supply. Spraying areas must be kept free from accumulation of combustible residues. The spray booth and operator's working area floor surface should be covered with a noncombustible surface for removal of and safe cleaning of residue.

"No Smoking" signs must be displayed throughout the model shop.

Personnel Protective Equipment

Protective eye and face equipment are required for most of the model area. Eye protectors must be provided where machines or model operations present the hazard of flying objects. Proper clothes protection (overalls, apron, lab jackets, etc.) should be required of all modelers.

Machinery and Machine Guarding

Machine guards, shields, and walls should be provided to protect the operator and fellow workers in the machine area from hazards such as rotating parts, flying chips, and sparks. Attach guards to the machine where possible; and if attachment to the machine is not possible, attach guards elsewhere or provide walls or shields.

Stationary machines must be securely anchored to prevent their moving or "walking."

Safe operation of the circular saw includes use of backup sticks, pushsticks, blade adjustment, and safety glasses. Push sticks will permit the operator's fingers to remain at a safe distance from the "point of operation." Backup sticks give the operator control of the material, to eliminate binding between the fence and the saw blade.

Color Code for Marking Physical Hazards

Green — Safety
First-aid equipment
Yellow — Caution signs
Hazardous parts of machines
Orange — Dangerous parts of machines
Energized equipment
Red — Fire exit signs
Fire protection equipment
Emergency stop bars, stop buttons, or electrical switches
Danger signs
Sprinkler systems

Portable Fire Extinguishers

Portable extinguishers must be maintained in proper operable condition and kept in designated places at all times when they are not being used. Extinguishers must be located along normal paths of travel, be readily accessible, and be immediately available.

Emergency Equipment

Emergency equipment should be available in or near the model area:

- First-aid box (equipment)
- Axe
- Sledgehammer
- Stretcher
- Rescue blanket
- Pinch bar
- Asbestos gloves
- Emergency lantern
- Two pairs of Jones' visor goggles
- Two 50' lengths of manila rope (1/2" diameter)
- Wool blanket
- Phone numbers for ambulance, doctor, hospital, police displayed for easy reference

Summary

Because model building entails the use of power tools and hand tools that are extremely hazardous if the proper operating procedures are not adhered to, it is important to institute a serious safety and housekeeping program in conjunction with any model-building class. The Occupational Safety and Health Administration standards should be closely followed in any model-building situation. All persons involved in a model-building program should go through the required safety and maintenance rules and conditions necessary to keep the modeling area a safe working place. The most serious accidents can occur through the use of power tools, including saws, sanders, drills, lathes, and other equipment that can cause serious bodily injury to the operator and those in the surrounding area, if not properly maintained and operated.

Hand tools, including knives, and saws, hand drills, razor cutters, and scribers, all present safety problems if the student or worker is not properly trained in their use.

Solvents, cements, and other flammable materials can cause serious environmental hazards if improperly used and maintained. Sloppiness in the model room, and the buildup of dust, plastic chips, paint supplies, and rags, are all fire hazards. Also, all electrical equipment must be properly maintained, recognizing the problems involved concerning the use of extension cords, electrical outlets, on and off switches, and so on. Air contamination by the use of solvents and power tools must also be considered. Proper ventilation of the working area is essential.

Model Shop Guidelines

The following is a set of guidelines for the model shop, including the use of machine and hand tools and maintenance of good, safe, working conditions.

1. Use safety glasses when using both machine and hand power tools and when cutting with hand saws.
2. All students and workers should be trained in the safety rules before using the model shop area.
3. Safety rules, regulations, and hazard conditions training should be set up and instituted with periodic drills and problem run-throughs to acquaint the users of the model area with the procedures necessary in case a safety problem should develop.
4. It is important to maintain all the necessary power and hand equipment in excellent shape, including the electrical aspects of the building.
5. A set of rules and safety procedures should be posted in the model area.

6.   Protective clothing should be worn whenever working with solvents, paints, and machines.

7.   All equipment should be maintained with the proper safety devices in good working order.

8.   A standard set of evacuation and/or accident procedures for fire or individual safety problems or other emergencies should be provided and used.

9.   The model area should be maintained in a clean, orderly manner.

10.   The model room is not a play area. Only serious-minded students and workers should be allowed to participate in any program involving the use of model equipment.

11.   Maintain a vigilant attitude toward the surrounding area when working with power and hand tools, making certain that people in that area cannot be harmed by the use of equipment.

12.   Loose clothing, gloves, and long hair can sometimes present unsafe working conditions, and care should be taken to avoid such situations while around working equipment.

13.   Know and understand all the types of equipment and materials, their proper use, and any problems that may develop through improper use.

14.   Danger signs should be posted in areas where any hazardous work may take place.

15.   Any area in which work is done with hot materials, such as a hot wire or any heating area, should have equipment posted as being hot.

16.   When electrical equipment is not in use, the power supply should be disconnected.

17.   The model shop should never be used by only one person, especially when the use of power tools is necessary.

The following is a set of housekeeping rules that will enable the model room to be kept in top shape, eliminating many inherent dangers in the use of power and hand tools and the associated materials necessary for model building.

1.   All tools should have designated areas in which they can be placed when not in use.

2.   The electrical wiring of the model shop should be done in such a manner that extension cords and other problem electrical equipment cannot cause injury to the user.

3.   The model shop should be kept in top order, including daily cleaning, sweeping, and wiping of all equipment.

4.   Solvents, paints, and other flammable equipment must be stored in a safe, orderly fashion in a designated area.

The following precautions should be noted when working with power equipment.

1.   Training in the proper use of all power equipment should be a prerequisite for the use of the model room.

2.   Areas where power tools are used and maintained must be kept clean and clear.

3.   When using power tools, always wear safety glasses.

4.   Always operate machines properly, and do not force any tool or machine that will not operate. Disconnect and consult your instructor.

5.   Use clamps or other aids whenever possible to perform the necessary power tool assignments.

6.   Always disconnect or shut off a machine after use.

7.   Be aware of the surrounding workers when cutting plastics or materials that could chip and become hazardous, flying objects.

8.   Always disconnect machines before servicing.

9.   Always use the guard where possible when cutting pieces of material on the circular saw.

10.   Where possible, use push sticks to avoid placing fingers and hands near the saw blade.

11.   Always use the proper tool for the job. Do not try to alter the tool in any way to conform to your predesigned project.

The following rules apply to the use of hand tools:

1.   Always wear safety glasses when using saws, wire cutters, or any other hand tool that might create a flying object.

2.   Always use the proper tool for the job in question.

3.   Do not carry tools or sharp objects on your person.

4.   Always note your surrounding workers' situation before commencing a job that might be hazardous.

The following list provides a set of safety rules and possible hazard situations for the handling of the various materials used in model building.

1.   All materials such as lacquers, paints, flammable solvents, and cements must be properly stored.

2. When using hazardous materials, the area of construction must be well away from any heat zone or electrical outlet.

3. It is important to maintain high air quality in the model room, especially in areas where spray painting or the use of solvents, cements, or lacquers could create hazardous situations for the worker. All model areas must be properly ventilated.

4. Large objects weighing more than 80 pounds should be moved only by authorized individuals using the proper equipment.

5. When lifting heavy objects, use the leg muscles, not the back muscles.

6. Use leather gloves whenever possible when moving large materials.

7. All floor areas should be kept free of oil, grease, or other substances that could cause bodily harm when moving objects or working in the model room.

8. All model rooms should be constructed so as to facilitate safe handling of the equipment and storage of component parts.

9. All caustic materials, acids, paints, and other objects that are in breakable containers should be stored properly at below-eye-level heights.

10. For the moving of large objects, proper safety shoes should be worn.

11. Use dollies or carts when moving large objects.

12. Never try to move large objects without help.

13. All sharp objects on materials and equipment should be blunted.

14. All material should be stacked, piled, and stored in a way that provides easy access and will not cause any safety problems.

15. When using materials such as lacquers and paints, properly ventilated spray booths should be provided to prevent air contamination or possible combustion problems.

16. "No Smoking" signs should be placed throughout the model area, and no one should be allowed to smoke near the model building area or in a drafting room.

17. When using equipment, materials, or constructing any item in the model room, the proper safety protective equipment should be worn, including lenses, goggles, safety glasses, protective shoes, and protective clothing.

The foregoing lists of rules and problems that may be encountered in the model area are, of course, not exhaustive. One of the primary objectives in setting up and utilizing the model area should be the reduction of possibly hazardous situations to an absolute minimum. Hazardous situations in the model room cannot be totally eliminated, but they can be minimized if proper care of the equipment and model shop is given top priority by the controlling group.

QUIZ

8-1. What is OSHA? How does it affect a model program?

8-2. Name five hazards associated with the use of hand tools.

8-3. Name five hazards associated with the use of machine tools. Describe the tool and the hazard.

8-4. Why is it necessary to keep the model area clean?

8-5. Name three hazards associated with the use of electrical equipment.

8-6. Why is it important to provide adequate ventilation for the model room and spray area?

8-7. Why is it important not to smoke in the model area?

8-8. What are machine guards or shields, and how are they used to prevent accidents?

8-9. What emergency equipment should be present in a typical model?

8-10. Name five hazards associated with the use of paints, solvents, and cements. How can they be eliminated or reduced?

8-11. Why is protective clothing necessary?

8-12. When is it necessary to use safety glasses?

8-13. Name 10 ways in which the model room can be made safer.

Standard Model Components

FIGURE 9-1 Petrochemical model. (Model photographs courtesy of Badger America, Inc., Cambridge, Massachusetts.)

Today, a vast selection of model materials and components are available to the designer using the three-dimensional technique. The selection of components in many scales and colors enables designers to present their efforts in a professional manner with the least amount of time expended in model work. Time savings are the principal reason why new products are constantly being developed to improve techniques. Examples of the available components are shown in the figures of this section.

MODEL COMPONENTS

Model components are available through a variety of commercial sources. In this book, Engineering Model Associates is the only company mentioned as the supplier of standard model components, but there are others (in Europe).

The model industry has been successfully standardized in many areas, thereby eliminating the necessity of creating component parts from scratch in the model room. Petrochemical models,

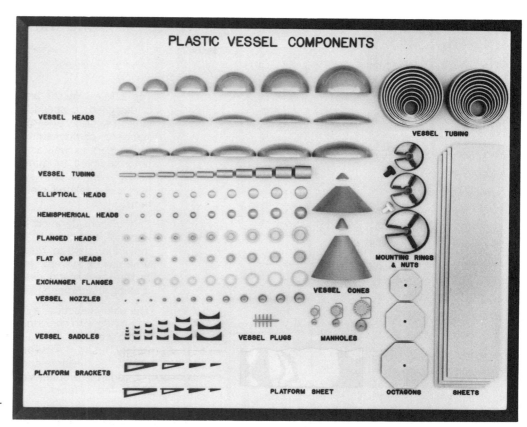

FIGURE 9-2 Plastic vessel components.

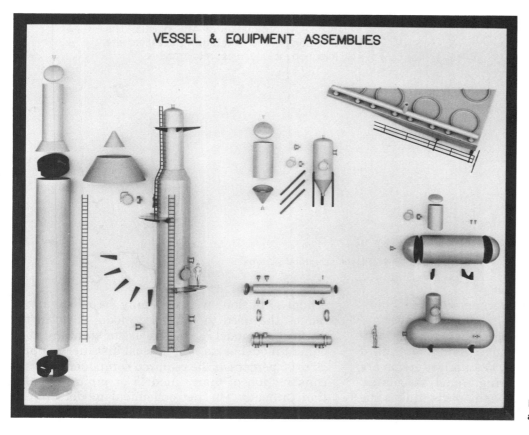

FIGURE 9-3 Vessel and equipment assemblies.

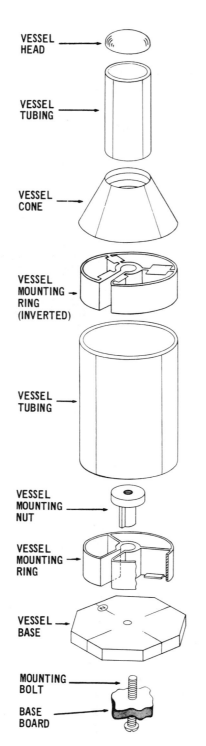

VESSEL HEAD

VESSEL TUBING

VESSEL CONE

VESSEL MOUNTING RING (INVERTED)

VESSEL TUBING

VESSEL MOUNTING NUT

VESSEL MOUNTING RING

VESSEL BASE

MOUNTING BOLT

BASE BOARD

PLASTIC STRUCTURAL SYSTEM

The E.M.A. Vessel and Equipment System is designed to speed the fabrication of the large majority of equipment pieces from standard components. Small vessels, heat exchangers as well as tanks and towers can be assembled in minutes - accurately and neatly - with a total system that is compatible to the related piping and structural systems.

Careful consideration has been given to the material and production technique of each individual part to result in this logical and time saving system. Intense care was given to the mechanical design for mounting and making attachments.

The color selection, a medium shade of gray, was made with consideration for photographic contrast and to be consistent with what is most widely used. Availability in color now eliminates the time consuming task of painting - and the problems of making attachments to painted surfaces.

Color coding equipment by areas can be achieved by using a band of colored tape or colored equipment name or number labels.

All Vessel Tubing is precision extruded in a high quality formulation of ABS plastic. The Heads, Cones, Mounting Rings, Bases, etc. are all injection molded to exact tolerances.

FIGURE 9-4 Plastic structural system.

process piping models, power-generation models, and others, and their uses in industry have contributed to the research necessary for the construction of a comprehensive list of standard model components. Over 6000 standard items are available through Engineering Model Associates. The use of standard component parts makes the assembly of models much easier, especially in the

school situation, where it may be necessary to reduce the need to fabricate model parts in the drafting or model room. The use of standard component model parts can, in most instances, supply 80 to 95 percent of the required components for the construction of many models or piping installation projects. The petrochemical model projects provided in Sections 25 to 28 can be entirely constructed from component parts with only slight modifications. The large model projects in Sections 29 to 31, on the other hand, require that 60 to 70 percent of the components be fabricated from wood or plastics.

Model component companies offer high-quality, precise components, representing many types of equipment for structural, piping, electrical, HVAC, vessels, and other equipment. Figure 9-2 shows the items available for plastic vessel components from Engineering Model Associates, including vessel heads, tubing, elliptical heads, hemispherical heads, flanged heads, flat cap heads, exchange flangers, vessel nozzles, vessel saddles, platform brackets, octagons, sheeting, tubing, mounting rings, and platform sheets. Figures 9-3 and 9-4 show vessel and equipment assemblies that are possible by the use of plastic vessel components in Fig. 9-2.

After working with model components and experiencing many alternative arrangements, the model maker or piping design student will be able to fabricate a wide array of vessels.

Figures 9-5 to 9-7 show the available plastic structural system components available, together with the plastic platform sheeting.

Fabrication of noncommercial structures such as concrete columns and/or steel structural shapes are very time consuming compared to construction with commercially available structural shapes. If at all possible, the model scale should be chosen so that the majority of structural shapes can be purchased from ready-made stock rather than requiring special setup in the model shop.

Figure 9-8 shows the available plastic valves and valve equipment that are available from Engineering Model Associates. Figure 9-9 is the "meat" of the model components, by which is meant the piping, including pipe types and sizes, in a variety of colors (color-coded), insulation, and fittings, including elbows, flanges, bends, tees, reducers, and caps. After working with standard component parts, the student will become quite familiar with possible variations that can be constructed. Only experience will bring this necessary knowledge.

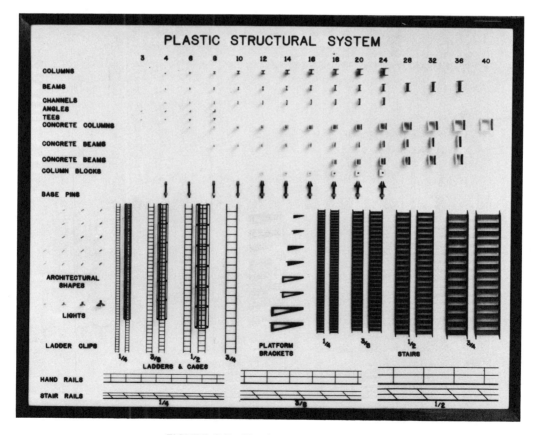

FIGURE 9-5 Plastic structural system.

ASSEMBLY DETAILS

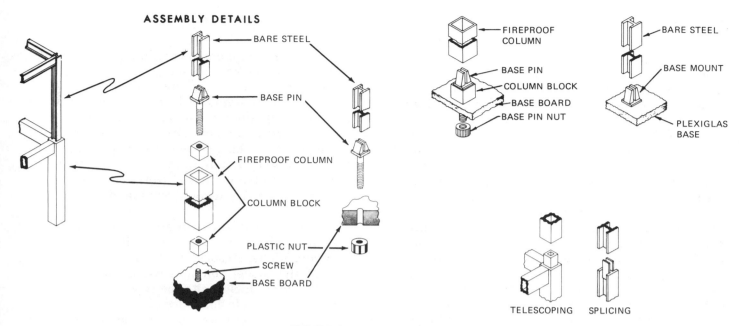

FIGURE 9-6 Plastic structural system.

PLATFORM SYSTEM

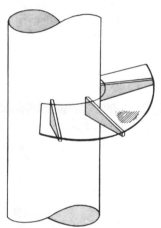

ASSEMBLY DETAILS

THE SOLID PLATFORM

The clear butyrate sheet allows for cutting solid platforms to size in the safest and most efficient way. Simply lay the plastic sheet on the template and scribe the required arcs with sharp dividers and break the platform section from the sheet. Straight platforms can be made by scribing with the use of a straight edge. Scissors or tin snips may also be used to cut the butyrate sheet.

TEMPLATE VPT-I

VESSEL PLATFORM TEMPLATE

The platform template is designed with circles the same sizes and code numbers as the Vessel Tubing. Radial orientation lines are at 15° spacing. This template, printed on high quality paper, may also be used for other orientation purposes.
SIZE: 12" x 12".

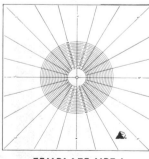

CLEAR
BUTYRATE SHEET
12"×12"×.040"

PLATFORM SHEET VP-40

FIGURE 9-7 Platform system.

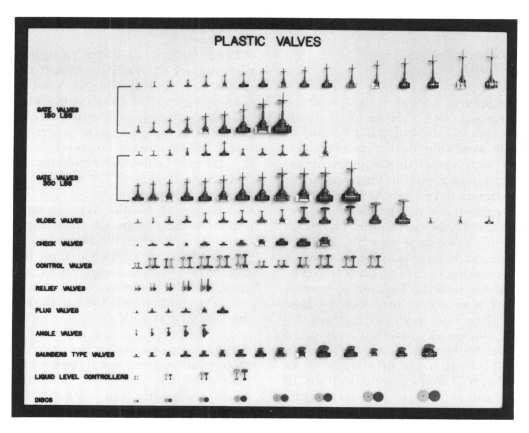

FIGURE 9-8   Plastic valves.

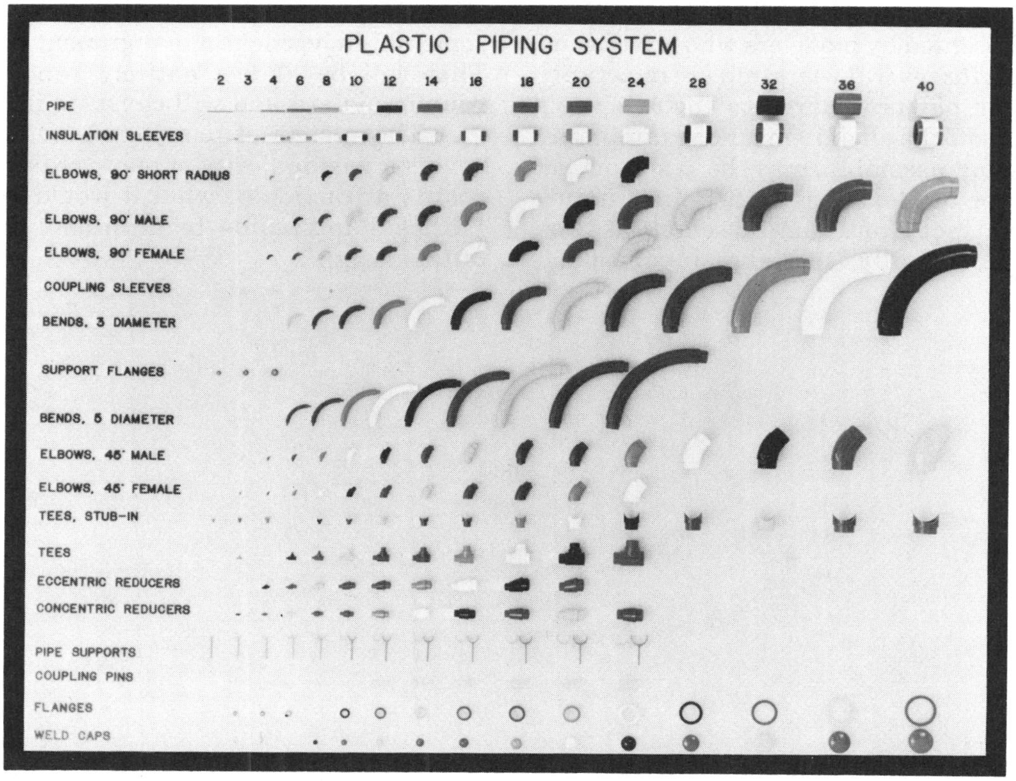

FIGURE 9-9   Plastic piping system.

EQUIPMENT COMPONENTS:
TO BUY OR TO BUILD

The choice of equipment should always be those that are commercially available items, if at all possible. The figures in this section show many of the commercially available plastic vessel components, together with vessel and equipment assemblies. EMA catalogs are available for ordering these and many items not shown here, including HVAC ducting, cable trays, pump assemblies, etc.

Equipment should always be fabricated from vendor equipment drawings if possible. In some cases, the equipment builder may have to work from designer's sketches or catalog data. Simulating the scaled shape and the location of nozzles and piping is of paramount importance rather than trying to fabricate intricate features for aesthetic value. Equipment building techniques vary from model builder to model builder. An important aspect is to minimize details and maximize accuracy of overall shape and connections. In some instances, components of standard equipment and vessels can be used in more detailed arrangements of large pieces of equipment. There is a wide variation in the modeling industry regarding the amount of detail to be shown on equipment. At one extreme is the modeler who uses excessive detail and tends to "gild the lily," while the other extreme is represented by modelers who have been building models for several years and are reluctant to change their old procedures to include new technology and off-the-shelf items. For example, a pump and motor assembly may be cut from a rectangular cube of plexiglass rather than simulating the actual motor and pump assembly as two different items. Actually, the labor involved in

cutting this cube and then painting it, drilling it, scraping off the paint to attach the piping and finally touching up the paint is far more costly than using an off-the-shelf pump/motor assembly.

One example of a purchasable assembly is the EMA pump and motor assembly system, the result of extensive research into standards throughout the processing industries. The simplified design enables EMA not only to offer a wide range of end and top suction configurations, but makes it easy for the average model facility to duplicate the design for sizes larger than those currently available commercially. The pump, motor, and base are sold as a single unit. The pump and base are color-coded vessel and equipment gray, and the motor is electrical green.

The front and top faces of the pump represent the face of flange locations, and centerlines are scribed to facilitate nozzle location. Pumps and motors are slotted to fit the keyway on the baseplate, thus assuring simple and perfect alignment. All components are precision injection-molded to guarantee quality and compatibility with the related systems. Charts provided in EMA's ordering catalog allow pump selection either by "Suction and Discharge Nozzle Sizes" or simply by dimensions.

Because of the large number of combinations of pumps and motors, there may occasionally be some slight vertical misalignment of the shafts. This will be almost entirely concealed by the coupling guard and will cause no inconvenience.

The system of pump and motor assemblies covers a vast majority of pump requirements. The cost is a fraction of what it would be to custom-fabricate and paint—regardless of the simplicity of the design.

10

Introduction
to Model Materials

FIGURE 10-1 Fossil-fired furnace. Scale: 3/32 + 1'0"; material: plastic; purpose: promotions and training aid. (Courtesy of The Scale Model Makers, Cleveland, Tennessee.)

Besides the standard component parts, many materials are used in the construction of models, such as plastics, wood, metal, solvent, cement, and paint. The model maker and piping designer must know how to use these materials in conjunction with each other, using the proper bonding and cementing procedures, which differ depending on the types of plastic, wood, or metal that are required for the production of a particular model.

This section gives a brief description of the commonly used raw materials in the fabrication of models.

The training in materials will encompass the correct choice and use of:

- Wood: pine, poplar, balsa
- Plastics: acrylic, butyrate, acrylonitrile butadiene styrene (ABS), foam
- Solvents
- Adhesives
- Cements
- Paints
- Expendable materials and supplies
- Metals

All standard component parts consist of molded plastics and can be easily cemented together with solvent to form intricate configurations for the piping system. Whenever possible, these plastics should be used in place of expensive metals or woods, which may not hold up as well in the production or use of the model. Use of standard component parts has greatly reduced the need to fabricate parts from heavy plastics, wood, or metal, as was formerly common in the model room.

Familiarity with materials and their most suitable application is a must for the piping designer and model builder. The proper materials for different types of models must also be considered. The preliminary model, since it is used only for a short time, should be constructed of materials that are cheap and can be either reused or discarded without problems in economy.

Architectural models and topographical models are constructed from materials unlike those in the piping field, although sometimes the piping designer or model builder will use balsa wood and other materials which are more commonly associated with the architectural field. In general, process piping and nuclear piping models are constructed from plastics and standard model components. Plastics, such as acrylics, butyrate, acrylic sheets, styrene sheets, and extruded rod, tube, and molded forms are all available for the model builder. Wood is also used.

Balsa, poplar, and pine can be used in the construction of model parts. Plywood or fiberboard may be used as a base, with plastic sheets over the top. Total model cost will vary drastically when using the different types of materials. For the sake of economy, schools may choose to use the cheaper fiberboard for the model base and not cover it with expensive acrylic sheets, although this detracts from the appearance and accuracy of the model.

Labor usually accounts for 80 to 90 percent of the modeling cost. Materials usually only run 10 to 20 percent of the total modeling construction, although for schools, labor is not a problem. In some instances, schools can afford to keep a large inventory of model items and sell them to the students as they are needed, although this is often not possible because of the expense entailed in the original purchase of the items and also in the storage facilities required to handle certain bulky items. In general, when doing projects in this book, if the school cannot afford to have standard component items stocked, the student should do a material take-off from the book while completing the drawings to build the model (if, of course, drawings have been assigned). This way, a ma-

jority of the components will be available when the drawings are done, instead of waiting for the order to be filled after the drawings have been completed. This arrangement is, of course, dependent upon the particular school's situation. EMA's two standard kits eliminate the need to order individual components or to construct a stock list. The compiling of a list of standard and raw materials would be extremely useful in any classroom situation to familiarize the student with the wide variety of standard and raw materials that are available, and should be required at some time during the course of the class.

The modeler will come in contact with wood, plastics, solvents, adhesives, and paints. The most common types of wood used for school model building will be balsa wood and pine, because of their lightness and ease of working. Fir and poplar are also used for intricate equipment, being tougher and of closer grain. Plywood is used for model base tops, table tops, and the like. It may also be necessary to fabricate model tables from pine for framing and legs (see Section 14). Poplar is also a popular wood to use in model working, although balsa wood can be used in classroom situations because it is easier to work with than the other materials, especially when a woodshop is not available.

WOOD

The following types of wood are used in a typical industrial modeling program.

First-Quality Select White Pine

This wood has good grain and a negligible amount of resin and gum deposits. It is used for stiffening sleepers and base legs (the quality of wood will help reduce warpage and twisting).

Poplar

First-quality kiln-dried poplar is used for those items of equipment where wood is best suited; however, plastic (wherever feasible) should be considered as a first choice.

Fir

A good grade of fir is commonly used for base legs.

Plywood/Chipboard

A good grade of plywood or chipboard is often used for the table-top underlayment. In model areas where weight causes base tops to sag out of alignment, plywood or fiberboard should be used underneath as a stiffener.

Hardwood

Because of cost, the use of hardwood should be kept to a minimum in schools. Hardwoods may be used for large turnings, odd-shaped equipment, and in situations where plastic or other woods cannot be used.

Balsa

Primarily an architectural medium, balsa can also be used in some industrial modeling situations.

PLASTICS

Plastics include acrylic, butyrate, ABS, and foamed varieties. Foamed plastics include polyurethane and polystyrene. These materials are used predominantly for the preliminary model because they are easy to work with and can be fabricated into complex shapes. Hot-wire cutters are a very practical tool to have access to when using foamed plastics. Certain types of glues and paints are not as successfully adaptable to the use of foamed plastics, and these should be tried out before using them on the model.

ABS is a commercially available material that can be used for many types of equipment in model construction areas. It is a fairly rigid plastic which can be accurately machined and is somewhat flexible. Butyrate is a type of plastic that is commercially available, usually from model companies, as it is used in the production of certain components. The majority of piping and fittings are made from this material. It is a soft but firm plastic. Acrylics, which are also referred to as Lucite and Plexiglas in trade names, are very common materials that are used throughout the model room. They come in sheets and extruded shapes, tubing, and rods, and can be used on the model to simulate equipment pieces and to cover the base top, or for concrete walls and sections. Acrylic is a much harder and brittle plastic than some of the others and does not lend itself as well to machining. Also, high-speed machining will tend to melt acrylic, whereas it will not melt many other types of plastics. When this happens, a sander is very handy to take off the burned or melted edges. Most plastics can be machined, **drilled, turned, painted, and cemented quite easily**, although all of them have differences in the types of cements and paints that should be applied.

The following is a list of common plastics found in the model shop.

Acrylic

The normal stock items are sheets in thicknesses ranging from 1/16″ to 1/2″ and in varying colors. The sizes available will, in general, accommodate 2″ increments at a scale of 3/8″ = 1′. Acrylic is used for base tops, pump foundation pads, piers, and for some pieces of equipment. Tubing is also available up to 18″ in diameter for very large vessels. It cements well to either butyrate or ABS.

Butyrate

Butyrate is the plastic used to manufacture almost all of the piping components. It has proven to be ideal because it is so convenient to work with; it can be cut, turned, drilled, painted, and easily cemented. It is a stable product and available in a wide range of colors. Its characteristics are best suited for the requirements of color, machinability, cutting, solvent bonding, and cold forming. It is also available in clear sheets for use as platforms and similar applications.

Butyrate is available in clear tin sheets .020″, .030″, and .040″ thick. It is the plastic used to manufacture piping components. Sheet stock is used where curved surfaces are formed, as in chutes, cones, and ducts; and for large equipment items such as boilers, reactors, or storage tanks, where it is desirable to keep down the weight of the model. The pipe sizes and fittings, which range from 1/16″ to 1 1/4″, are utilized extensively for small items of equipment. Vessel saddles in butyrate are available in sizes up to 3″ in actual diameter.

Acrylonitrile Butadiene Styrene (ABS)

ABS is used for structural members for both preliminary and final models, colored heads, and tubing from 3/8″ through 6″ diameter. Many model components are available in this material. It is very compatible with other plastics.

ABS is the plastic selected for the entire EMA structural system and the complete vessel system. It has excellent working qualities, cements well, and has all the mechanical properties required for the desired applications. Sheet material is also available, in matching colors, which can be heat-formed or easily fabricated for shutes, ducts, and other large equipment pieces, such as boilers, heaters, coolers, and storage vessels. It is available in several sizes and thicknesses of sheet stock and strip stock and in the appropriate colors for normal use.

Foamed Plastics

The cellular plastics, known as styrofoam, sta-form, and urethane foam, are used for preliminary models. Styrofoam cylinders are available in a wide range of diameters, and they can be quickly cut to length to make a preliminary model vessel. These foamed plastics can be easily cut to form replicas of other equipment, concrete structures, walls, and so on.

Usually, the foamed plastics are not dense enough to be used on final models except where attachments are not required. All but the urethane foam will decompose under the action of the solvents and cements used with acrylic and butyrate plastics.

Artfoam (product of Strux Corp.)

Artfoam is a rigid urethane material produced in block form and sold by the board foot. The standard type is white in color; the fire-retardant type is light tan.

Artfoam has excellent carving characteristics and is ideal for the construction of scale models, molds, patterns, prototypes, mock-ups, jigs, and fixtures.

Outstanding features of this product are:

- It combines strength and light weight—even in thin sections.

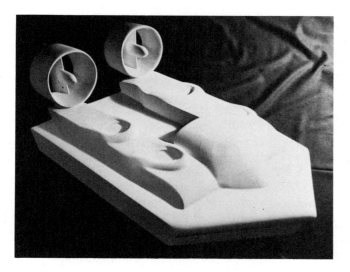

FIGURE 10-2   Model of a hovercraft produced by direct carving and fabricating of Artfoam (rigid urethane), a product of The Strux Corporation, Lindenhurst, New York.

- It carves easily, permits excellent detail, and substantially reduces working time. Artfoam has no grain and therefore can be carved without cracking, checking, or splitting.
- Regular woodworking tools may be used with Artfoam, and it is easily turned on a lathe.
- It has a closed cell structure and offers excellent insulation and flotation properties.
- It is not subject to solvents, takes a wide range of finishes, and is nonporous.
- It is dimensionally stable under a wide range of temperature and moisture conditions.
- Mistakes are easily corrected by bonding a new piece of foam and reworking.
- Artfoam has a temperature limit of 250°F. *Do not expose to open flame.* The dust is inert and nonallergenic.

SOLVENTS, ADHESIVES, AND CEMENTS

Plastic cements and applicators are available from Engineering Model Associates. The type of material must be taken into account when using certain bonding procedures.

The strength of a bond between any two materials depends largely on the amount of surface contact or gluing area. This is especially true with model structures. The joint will have maximum strength when cuts are square and total contact is achieved. Since the solvent used has no filling effect, gaps between two pieces of material cannot be filled. If a gap condition exists between a beam and column, soak the end of the beam in a shallow solution of solvent (1/8" deep) for 30 seconds or on a saturated blotter until the plastic is softened. The softened plastic will now make a total contact and form a strong joint. (*Note:* New SAC fittings have eliminated this problem.)

Acrylics, ABS, butyrate plastics that are used for model making are cemented and bonded using simple solvents. The solvents are available commercially and are easily applied to the bonding area.

Many types of glues are available, including resins. Plastic resin glue is excellent for bonding wood to wood. It is not to be used when bonding plastics. There is also hot-melt glue, which is used for bonding foam plastic to itself or to other materials. This type of glue is excellent for providing quick, long-lasting joints.

It is important to never overcement areas, as this will cause waste and running and may damage the surrounding component parts. Some of the procedure items that may be necessary to take into account when using solvents are:

- Never wipe solvent that has been spilled on a model part; let it evaporate.
- Always use the correct amount of solvent that is necessary to bond the elements.
- Too much solvent is as bad as too little; it will weaken and collapse the pipe wall, throwing it out of alignment.
- Solvent is not used on a painted surface because no cementing action is possible; the object would only tack to the paint surface (excessive solvent attacks and lifts a painted surface).
- The bond between butyrate and ABS, although adequate, is not as strong as it is between like materials. Butyrate attached to an ABS pipe bent can be readily removed, which is an advantage.
- Butyrate pipe fittings are inseparable when once solvented, so butyrate is used only where it becomes necessary to adequately secure the pipe configuration.
- Two flat plastic surfaces can be easily joined by the capillary flooding action of solvent.
- Although it is possible to use snap-together parts, these should not be cemented together unless it is absolutely necessary, as the commercial fittings are usually made of butyrate plastic and become inseparable when cemented. Certain types of glues are also necessary for model construction, and these must be considered separately from solvent, cements, and adhesives (see below). Certain glues have gap-filling qualities that may be necessary for the construction of special items, especially vessels.
- When strong, durable, butt-ended joints are to be made, remember that the solvent has no gap-filling qualities as do viscous cements. The ends of the plastic should be soaked in the solvent for approximately 30 seconds or until a little mushy so that the material will flow, spread, and cushion out against the mating surface.

Solvents

One of the significant advantages of using ABS, acrylic, and butyrate plastics in model construction lies in the fact that a simple solvent will bond like materials together and unlike materials to each other. The solvents used are basically ethylene dichloride or methylene dichloride and are available under several brand names.

EMA's Plastic Piping Cement (PCC-2): This cement is for specific qualities, such as the slight retarding of "setup" time to allow small adjustments to be made, and the addition of another chemical to the formula to prevent "blushing" or whitening at the bond. This solvent cement allows the cementing of similar plastic materials normally used in model construction (i.e., butyrate to butyrate, ABS to ABS, or either to acrylic).

EMA's General Purpose Cement (GPC-2): This bodied formulation allows the cementing of dissimilar plastic materials normally used in model construction, such as piping (butyrate) to structure (ABS). This is a solvent cement formulated to bond unlike plastic materials and is slightly "bodied" or thickened to achieve better gap-filling qualities.

Adhesives

Duco Weld-On No. 16: This is a general-purpose glue used in model work as a secondary cementing agent. Note that it is a glue, not a solvent; it has certain gap-filling qualities and a reasonable setup time. These characteristics make it useful in applications where additional solvent cannot achieve a better joint than the one already existing: for example, between a curved surface (pipe) and a flat one (the horizontal pipe rack).

(Elmer's) Plastic Resin Glue: This glue is used for all wood-to-wood joints. It is a white, viscous material, soluble with water before drying. This is the glue frequently used today as an all-purpose home adhesive. It is basically an acid that dissolves the fibers of the wood, and is therefore not effective when used with acrylic or butyrate plastics.

Cements for Foamed Plastics

There are few adequate, fast-drying cements or glues available to join foamed plastics. Plastic resin glue will give a bond of sorts, but requires from several hours to several days to cure. Various rubber cements have been tried, but none have proven satisfactory. For modeling, styrofoam double-sided adhesive tape, T-pins, and clear cellophane tape have proven adequate. A hot-melt glue gun works well with urethane but must be handled carefully to prevent skin burns. Some companies use the following in bonding foam to plexiglass or lexan, with some success.

3M Contact Cement No. 1357: To cement preformed plexiglass to foam, brush cement on

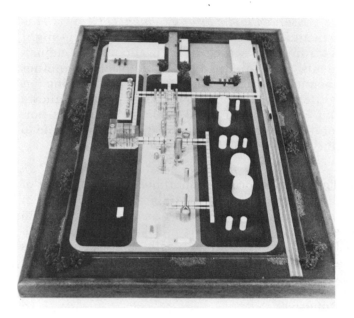

FIGURE 10-3 Presentation model. (Model photographs courtesy of Badger America, Inc., Cambridge, Massachusetts 02142.)

both surfaces and dry-bond. If the cement color is objectionable, a heavy coat of white spray can lacquer seals and foam and cover the glue. Use the same procedure for bonding styrofoam to lexan and polyurethane to lexan. Caution must be used, as this cement is highly flammable. The work shall be performed in a ventilated room.

3M No. 5034 or No. 2226: This is a water-base latex cement which may be used in dry-bonding urethane to preformed plexiglass as well as urethane to lexan, although the drying time is slower than 3M No. 1357. The joint is satisfactory as long as it is not under tension.

Five-minute Epoxy: This two-part cement has been used with great success in bonding small sections of styrofoam and polyurethane foam.

Styrofoam two-sided tape: This material has proved satisfactory for many applications.

Hot glue: The most adequate method of joining foam is with the electric hot-glue gun. This tool should be used for relatively permanent applications. If an item is to be bonded temporarily, double-sided tape or clear cellophane tape can be used.

PAINT

Paints are another material used throughout the model building area, and include types of lacquers

or other coatings that may be necessary. Paints bond easily to wood surfaces, of course, although certain types of plastics are harder to cover. It is possible to use either water-base paints or lacquer-soluble paint, depending on what colors are available. It should be noted that mixing the two on one model should be avoided wherever possible.

Vessels can be painted unless the model is to be torn apart and reused. The modeling student who uses this book should attempt to make model projects as accurate and attractive as possible for show purposes. In industry, most of the vessels on the model will not be painted. Painting is sometimes necessary to provide color coding for the different systems that are encountered in a model project. Enamel paints in aerosol cans are also used for a variety of work, as are specialized paints, such as wrinkle paint, which gives an interesting surface texture to certain components, such as concrete areas. Spray booths should be constructed in the model room in situations where spraying many model parts is necessary. This will reduce air contamination and other hazardous conditions.

The slick surface of plastics should be broken by light sanding or rubbing with steel wool prior to painting. The plastic must, of course, be clean; a rag or paper towel moistened in solvent will work well as a cleansing agent. However, commercial antistatic and plastic cleansers are available and are recommended.

A flat surface that has been spray-painted and then marred during model work may be restored to the appearance of a sprayed surface (i.e., no brush marks) by thinning the paint down to the consistency of milk and then flooding it on the surface, rather than by brushing it on.

The following types of paints and sealers are in common industrial use.

Spraymatch Paint (Lacquer)

This paint is packaged in aerosol cans and is available in colors to match all plastic components used on the design model. Normally, little painting is required because of the many materials available in colored plastic. However, when a special component is fabricated from wood or plastic, it can be finished quickly to match the other model colors.

Spray cans are available to match piping and equipment colors. Pint cans in all the appropriate colors are also available for brush "touch-up," or the paint can be thinned with lacquer thinner for spray painting. Paint will be touch-dry in 15 to 20 minutes.

Latex Lucite

This is a flat (nongloss) paint thinned with water. It is used to apply color, if desired, to wooden members of bases. Cleanup before the paint dries is accomplished with water, thereby allowing the use of this type of paint throughout an entire operation with no danger from hazardous fumes.

Lucite and latex-base paints can be used for many colors. Both are soluble, prior to drying, in water; both are touch-dry in 20 minutes to 1/2 hour.

The reason for not using either water- or lacquer-soluble paint exclusively is that the bright, deep pipe colors can only be duplicated in lacquers, whereas the softer, flat, relatively odorless and fire-resistant paints are found in the water-soluble brands. All of these paints may be sprayed as well as brushed.

Wood Sealer

This should be used if the wooden base frame and legs are to remain unpainted. It should also be used if the wood is to be stained or varnished. Sealers require volatile thinners and cleaning fluids but are quick-drying and very easy to apply. Cleanup can be minimized by using inexpensive brushes which can be discarded after a day's use.

EXPENDABLE MATERIALS AND SUPPLIES

The following items are supplies that facilitate the construction of design models. Each model station should have a supply of the following:

- Small supply of structural shapes, including ladders and stairs
- Clear plastic strips for fictitious supports (1/16″ × 3/16″, 1/8″ × 3/8″)
- Sheet plastic (square foot of each thickness)
- Sandpaper (assorted grits)
- Industrial wipers
- Plastic marking pencils and colored pencils (red, yellow, and brown)
- Brass chain
- Chart-Pak tapes
- Line tags and tagging material
- Duco cement (tubes)
- Weld-On No. 16 (tubes)
- Plastic solvent
- Paint brushes (artist-type)
- Pointers
- Scale men
- Stationery (scratch pads, pencils, erasers, etc.)
- Lettering pen

Certain metal items, usually constructed of brass, are also used in the model shop, as are simpler materials, such as cardboard, illustration board, and a variety of materials that are available at a drafting supply store or an artist materials shop. Color coordination and the ability to use materials only come through experience, and although a student's efforts may not create a perfect, beautiful model in the beginning, after the construction of one or two models, the experience will definitely be reflected in the quality of any project that he or she undertakes.

QUIZ

10-1. Name five materials used in building a typical model.
10-2. What materials are used more often on architectural than on industrial models?
10-3. What percentage of the costs of a typical model are for materials?
10-4. When is hardware used on models?
10-5. What types of plastics are used in models?
10-6. What is the difference between foamed plastics and acrylic?
10-7. Describe the type of solvents or adhesives that work better with various plastics, such as acrylics, ABS, butyrate, and so on.
10-8. Name five precautions to follow when using solvents.
10-9. When is general-purpose cement used?
10-10. Is it possible to use cements for foamed plastics? Explain.
10-11. What portions of a model are normally painted?

11

Model Specifications

FIGURE 11-1   Power plant.

As mentioned previously, there can be variations in a given plant design as far as the amount of detail that is shown on a modeling project. In order to establish the definition for a modeling project, a model specification is required. The model specification provides a documented definition to model designers, model builders, clients, and appropriate management personnel in order to coordinate or communicate the model detail that is required on the project. A model specification should establish the type of model, the scope of the project, the planned use of the model, the method of construction, the materials that are required for the model,

and the color scheme or color-code system that will be utilized on the model.

Some companies have a standard model specification that only needs to be filled in to define a model project. This type of form certainly has its advantages, in that a consistent modeling procedure can be maintained within a design office or company. Another advantage is that a form of this type usually evolves into one that covers all possible questions that can come up on a project. One distinct disadvantage is that those writing a model specification for a new project (filling out a form) may tend to include model requirements that are "standard" but not actually required. The form approach also tends to stagnate or hinder innovative or new model ideas.

The model specification should be a rigorously analyzed and thoroughly digested piece of work. It should not be considered as a necessary evil that must be accomplished in order to progress to the heart of the model project. The model specification must be approved and reviewed by the client, the project engineer, appropriate management, and other appropriate personnel before an estimate is made.

The model specification is the control document for the entire model program. For example, if a model is required to have significant detail in certain portions of the plan and be rather skimpy on detail in other portions of the plan, this should be specified in the model specifications. A sample model specification, together with appropriate comments depicting the various attributes in the specification, are provided on the following pages.

SAMPLE MODEL SPECIFICATIONS

General

Example: This specification describes the type, scope, method of construction, materials, and color scheme of the piping design model.

Comments: If a company desires to build up a set of specifications for different types of models and various design reference documents, it should be stated in this section. Any drawings that will be made, in addition to piping and equipment arrangement and isometrics, must be specifically called out. If this specification covers an after-the-fact, study, preliminary, or other type of model, it should be stated in this section.

Type of Model

Example: The model will be a full-line-type piping design layout model. All equipment, concrete, and steel is modeled to a scale of 3/8″ = 1′0″. Vessels and heat exchangers will be modeled from plastic tubing of the nearest commercially available tubing size. Pumps and compressors will be modeled with minimum detail, just by showing general outline. Generally, out-of-scale construction of equipment will be held to 2″ maximum at 3/8″ scale. The shape of structural members will be modeled to within 2″ maximum at 3/8″ scale. Insulation thickness of insulated equipment and piping will not be included in the scale dimensions of the model components.

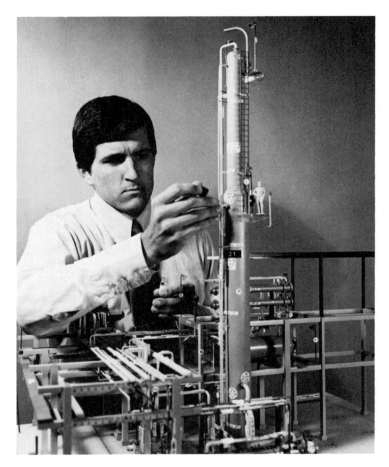

FIGURE 11-2 EMA model.

Comments: Should any critical or exotic piping material be required on the preliminary model, it should be so specified. In some cases, a larger-scale section of a particularly congested area may be required.

Scope

Example: The areas to be modeled will be only those for new construction. New equipment in existing areas will not be modeled. The new storage area will not be modeled. The underground will not be modeled.

Comments: Some new areas within an overall plant may not require modeling. These areas should be specified in this section.

Intent of the Model

Example: The intent of this model is that the company engineering groups use it as the focal point for all communication and coordination of the plant design. It will be used to communicate to the client the design and the design status. All isometrics for field- and shop-fabricated pipe will be developed from the model. After model design completion, the model will be used for a construction guide or tool at the plant site and, finally, for training of personnel and as a plant maintenance guide.

Comments: Should a model have any unusual intent or shipping requirements, such as shipping to or through extreme temperature and/or handling situations, note of it should be made in this section.

Ladders, Platforms, and Equipment Nozzles

Example: Ladders and stairways will be shown with cages and hand rails omitted. Platforms will be shown in outline form only, with hand rails omitted. Vessel manways will be modeled. Equipment nozzle and valve mating flanges will not be shown.

Comments: Should the client specify cages and hand rails or should they be desired to establish clearance in congested areas, they are available as off-the-shelf items.

Plot Boards

Example: All equipment will be mechanically attached or solvent-welded to plot boards. Plot boards will be sized to accommodate the process areas with a desirable maximum width of 29″. All plot boards will be constructed to accommodate removable legs, adjustable in height. Tops are to be constructed with 1/4″ plexiglass.

Comments: The size and/or shape of the plot boards is dictated by the equipment and/or plant layout. If at all possible, do not split vessels, equipment, or heavily concentrated areas of piping. The maximum width of 29″ was established as the maximum table width that can be carried horizontally through a standard 30″ door. Plot boards should not exceed the standard maximum unless it is absolutely necessary. Such cases would be to avoid splitting a problem area or a complicated piece of equipment, and then only if no item on the board exceeds 25 inches in height. An overwidth board must be tilted 90° to pass through a standard door. This is at best a risky situation. The strong recommendation is to make every reasonable effort to avoid overwidth boards.

Piping

Example: Piping 2″ and smaller is shown by 1/16″ plastic coated wire. Piping 3″ and larger will be shown full scale. Line tags are attached to

the model piping to show line size, line number, material specifications, insulation, tracing, or electrical heat, commodity, and flow direction.

The following will show on the model:

- Utility stations in block form, but without piping running to them, except for one typical station at grade.
- Drain funnels indicated with 1/4″-diameter black labels.
- All process piping, except as stated herein. All other piping 2″ and larger.
- All piping in pipeways, regardless of size.
- Equipment process vents and drains that appear on flow diagrams.
- Bridle block valves.
- Steam trap boot legs.
- Spring hangers, rod hangers, and base elbow supports.
- Emergency showers in block form (no piping).
- Sample coolers in block form (no piping).
- Vessel access openings with black tape cutouts.
- Where multiple items have typical piping, such as furnace burner piping, only one unit will be piped completely.
- Furnished piping at equipment will be full-scale, painted the color of the equipment.
- Chain operators for valves will be indicated by a loop of small link chain sandwiched to the valve handwheel with a disc the size of the handwheel.
- Railroads, sumps, trenches, catch basins, and surface drains indicated with black tape.
- Fences and buried existing process lines indicated with dashed black-and-white tape.
- Pipe shoes will be shown as a 4″ square by 1′0″ ± length of clear plastic.
- Insulation as a white snap-on sleeve.

The following items will not show on the model:

- 1 1/2″ and smaller piping, except in pipeways and as deemed necessary by the project coordinator for process clarity.
- Piping hydrostatic test vents and drains, including control valve loop drains.
- Exchanger thermal relief valves.
- Test connections on exchange nozzles or the exchanger itself.
- Threaded (screwed) fittings such as unions, swages, caps, and couplings.
- Instrumentation valving.
- Weld reducers in lines 3″ and smaller in size.
- Equipment elevators.

Comments: These lists showing items that will or will not be shown were developed based on design definition suitability versus cost. There will probably be instances where exceptions to these lists will be required. It is of utmost importance that all responsible parties (the client, above all) understand the detail that will and will not be included on each model before any project goes past the specification stage.

Model Tags

Example: Horizontal tags, when possible, will read in the same direction as the plot plan is lettered. Lettering must be of finished drawing quality.

Vertical tags will be located so that they may be read in the same direction that the plot plan is lettered and from the bottom up. The following will be tagged:

- All equipment, with its item number.
- Piping; where space is limited, indicate line size only.
- Pipe support numbers and top of support elevation, one support each board.
- High point of finished grade on each board.
- North on each board.
- Platform elevations.
- Fire hydrants, hose boxes, hose reels, etc., with white labels.
- Centerline coordinates of roads.
- In-line and vessel instruments at the tap location.
- Sample connection (SC) and steam outs (SO), with adhesive buttons at connection locations.
- Utility stations with letter designations: A—air, W—water, S—steam.

Comments: An engineering design model is completely useless as a design tool unless it contains complete, accurate, and legible tagging. Good lettering quality goes a long way toward maintaining a professional image. It is also generally accepted that vertical lettering on tags is more legible from any angle than is slanted lettering, either to individuals or in photographs, and is therefore most commonly used. At any rate, consistency in style is called for.

Model Colors

Example: Colors are as noted below:

Equipment: EMA Equipment Gray—Equipment in the various process areas may be shown with different colors.

Piping: Red—process alloy pipe.

Yellow—process carbon steel pipe.

Pink — instrumentation — orifice flanges, controllers, loops, and relief valves.

Light green—electrical components.

EMA Steel Gray—bare steel, equipment ladders, and stairs. Items furnished by piping, such as rod hangers, spring hangers, dummy supports, field supports, etc.

EMA Valve Gray—manufactured valves.

EMA Concrete Gray—concrete and fire-proofing.

(*Note:* Clear plastic will be used for "ghost" or fictitious supports. These are used for model support and do not physically exist.)

Comments: A consistent color-code system should be established for all model projects to facilitate "model reading." Although a different color-coding system may be established, this one is consistent with commercially available materials.

Electrical Work

Example: Light fixtures will be shown. Conduit raceways, starter racks, and electrical panels, where size or location may indicate possible interferences, will be shown in block form. Individual conduits will not be shown. Only the main raceways will be shown in block or strip form.

Instrumentation

Example:

- Main instrument racks, junction boxes, and instruments will be located on the model.
- All instruments will be tagged with a plastic button with the flow-sheet nomenclature lettered on it.
- Temperature and pressure connections on piping and equipment will be shown as a plastic button.
- Pedestal and line-mounted transmitters will be indicated on the model as accurately as is possible with commercially available model components or in block form.
- Level instruments, gauge glasses, level controllers, and switches will be shown as a wire loop to indicate scale. Individual valving will not be shown.

Model Review

Example: At various phases of the design, the model will be available to the client for review. The project manager will establish a date with the customer for review. The piping design supervisor will furnish prints of up-to-date flow diagrams, pointer, model scale, the model, and a 3/8″ scale man for the review. When the customer review comments are resolved and the model has been corrected as necessary, the customer will be notified to arrange for a final review. The plant design shall be considered complete and not subject to revision after final customer approval.

Comments: Any in-process reviews that the client desires should be clearly specified in this section. It is best to plan reviews based on completion of key phases of a project rather than based on time frames, such as biweekly reviews.

Typical client review periods are indicated below.

- After preliminary model is complete.
- After 30 percent of piping is installed.
- After 60 percent of piping is installed.
- Final model review.

Note: Basic model review is unnecessary, as the basic model is only a correctly scaled preliminary model, which has already been approved.

This section will have introduced the prospective modeler (student) to the type of specifications that may be found "in the field." It is important to remember that each company (and each project) will have a new set of "specs." The modeler must be able to adapt to any given situation (job). Although this book describes the most commonly used specifications throughout the model industry, it by no means covers all the variations that are in existence.

12

Models and Color Coding

FIGURE 12-1 Fossil-fuel steam generator.

Identification of piping systems and, in general, being able to read a given model is accomplished through tagging and color coding. There are many different approaches that can be used to color code models. Each company or client will often have its own standard color-coding system. A color code is normally included in the legend plaque attached to one of the model bases or, in the case of a multiple-unit project, to a model base in each unit. The following categories are almost universally differentiated by color code:

- Piping
- Structural
- Equipment
- Electrical
- Instrumentation

Piping is often further broken down by color code. There are two general methods for this: a piping specification code or a commodity code. If the model is going to be used basically as a construction tool or guide, piping can be color-coded to show the different materials. For example, process carbon steel pipe may be shown as yellow, process alloy or other special materials as red, and heavy wall carbon steel as blue in the pipe specification system. If a model is to be used basically to show

FIGURE 12-2

the various processes involved, the process piping (and equipment if desired) associated with a given process will be one color while other processes will be distinguished by their own specific color code.

The following color codes are considered industry-standard:

- Electrical components—light green
- Instrumentation components—pink
- Equipment structures—gray

Listed below is a typical color-code system for a petrochemical model:

- Equipment—gray; equipment in different process areas may be shown with different colors, but this requires painting and adds considerably to the cost of the basic model and creates problems with attachments.
- Piping
    —red (alloy pipe)
    —yellow (carbon steel pipe)
    —pink (instrument orifice flanges, controllers, loops, and relief valves)
    —light green (electrical components)
    —black (cast iron)

    —orange (synthetic or glass)
    —blue (heavy wall carbon steel)
- Valve—gray (manufactured valves)
- Structures
    —steel gray
    —concrete gray (concrete and fireproofing)
- Clear plastic—fictitious or ghost supports used for model support; do not exist physically except on the model
- Insulation on pipe
    —white sleeve (hot)
    —purple sleeve (cold)
    —light blue sleeve (steam-traced)
    —light green sleeve (electrically traced)
- Insulation on equipment—indicated by a "cloud" of pressure-sensitive white label labeled with the proper insulation thickness.

COLOR-CODING METHODS

Standard component parts come in a variety of colors. Almost all the components are available in yellow, blue, orange, pink, green, white, gray, red, light blue, brown, and black. All models are constructed with a color code in mind, and this may differ among companies, although there are certain standard procedures. In general, it is suggested that there are three different ways of color coding a model.

- Service
- Materials
- Process and service

When grouping by service, it is suggested that the following be used:

- Process—yellow.
- Utilities—blue; or they can be broken down into: steam and condensate—orange; water—blue; air—white; gases—black or brown; fire protection—red.
- Existing piping—white.
- Valves—gray.
- Insulation—white; or broken down into: insulation, hot—white sleeve; insulation, cold—purple sleeve; insulation, steam traced—light blue sleeve; insulation, electrical traced—electrical green sleeve.
- All electrical items, including trays, electrical equipment, and conduit should be green.
- Heating, air conditioning, and ventilation can be done in buff, or preferably in light or dark blue.
- Roads—brown.
- Plot plan or limits, including battery limits—black tape.
- Building walls—black tape.
- Trenches—black outline.
- Underground piping—black centerline tape.
- Underground electrical—electrical green tape.
- Underground instrumentation—instrumentation pink tape.

When color coding by materials, the following should be used:

- Carbon steel—yellow
- Alloy—red
- Special materials—orange
- Electrical—green
- Galvanized—buff or blue

The following general list can also be used:

- Structural steel—gray
- Existing structures—white
- Future structures—gray with speckles
- Concrete—gray

- Equipment—gray
- Existing equipment—white
- Future equipment—valve gray with speckles
- Electrical—green
- Instrumentation—pink
- HVAC—light or dark blue
- Fictitious parts—transparent clear
- Safety equipment—red

When grouping by process and service, the following is suggested:

- Process—yellow
- Utilities—blue
- Special service—orange
- Electrical—green
- HVAC—buff or blue

Existing piping should be the same as the base color or speckled, or some companies use colors exclusive to their company. The important thing is that the existing equipment be generally recognized as such so that the construction crew will not duplicate it.

In general, fittings come in the color of the piping: white, black, or gray. The use of colors for fittings will depend on the standard procedure for the particular company. Component manufacturers vary in their use of some colors for different items, such as valves and instrumentation. Usually, it is best to use either gray or black for valves and to keep all instrumentation in pink. One thing that is important when constructing small models is not to use too many different colors of piping, giving a Christmas tree effect to the model. This includes the use of colors for painting, which should be kept to a minimum. Equipment should generally be sprayed either gray or rust red.

The following code has been used in EMA's training models and this can be used for all of the model projects herein, although it would be advantageous to attempt different projects with the other coding systems, using service or materials or process as a basic code, in order to experience all three methods.

It is unfortunate that this book could not be printed in color, so as to more accurately represent the actual industrial model.

EMA COLOR CODING

Piping, structural, equipment, electrical, and instrumentation details will be color-coded on each project for the purpose of identification. Every effort will be made to use a standard color code on all projects. A color-code plaque will be made for each modeled project and attached to the model before final review.

General

Structural steel	Steel gray
Existing structure	White
Future structure	Steel gray with white speckle
Concrete	Concrete gray
Equipment	Vessel and equipment gray
Existing equipment	White
Future equipment	Vessel and equipment gray with white speckle
Electrical	Electrical green
Instrumentation	Instrument pink
HVAC (ducts and equipment)	Light blue
Fictitious (model) supports	Transparent
Safety equipment	Red

Piping

Note: Piping color is entirely by company selection. The following is only intended as a suggestion.

Process	Yellow
Utilities	Blue
Alloy, exotic, lined, or heavy wall	Orange
Existing pipe	White
Fire protection	Red
Valves	Valve gray
Vendor engineered piping (generally excluded)	Vessel and equipment gray
Insulation—hot	White sleeve
Insulation—cold	Purple sleeve
Insulation—steam-traced	Light blue sleeve
Insulation—electrically traced	Electrical green sleeve

Grade of underground

Roads	Brown (paint or tape)
Plot limit	Black plot limit tape
Building walls	Black tape (to scale)
Trenches	Black outline
Dropout areas	Black outline
Underground piping	Black centerline tape
Underground electrical	Electrical green (paint or tape)
Underground instrumentation	Instrument pink (paint or tape)

The following code is an example of a typical nuclear power plant color code.

ASME Section I Piping	Purple
ASME Section III Class 1 Piping	Red
ASME Section III Class 2 Piping	Orange
ASME Section III Class 3 Piping	Yellow
ANSI B31.1 Piping	Green
Fire protection piping	Brown
Roof drain and sewer piping	Black
Equipment	Gray
Concrete—structural or foundations	White
Steel—structural	Dark gray
Equipment laydown areas	Transparent
Fictitious (model) supports	Transparent
Grating or checker plate	Transparent grated
HVAC	Light blue
Instrumentation	Pink
Electrical	Green

QUIZ

12-1. Why are models color-coded?

12-2. Name three methods of color coding.

12-3. How are battery limits delineated on the model, and with what color?

12-4. What items are usually green?

12-5. HVAC is usually represented in what color?

13

Preliminary/Study Model

FIGURE 13-1 Preliminary model. (Model photographs courtesy of Badger America, Inc., Cambridge, Massachusetts 02124.)

The main purpose of a preliminary model is to determine the ultimate or most efficient equipment arrangement, together with the determination of the location for major and/or critical lines. In cases where exotic or critical piping is involved, it should be added to the preliminary model. Other piping should be excluded. Critical or exotic lines are defined as lines that must have stress analysis performed before the fittings are ordered or are of such complexity, size, or long delivery time that they must be ordered very early in the project. Figures 13-1 and 13-2 show two views of a typical preliminary model.

Several alternative equipment arrangements should be made to determine the ideal arrangement. Polaroid photographs should be made of these arrangements, together with appropriate notes. Use of these photographs will minimize the drafting effort. Prior to the start of a preliminary model, the following information is required:

- A list of vessels, towers, exchangers, heaters, compressors, and pumps, and their approximate sizes
- Mechanical or process flow diagrams
- Special structural requirements

FIGURE 13-2 Preliminary model. (Model photographs courtesy of Badger America, Inc., Cambridge, Massachusetts 02124.)

Normally, a scale no larger than 1/4" = 1' should be used. Scales commonly used are 1/8" = 1' or 1" = 10'. However, there are occasions where larger scales will be required to develop equipment arrangements in congested or multilevel areas.

Because the preliminary or study model is only a preliminary tool or at least a temporary tool, it can be fabricated from less-durable materials. Depending upon the durability and life-expectancy requirements for the study or preliminary model, the base board can be made out of poster board, heavy cardboard, plexiglass, styrene, or plywood. It is suggested that foam blocks be cut to appropriate size to simulate equipment and vessels. Foam blocks should be labeled with equipment name and attached to the preliminary or study base with double-sided tape. Equipment locations, pipe racks, and bays should be represented on the model using a preliminary plastic structural system.

Preliminary structural kits are available for this purpose. Some include scale figures, ladders, stairs, and scale rules, together with columns, column crosses, base footers, beams, beam crosses, beam supports, beam splices, and all necessary components. Using this type of preliminary structural system, column spacing and beam elevations, as well as locations, are easily changed. Space relationships, accessibility, mechanical flow, and supports are immediately obvious.

There is no waste in this type of kit because when the design is optimized, the structure can be disassembled and the parts can be used again to evolve other configurations. Kits are available in 1/4", 3/8", 1/2", and 3/4" scales. Figures 13-3 and 13-4 show examples of a preliminary structural system.

The use of polyurethane or polystyrene foam as a material for stimulating vessels and equipment is quite common on preliminary or study models. A hot-wire saw or hot-wire foam cutter is a valuable asset when cutting the foam blocks. A bandsaw also works well, although it creates "dust" from the foam being cut. Nevertheless, the best overall choice between the commercially available hot-wire cutters and bandsaws is the bandsaw, because of the ease of cutting large blocks of foam. The material cost required to assemble a study or preliminary model is inconsequential compared to the labor cost and is rarely a factor to be considered in the overall cost of the program. Many companies utilize preliminary models in their estimate or bid preparations. Some preliminary models become a little more elaborate as the equipment location is evolved and are sometimes used in sales and bid presentations.

After several arrangements have been put together and photographed, the one that is considered by the layout personnel to be the optimum arrangement is reconstructed. Now the preliminary model review meeting should be held. It is essential to solicit a wide degree of participation at the preliminary model review. All engineering groups and/or disciplines should be involved in this review. One of the chief assets of the use of a preliminary model versus drawings is that it stimulates criticism from the experienced personnel in design, operations, construction, management,

FIGURE 13-3   Preliminary structural system.

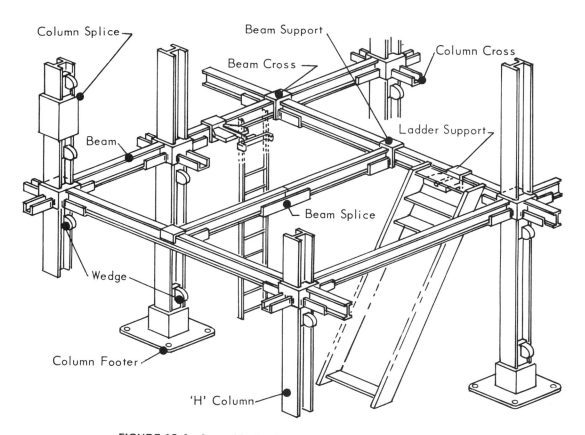

FIGURE 13-4   Assembly details for preliminary structural system.

and process fields on a given job. This constructive criticism can be evaluated and incorporated into the model at the preliminary review meeting at very little cost to the overall project. After various equipment arrangements have been developed, evolved, and evaluated, a firm plot plan can be developed and the client review can be called.

Only after client approval of the preliminary plot plan should the plot plan drawings, layout drawings, and equipment layout drawings be prepared and issued. For plot plans that are made up of several process units and/or attendant facilities, an overall plot plan should be developed for each process unit or attendant facility that consists of major units. It is important to establish the equipment and vessel coordinates as early as possible so that modeling can proceed to the design modeling phase. Structural and grade mounted equipment coordinates should be detailed on the plot plan. All structures and equipment should be

located by coordinates and elevations rather than by dimensions. Ideally, only upon final arrival of the plot plan drawings should the design model bases be actually started, so that optimum model base cuts can be determined. (See Section 2 for other photographs of preliminary study models.) A possible class project building a preliminary model would greatly help student understanding of the use and advantages of completing a preliminary model before construction of the final model.

Using foam shapes, an inexpensive base, double-sided tape, and preliminary structural system (Figs. 13-3 and 13-4), the class should experiment in alternative equipment locations for projects such as those found in *Piping Systems Drafting and Design.* Building preliminary models for projects in Sections 25 to 31 would also be helpful to student understanding of these assignments.

QUIZ

13-1. What is a preliminary model, and how is it used in industry?

13-2. What drawings does a preliminary model substitute for?

13-3. Prior to the start of a typical preliminary model, what information is necessary?

13-4. What scale is a typical preliminary model constructed at?

13-5. What types of equipment are usually shown on a preliminary model?

14

Model Table
and
Base Construction

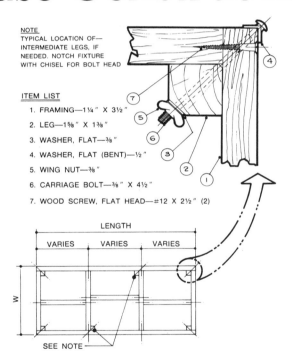

NOTE
TYPICAL LOCATION OF—
INTERMEDIATE LEGS, IF
NEEDED. NOTCH FIXTURE
WITH CHISEL FOR BOLT HEAD

ITEM LIST

1. FRAMING—1¼″ X 3½″

2. LEG—1⅝″ X 1⅜″

3. WASHER, FLAT—⅜″

4. WASHER, FLAT (BENT)—½″

5. WING NUT—⅜″

6. CARRIAGE BOLT—⅜″ X 4½″

7. WOOD SCREW, FLAT HEAD—#12 X 2½″ (2)

LENGTH

VARIES   VARIES   VARIES

W

SEE NOTE

FIGURE 14-1   Wood table substructure and legs.

The following section covers the construction of model bases and tables. The first step is the determination of model scale, which is dependent upon the accuracy and detail required and the congestion of the area or areas to be modeled.

The second step in the construction of model bases is to divide up the plot plan into the number of bases or tables that will be required. Throughout this discussion, the term table or model base will be used interchangeably. The division of the plot plan should be made by the project engineer and model shop supervisor. The responsibility should not be delegated to the group that makes the model

tables because the table dimensions cannot be arbitrarily or conveniently set. *The division of the plot plan must dictate the table sizes, not vice versa.*

There are some very specific guidelines that should be followed in determining table sizes.

Table tops should, in general, be less than 29″ wide and 6′ long. The main reason for this determination is to permit movement of the completed model through standard hallways, doors, and elevators. However, when tables approach the 6′ length and longer, extra support legs are often needed to ensure a level work surface. Since tables are all custom-made, top sizes can as easily be built to 28 3/16″ as one to 28 1/2″. On the other hand, should a number of tables, such as five or ten, be required of the same size, this allows for more efficient fabrication of the tables, and therefore certain economies can be expected in making or ordering these tables. Also, consideration should be given to splitting the bases so that they will be in even 1′0″ or 6″ scale increments, in length and width. This will make design calculations easier and help eliminate mathematical errors when working from base to base or from a base edge.

Equipment and vessels should not be split if possible. However, splitting of equipment and vessels is a better choice than permitting the equipment or vessels to overlap a table edge. Overlapping enhances the possibility of equipment being damaged during both the design stage and shipping, and also gives a false representation of available space on the base adjacent to the base containing the overlapping equipment.

When determining the number of bases, consideration should be given to process or equipment areas. It is desirable to maintain all of a given process area or equipment area on one table top.

Column centerlines represent an ideal place to split a given plot plan. Splits that do not fall on column centerlines require fictitious supports.

When constructing models with more than one level, the split should be made at the edge of the table with no levels overhanging. It is often difficult to determine the proper place to make this split, in that various levels may have equipment and/or processes that should not be split or separated. When this occurs, it is best to look at the overall effect of the model and make the split along the line that would have the least adverse overall effect.

Model bases should not extend beyond the plot limits of the current project. The purpose of this is to provide space for future projects to be added on additional model tables.

Basic models can be subdivided into three phases of construction: first, the actual substructure of the model table along with the supporting legs; second, the table-top material that all the equipment and structures are attached to; and third, the equipment and structural items that are mounted and prepared to receive piping. The third phase is covered in Section 15.

TABLE SUBSTRUCTURE AND LEG ASSEMBLY

There are many different configurations of the table substructure and leg assemblies used in the

model industry today. A simple way of looking at the table substructure and legs is that it provides a means to hold the table top and model equipment at a working level. Models, with the exception of nuclear models, are typically constructed at the 30″ table-top height. Legs are included as part of the substructure, so that additional tables will not need to be in the design office or field site to hold the models. Nuclear models are often constructed at a much lower base height because of their larger scale and multilevel construction, which often requires them to exceed several feet in height. (*Note:* There are several illustrations of different configurations in this section. Their presence does not necessarily make them acceptable. Please refer to the text that goes along with each table description.)

A wooden substructure with removable wooden legs is probably the most widely used table configuration in the model industry today (Fig. 14-1 shows this design together with the materials list). The frame is made from 5/4 kiln-dried white pine. The legs are often made from 2″ × 2″ fir. Substructures are typically glued and screwed together to provide adequate rigidity. Extreme care must be taken in fabrication to achieve straight and flat base surfaces. An alternative design is shown in Fig. 14-2. Construction is from 2″ × 2″ No. 1 fir.

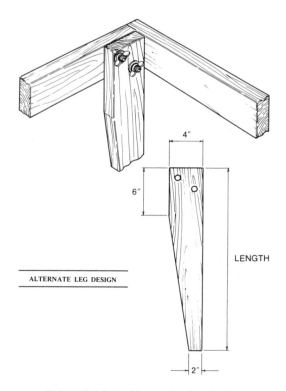

FIGURE 14-2 Alternative leg design.

The removable legs have three basic purposes: one, more compact shipping crates can be utilized with the legs removed; two, tables exhibit more stability with the legs removed for shipping purposes; and three, photography can be more easily achieved with the table legs removed. Another type of wooden substructure currently being used is constructed from 2″ × 4″ lumber in very much the same manner as the 5/4 white pine substructure with the addition of either 1/2″ or 3/8″ plywood fastened to the top and bottom to create a laminated-type structure. This configuration, often utilizing folding steel legs, is sometimes used for preliminary model layouts where there are no permanent attachments to the surface to be considered (see Fig. 14-3). A variety of folding steel

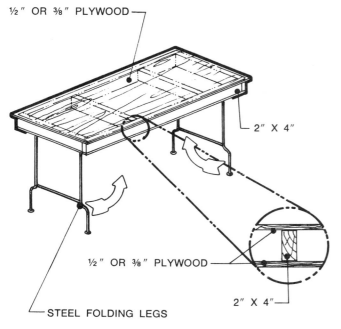

FIGURE 14-3 Laminated plywood and 2″ × 4″ wood substructure with metal folding legs.

table legs are commercially available that can be attached to various table substructures. It is necessary to provide adjustable leg glides on any type of leg, whether it be of wood construction or steel construction. The main purpose of the adjustable leg glides is to simplify table-top leveling and base-edge matching when piping from base to base, during reviews and for photography.

A relatively new type of construction is plywood, or plexiglass laminated to plywood, mounted on a substructure of a commercially available steel frame with folding legs (Fig. 14-4). These table substructures can be procured in almost any size required by the modeling industry. Being a mass-production item, they offer several

FIGURE 14-4 Steel substructure and steel folding legs with plywood top.

advantages over the wooden frame, such as a more uniform high quality, table consistency, and lower purchase price. A disadvantage of steel frame construction is that without cross members or struts under the base surface, there will be potential problems of warping and racking.

However, a model table is produced and marketed by EMA Services, Inc., which combines the metal frame and folding leg with a tubular steel grid to which any type of surface material can be attached. This arrangement provides a rigid frame upon which sheet plexiglass can be mounted without requiring an underlayment. The legs fold and lock for shipping or for the convenience of lowering to floor level for photography (see Fig. 14-5).

When choosing the type of table that will be utilized on a given plant model, several considerations need to be made. Of prime importance is the overall environment that the table will be exposed to during transit and at its final destination. Because of the expense of models alone, they need to be handled with special care. However, handling becomes a special problem when a model must be shipped by commercial means, particularly by air freight, rail, or cargo ship. The packaging and crating plays an important role in protecting the model during shipment. If a model is going to be set in a design office or laboratory with stable temperature and humidity control for comfort conditions, very little consideration needs to be given to the model substructure design and construction.

Models that will be exposed to large temperature and humidity extremes during shipment and use require special consideration when determining the substructure design. For example, high-

FIGURE 14-5   Standard EMA table metal frame, folding legs, tubular steel grid.

humidity conditions can often cause warping and swelling of the model substructure, together with model components and model tops. Large temperature extremes have very little effect on wooden substructures in that they have a relatively low coefficient of thermal expansion. However, plastic components have a relatively high thermal coefficient of expansion compared to either wood or steel. Therefore, the connection between the plastic and wood or the plastic and metal must be designed to permit these movements. Insufficient design will cause table buckling and subsequent breaking of equipment or joints. Although these problems can be serious, they are relatively easy to overcome with proper design concepts.

Another consideration to be made when choosing a model substructure or model design table is the mass or weight that will be applied upon a given model base. Nuclear models, in general, require considerably more bracing in the table substructure as a combined result of their larger scale, more densely populated equipment and piping, and their multilevel construction. This is not to say that the table or substructure design is inconsequential when refinery, chemical, soap plant, and big industrial models are being fabri-

cated. However, it is true that the average refinery, petrochemical, or other nonnuclear model can be built on any of the aforementioned substructures with adequate results. When the refinery or any given class or model becomes highly congested with equipment and multilevels, consideration must be given to the type of table substructure.

One of the best measures of table rigidity is racking. Racking can be defined as the amount of out-of-flatness that is created when one corner of a model table is elevated independently of the other three corners. This out-of-flatness condition, if not controlled, will cause twisting and subsequent popping of bond joints, as well as possible breaking and cracking of structures and lines. In one sense, racking is an academic question, in that tables are normally not picked up or moved about by lifting one corner. Tables are normally carried in a level position by applying lifting forces on all four corners, thereby minimizing the racked condition. On the other hand, the racked condition can occur during movement of the table by one person or during initial setup of the table by one person or during initial setup of a model, particularly in a construction area where the floor may not be level. This, incidently, is another reason for the necessity of leg leveling glides.

Since the wooden substructure type of table with wooden legs is the most common in the industry today, several tables have been evaluated using the wooden table as a standard for comparison. It was determined that the standard wood table (Figs. 14-1 and 14-6) and the metal table with the grid platen substructure are superior to other commonly used tables in regard to racking when loaded with a 63-pound distributed load and a 90-pound point load.

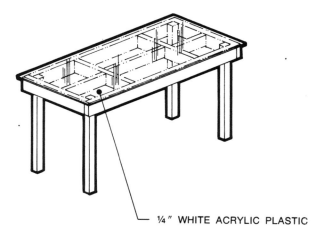

¼″ WHITE ACRYLIC PLASTIC

FIGURE 14-6   Wood structure with ¼″ acrylic plastic.

TABLE-TOP CONSIDERATIONS

Compatibility is the key word when looking at the table-top materials that are available. Virtually all the items that are to be fastened to the table top, such as structural, vessels, and equipment, are now commercially available in plastic. Plexiglass tops have therefore been widely adopted, because attachments can be made by simply solvent-cement bonding rather than by mechanical attachments with screws and bolts. There may, however, be considerations for alternative selections. If backlighting for photography is a requirement, for example, a plywood or Formica surface would not be feasible. This requirement would automatically dictate the use of the tables shown in Figs. 14-5 and 14-6, with 1/4" plexiglass tops.

Either 1/8" or 1/4" plexiglass can be used as a top when plywood or flakeboard is used as an underlayment (Figs. 14-7 and 14-8). This top configuration can be utilized with any of the aforementioned structures. The 1/8" top is obviously more economical. Another advantage of the 1/8" thickness is that with the commercial tolerance of ±10 percent of the thickness, one can be assured of one-half the variation.

When attaching plexiglass to either a metal or a wood substructure, care must be taken to permit differential movement due to the varying thermal expansions of the differing materials. When using screws to mechanically hold down the plexiglass, the center screw only should be flat-headed, countersunk, and snugged into the countersink. Corner holes should be at least 1/8" oversized and the screws should be oval-headed with a finish washer (see Fig. 14-7). These screws should also be only "snugged up," not severely tightened.

Another top configuration can be created by bonding plexiglass to the plywood underlayment (Fig. 14-8). One distinct disadvantage of introducing an adhesive or bonding material is that an automatic increase in labor and possibly more extensive shop equipment is required. The most compatible adhesive that one could use when bonding plexiglass to either plywood or flakeboard underlayment would be a silicon-type adhesive. This adhesive requires a primer to be applied to the plexiglass and also requires pressure to be applied to the surface during the cure cycle.

The second type of adhesive would be a standard Formica-type contact cement. This approach is not recommended, in that crazing of the plexiglass can occur as a result of the solvent

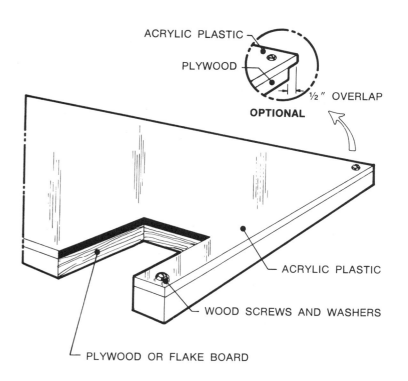

1/4" ACRYLIC PLASTIC

NO 8 X 3/4" OVAL HEAD WOOD SCREWS

NO 8 COUNTERSUNK WASHERS

1/2" OR 3/8" PLYWOOD OR FLAKE BOARD

FIGURE 14-7 Table top—detail of acrylic plastic attached to plywood with screws.

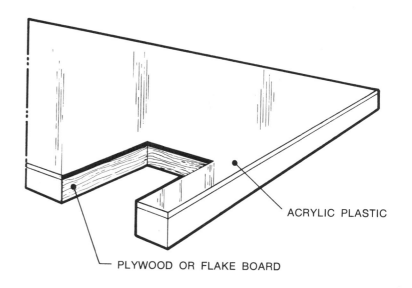

1/8" ACRYLIC PLASTIC

1/2" OR 3/8" PLYWOOD OR FLAKE BOARD

SILICONE ADHESIVE

FIGURE 14-8 Table top—detail of acrylic plastic attached to plywood with adhesive.

attacking the plexiglass. A second disadvantage is that delamination may occur. A third disadvantage is that a similar backing material should be applied to the back of the underside of the table top to stabilize and prevent curl during temperature extremes.

Another consideration for top materials is the application of Formica to an underlayment (Fig. 14-9). A white or matte-finish Formica creates a very desirable working surface. However, problems occur because of additional labor needed to apply the contact cement, and additional shop venting and shop space that may be required. Again, a Formica backing material is required to minimize curl. Another disadvantage of Formica is the incompatibility of current modeling components, in that solvent welding cannot be effectively utilized. However, several other adhesives are available which offer quick setup time and effective bonding.

One big disadvantage of the laminate-type material (thin plexiglass or Formica) is that a more complicated manufacturing process for the tops is required. This normally evolves into more shop space, more equipment, more time, and

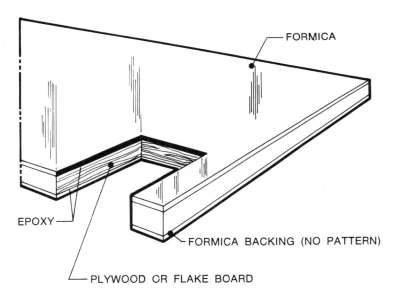

EPOXY ⌐

└ FORMICA BACKING (NO PATTERN)

└─ PLYWOOD OR FLAKE BOARD

●—FORMICA

●—PLYWOOD OR FLAKE BOARD

●—FORMICA BACKING

●—EPOXY BONDING MATERIAL

FIGURE 14-9 Table top—detail of formica bonded to plywood or flake board.

therefore more dollars. However, the lower cost of these laminated materials can possibly offset the added labor and be competitive with the relatively high cost of 1/4″ plexiglass. The top surface of the plexiglass must be such that no glare of lights will take place during photography. The plexiglass can be purchased in a frosted condition. The same effect can be achieved by applying a medium-grit sandpaper to the surface.

The overall cost of a substructure and top for a model base is very small compared to the overall cost of the basic model and almost insignificant compared to the cost of the overall design model. It should be emphasized at this point as a result of these facts that the compatibility of substructure and top to the use and environment of the finished model, as well as good delivery, are far more important considerations than the cost of table and substructure.

One approach that has been tried, but not with much success, is the use of a painted plywood table top. This seems to be an economical approach on first thought but is a good example of why a thoroughly experienced model shop supervisor is so important. The painted tops create so many new, time-consuming problems in the actual construction of the model that the acrylic tops will be paid for many times over in the time saved during the course of the project.

CONSTRUCTION AND ASSEMBLY OF BASIC MODELS

The preferred way to construct and assemble a basic model is to segregate the building of the substructure and table top in a certain area of the overall model shop and then provide a relatively cleaner area for the fabrication and attachment of the equipment and structures. As a medium, the basic model work should all be confined to the model shop rather than trying to build equipment and attach structures on the design floor. As previously mentioned, there are some companies that do perform the equipment fabrication and attachment of the structures on the design floor, but as a rule of thumb, this is undesirable because of the noise, congestion, and basic confusion. Also, by not doing basic model work on the design floor, a company is able to segregate the various skill levels in order to control the work.

Using the model index drawings or a marked-up plot plan drawing that defines the size and location of each model table top, the first step after completion of the model table is to lay out all major structures and equipment. It is important to check with the project engineer or the engineering print issue control center to determine the latest issue of the plot plan or model index drawings.

It is necessary to use the coordinate system on model projects. Actual dimensions create too many problems as to points of reference. In many cases, they are impossible to use simply because the model is three-dimensional. Figure 14-10 illustrates this procedure.

Coordinate lines should all be checked prior to drilling of holes or attaching any equipment or components to the table top. It is best to have this checking performed by a model technician or designer other than the one who originally laid out the coordinate lines.

Before a model technician or designer can effectively lay out the model base, he or she must be totally familiar with the scale-model compo-

nents that will be used. For example, he or she needs to know the components that are commercially available, as well as their method of attachment.

At this point in the design modeling project, the following information must be available to or developed by the design group:

- Model specifications, including model scope.
- High point of finished grade; typically established at elevation 100'0".
- The elevation for the top of grout.
- Latest issue of flow diagrams.
- Aboveground piping plan—this routing diagram can be made on an ozalid of the plot plan. This is simply a study and not a formal drawing. It provides the general routing of the major lines and is usually accomplished during the plot plan development phase,

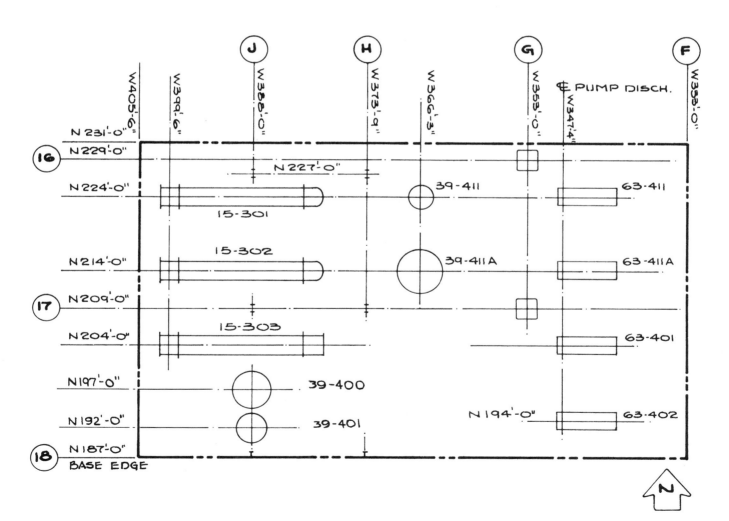

FIGURE 14-10 Table plot plan layout.

since major lines routing is a major factor in equipment location.
- Location of all main structural columns.
- Elevation of all structures along with the required platforms.
- All available equipment drawings.
- Pipeway information: widths, bent spacing, top of support elevations (spacing of multiple

levels), and a structural department "best guess" on sizes.
- Space requirements and locations of instrumentation and electrical conduit banks and major pieces of equipment, such as switch gear and control panels.
- All equipment orientation, piping sketches, and studies previously accomplished.

QUIZ

14-1. In what area are the table and base constructed?

14-2. What are the normal maximum sizes for table tops?

14-3. What are the first two steps in a typical base construction?

14-4. What are bases normally constructed of?

14-5. What is a typical table top normally made of?

14-6. Should model bases extend beyond the plot limits of the current project?

14-7. Where should a model be split or sectioned? In what area should it not be divided?

14-8. Is there a difference in the construction of the base of a preliminary versus a final design model?

14-9. Where is plywood used on a typical model base or table?

14-10. What thickness of plexiglass is usually used for table tops?

14-11. What are the disadvantages of using thin plexiglass or Formica?

14-12. Why is it usually not standard procedure to use flat-painted plywood for model tops?

15

Model Construction (Basic Model Stage)

FIGURE 15-1 Basic model (this is a photograph of the project in Section 25).

The preferred way to construct and assemble a basic model is to segregate the building of the substructure and table top in a certain area of the overall model shop and then provide a relatively cleaner area for the fabrication and attachment of the equipment and structures. As a minimum, the basic model work should all be confined to the model shop rather than trying to build equipment and attach structures on the design floor. As previously mentioned, there are some companies that do perform the equipment fabrication and attachment of the structures on the design floor, but as a rule of thumb, this is undesirable because of the noise, congestion, and basic confusion. Also, by not doing basic model work on the design floor, a company is able to segregate the various skill levels in order to control the work. In general, schools will combine the basic model and design model areas into one model room.

The design model is constructed in two stages: the basic model stage and the final model stage. The basic model (Fig. 15-1) stage is constructed first. It includes all major structures, and all equipment with nozzles and tagging installed ready for piping to be added. Completion of the basic model is ideally accomplished before the model is removed from the model shop area. However, this goal normally may not be achieved. Some equipment structures and vessels are incomplete or not available at this time. Once the basic model has been moved to the design area, the piping design effort commences. All information on the model should be checked at this time. A discussion of checking is included in Section 19. Piping, electrical, and instrumentation is normally added directly onto the model with only a minimum of sketches along with study and informal drawings.

MODEL SCALES

A typical scale for petrochemical and refinery models is $3/8'' = 1'$. However, $1/2'' = 1'$ and $3/4'' = 1'$ are frequently used, particularly when a given area of a plant is going to be remodeled and only one or two model bases are involved. Frequently, these larger-scale models are built for training purposes. This permits the operators and personnel being trained to be able to better visualize the equipment detail and relative location of equipment. Nuclear models are typically of the larger scales due to their complexity and their need for more accuracy. The common scale for nuclear models is $1/2'' = 1'$. For example, accuracy of within 2 scale inches can be readily achieved with $3/8''$ scale. But accuracy to within $1''$ can be attained with $1/2''$ scale.

Determination of model scale is dependent upon the accuracy required, the required detail, and the congestion of the area or areas to be modeled. Construction of model bases was covered in the preceding section.

Determination of the design model scale is extremely important. The preliminary model or site model scale is usually 1:200 or $1/4'' = 1'$.

FIGURE 15-2 Cutaway (dodged) piece of model wall.

Topographical or architectural models are constructed as small as $1'' = 50'$. In general, the final-design-stage models are constructed from $1/4'' = 1'$ to $3/4'' = 1'$, depending on the complexity and size of the intended plant. In some cases, $1 1/2''$ or $3''$ to a foot are used, and some engineering firms will prepare full-scale models of problem areas, such as access areas to instrumentation on nuclear reactors and/or the modeling of the control room for placement of instrumentation and operating controls. Some of the factors that will determine the scale are the degree of complexity or detail that is necessary on the project, the relationship of this scale to the available model components, the amount of available space for model construction, and the economics of model construction at a particular scale.

In most cases, the use of $1/2'' = 1'$ to $3/8'' = 1'$ are the most common in the petrochemical and power-generation fields. Petrochemical plants (refineries) and process plants all offer more space than nuclear or conventional power plants, mainly because the power plant must be confined within a building, whereas a petrochemical installation is very seldom confined to a single structure and can therefore be spread out over a wider area.

The total physical size of the plant in its model stage is an extremely important factor in the determination of the scale. The total height of the building and/or project must be taken into account when this scale is decided upon. If the scale is too large, the available headroom in the model shop and design department may not be sufficient, requiring sectioning both horizontally and vertically, which will increase the cost of the model. In situations where the model depicts an industrial complex that is spread out and composed of equipment that is separated by roads and other areas because of safety reasons, the $3/8'' = 1'$ is an excellent scale, providing a sufficient amount of detail and exposure to be photographed when recorded.

When determining the scale, it is also important to take into account the cost of the construction of bases and items that cannot be ordered. Fabrication of equipment, vessels, bases, and other items that cannot be ordered from a catalog may increase the total cost of the project considerably. The amount and size of piping to be shown and constructed on the model will also help to determine the scale. In problem areas, piping down to $1''$ must be constructed on the model. Although this presents a variety of problems,

Section 29. The smaller projects provided in the text can be modeled to a larger scale, so as to provide for more detail. This will increase their value as teaching aids, but also their cost.

SECTIONING OF MODELS

In situations in industry where the overall model is of a large scale and/or the plant is of sufficient size, models must be constructed with breakaway or sectioning ability (Fig. 15-5), which enables portions of the model to be disassembled or unfastened so that the designer and/or construction crew are able to view project interiors. A typical nuclear power plant may have as many as 30 sections that can be pulled apart and viewed separately, ranging in sizes and on bases of 2′ × 4′ or 2′ × 5′. This breakaway sectioning ability is extremely important in the modeling of large, important complexes. Figure 15-5 shows an example of how a model can be sectioned and hinged together, enabling the users of the model to swivel the sections apart and have access to interior areas of the equipment and piping.

The many photographs provided in this text

FIGURE 15-3 Steam generator of a power plant.

including overcomplication of certain areas to be modeled, in general the basic procedure is to model all piping 2″ outside diameter (OD) and above, unless smaller piping of extremely critical areas is necessary. The smallest-diameter pipe available from model component companies is 1/16″. Therefore, this will determine its use as a minimum-OD pipe size. Larger scales may be necessary where small piping must be constructed on the model. Another problem, when determining the scale, is the necessary intricacy by which the model must be made. If the scale is too small, it may be impossible to construct certain areas, and will also provide problems in the taking of isometrics from the model. Large-scale models can increase the cost of the total engineering production and require the use of fictitious supports.

A majority of the models that can be constructed from this book can be done in 3/8″ = 1′, although in Section 30 that would present size and economic problems. The power plant in Section 30 should be modeled at a maximum of 1/8″ = 1′ or 3/32″ = 1′. The same is true of the nuclear reactor in

FIGURE 15-4 Steam generator model. No piping or detail is shown on the model at this stage.

FIGURE 15-5 Model has been split (sectioned) vertically in this nuclear power plant.

show piping installations, closeup views, and overall views of industrial piping models and should be studied carefully in order to understand many of the possibilities for the construction of model configurations. Figure 15-2 and Fig. 15-6 show the use of white plastic sheets with large wavy cutouts (dodges), which enables the users of the model to see into the depths of the equipment areas.

Because of size limitations concerning such items as model movement in and out of standard-sized doors, shipping cartons, and size restrictions on space for the shipping of models, the maximum size is usually limited to 6' × 2'6". Standard model tables are also available in these dimensions. Because of size restrictions, a significant percentage of models must be sectioned to form smaller

FIGURE 15-6 Closeup view of power plant model; notice the wavy wall cutouts. This procedure eliminates weight and provides access to the model interior for photographing and construction.

units. This sectioning appears in Fig. 15-5, which shows a large nuclear model split so as to view the inside of the model area while maintaining the required 2′6″ × 6′ standard table size. Models can also be split horizontally, especially in situations where the model reaches a height of 30″ or more. When splitting the model into sections, the splits should be along coordinate lines or obvious breakpoints in the model, if possible, such as on column centerlines. Sectioning facilitates the accessibility to the interior parts of the model for both the designer and construction crew. The following is a list of recommended procedures when sectioning the model. These must be considered in the preliminary stages of the design model, so as to facilitate the actual construction process:

- Maximum base size should be limited to 2′6″ × 6′0″.
- Models should be built with a minimum 3″ margin on the outside edges, never permitting the model to overhang the edge of the base. (This may not be possible where model bases are put edge to edge to form a complete facility.)
- Split models at centerlines of columns, never through pieces of equipment or at places where the sectioning will cause undue work for both the model maker or pipe designer.
- Never split the model down the center of a

pipe rack, and avoid piping and equipment areas that are congested.

DESIGN MODELING PROCEDURES

Each company using design models will have methods or procedures that differ from other companies, just as the drawing methods and procedures differ. There are, however, certain practices that are accepted by the large majority of model users and these can be stated as standard practice.

Types of Models

Preliminary or equipment arrangement model

This model is used to develop optimum arrangement for equipment and facilities to produce a plot plan. This model is primarily for plant layout development. It is made of rough foam or plastic shapes scaled at 1/8″ = 1′0″ or 1/4″ = 1′0″ (larger scales can, of course, be used, depending on the size and complexity of the project). These shapes are determined by consulting rough sketches or preliminary vendor data and prints. The preliminary structural system is used to show pipe racks and structure. This snap-fit system permits rapid changes of column spacing or beam locations as new ideas present themselves. This allows quick changing of components as basic

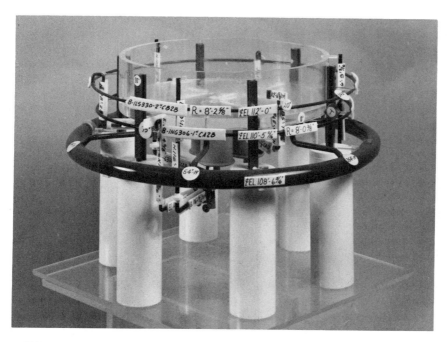

FIGURE 15-7 Small assembly which is constructed separate from the model and added on as a complete unit.

FIGURE 15-8 Simplified preliminary model.

plant and equipment arrangement evolves and also allows for the reuse of the plastic parts.

Before model fabrication begins, the following information is required:

- Process flow diagrams
- Plot area and rough general layout of equipment and structures
- List of equipment with approximate overall dimensions for blocking-in
- General structural requirements

The engineers and designers assigned to the project first arrange the components to conform to the rough general layout.

Alternative arrangements are made, with each being discussed and photographed. The model is rearranged to conform with the best advantages of each alternative. Then a detailed internal review is conducted. The preliminary model is reviewed for:

- Economy of arrangements and pipe runs
- Construction feasibility
- Foundation and underground
- Accessibility
- Clearances
- Maintenance

Fullest participation by all engineering groups concerned is essential for review and to give final approval of the modeled plot plan.

After approval of the preliminary model, the plot plan drawing is prepared and issued according to the approved arrangement.

Design model

The design model is used as a tool to aid in the development and coordination of the project, as well as a means of clarifying the design. It includes all equipment, structural, piping, instrumentation, and electrical features necessary to transform idea and theory (the design) into a finished plant. Scale-model cranes are also used for evaluating construction access.

The design model is constructed in two states: basic model and final design model.

Basic model: This includes all bases, structures, platforms, and equipment tagged and in place, ready for piping to begin. Construction of the basic model is completed, as far as possible, in the model shop before it is delivered to the design area.

Final design model: Once in the design area, the addition of later design information begins. Such items as piping, electrical, and instrumentation are designed or located on the model, with a minimum of sketches, until all desirable features are represented.

Work on the design model will be performed by the piping designers, except as specifically noted in later subsections. (*Note:* The modeling group should be called upon to make and/or install items on the models that have been designed on paper, such as structures, equipment, pipes in the pipeways, or duplicate piping involving extended installation time. This frees the designers to do design work, making their efforts most effective.)

Planning

The following information must be developed under the supervision and with the approval of the project engineer; design sketches will not be used unless necessary to develop these data:

* Mode of shipping model (e.g., van or aircraft).
* Model scale (if other than 3/8″ = 1′0″, the modeling group supervisor should be consulted).
* Color code, if other than standard.
* Area to be shown (also area to be excluded or blocked-in, if any).
* High point of grade (preferably called elevation 100′0″).
* Top of grout for setting equipment.
* Model schedule.
* Scope of model, which includes minimum-size lines to be shown and extent of detail or any special features of the project.
* P&ID transposition or routine diagram made on a sepia of the plot plan. (This drawing is schematic and used to lay out the general runs of piping for economical routing. Details of routing are developed later on the model.)
* Design study sketches to determine orientation and elevation of nozzles, manways, piping, platforms, ladders, and instruments. (*Note:* When design study sketches for columns (towers) are forwarded to the model shop, the model group will attach all platforms, ladders, davits, and nozzles with piping, instrumentation, etc.)
* Pipe rack widths, spacing of bents, and top of support elevations.
* Location of all major structural columns (stanchions).
* Elevation of other structural levels and extent of platforms required.
* Model base index, showing match lines for model bases marked on plot plan with sizes and numbering sequence.

The project engineer and the modeling group supervisor will confer as to the optimum location of model base match lines. Horizontal cuts must be carefully considered and approved by the modeling group supervisor. Following approval of the base index drawings, they are sent to the model shop together with a priority schedule for model shop completion. Every effort must be made to have as much as possible of the equipment, structures, pipeways, and tagging installed on the model bases by the shop prior to delivery of the bases to the design area.

General Specifications

Base and frame

Maximum base size will be 6′ long by 2′6″ wide. This is to permit moving through standard doorways and to permit turning corners in a standard hallway. However, if the equipment on the base does not exceed 2′ in height, it is acceptable to exceed the 26″ foot base width. In such cases, the wider base can be turned sideways to pass through standard doorways.

When attaching a plastic base top to its wooden frame, always be sure that the corner hold-down screw holes are drilled at least 1/8″ oversize. The top is secured in the center by tight screws, but both ends are allowed to "float" around the oversize holes, thus compensating for moderate swelling or contraction of the wood sleepers. A warped or poorly fitting top, not lying flat and level on the sleeper supports, must be repaired. Plastic is a very brittle material, and stresses caused by large equipment and poor fit can cause the top to crack.

FIGURE 15-9 Model base showing coordinates and boundaries established by the use of tape. Column footers have been attached to the base using double-sided tape.

Always provide sufficient clearance, from 1/64″ to 1/16″ (the amount will vary depending on the intended use) for every base hole drilled to accommodate equipment or structural members. This clearance eases strain and allows slight adjustments to be made.

Pipe bents and structures of structural steel are secured to the base with EMA base pins or base mounts, of the correct size to accept the size of structural members being secured, or they are solvent welded to base.

Fireproofed or concrete columns are secured to the base with column blocks and/or self-tapping screws.

In securing structures to the base, start at one corner column and square each column before bonding or tightening. This will eliminate strain caused by hold-down screws or pins being inserted at an angle.

Structural and architectural

Only column and primary steel sizes are needed to start model fabrication of structures. The civil/structural section will supply sketches or drawings covering information "for model only" in order to expedite model construction. Secondary steel, tertiary steel, and bracing should be excluded on the design model, except in cases where interference is likely or where it is required for equipment support and structural design evaluation. This will be determined by the piping design supervisor as model design is developed.

Steel and concrete members are within 1/16″ of true shape and size.

Column footers are shown on the model only when they project more than 6″ past the edge of the column; otherwise, the column is extended to the model base.

Building walls are shown in two dimensions using black tape the width of the wall thickness to scale.

Doors are shown as an opening or void in the tape that represents the wall.

Grating and checkerplate are indicated with plastic screen or printed transfer film cut to dodged or uneven outlines and bonded to the corners or edges of the platforms or floors.

Siding is shown with small dodged pieces of appropriate material and kept to a minimum.

Platforms, ladders, stairs, and supports

Platforms requiring a circular cut for modeling such as those on vertical columns are fabricated from .040″ butyrate sheet (VP-40).

Platforms not connected to equipment will be fabricated from structural shapes to centerline and top of platform dimensions, or from sheet plastic.

Ladders and stairs are shown to scale. Hand rail, stair rail, and ladder cages are shown where interferences are likely (or by request of the customer) (Figs. 15-11 and 15-12).

Supports for piping, such as vessel clips or

FIGURE 15-10 View of design model, showing platforms, ladder, cages, and so on.

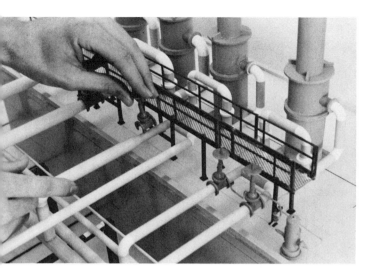

FIGURE 15-11 Wharf model is in the piping stage, with the attaching of valves to the model.

FIGURE 15-12 This model needed to have many parts fabricated from basic model tubing and sheet stock.

FIGURE 15-13 Student modeler installing platform for wharf project.

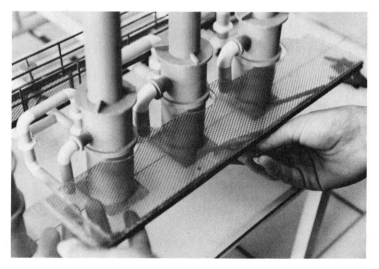

FIGURE 15-14 Checking accuracy of cutouts in platform.

base supports (or other where interference is unlikely) are not shown on the model in three dimensions. These support points are tagged on the pipe using legend markers. Fictitious supports, sufficient to suspend the piping, are installed as required during design, and tags indicating type of supports are applied when the design of the line is reasonably firm.

Valves

Valves are ordered as components and altered if necessary (see Figs. 15-15 to 15-19).

GENERAL MODELING HINTS

Equipment

Never drill a hole larger than 1/8″ in a piece of equipment. A hole larger than 1/8″ poses particular problems should the nozzle or connection be moved only a few degrees or inches. Also, the larger the hole, the more difficult an acceptable repair becomes should it be necessary to plug it. An EMA vessel nozzle plug (VNP-4) is used to quickly plug an 1/8″-diameter hole.

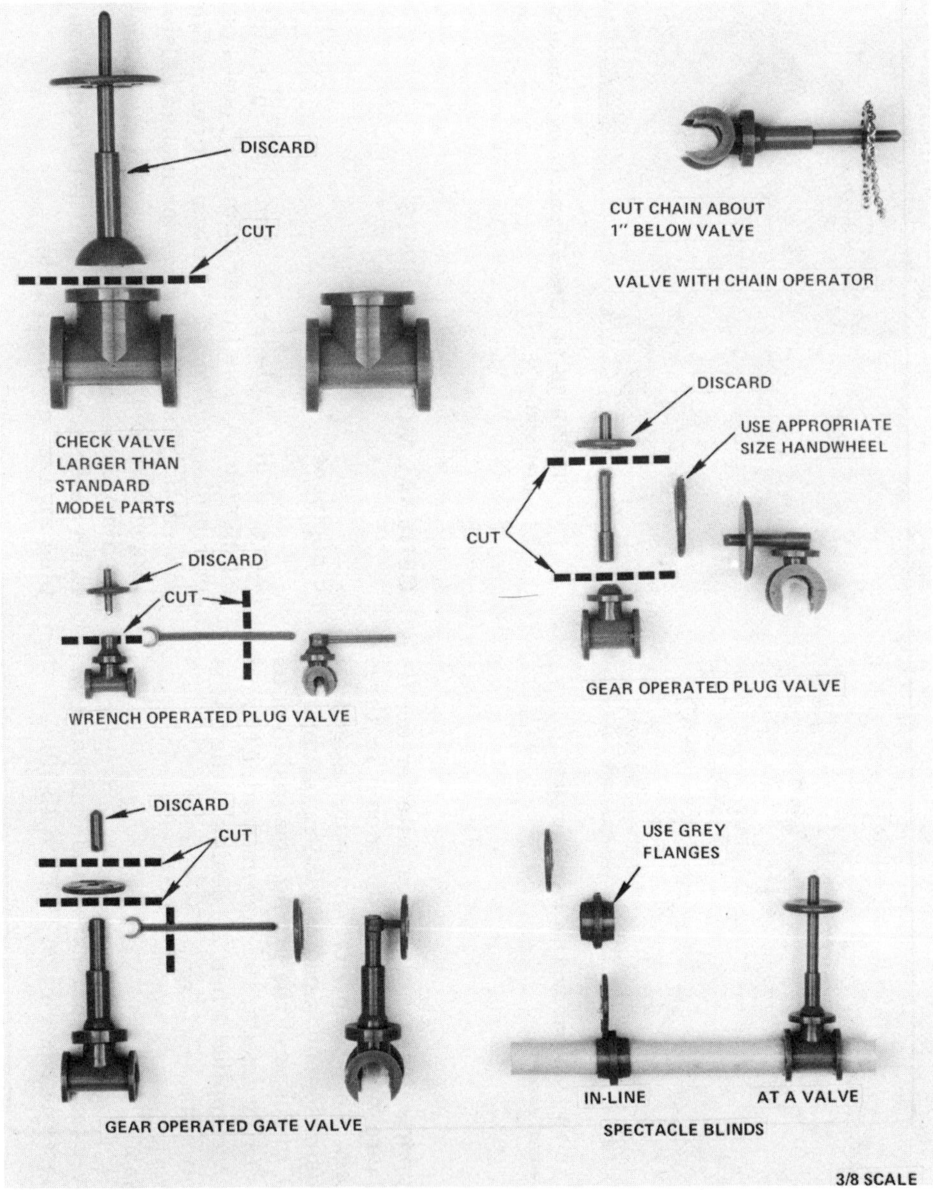

150# GATE VALVES
(LARGER THAN STANDARD MODEL PART)

USE PARTS FROM 24" 150# VALVE

USE PIPE TO EXTEND STEM

Discard

Discard

Cut

Paint Gray

3/8" SCALE

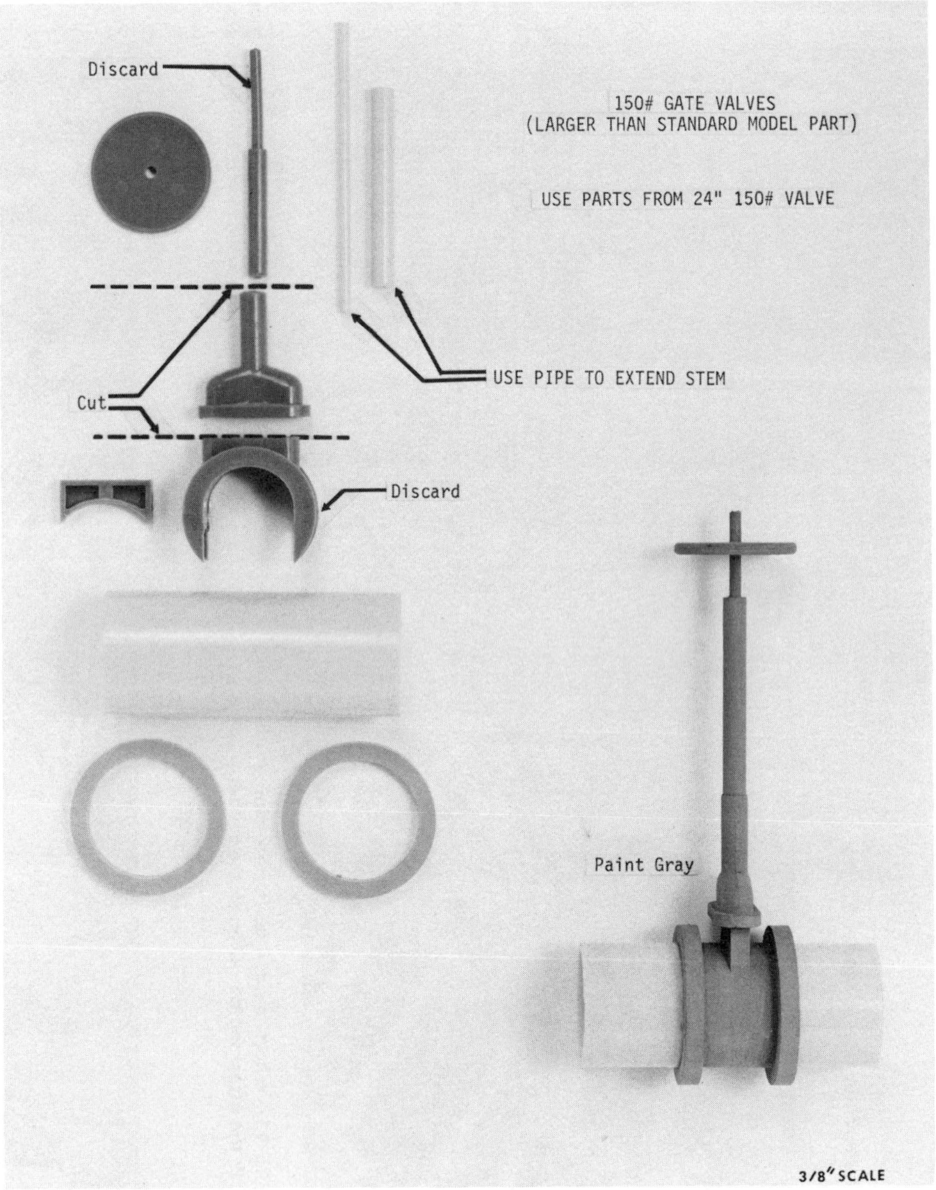

FIGURE 15-16 Valve variations.

CUT CHAIN ABOUT
1" BELOW VALVE

VALVE WITH CHAIN OPERATOR

DISCARD

USE APPROPRIATE
SIZE HANDWHEEL

CUT

GEAR OPERATED PLUG VALVE

USE GREY
FLANGES

IN-LINE

AT A VALVE

SPECTACLE BLINDS

3/8 SCALE

DISCARD

CUT

CHECK VALVE
LARGER THAN
STANDARD
MODEL PARTS

DISCARD

CUT

WRENCH OPERATED PLUG VALVE

DISCARD

CUT

GEAR OPERATED GATE VALVE

FIGURE 15-15 Valve variations possible from standard EMA components.

136

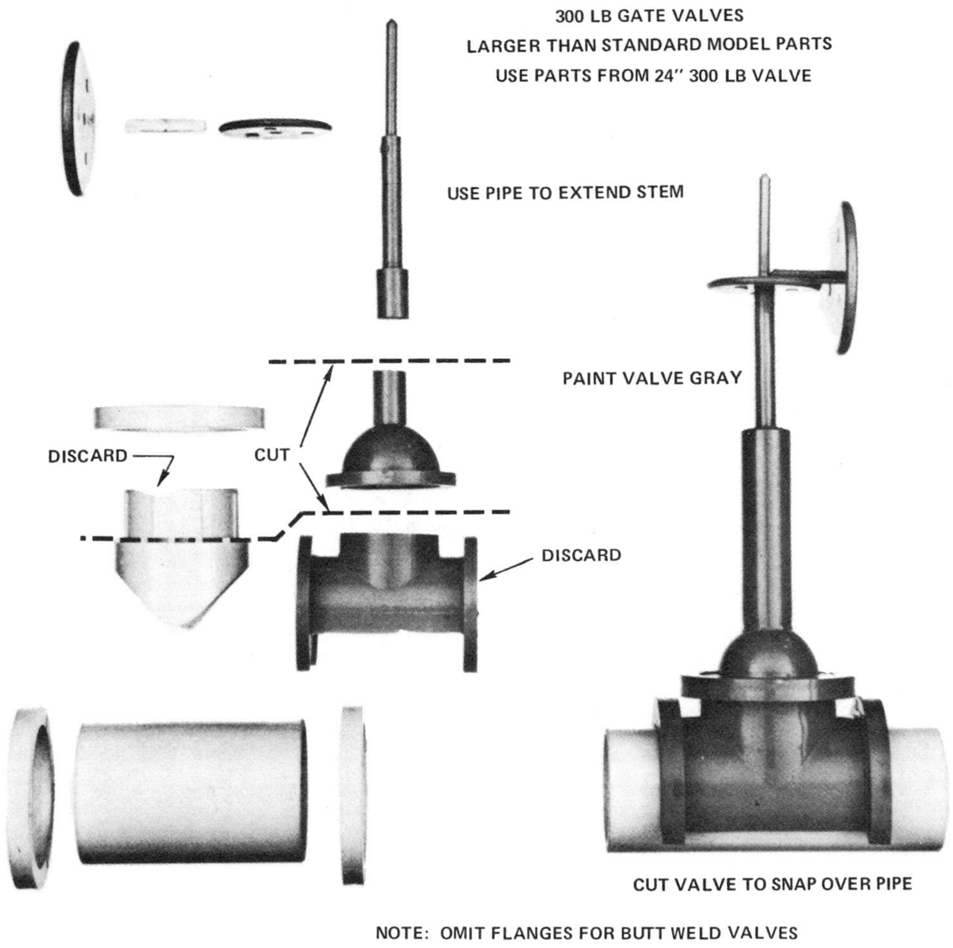

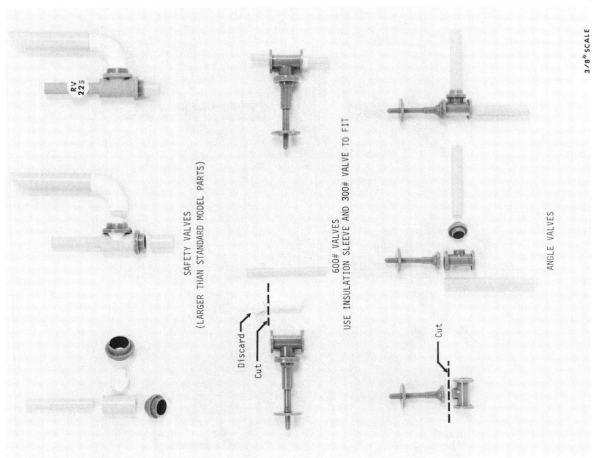

SAFETY VALVES
(LARGER THAN STANDARD MODEL PARTS)

600# VALVES
USE INSULATION SLEEVE AND 300# VALVE TO FIT

ANGLE VALVES

Discard
Cut

Cut

3/8" SCALE

FIGURE 15-18 Valve variations.

300 LB GATE VALVES
LARGER THAN STANDARD MODEL PARTS
USE PARTS FROM 24" 300 LB VALVE

USE PIPE TO EXTEND STEM

PAINT VALVE GRAY

CUT VALVE TO SNAP OVER PIPE

NOTE: OMIT FLANGES FOR BUTT WELD VALVES

DISCARD

CUT

DISCARD

FIGURE 15-17 Valve variations.

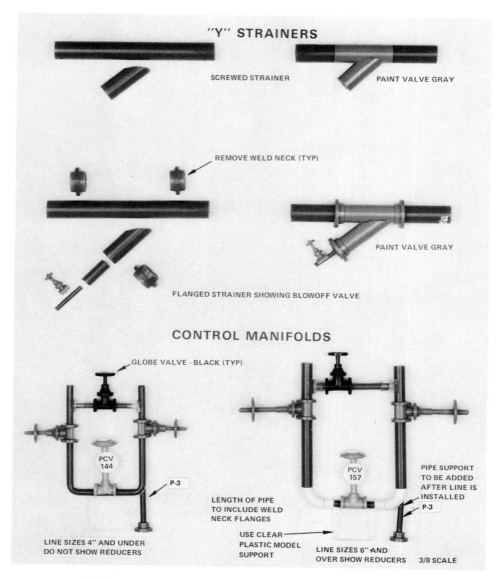

FIGURE 15-19 Fabrication of Y strainers and control manifolds.

Right-angle nozzles on equipment should be left free to rotate and not permanently set until location is final.

Always ensure that the center and/or reference lines are scribed on the fictitious base or actual pad used to support equipment. The equipment should then be assembled on this pad outside the model. Matching reference lines are then drawn on the model base and the equipment slipped into place. For example, it is far easier to align and set to elevation a four-legged vessel on a rectangular pad having scribed centerlines and leg-supporting holes while the base is outside the model than it is to drill holes in the model base and locate in the area crowded with equipment.

When making up exchangers from other than a final vendor's print, leave the cap ends off and cut to the tube length. If this practice is followed, it will save replacing the entire unit in many final models. Practice has shown that the diameter of an exchanger usually remains within modeling limits, and if the exchanger is cut only to the tube bundle length, the final overall dimension cannot be shorter. We can easily add to the length, but to shorten a unit it must be removed from the model.

Large equipment on legs, such as heaters or furnaces, are provided with either a fictitious clear block or hold-down to base or with supports drilled and tapped to receive screws.

Columns and other vertical vessels are provided with an EMA vessel mounting ring and

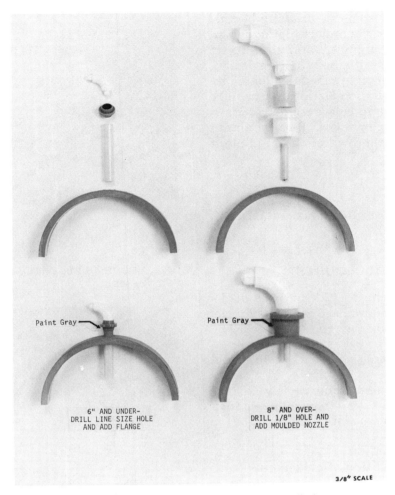

FIGURE 15-20 Nozzle fabrication and installation.

vessel mounting nut. A 1/4-20 stove bolt with a flat washer is used through the base top to secure the vessel.

Small equipment, such as pumps, heat exchangers, and filters, are held to the base with a small amount of solvent. After acceptance of the location and piping attached to the particular piece of equipment, the item is cemented to the base with additional solvent.

Structures

Weak butt joints are common in plastic model structures. Because acrylic solvents do not have gap-filling properties, structural components and pipe bents usually do not have large mating and gluing surfaces and frequently break because the contact area that the solvent has bonded is too small.

Joints with imperfectly cut mating faces and joints positioned at 90° angles may also experience such problems.

All platforms are made from 1/8" transparent gray plastic to eliminate the need for additional material to indicate grating or checkerplate.

Concrete floors are shown using white or clear sheet plastic cut in a dodged pattern along the edge and/or corners. The rest of the floor is left open so as not to obscure items below.

Model Assemblies

Model components that are commercially available should be used in every practical instance because of the time saved. However, there are some instances in which a particular part is not available and must be fabricated.

Review

Regular viewing of all design steps by project engineers and designers is necessary to forestall undesirable design features or possible problems. Review of all design is made of the modeled plant, by area, before piping isometric drawing begins. This review is made by the project piping design engineer, the project engineer, and the project manager for the purpose of approving the design.

A review by the client is scheduled for a date when design and installation on the model will be essentially completed and before isometric drawings are started. This review is held to obtain comments on and/or approval of the final plant design.

Checking

Checking the model is essential for coordination of the design effort.

OTHER MODELING PROCEDURES

Where modeling is done for the purpose of developing design, procedures are required for accomplishing other tasks, such as:

- Production of piping isometrics from model information.
- Setting up and conducting reviews of the model by both in-house and client personnel.
- Photographing the model.
- Shipping the model.
- Insuring the model.
- Control and accounting of model materials.

These procedures will differ from company to company and will not be of concern to us here. We mention them to emphasize that careful control of all phases of this work is necessary to maintain consistency and achieve maximum value from design models.

EQUIPMENT LAYOUT

When laying out equipment on the model base, the following simple guidelines should be used:

- Line up centerlines of pump discharge nozzles. This allows piping design to proceed from a fixed set of coordinates even though pump drawings may not yet be available.
- Line up the pipe rack end of pump foundations where possible by extending the pump foundation if necessary, but within practical limits.
- The centerlines of channel nozzles should be used to locate exchangers. This gives a definite set of coordinates on the plot plan and

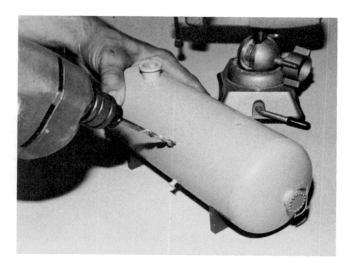

FIGURE 15-21   Drilling a hole in a horizontal vessel.

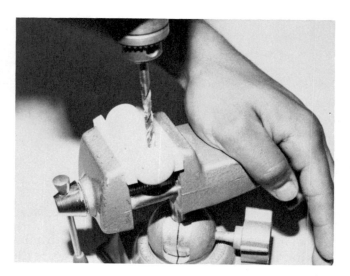

FIGURE 15-22   Using a vise to hold a component while drilling.

consequently speeds up model design and isometric input, results in fewer changes, and provides for easier and faster checking.

These items are normally covered in a company's standards. If they are not, or are not conducted as indicated above, serious consideration should be given to revising the standards. Especially in regard to the first and third guidelines above, considerable amounts of design time can be saved by the use of these procedures.

After the model coordinates have been checked, proceed to lay out all underground utilities, piping, and drains, using the correct tape as described in the model specifications and installed in the correct scale width.

STRUCTURAL LAYOUT

Structural steel and concrete members should be as close to the actual shape as possible. They should be dimensionally accurate to within 1/16". In all cases, go to the next larger size when the actual size is not available. Depending on the progress of the project, the structural group will provide either sketches or drawings defining the column and primary steel sizes. In cases where commercial steel and concrete shapes are not available, they can be fabricated from available plastic stock in the correct color.

CIVIL LAYOUT

Colored tape can be used to identify such items as road centerlines and extremities—1/16"-wide black tape—and plot limit—1/16"—wide black tape (see Fig. 15-9).

ARCHITECTURAL LAYOUT

Building walls can be shown in two dimensions using black tape to the proper scale or with white plexiglass. When using black tape, doors are shown as openings or voids in the tape representing the walls. When plexiglass is used to represent walls, it is common to show only the corners and/or sections where walls meet and, in some cases, to show sections of the walls where piping passes through. A third possibility is to use a combination of black-and-white diagonal-hatch tape to represent building walls and openings, and plexiglass sections to show corners and wall intersections. Clear plexiglass is often used to indicate transite wall sections.

STRUCTURAL COMPONENTS

Clear plastic will be used for fictitious pipe supports. Actual pipe supports should be color-coded gray or the same color as other structural components in an area. In general, hand rails and ladder cages will not be shown on the model except in cases dictated by the model specification or in areas where congested piping arrangements and/or equipment require modeling of the hand rails and ladder cages in order to assure clearances. Stairs and ladders will be shown to scale. Platforms will be modeled with clear 1/16" plastic. Much of the bracing and secondary members, along with platforms, cages, and hand rails, will

be installed in the design office after piping design commences. In some instances, model shop personnel perform this work in the design office. However, more often the piping designers perform these functions.

Fabrication of noncommercial structures such as concrete columns and/or steel structural shapes are very time consuming as compared to utilizing commercially available structural shapes. If at all possible, the scales should be chosen such that the majority of structural shapes can be purchased from ready-made stock rather than requiring special setup in your own shop.

EQUIPMENT COMPONENTS

The choice of equipment should always be commercially available items if at all possible. Section 9 shows the commercially available plastic vessel components, vessel and equipment assemblies, and pump motor assemblies. Equipment should always be fabricated from vendor equipment drawings if at all possible. In some cases, the equipment builder may have to work from designer's sketches or catalog data. Simulating the scaled shape and the location of nozzles and piping is of paramount importance, rather than trying to fabricate intricate features for aesthetic value. Equipment building techniques vary from model builder to model builder. An important aspect is to minimize details and maximize the accuracy of overall shape and connections. In some instances, components of standard equipment and vessels can be used in more detailed arrangements of large pieces of equipment. There is a wide variation in the modeling industry regarding the amount of detail to be shown on equipment. For example, a pump and motor assembly may be cut from a rectangular cube of plexiglass rather than simulating the actual motor and pump assembly as two different items. Actually, the labor involved in cutting this cube and then painting it, drilling it, scraping off the paint to attach the piping, and finally touching up the paint is far more costly than using an off-the-shelf pump/motor assembly.

Most pumps and vessels can be modeled from commercially available components. When fabricating heat exchangers, columns, vessels, and towers, *it should be remembered to go to the next larger scale of tubing if the exact size is not available from commercial stock.* Some companies require such intricate detail on their equipment that it is feasible to fabricate room-temperature vulcanizing molds and case these components or equipment pieces. A semi-mass-production technique can be accomplished in this manner. The time required to fabricate equipment is one of the most elusive things in a model estimate. Therefore, the model specification should determine the degree of detail.

ATTACHMENT OF EQUIPMENT AND STRUCTURES TO MODEL BASE

In general, it is best to attach major equipment and major structures that require mechanical connection prior to mounting other components.

Always provide sufficient clearance, from 1/64″ to 1/16″ (the amount will vary depending on the intended use), for every base hole drilled, to accommodate equipment or structural mounting bolts. This clearance eases strain and allows slight adjustments to be made.

Pipe bents and small structures are secured to the base with plastic bolts and nuts of the correct size to accept the size of structural member being secured. (*Note:* Many companies glue these items instead of bolting. Schools should use both procedures for experience.)

Larger items such as vessels are secured with mounting nuts or a plastic boss built into the base of an item (furnace, preheater, etc.) and tapped to receive a 1/4-20 stove bolt. Extreme care must be taken prior to shipment of a model to check that all columns, exchangers, structures, furnaces, large compressors, and the like are fastened securely by positive mechanical means.

FIGURE 15-23 When cutting pipe with table saw, set angle of cut first, then hold both sides of pipe so as to reduce the possibility of flying pieces.

Fireproofed or concrete columns are secured to the base with column blocks and self-tapping screws or the plastic model bolt and nut as used to mount bare steel, or just glued to the base.

In cases where structure or equipment items fall over a base sleeper, they must be doweled to the base using appropriate pieces of model pipe as dowels. Exceptions to this are described in the following paragraph.

Small equipment such as pumps, heat exchangers, and filters are held to the base with double-sided tape or solvent tacked. After acceptance of the location and piping attached to the particular piece of equipment, the tape is removed and the item is solvent-welded to the base.

Large equipment on legs, such as heaters or furnaces, are provided with either a fictitious clear block for securing to base or with supports drilled and tapped to receive screws.

Towers and cylindrical vessels are provided with a vessel mounting ring and vessel mounting nut. A 1/4-20 stove bolt with a flat washer is used through the base top to secure the vessel.

Structures

The strength of a bond between any two materials depends largely on the amount of surface contact or gluing area. This is especially true with model structures; therefore, the joint will have maximum strength when cuts are square and total contact is achieved. Since the solvent used has no filling effect, gaps between two pieces of material cannot be filled.

All platforms, whether circular or rectangular, are made of vessel platform clear plastic. Grating, represented by cross-hatch decal, is dodged along an edge or corner for definition. The rest of the platform is left clear so as not to obstruct the view of adjacent areas.

When indicating floor plate or concrete decks on the model, only the necessary number of dodged sections should be used to clarify extremities and support equipment. Transparency is possible only if the specified color code is violated. Generally, specification violations should be avoided because they create more questions than they solve.

Equipment

Commercially available systems should be used for vessel fabrication.

Right-angle nozzles on equipment should not be permanently set to a study orientation but should be left free to rotate.

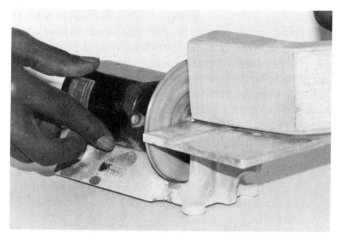

FIGURE 15-24 Using a small sander to even out wood (balsa) ducting.

The nozzle should always be left unglued to allow a small amount of play in the nozzle setting. This compensates for two possible faults. First, the pin hole is frequently at a slight angle; this will cock the nozzle and throw the connecting pipe out of alignment. Second, the pipe itself may have slight fabrication errors and a little play in the nozzle will generally correct this error.

Always see that center and/or nozzle reference lines are scribed on the fictitious bases or actual pads used to support equipment. The equipment should then be assembled on this pad outside the model, matching reference lines drawn on the model base, and the equipment then slipped into place. Smaller rectangular pieces of equipment (package units, etc.) should be "boxed" with gray sheet stock to maximum dimension.

FIGURE 15-25 Applying extra cement at joints of structural elements.

Vertical vessel platforms are to be made of clear plastic sheet, top of plastic to be T.O.S.EL. Supports are to be made of clear platform brackets. (*Note:* Supports = T.O.S.EL. less 1″.) Supports are to be radial. End supports are oriented by arc or inner diameter. Use one support for platforms less than 45°, two for platforms up to 90°, three for platforms up to 180°, four for platforms more than 180°. Supports are trimmed to the width of platform. Finish platforms with cross-hatch dodging and tag, giving platform number and T.O.S.EL. Where desirable to indicate actual supports, they will be modeled in steel gray.

OUTLINE OF CONSTRUCTION STEPS FOR THE BASIC MODEL

The physical construction techniques, the time required for the construction process, the ordering procedures, the tagging techniques, and the base and model layout procedures are all items in the total construction effort of any industrial model project.

Whenever possible, in classroom situations, the construction of the basic model should be kept as simple as possible in order to keep the total project cost to a minimum. A number of cost-saving techniques can be used, such as the use of a wooden base instead of plexiglass, the bending of the majority of small-OD pipe bends, and preplanning of the ordering of component parts so as to minimize waste of materials, such as those for vessels, tubing, and pipe. Also, it is possible to fabricate many items as block-type equipment instead of using component parts. Where cost is a major factor and time and construction effort are available, these cost-saving procedures can be implemented.

For the classroom situation where one wishes to *minimize* the fabrication of parts, it is suggested that all components be ordered instead of fabricated, including structural steel and piping elbows, instead of bending the pipe. This also includes the ordering of standard equipment such as pumps and lighting fixtures, which will help eliminate a good percentage of the total fabrication time and effort.

Following is a loose description of construction techniques for the fabrication of an industrial piping model. Although these can vary from company to company, they should be adhered to as to the general outline of sequence of events for the construction of the model.

Procurement and Setup of the Base

The model base should be cut to the minimum requirements that are necessary to provide a 3″ margin around the outside of the model and should be sectioned appropriately if the base is too cumbersome.

The plot plan north arrow orientation should be set up, thereby providing the directional information necessary for the model and project orientation.

A reference work edge at the south and west sides of the base should be established.

All major equipment and structures should be laid out on the base. This includes structural centerlines, piping, pipe rack, orientation, and equipment location.

Locate all equipment on the base by the use of a black film marker or pencil.

Tag all the coordinates for equipment locations, vessels, pumps, battery limits, and so on.

All underground utilities should be laid out at this time, including piping and drains. The use of color-coded centerline tape is the best method for doing this.

On models that will have a basement modeled, use clear plexiglass for the major base, because it is then possible to construct a subbase and be able to view the equipment, piping, and so on, that exists in the basement through the base at ground level.

Structural Elements: Construction and Installation

The structural elements on a model are usually referred to as model framing. In situations where the total cost of the model should be limited by the fabrication of the structural elements, it is possible to use plexiglass or acrylic that is shaped on the

FIGURE 15-26 Spraying ducting to conform to preestablished color code.

various power tools provided in the model shop. Standard component parts such as structural shapes, ladders, stairs, handrails, and platforms are also available, and these will, of course, speed the total construction effort and assembly of the project. It is suggested that the first models that the student completes utilize the second method.

A variety of basic acrylic shapes are available for the production of structural items and can be altered by the use of the power tools available in typical model shops. In general, when fabricating these items, they should be cut slightly oversized and then planed down to the required dimensions and the ends sanded square to provide for accurate vertical and horizontal alignment.

Structural Shapes and Assemblies

The structure should be assembled by the use of prefabrication of the various structural items, such as pipe racks, column rows, or what are referred to as bents.

When assembling pipeways or bents, a small jig should be constructed so as to provide the fabricator with the ability to produce the shapes in the required number accurately and to the required dimensions without misalignment. (See Section 25.)

Small pieces of screen or clear plexiglass should be used to represent platforms.

Tag all structures top of steel elevations and platform elevations.

When splitting the model horizontally, it is important to provide a break at each floor level. Where components extend from floor to floor, such as stairwells, staircases, ladders, and piping, it is sometimes normal procedure to terminate the particular equipment at the floor. Where models are not split horizontally, it is possible to extend the equipment through the floors, which is the preferred situation in many cases.

All structural pieces are to be made with strong joints and should be provided with the necessary structural bracing. In situations where it is necessary to create an extremely strong, stable model, the use of fictitious supports is advised. Fictitious supports are usually shown in clear plastic or in an established color code.

In situations where the model needs to be sectioned, it should be cut in places that are logical breakpoints, such as column centerlines.

Where possible, the use of plastic to represent walls should be kept to a minimum, although in many projects such as those for large nuclear plants, walls and concrete must be represented on the model. It is generally an accepted practice to cut away (as in Fig. 15-2) a majority of the walls so as to provide access for the model builder and visual access for the construction crew.

Pump Assemblies

In situations where the desired pump size or configuration cannot be procured from the component company or where fabrication of the pump in a simplified block form is preferred, the basic overall dimensions of the pump must be adhered to in order to accurately represent the pump, motor, and base. In general, it is advisable to use either wood or plastic shapes, wood of course being cheaper, making sure to cut the overall dimensions of the block which will accurately represent the pump system. The suction and discharge points can be drilled into the block form. It is essential that the model builder correctly set up these two dimensions. The following set of procedures can be used to assemble the pumps and drivers (motor, etc.).

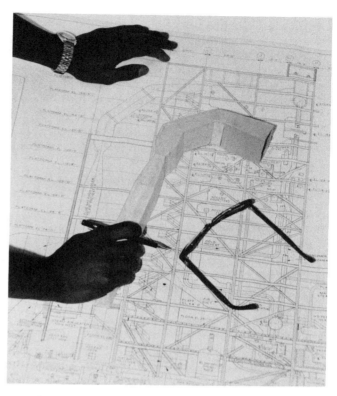

FIGURE 15-28 Flue gas ducting being checked to drawing.

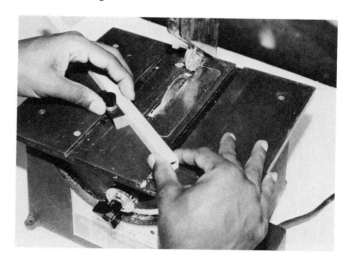

FIGURE 15-29 Using designer table saw to cut plastic fireproof column; notice that the guard is up when cutting small items.

- To assemble pumps, first locate the discharge.
- Attach the pumps to the base plate, utilizing the dimension from the face of the base plate to the centerline of the discharge.
- Attach the motor so that the dimension between the face of the suction nozzle and the end of the motor will be accurate.

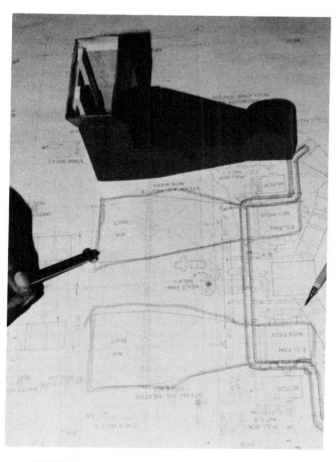

FIGURE 15-27 Print shows configuration of ducting with finished piece next to outline.

- Locate the discharge centerline from the centerline of the pump, and at this point, drill a nozzle-size hole (1/8″).
- Locate the suction centerline and drill the nozzle-size hole (1/8″).
- Pumps can either be top-suctioned or end-suctioned and the location of the suctional discharge must be oriented in accordance with the particular type of pump that is used.

Vessels, Both Vertical and Horizontal

Acrylic tubing is available from component manufacturing companies for the fabrication of tanks and vessels. Also included are the appropriate heads that may be necessary, such as elliptical or spherical.

The following paragraphs describe the specifications for construction of vertical and horizontal vessels.

Whenever possible, use standard component items for the construction of all vessels.

As a first step, locate the bottom tangent line on the vessel tube and scribe a line around the circumference. At this point, wrap a piece of paper or tape around the tubing, making sure that one edge is perfectly straight. This will enable the fabricator to scribe a line that will represent the cutoff point of the vessel.

The tubing should be cut by the use of a power saw or hand saw, giving careful attention to the maintenance of a square end.

All vessel ends should be sanded to achieve a perfect 90° edge.

At this time, for horizontal vessels the saddle should be located and lightly bonded in the appropriate position. It is also possible to use double-sided tape, providing for the disassembly of the vessel from the saddle. At this point, all nozzle holes should be drilled after accurately marking the necessary dimensions for the positioning of the nozzle. The nozzle should be attached to the vessel at this point. Any other materials, such as level glasses and controllers, should also be installed, including the vessel heads. The last procedure for a horizontal vessel should be the tagging of all the appropriate aspects of the vessel.

For the construction of vertical vessels, it is usually necessary to fabricate the transition from the lower larger-diameter to the upper smaller-diameter tubing, using a cone for the transition area. The upper and lower portions of the vertical vessel and transition piece should be securely and accurately constructed, giving special care to the maintenance of an accurate, vertical shape. The tower head and base should also be securely mounted. After this, all nozzles, manways, and so on, should be located and the attachment hole drilled in the appropriate place. The next procedure should take into account the location of the platform elevations, marking a horizontal line around the vessel at the appropriate points. All ladder support holes and pipe support holes should also be drilled at this time. After this, the accurate construction of the platform and platform braces should take place, then the assembly of the ladder clips, ladders, cages, and any other components that must be attached to the vertical vessel. (See Section 25 for a detailed explanation of model equipment construction.)

QUIZ

15-1. What is a basic model stage in the construction of a typical industrial installation?

15-2. In what area is the basic model usually constructed?

15-3. What scale is normally used for the construction of industrial models?

15-4. What is the job of the project engineer or modeling group supervisor?

15-5. Describe four specifications for the base and frame.

15-6. How is it possible to eliminate weak butt joints?

15-7. What is a fictitious support, and when is it used?

15-8. When is it advantageous to use double-sided tape?

15-9. What are vessel platforms usually made of?

15-10. What is model framing?

15-11. When should nonstandard components be used?

15-12. What is a cone, and how is it used?

16

Piping the Model (Design Model Stage)

FIGURE 16-1 Small complete design model.

The final design model is the heart of any model design effort. Typically, the final model design effort commences at the completion of the basic model fabrication level. The basic model is considered complete when the structures and equipment with nozzles are in place and ready for piping. As previously mentioned, the basic model is usually fabricated in the model shop area while the final design effort takes place on the design floor. Prior to the start of the installation of any piping onto the design model, it is of the utmost importance to be totally familiar with the available model piping systems and components.

At this point in the model design program it is feasible to utilize either the full-scale piping system or the centerline piping system or a combination of the two. Figures 16-1 and 16-2 depict the full-scale piping system components while Fig. 16-4 illustrates centerline piping. It should be noted that most of the full-scale components, with the exception of pipe, are used in either system. It is suggested that all projects in this text be done only with the full-scale method.

The names of the two different piping systems (*full-scale piping system and centerline piping system*) define the difference between the two

FIGURE 16-2 End view of pipe rack and wharf piping.

piping systems; that is, the full-scale piping system depicts all the pipes, elbows, valves, and other components in the model's full scale, while the centerline piping system utilizes 1/16″ plastic coated wire which can easily be formed by hand. Both the plastic wire that simulates piping in the centerline system and the full-scale plastic pipe in the full-scale system are available in 10 different colors. This feature eliminates the need of painting to achieve color coding. Line sizing sleeves, available in valve gray, are used to indicate the scale pipe diameter and serve as adapters for all other snap-on components and fittings, such as valves, flanges, and insulation sleeves. However, for heavily insulated pipelines, white line sizing sleeves are recommended to indicate the outside diameter of insulation. Both systems indicate the true centerlines of all piping. This is achieved automatically in the full-scale system and is accomplished in the centerline system by the use of the sizing sleeves. Pipe guides, supports, and shoes are represented with equal ease in either system. The centerline system is advantageous where a photograph/drawing technique is utilized. The color selection allows for the differentiation of coding, and the problem of lines being hidden behind other lines is minimized. Centerline piping can be replaced on the model with full-scale piping with minimum loss of material if the need arises. Full-scale piping provides one type of check, because it results in a more accurate representation of the piping on the finished model. (This method is also far more common in industry.)

In comparison, the centerline system is slightly more economical from a model material cost and inventory standpoint, but must be used in conjunction with photographs or finished drawings as well as isometric or spool sheets. It is an ideal system for preliminary routing, but it requires more calculating when installing piping because of the inaccurate visual presentation. Also, the fact that so much is left to the imagination reduces the value of the centerline system when compared with the full-scale system in the elimination of interferences and design errors.

In general, personnel involved with installing the piping on the model will be designers with significant background in piping who have been

FIGURE 16-3 Wharf model in piping stage using full-bore piping.

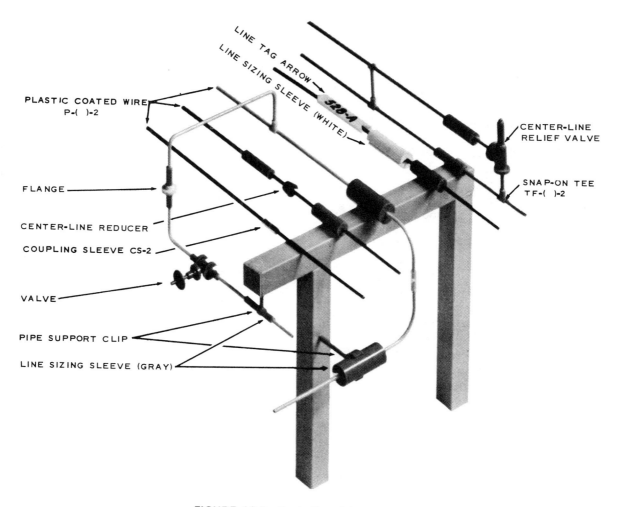

FIGURE 16-4 Centerline piping system.

FIGURE 16-5 Wharf model.

trained in the technique of designing and installing plastic components directly on the basic models with a minimum of drawings and sketches. Piping design on the model occurs very much in the same manner that piping design occurs on drawings. Like any skill, the efficiency of piping design on the model will increase with appropriate training and practice. Layout of piping on the model is accomplished in very much the same manner that layout occurs with actual piping in the field. Therefore, every effort must be made to lay out and locate piping in such a manner as to minimize tolerance buildup and errors. The following considerations should be given for accurate and efficient installation of model piping.

- Locate pipes from structural columns and equipment centerlines, *never* from other pipes. This procedure serves as a check of the other pipe on the rack. Locating from one pipe to another pipe could compound the tolerance buildup and/or error for each measurement that could accumulate across the rack.
- Always provide ample supports for pipe. Install as many supports as possible prior to fitting the pipe into the model. This serves

three major purposes: one, it checks the accuracy of the new pipe; two, it eliminates the need of temporary supports; and three, it facilitates pipe installation.

- Where no permanent support can be attached to the model structure or equipment, install a temporary support prior to installing the spool.
- Remake pipe where inaccurate. Do not try to salvage bent pipe. Do not piece together numerous short lengths.
- When bending pipe, always make every effort to fabricate the entire spool from one continuous piece. If pipe must be cut in order to fit into the model, do so after bending and rejoin the cut with a coupling sleeve.
- Make sure that all previous bends are true and square before proceeding to the next consecutive bend in a continuous line.
- Piping should be preassembled outside the model where possible. This practice will in many instances increase speed and accuracy. Manifolds, valve stations, and control sets are examples of sections that can be assembled outside the model.
- Actual pipe supports are usually modeled in a simplified form to indicate location. Special types, such as spring hangers or unusual brackets, are shown with a more realistic configuration both for the more accurate picture and to reserve the space. Fictitious supports should be installed to provide adequate support to any line or item needing them. In keeping with an industry-wide standard, fictitious supports, commonly called "ghost" supports, are modeled of clear plastic. If possible, ghost supports should be placed as inconspicuously as can be managed and still fulfill the primary function of providing adequate support.
- It is often necessary to use temporary supports. These supports are often needed where structures or stanchions are not yet designed and therefore are not on the model. They should be constructed of clear plastic because they may be needed as a ghost later. They may also be left in place if they are not obstructive. This will save reconstruction or removal time.
- To accurately determine the length of the horizontal leg of a pipe from a tower nozzle, it is essential to check the model vessel diameter against the true vessel diameter to make necessary compensations so as to maintain the correct dimension from the centerline of the vessel to the center leg of the pipe.
- Check the accuracy of spools on the bending board by edge-to-edge readings rather than by centerline readings.
- Do not show mating flanges on nozzles or valves except blind flanges, which are gray discs.
- As a general rule, do not bond any pipe assemblies or joints unless required to hold them in position. It may be emphasized that a minimum of bonding should be done until all piping has been accomplished and checking has been completed.
- The minimum size of line to be shown on the model is dictated by the model specifications for each project. However, it is normal to show all process lines plus all the utility lines 2″ and larger in diameter, or the diameter of the smallest utility line in a welded specification.
- Chain operators, gear, and pneumatic and extension hand wheels should be shown to scale on the model.
- Electrical tracing should be shown with a light green snap-on sleeve.
- Steam tracing should be shown with a light blue snap-on sleeve.
- Insulation is indicated with a white snap-on sleeve for hot lines and a purple snap-on sleeve for cold lines. Personnel protection insulation is a white sleeve with a "PP" tag.
- Utility hose stations should be shown, at least in one typical case, with pipe and valves unless otherwise stated in the model specifications.
- Steam traps and steam trap assemblies shall be blocked in as much as possible and tagged with standard detail or other information set forth in the model specifications.
- Safety showers and eye washers shall be shown on the model and color-coded the same color as other safety equipment.
- Relief valves shall be instrument color and tagged with number and other applicable information.
- Various types of branch connections should not be differentiated on the model. This will be determined by the isometrician in accordance with piping specifications.
- Sprinkler systems would normally not be shown, but an area will be provided for this piping with a building. Where it is advantageous to show the sprinkler headers, they

shall be the same color as that used for safety equipment.

Because piping takes up the major space, it must have prime consideration and is therefore assembled onto the model first after all possible equipment and structures are placed.

COORDINATION AND RESPONSIBILITY OF THE FINAL MODEL

The project piping engineer has the total responsibility and authority for design of the final model, even though many different subgroups have responsibility in various areas of the model. For example, the piping design group is responsible for the installation of all piping and associated valving on the model. The instrument group is responsible for location of instruments on the model even though the actual installation may be performed by the piping designers. Location and installation of electrical items is the responsibility of the electrical group even though the piping designers may do some of the actual installation of electrical equipment. Since the bulk of the work on the final model is performed by the piping designers, the coordination of the installation of the instrumentation, electrical, and whatever structural and HVAC work is involved remains the responsibility of the piping design group. However, the instrumentation, electrical, and HVAC groups have overriding authority in their specific areas of design. The project engineer historically maintains overall design authority and is the final arbitrator on conflicts between groups or within a design group.

FIGURE 16-6 Closeup view of small component and piping.

DESIGN MODEL CONSTRUCTION

The piping design and engineering department will coordinate the overall construction of the design model. Therefore, all subgroups, such as electrical, HVAC, and instrumentation, must deal directly with the model coordinator. This will help eliminate problems in the use of space on the model that may be allocated for the various types of equipment. The design model after the basic modeling stage, is usually located in the drafting department.

Any necessary plan, section, and elevation drawings that may be needed can be taken directly from the basic model. The plan layout drawings, when used, become a working document of the prospective plant and can be distributed to subgroups in the engineering department for detailing and location of equipment such as HVAC, ducting, electrical trays, ladders, platforms, electrical components, instrumentation, and valves. The model offers an opportunity for a constant state of review and approval by the various design groups. Major electrical conduit runs and ductwork can be added to the model in the earlier stages, along with any small equipment that is not manufactured and located in the model department. Simple freehand sketching can be used to offer design options for the running and routing of pipe and the location of in-line valves and instruments. On the average, it may take two or three changes to obtain the best possible pipe routing situations. Any minor steel, ductwork, conduit runs, or small equipment can also be added at this time. After the piping designer has established all the major piping runs and connections that will produce the required process, the model is then made accessible to the process and instrumentation engineers for review.

A continuous overview is maintained by all engineering groups so that interferences and design problems can be worked out in the earliest possible stage. This feature, of course, is not available when using orthographically projected drawings. The actual design and construction progress can also be documented much more easily on the model than on the drawings. At this stage, the model offers complete and correct plan design possibilities and have almost totally eliminated the need to make complicated orthographically projected piping drawings. From this model, using the basic coordinates and locations for pipes and equipment, drafters and detailers are able to produce the required isometric views of each line and

FIGURE 16-7   Plan view of pipe rack and fin-fan air cooler.

FIGURE 16-8   Elevation view of fin-fan project.

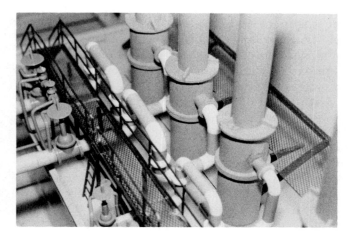

FIGURE 16-9   Closeup view of wharf model piping.

provide all the fabrication dimensions necessary. Or, when using the computer and plotter, the drafter will simply establish the necessary coordinates to enable the computer to do the drawing. In some cases, for racked piping, it is more advantageous to use plan drawings than isometrics, because racks consist primarily of straight runs. When using this method, the rack plans and isometrics are the only major drawings necessary for the construction of the overall project.

By carefully coding and coordinating the construction sequence on the drawings and model, the construction crew is able to fabricate and install the necessary pipe sections with a minimum of difficulty. Piping fabrication of components that must be shop-constructed can be ac-

complished previous to the building construction and equipment placement.

When using models in the design stage, accuracy and establishment of allowable tolerance is a primary concern. The design group checker must review the completed design model and check dimensions for accuracy. At this time, it is also possible to redesign areas in the plant that may have interference or process problems.

INSTALLATION OF PIPING

The information supplied in this book is similar to that which is available to the model designer for the purpose of designing piping using the model on an actual project.

FIGURE 16-10 In some cases, even small-diameter pipes will be shown on the model.

The major purpose of model training is to develop the ability to think in three dimensions. Training in drafting, on the other hand, encourages the student to think in two dimensions. When studying a plan drawing of an object, he or she is required to visualize and draw other two-dimensional views of that object. We normally think in three dimensions and if we practice working in three dimensions by avoiding the use of sketches or other immediate steps, our thoughts will be more precise and infinitely easier to convey.

At this point in an actual project, the model has been tagged with dimensional and other in-

FIGURE 16-11 Design model in final stage.

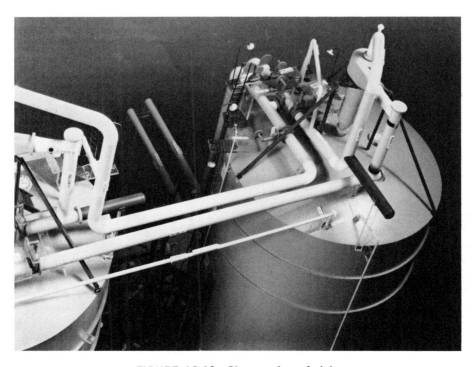

FIGURE 16-12 Closeup view of piping.

formation sufficient for the designer to install the piping. The documents he or she will require to do this design are listed below with a brief description of the uses for the documents.

1. *The piping and instrument diagram (P&ID):* This is the "Bible" as to where a pipe begins and ends, its size, number, specifications, and types of instruments and valves required. (See Section 25.)

2. *Line summary:* This information is developed to give temperatures, pressures, services, insulation specifications and requirements, as well as other design and operating conditions. (See Section 25.)

3. *Vessel orientation sketches:* These are developed to establish nozzle, manway, platform, ladder, davit and pipe downcommer locations, as well as vessel connections for pipe supports and guides. (See Section 25.)

4. *Routing diagram:* Sometimes called the P&ID transposition drawing. This is developed to establish the general routing of pipe and to determine pipeway widths and miscellaneous pipe support requirements. This drawing is normally made on a sepia of the plot plan.

5. *Piping standards:* Standards covering details of design methods are developed for each project from either contractor or client standards. When working on an actual project the designer must follow all applicable standards for that job.

6. *Design guides and dimension charts:* Design guides aid the designer in line spacing, control manifold design, and in other details of design, such as clearances required around equipment and preferred hook-up of pumps. Dimension charts are references for the designer in determining pipe and fitting dimensions, valve dimensions, and so on.

The starting procedure for detail piping design is performed in a logical order based on priorities. The alloy, exotic, or heavy wall piping is installed first. These pipes are usually the most critical and the most expensive, so they are given the "right of way," and also fabrication and delivery time is longer so that ordering (purchasing) must be done early enough to have the fabricated pipe at the job site on schedule. Piping design, which would affect the location of nozzles on equipment requiring a long delivery time, would also be of high priority regardless of material or size, so that the equipment piece could be specified and purchased.

Piping Specifications

Piping will be installed on the model by the piping designer without the use of sketches or drawings, except where extremely complex piping is involved. Where they are required, sketches are to be kept as simple as possible.

- Model tolerance for piping will be 1/6″ actual or 2 scale inches (3/8″ = 1′0″ scale).
- All process and utility headers will be shown on the model.
- Piping on shoes on the pipeway or other locations will be installed at the proper elevation. This will help minimize the possibility of error.
- Underground piping will be shown on the model by use of centerline tape. Hubs and floor drains will be shown using black dots for hubs and black squares for floor drains.
- Mitered ells will be made in the model shop. Requirements for these should be determined by the piping design supervisor and sufficient information for fabrication should be forwarded to the model shop at the time of basic model construction.
- Utility hose stations will be shown as a block painted to match the color for utility piping and will be tagged with appropriate information.
- Steam traps and steam trap assemblies will be blocked in as much as possible and tagged with standard detail numbers or other information.
- Safety showers and eye washers will be shown on the model and painted the color used for safety equipment.
- Relief valves will be of instrument color and tagged with the appropriate information.
- Field-welded branches, sweeps, weldolets, and weld tees will not be distinguished from one another on the model.
- Insulation will be shown on the model by white plastic sleeves for hot insulation and purple sleeves for cold insulation.
- For personnel protection, insulation sleeves will be tagged "PP."
- Steam tracing will be shown by a light blue insulation sleeve.
- Electrical tracing will be shown by a light green insulation sleeve.
- Sprinkler systems will normally not be shown, but an area within a building will be provided for this piping. Where it is advan-

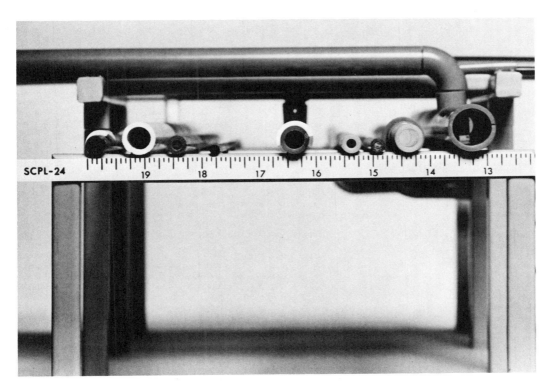

FIGURE 16-13   End view of pipe rack.

tageous to show the sprinkler headers, they will be the same color as fire protection.

- Chain operators, extension handwheels, and gear and pneumatic operators will be shown to scale on the model.
- Mating flanges will not be shown on nozzles, valves, or instrument connections, except where model components include them.
- Building piping (plumbing) will be shown on the model; it should be installed early in the development of piping to show possible interferences.
- Flexible hose or flexible piping will be shown using black pipe, either as short stub or cut to the length of the actual hose or pipe.
- Sample, vent, drain, and test connections will be shown on the model at the desired location. They will not be tagged with coordinates on the model unless location is critical. Hydrostatic vents and drains will be shown on isometric drawings only.
- Touch-up painting of such things as dummy legs, extended nozzles, and specialty items should be done after an area is reasonably firmed up, not upon first installation.
- Pipeway drawings showing location of lines in main pipeways will be prepared and issued to the field at an early date to allow installation of straight-run pipe. Each deck of multi-decked pipeways should be laid out on the

same drawing whenever possible. Branch connections and/or isometric continuation references will not be shown.

General Procedures

- The subassembly of pipes outside the model prior to installation will often aid speed and accuracy. Manifolds, valve stations, and control stations are prime examples.
- Do not attach valves on control manifolds or other assemblies prior to installing on the model. This practice allows for aligning the pipe with a square or triangle against the pipe prior to cementing in place. Valves are snapped on after pipe is in place.
- To accurately determine the length of the horizontal leg of a pipe from a vertical column nozzle, it is essential to check the actual model vessel diameter against the true vessel diameter and to compensate accordingly so as to maintain the correct dimension from the centerline of the vessel to the vertical leg.
- Where no permanent support can be attached to the model structure or equipment, install a temporary one prior to installing the spool out of clear plastic.
- Install as many supports as possible prior to fitting the pipe on the model. This serves three major purposes: it checks the accuracy

155

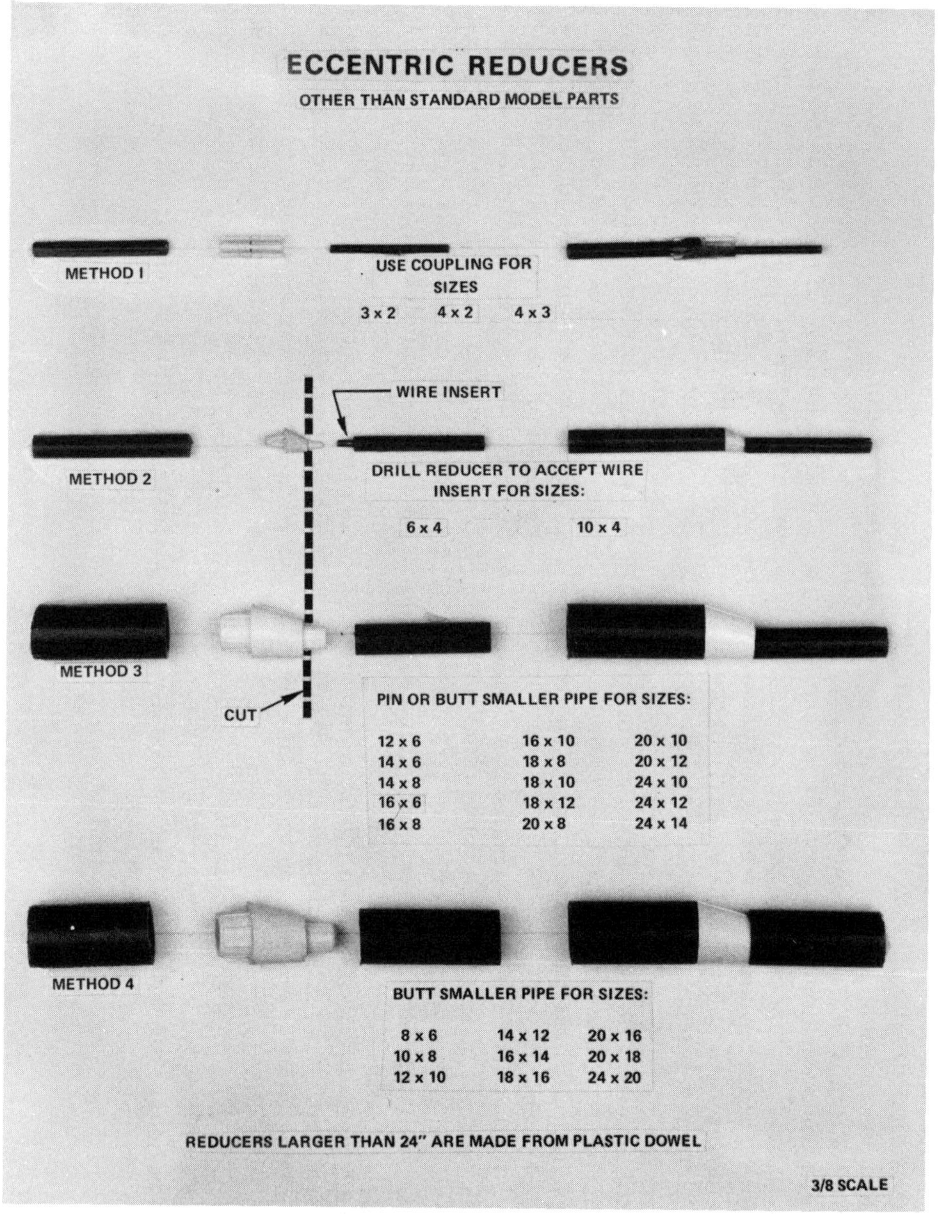

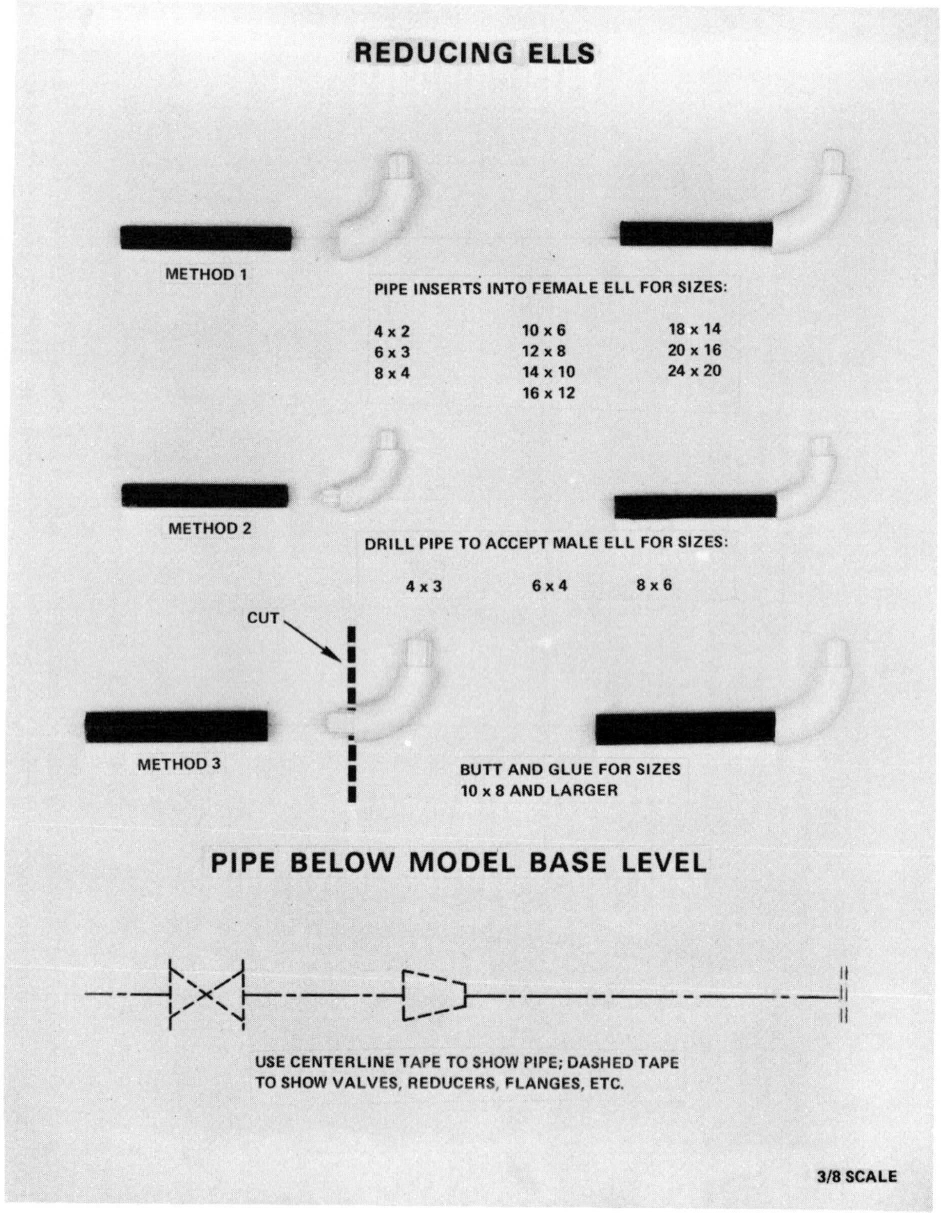

REDUCING ELLS

METHOD 1

PIPE INSERTS INTO FEMALE ELL FOR SIZES:

4 x 2	10 x 6	18 x 14
6 x 3	12 x 8	20 x 16
8 x 4	14 x 10	24 x 20
	16 x 12	

METHOD 2

DRILL PIPE TO ACCEPT MALE ELL FOR SIZES:

4 x 3	6 x 4	8 x 6

METHOD 3

BUTT AND GLUE FOR SIZES
10 x 8 AND LARGER

CUT

3/8 SCALE

PIPE BELOW MODEL BASE LEVEL

USE CENTERLINE TAPE TO SHOW PIPE; DASHED TAPE
TO SHOW VALVES, REDUCERS, FLANGES, ETC.

FIGURE 16-15

ECCENTRIC REDUCERS

OTHER THAN STANDARD MODEL PARTS

METHOD 1

USE COUPLING FOR SIZES

3 x 2   4 x 2   4 x 3

METHOD 2

WIRE INSERT

DRILL REDUCER TO ACCEPT WIRE
INSERT FOR SIZES:

6 x 4   10 x 4

METHOD 3

CUT

PIN OR BUTT SMALLER PIPE FOR SIZES:

12 x 6	16 x 10	20 x 10
14 x 6	18 x 8	20 x 12
14 x 8	18 x 10	24 x 10
16 x 6	18 x 12	24 x 12
16 x 8	20 x 8	24 x 14

METHOD 4

BUTT SMALLER PIPE FOR SIZES:

8 x 6	14 x 12	20 x 16
10 x 8	16 x 14	20 x 18
12 x 10	18 x 16	24 x 20

REDUCERS LARGER THAN 24" ARE MADE FROM PLASTIC DOWEL

3/8 SCALE

FIGURE 16-14

of your pipe fabrication; it eliminates the need of temporary supports; and it facilitates pipe installation.

- Valve orientations are taken directly from the model. If a valve is not cemented correctly, it can be rotated accidentally out of position and a corresponding incorrect installation can result in the field.
- When installing pipe, mark the pipe where it crosses structure reference lines and, in turn, mark the structural member where the pipe crosses it. This facilitates accurate assembly of pipe in the model.
- Locate pipes from structural columns and equipment centerlines—never from other pipes.
- Wherever a series of dimensions exists, as in a pipeway, add the dimensions so as to locate any one particular line from the base reference point, usually the centerline of a structural column.

Measuring Specifications

- To reach difficult locations, use a piece of 2″ pipe bent to a right angle and registered with blackened knife marks. The registered section can be formed into an arc of the diameter of a vessel and marked with increments of arc to orient points. Plastic scales can be cut to special lengths. For particularly inaccessible jobs, handles can be cemented to segments of the scales.

- To determine the circumference of a vessel, wrap strips of paper about 1/2″ wide around it and then divide into appropriate increments of orientation.
- Care should be taken in the use of secondary reference points: for example, when measuring from a platform be certain of its accuracy.
- Dividers are useful not only in transferring linear measurements but can also be used to transfer segments of art by cord measure.
- Use inside calipers or short lengths of cutoff wire to establish elevations of nozzles on the underside of vessels too close to the base to be measured with a scale.

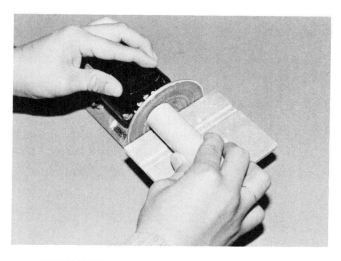

FIGURE 16-17   Student evening out ends of pipe before installation.

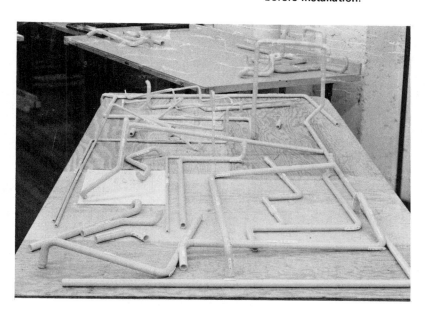

FIGURE 16-16   Major piping for large projects are sometimes fabricated and tagged in the model room and then sent to the design floor for installation.

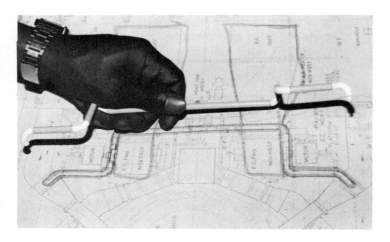

FIGURE 16-18   Modeler checks pipe configuration with print.

FIGURE 16-19   Cementing piping.

- Squares and triangles can be used to extend orientations up or down vessels. Squares taped to bases can be used to extend primary reference points to an elevation convenient for working over other equipment.
- Chalk lines are useful in extending orientations up or down vessels. Chalk lines can be improvised from blackboard chalk and string.

THE BENDING BOARD

One of the most valuable tools model designers will use is the bending board (Fig. 16-20). It will enable them to work with maximum speed and accuracy and the importance of its use cannot be overemphasized. Therefore, each beginning model designer should master all facets of the use of the bending board.

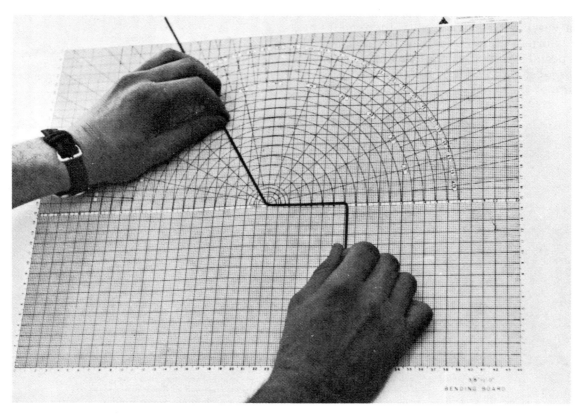

FIGURE 16-20   EMA bending board.

This portion of the training will cover the basic uses of the bending board for:

- Layout of dimensions
- Layout of angles and offsets
- Adding and subtracting
- Checking accuracy of pipe bends
- Checking piping configuration
- Alignment of pipe runs

Piping, 4″ and under, is bent to desired configuration using long-nose pliers (flat-nose, duck-bill, or electrician's pliers can be substituted). Diagonal cutting pliers are used for cutting the pipe.

As in most techniques of craftsmanship, the basics are the most important to master. The simple matter of making a bend on the plastic coated wire used for piping, if properly mastered, can have a long-range influence on your speed and accuracy. Accuracy is stressed at this point; speed will come later.

In making the first bend, hold the pipe in the bending pliers in the right hand with the flat portion in the horizontal plane and the shorter portion of pipe to the left. Using the left thumb, push the pipe down (always away from the body), keeping it as close to the pliers as possible. As the pipe is being bent, "eye-ball" the portion to the left to judge when it is bent slightly more than 90° (or

desired angle) to the part held in the pliers. Firm, continuous pressure should be applied by the left thumb until the bend is completed. Do not stop in the process of bending and then resume the action, because this may cause the bend to be less than 90°, making it more difficult to square up. The bend is now checked for desired angle on the bending board by aligning both legs with the lines on the board (Fig. 16-21).

In bending pipe for installation in the model, the first and last bends are "free" bends, so called because exact measurements are not required at the time of bending. Always allow more length than required for the first and last bends and snip off the excess when fitting the pipe into the model (Fig. 16-22).

All subsequent bends are made to specific centerline-to-centerline dimensions. Set the previous bend on the bending board at the correct centerline dimensions and mark the pipe at zero with the marking pencil. Hold the pipe in the pliers with the previous bend to the right of the pliers and mark for the next bend to the left. The mark should be about three-fourths to one diameter of pipe to the left. Align the pipe in the pliers so that it will bend in the proper direction in relation to the previous bend as it is bent vertically downward. Make each bend slightly past the desired angle. It will remain straighter when adjusted from an "overly-bent position" (Fig. 16-23).

FIGURE 16-21

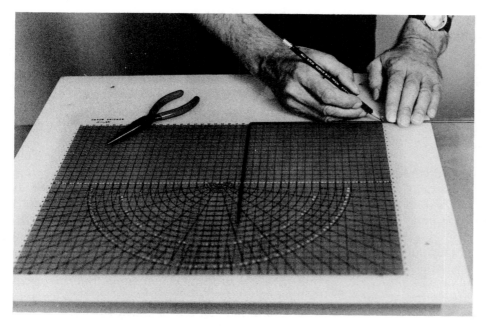

FIGURE 16-22

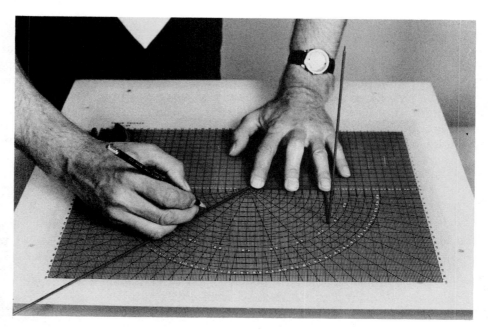

FIGURE 16-23

Always use the bending board to check the bend for configuration, dimension, and alignment before proceeding to the next bend.

Any excess is trimmed with side cutters after all other bends are made and the pipe is ready for installation on the model (Fig. 16-24).

The fabrication of piping 6″ and larger in diameter requires spools to be cut to various lengths. The 6″ through 10″ pipe should be cut using a shoe knife, never an X-Acto knife. Merely roll the pipe parallel to the horizontal lines on the bending board with the knife aligned with the

vertical lines. Do not attempt to cut through the pipe. Deep scoring will permit the pipe to be "snapped" with a clean, straight edge. This technique saves time since it completely eliminates use of the marking pencil (Fig. 16-25).

The 12″ and larger pipe, which is more difficult to score and snap, should be cut on the designer's saw. When using the designer's saw, heed the caution sign. Follow instructions as given during the machine demonstration. Unless completely sure of safe operation, get competent advice (Fig. 16-26).

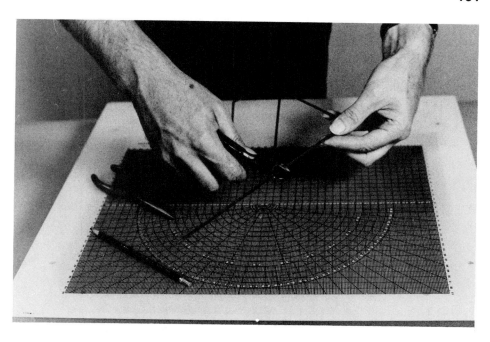

FIGURE 16-24

FIGURE 16-25

The bending board should be used in adding and subtracting dimensions graphically, when possible. This practice will eliminate many errors that might be made if done mathematically and also act as a check on the model and pipe configurations. An example of this procedure is when running a 4″ or smaller line from one known point to another, say from nozzle centerline elevation 133′-1 1/2″ to a horizontal turn at elevation (centerline) 125′-9 3/4″.

Simply place the first bend (the one that represents the elbow at the nozzle) on the bending board at the point marked 33′-1 1/2″ and put a mark on the pipe at the point marked 25′-9 3/4″. If bent properly, the pipe will be at the proper elevation when installed and you will have avoided working out the length of run of pipe, which is superfluous information. When this technique can be applied, your speed and accuracy will improve.

The bending board can be used to advantage in layout, fabrication, and checking piping of 6″ size and larger. To cut a spool length of pipe (the length between two fittings), set the end of the pipe

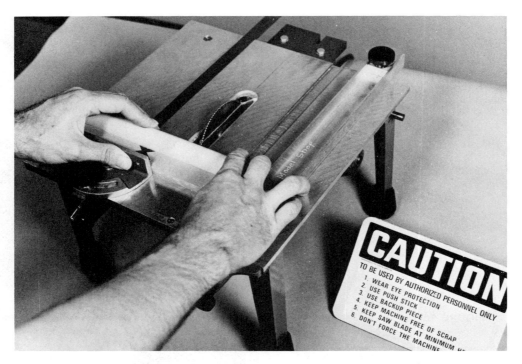

FIGURE 16-26

on the bending board at the proper centerline-to-centerline dimension and score the pipe at the dimension from the zero point that equals that of the two fittings (Fig. 16-27).

This technique, similar to that in the preced-

ing paragraph, results in an accurate graphical solution without the necessity of mathematical computation prior to marking and cutting of the pipe. Continued use of this technique will increase proficiency and decrease the time required to

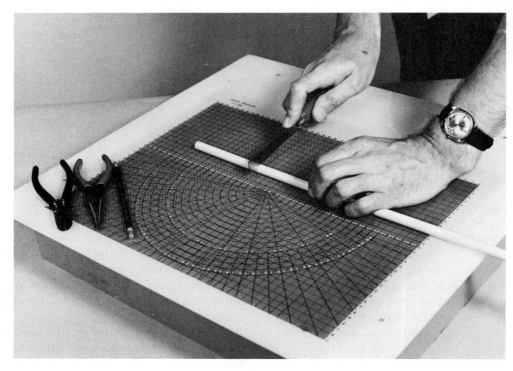

FIGURE 16-27

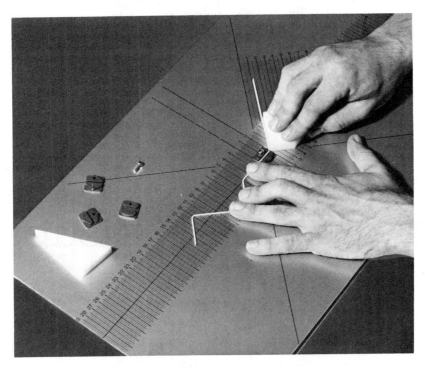

FIGURE 16-28   EMA pipe bending jig.

fabricate the piping. This will allow the designer to concentrate more fully on design criteria, with minimal effort expended on the model work.

Following are some important hints related to bending pipe and the use of the bending board:

- When bending pipe, make every effort to fabricate the entire spool from one continuous piece. If the piece must be cut in order to fit into the model, do so after bending.

- Make absolutely sure that each bend is true and square before proceeding to additional bends in a continuous line.

- Remake pipe where inaccurate. Do not try to salvage bent pipe. Do not piece together numerous short lengths.

- Check the accuracy of spools on the bending board by edge-to-edge readings rather than by centerline readings.

QUIZ

16-1. What is a final design model, and where is it usually constructed?

16-2. Describe the difference between a full-scale and a centerline piping system.

16-3. Name four factors to consider when installing model piping.

16-4. Are sprinkler systems usually shown on a model?

16-5. What drawings or documents are necessary for the installation of piping?

16-6. List 10 specifications for installation piping.

16-7. List four typical measuring specifications for the location of piping.

16-8. When is a bending board used?

17

Instrumentation, HVAC, Electrical, and Pipe Supports on the Model

FIGURE 17-1 Closeup view showing intricate instrumentation modeling and tagging of instruments.

INSTRUMENTATION

Instrumentation is one of the more important aspects of modeling and should be shown in most situations and appropriately tagged. Figure 17-1 shows an example of a variety of instrumentation that has been properly installed and tagged, including temperature instruments and pressure indicators.

Installation of instrumentation items onto the model is a joint responsibility of the piping designer, the model maker, and the instrumentation group. The overall responsibility for location and installation of instrumentation items is the direct responsibility of the instrumentation group. However, specific items may be added onto the model either by the piping designer, model builder, or instrument designer. The following instrumentation items are considered critical and therefore should be installed on the model unless otherwise stated in the instrument specification:

- Cable trays—included in the electrical cable space and shown transparent green.
- Pneumatic tubing racks—strips of the appropriate width and color to reserve the space.
- Pressure indicators, orifices, flow meters, con-

trol valves, and other in-line instruments should be shown.

- Transmitters and receivers, when not attached to the in-line instrument and it is necessary to reserve the space.

All items for which the instrumentation group is responsible for specifying should be the color designed for instrumentation.

The following instrumentation will be represented on the model:

- All in-line instruments, such as pressure indicators, temperature indicators, orifices, flow meters, and control valves.
- Pressure taps and couplings for thermowells and other sensing points will be represented by markers and tagged.
- All level gages, level controllers, level switches, and level alarms.
- Instrument pneumatic tubing trays or racks installed by, or under the supervision of, the project instrument engineer.
- All instruments on equipment.
- Control panels (blocked in).
- Transmitters or receivers that are not on in-line instruments. These will be shown to reserve space, when necessary, and will be installed by, or under supervision of, the project instrumentation engineer.
- Other instruments, such as analyzers, sample coolers, or heaters, that are not connected to piping or equipment. These will be shown only when necessary to reserve clearance space, and will be installed by, or under the supervision of, the project instrumentation engineer.

The following is a brief list of specifications for instrumentation on a model:

- All instrumentation should be color-coded pink.
- Instrumentation should be accurately fabricated and located on the model, providing operating room that may be necessary.
- Instruments should be located so as to be readily available to the operator, both visually and physically in the case of locally operated and read instruments.
- All instrumentation must be accurately tagged.
- Instrument tubing, panels, and piping must all be fabricated with extreme accuracy on models.

See Figs. 17-2 and 17-3 for types of instrumentation that can be constructed by using EMA standard components as is or altered.

HEATING, VENTILATING, AND AIR CONDITIONING

Including the heating, ventilating, and air conditioning equipment and ducts on the engineering model enhances the overall value of the modeling effort in that field routing of ducts will be minimized and overall allocation of space and efficient routing can be maintained. In some cases, such as dust collecting or fume collecting systems, special color coding may be advantageous to provide for safety reviews and operator training. Facilities engineering group and environmental group personnel will supervise this portion of the modeling effort. Either the piping designer or model maker will perform the actual model fabrication. The following procedures are applicable:

- Equipment should be blocked out and tagged appropriately.
- Smaller ducts can be modeled with solid plastic, while larger ducts can be modeled from polyurethane foam or thin sheets of plastic cut in form to shape any size duct. (It is best to stay away from polyurethane foam materials for permanent ducting because of their fragility. However, preliminary ducting may be cut from polyurethane foam to determine routing on the final model, if this has not already been accomplished on a preliminary model.)
- Interior duct design, such as turning vanes and diverters, should be located and indicated by a tag on the exterior of the duct containing the vane or diverter.
- Expansion joints and duct antivibration coupling devices will be shown with black tape and appropriately tagged.
- Instrumentation related to HVAC will be modeled to scale or indicated by sufficient tags. HVAC instruments should be color-coded the same color as other instruments on the model. (See Section 18 on Tagging.)

All heating, ventilating, and air conditioning equipment and ducts will be shown on the model.

- Every effort should be made to use the model for the routing and design of ducts, as well as for locating related equipment.

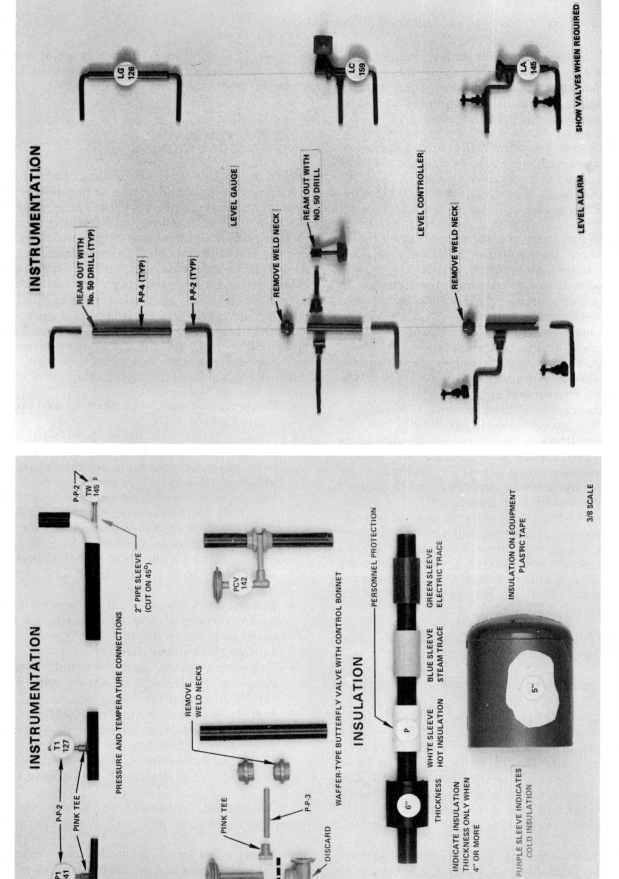

INSTRUMENTATION

P1
241

P-P-2

T1
127

PINK TEE

PRESSURE AND TEMPERATURE CONNECTIONS

REMOVE
WELD NECKS

PINK TEE

P-P-3

DISCARD

CUT

PCV
142

2" PIPE SLEEVE
(CUT ON 45°)

P-P-2
TW
145

WAFFER-TYPE BUTTERFLY VALVE WITH CONTROL BONNET

INSULATION

PERSONNEL PROTECTION

GREEN SLEEVE
ELECTRIC TRACE

BLUE SLEEVE
STEAM TRACE

P

WHITE SLEEVE
HOT INSULATION

6"

THICKNESS

INDICATE INSULATION
THICKNESS ONLY WHEN
4" OR MORE

PURPLE SLEEVE INDICATES
COLD INSULATION

INSULATION ON EQUIPMENT
PLASTIC TAPE

5"

3/8 SCALE

FIGURE 17-2

INSTRUMENTATION

LG
126

REAM OUT WITH
NO. 50 DRILL (TYP)

P-P-4 (TYP)

P-P-2 (TYP)

LEVEL GAUGE

REMOVE WELD NECK

LC
159

REAM OUT WITH
NO. 50 DRILL

LEVEL CONTROLLER

REMOVE WELD NECK

LA
145

LEVEL ALARM

SHOW VALVES WHEN REQUIRED

FIGURE 17-3

- Expansion joints will be shown by black tape and will be tagged.
- Turning vanes or diverters will be indicated by a tag on the model, referring to detail or drawing by vane or diverter number.
- Damper operators, temperature taps, and other instrumentation related to HVAC will be shown to scale, or indicated by tags, and will be instrument-color when modeled.
- All HVAC should be constructed with extreme care to produce true, accurate dimensions for all ducting and components for the heating, air conditioning, and ventilation system.
- HVAC construction must also include the positioning and tagging of insulation needs.
- Ducting should be completed at a fairly early stage in the model construction so as to provide the information regarding the location of all HVAC equipment and ducting, and eliminating interference problems with the other engineering groups, such as pipe layout, pipe support, and electrical equipment.
- Because ducting takes large amounts of space, early insulation will prevent interferences.
- Block shapes should be used to represent most HVAC equipment (coils, fans, filters, etc.).
- Use foam, plastic sheeting, or light woods for HVAC equipment, including instruments, panels, flanges, and rectangular ducting.
- Use plastic tubing for round ducting.
- Use standard components for fittings, elbows, and so on.
- Model *all* ducting true to scale.

ELECTRICAL

All electrical items that are to be modeled should be installed by the electrical group or under the supervision of electrical personnel, with the exception of electrical tracings on piping, thermal couples, and electrical motors on equipment. The following equipment items should be shown on the model in block form and color-coded light green:

- Cable trays (transparent)
- Conduit banks (transparent)
- Substations
- Switch gears
- Motor control centers
- Transformers
- Exceptionally large individual conduit
- Lighting panels

Lighting fixtures are typically modeled using available plastic scale figures together with 1/16" light green pipe. The following are electrical items typically not modeled but tagged:

- Welding receptacles
- Lighting receptacles
- Pushbuttons

All items shown on the model that the electrical group is responsible for specifying should be the color designated for electrical equipment.

Major Electrical Equipment

The following will be shown on the model in block form and will be the color designated for electrical equipment:

- Motor control centers
- Switchgears
- Cable trays
- Transformers
- Banks of conduits
- Substations
- Tower and pole lines

Small Electrical Equipment

The model will reflect the following, either to scale or by the use of tags, tape, or legend markers:

- Pushbuttons
- Telephones
- Lighting fixtures (to scale)
- Junction boxes
- Receptacles
- Underground conduit and duct banks (tape, to scale)

Many standard components are available that simulate the electrical systems that are prevalent on the modern industrial model, including cable trays, lighting systems, and in some cases, conduits.

The following is a list of specifications that can be utilized when constructing and installing the electrical system and the electrical needs on an industrial model:

- All conduits should be shown by the use of full-bore tubing, fittings, or plastic representation.
- All electrical needs should be shown on the model.
- Lighting systems, indoor and outdoor light-

ing, and so on, should all be located on the model.

- Standard cable trays are available and should be accurately positioned throughout the model.
- Substations, switching stations, control centers, switch racks, and other electrical needs should be represented with block shapes.
- Control stations should be modeled where appropriate.
- Always provide sufficient operation and maintenance space for all electrical equipment.
- All electrical equipment should be color-coded in green.
- Show junction boxes with color-coded tags or block shapes.
- All cable trays must be modeled at the earliest possible time so as to reduce interferences.
- Most electrical instruments are not modeled, just tagged.

PIPE HANGERS AND SUPPORTS

In the past, the use of the model for pipe support location and design was dependent upon the particular practice of the company. The most modern use of models for pipe supports has found the piping designer doing the actual design placement and location of major supports, which may number in the thousands for a large power project.

For pipe supports, the designing of the support on the model enables the pipe support department to use less drawing time and facilitate accurate spotting of the pipe support locations with regard to other equipment. In most cases, the model will totally eliminate the interference problem in the placement of pipe supports and will improve the overall planning for placement of pipe supports in combination with each other. By using a model, the pipe support group will greatly reduce

problems between different groups within the company, such as HVAC, electrical, instrumentation, and pipe support. The model should be used for evaluating all structural embedments and structural framing methods which are used for pipe supports.

Before locating pipe supports on the model, identify the surrounding important equipment, and objects that may influence the placement of the pipe support, such as piping runs and piping components, valves, and fittings; the building structural elements involved; electrical runs and trays; all heating, air conditioning, and ventilation ducts and equipment; and mechanical equipment and vessels. It is important to establish dimensions with respect to elevations and coordinates for the location of pipe supports.

In many cases, the pipe support drafter will be called upon to fabricate the pipe support for the model and place it on the model directly. When spotting pipe supports on a model, it is important to take into account the following information:

- The access and installation space necessary for the construction of pipe support in a particular area.
- Any common supports that may be used to support other parallel or close pipe runs.
- Beware of any situation on the model where an incomplete structural or concrete area is not shown.
- Allow sufficient pulling space for equipment when placing pipe supports close to the surrounding vessels and other components.
- Do not locate pipe supports too close to traps or pipe ends and drains.

Overall, a design model will enable the pipe support group to greatly facilitate the design and placement of the pipe support on a project, eliminating a great number of difficulties encountered when using only the drawing method.

QUIZ

17-1. What items are usually considered aspects of instrumentation?

17-2. What color is most instrumentation shown as?

17-3. What is HVAC, and what aspects of it should be shown on a typical model?

17-4. What is the usual material for the construction of ducting?

17-5. What is a cable tray, and what is its normal color code?

17-6. Name six electrical items that should be shown on the model.

17-7. Name five aspects of locating pipe supports on the model that must be taken into account by the designer.

18

Tagging the Model

FIGURE 18-1 Design model showing complete tagging.

All the photographs provided in this book show the liberal use of tagging. Tagging the model is one of the most important procedures for the communication of all dimensional information, equipment identification, and a variety of other uses. It is one of the most important aspects of model building.

Can you imagine producing a complete set of engineering drawings and leaving off necessary notes and dimensions to adequately define the design? Obviously, no good designer would purposely let this happen. This same philosophy must be carried over into model tagging. When insufficient tagging is applied, the value of the engineering design model depreciates in direct proportion to the insufficiency of the tagging. More specifically, the ultimate efficiency of the design model can be most nearly achieved only when the tagging is complete, correct, and legible. The goals of this section are to emphasize these needs and provide adequate guidelines so that they may be achieved.

It hardly seems necessary to mention legibility. However, it must be stressed that correct and complete model tag information is of no value unless it can be read. Therefore, a basic criterion for a modeler is to possess good lettering skills.

169

Average-quality lettering on a drawing may suffice, since drawing notes and/or dimensions are all on a flat plane and are in full view. However, tagging on a congested model is often troublesome to read as a result of being partially hidden by piping, structures, and/or equipment. High-quality, consistent lettering helps to alleviate this problem.

There are several ways to achieve good-quality (legible) lettering on model tagging. The industry standard is black hand lettering on commercially available pressure-sensitive tags. These tags are available in many sizes and shapes and preprinted with the most common legends, such as T.O.S.El. or ₵. Other approaches, such as typing or using transfer-type lettering, are much more time consuming and offer no recognizable advantage if the hand lettering is of consistent style and quality.

The style of lettering generally conceded to be the best for model tagging is uppercase vertical letters, these being the easiest to read from any angle in either actual or photographic situations. In any case, professionalism calls for consistency. Lettering criteria must be decided upon and clearly defined in the model specifications before actual model construction begins.

Since most of the commercial tags are made of a matte-finished vinyl plastic or of a plastic-impregnated paper, it is necessary to use fiber-tipped lettering pens that are quick drying and permanent. Ballpoints and fountain pens should be avoided, as they will either smear or puddle on the tag. As previously noted, typing is not advantageous, not only because of the extra time and handling involved, but also because typed tags must be sprayed with clear plastic to prevent smearing.

Assuming that professional-quality lettering has been achieved, the most important aspect of model tagging is at what stage the tags are applied. It is strongly recommended that tags be applied as the equipment is built or the line installed. It is a very short-sighted and costly procedure to delay tagging to a later stage just to "get something on the model quickly." This questionable advantage is far outweighed by the following problems and time losses it creates:

- Utility of the model in its untagged state is reduced to less than that of a flow diagram.
- Without tagging, all notes and sketches must be made and maintained for every facet of design.
- These notes and sketches must be rehandled at the later stage, requiring a second familiarization and orientation with the design.
- If complete notes and sketches are not made and filed, all calculations must be done a second time as tagging proceeds.

FIGURE 18-2 Notice intricate detail and tagging shown on this model.

• The human factor (not wanting to have to handle all information a second time or to "finish someone else's job") will invariably cause some necessary information to be omitted, thereby creating unnecessary loss of time during checking and correcting.

It is conservatively estimated that delayed or incomplete tagging will add 25 percent to the design time of a project.

The last aspect of model tagging is the actual application procedure. Again for reasons of professionalism and consistency, tags should be installed to read from the same orientation as the plot plan. In addition, vertical tags should read from the bottom up. These points may seem inconsequential to the uninitiated, but you will quickly recognize their importance as your project progresses. The following pages discuss many of the items that must be tagged.

FIGURE 18-3 Tagging on petrochemical model.

FIGURE 18-4 Closeup view showing the vast amount of tagging used on a typical design model.

FIGURE 18-5 Closeup view of pump station and tagging.

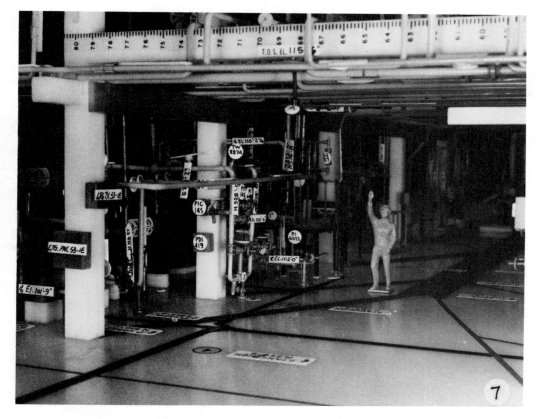

FIGURE 18-6 View of model and tagging beneath a pipeway. Notice the control valve manifold and appropriate tagging.

172

FIGURE 18-7

MODEL TAGGING PROCEDURES

Details of model tagging procedures differ from company to company, but basically the purpose is the same—to communicate dimensional and other information to model users.

For the purposes of this book, a workable tagging procedure is included. Using this procedure, sufficient information is applied to the basic model to enable the designer to establish pipe runs and subsequently locate them on the model with coordinates, using minimal reference documents. Properly applied information by the designer should be sufficient to complete piping isometric drawings from the model.

This procedure outlines minimal tagging requirements.

- Piping designers will be responsible for proper tagging to facilitate lifting information from the model for the preparation of isometric drawings.
- Where too little physical space is available for proper tagging, such as beside pumps or on small-diameter vessels with several nozzles, a model equipment information sheet will be filled in with appropriate information and attached to the model base by a clipboard (Figs. 18-9, 18-10, and 18-11).
- All necessary tagging will be applied immediately upon completion of equipment and pipe-run installation on the model.
- When possible, model tags will be placed so as to read from the same orientation as the plot plan. Tags in the vertical position will be lettered to read from the bottom upward. Tags will be lettered with drawing ink or special

pens; ball-point or fountain pens will not be used.
- To assure the adhesion of model tags, the following procedures must be employed:
  —Avoid excessive bending in removing tags from backing.
  —Clean line of any dust, dirt, or oil before placing tag.
  —Press tag firmly to pipe along full tag length, making sure the edges are sealed.
  —If a pipeline needs changing, make a new tag.
- All structural column, equipment, and pipe-run coordinate tags are to be centerline unless stated otherwise on the tag.
- Where coordinate tags are used for reference (such as the centerline of a stanchion on a pipe rack or the tangent line of a horizontal drum or any instance where a choice of two points may be made), the lower coordinate will be used so that related dimensions can be added rather than subtracted from the reference tag.
- Proper tagging is essential for supplying information to design groups and the construction department. It is the basis for the production of isometric drawings. All bases and equipment are identified by number; such items as equipment, structures, piping, trenches, and roads are dimensioned by using elevation and/or coordinate tags.
- Coordinate tags for structures and equipment, as well as nozzle tags, will be checked prior to placing pipe on the model.
- Tags on piping will be checked before isometrics are drawn.

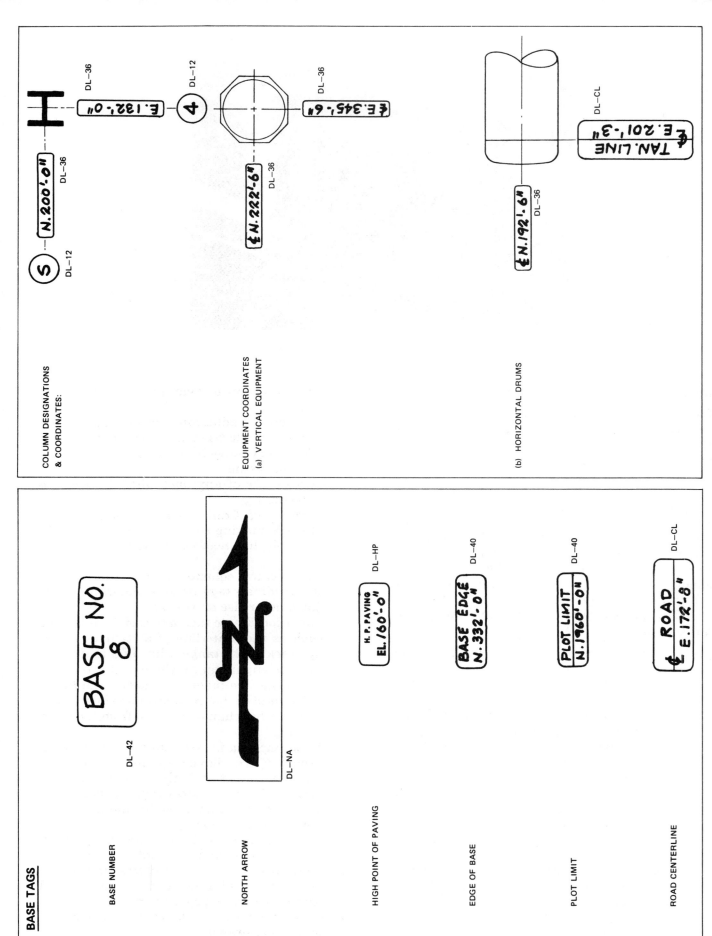

COLUMN DESIGNATIONS & COORDINATES:

N.200'-0"   DL-36
DL-12   S
E.132'-0"   DL-36
DL-12   4
DL-36   N.222'-6"
E.345'-6"   DL-36

EQUIPMENT COORDINATES
(a) VERTICAL EQUIPMENT

DL-CL
℄ TAN. LINE
E.201'-3"
N.192'-6"   DL-36

(b) HORIZONTAL DRUMS

BASE TAGS

BASE NO. 8
DL-42
BASE NUMBER

DL-NA
NORTH ARROW

H.P. PAVING
EL.160'-0"   DL-HP
HIGH POINT OF PAVING

BASE EDGE
N.332'-0"   DL-40
EDGE OF BASE

PLOT LIMIT
N.1960'-0"   DL-40
PLOT LIMIT

℄ ROAD
E.172'-8"   DL-CL
ROAD CENTERLINE

174

FIGURE 18-8 Tagging procedures.

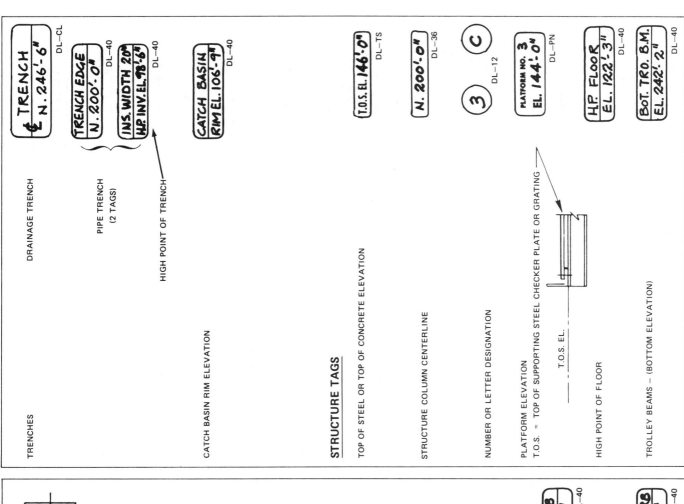

TRENCHES

DRAINAGE TRENCH

PIPE TRENCH
(2 TAGS)

HIGH POINT OF TRENCH

CATCH BASIN RIM ELEVATION

STRUCTURE TAGS

TOP OF STEEL OR TOP OF CONCRETE ELEVATION

STRUCTURE COLUMN CENTERLINE

NUMBER OR LETTER DESIGNATION

PLATFORM ELEVATION
T.O.S. = TOP OF SUPPORTING STEEL CHECKER PLATE OR GRATING

HIGH POINT OF FLOOR

TROLLEY BEAMS – (BOTTOM ELEVATION)

FIGURE 18-8   Continued

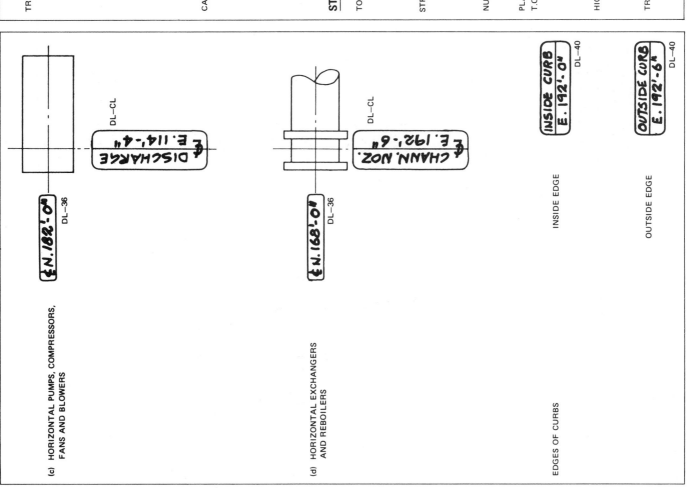

(c) HORIZONTAL PUMPS, COMPRESSORS,
     FANS AND BLOWERS

(d) HORIZONTAL EXCHANGERS
     AND REBOILERS

EDGES OF CURBS

INSIDE EDGE

OUTSIDE EDGE

FIGURE 18-8   Continued

EQUIPMENT TAGS

VERTICAL VESSELS

50-1101 DL-40

ACTUAL DIA. 4'-6" MODEL DIA. 4'-8" NO2. 300# R.F. DL-42

M1 146'-8" 18"-90°

N2 123'-2" 4"-270° 8'-6"

N3 168'-3" 3"-90° 18" DL-24

N6 110'-3½" 10'-60° 12" DL-24

NA 124'-3½" 6"-3'-0" 4'-10" DL-24

PLATFORM NO. 4 EL. 120'-0" DL-PN

LADDER 90° DL-CL

(a) MASTER TAG
  - EQUIPMENT NUMBER (DYMO TAPE)
  - ALTERNATE METHOD – USE DL-40 WITH RED MARKING PEN
  - ACTUAL VESSEL DIAMETER
  - MODEL VESSEL DIAMETER
  - NOZZLE RATING AND FACING

(b) RADIAL NOZZLES AND MANWAYS
  - IDENTIFICATION
  - CENTERLINE ELEVATION
  - SIZE/ORIENTATION FROM NORTH
  - NOZZLE PROJECTION FROM VESSEL CENTERLINE (MANWAYS EXCLUDED)

(c) TOP OR BOTTOM NOZZLES AND MANWAYS
  - IDENTIFICATION
  - FACE ELEVATION (MANWAYS EXCLUDED)
  - SIZE/ORIENTATION FROM NORTH
  - DISTANCE FROM CENTERLINE

(d) BOTTOM NOZZLE INFORMATION FOR PIPE PENETRATING SKIRT
  - CONNECTION POINT AND IDENTIFICATION
  - FACE ELEVATION
  - SIZE/ORIENTATION FROM NORTH
  - DISTANCE FROM CENTERLINE

(e) TANGENTIAL NOZZLES
  - IDENTIFICATION
  - CENTERLINE ELEVATION
  - SIZE/DISTANCE FROM PARALLEL CENTERLINE
  - PROJECTION FROM PERPENDICULAR CENTERLINE

(f) PLATFORMS
  - NUMBER AND ELEVATION
  - (REFER TO STRUCTURES–PLATFORM ELEVATION)
  - LADDER ORIENTATION

FIGURE 18-8 Continued

HORIZONTAL VESSELS

50-1202 DL-40

ACTUAL DIA. 4'-6" MODEL DIA. 4'-8" NO2. 300# R.F. DL-42

M1 8'-10" 18"-90° DL-24

N3 12'-2" 6"-0° 6'-6" DL-24

N8 116'-4½" 6"-14'-2" 10" DL-24

N6 114'-2½" 4"-10'-2" 4'-2" DL-24

℄ 50-1202 EL. 109'-6" DL-CL

PLATFORM NO. 2 EL. 118'-6" DL-PN

SLOPE ⅛"/FT. LTA-200

℄ W.P. EL. 112'-8" DL-CL

(a) MASTER TAG
  - VESSEL NUMBER DESIGNATION
  - ACTUAL DIAMETER
  - MODEL DIAMETER
  - NOZZLE RATING AND FACING

(b) RADIAL NOZZLES AND MANWAYS
  - IDENTIFICATION
  - DISTANCE FROM REFERENCE TANGENT LINE
  - SIZE/ORIENTATION FROM VERTICAL CENTERLINE (0° AT TOP. READ CLOCKWISE, VIEWING FROM REFERENCE END.)
  - NOZZLE PROJECTION FROM DRUM CENTERLINE (MANWAYS EXCLUDED)

(c) END NOZZLES AND MANWAYS
  - IDENTIFICATION
  - CENTERLINE ELEVATION
  - SIZE/DISTANCE FROM REFERENCE TANGENT LINE (MANWAYS EXCLUDED)
  - DISTANCE FROM CENTERLINE

(d) TANGENTIAL NOZZLES
  - IDENTIFICATION
  - CENTERLINE ELEVATION
  - SIZE/DISTANCE FROM REFERENCE TANGENT LINE
  - PROJECTION FROM PERPENDICULAR CENTERLINE

(e) CENTERLINE ELEVATION

(f) PLATFORM ELEVATION
  - (REFER TO STRUCTURES–PLATFORM ELEVATION)

(g) SLOPE
  - SLOPE TAG
  - WORK POINT ELEVATION (MIDPOINT)

FIGURE 18-8 Continued

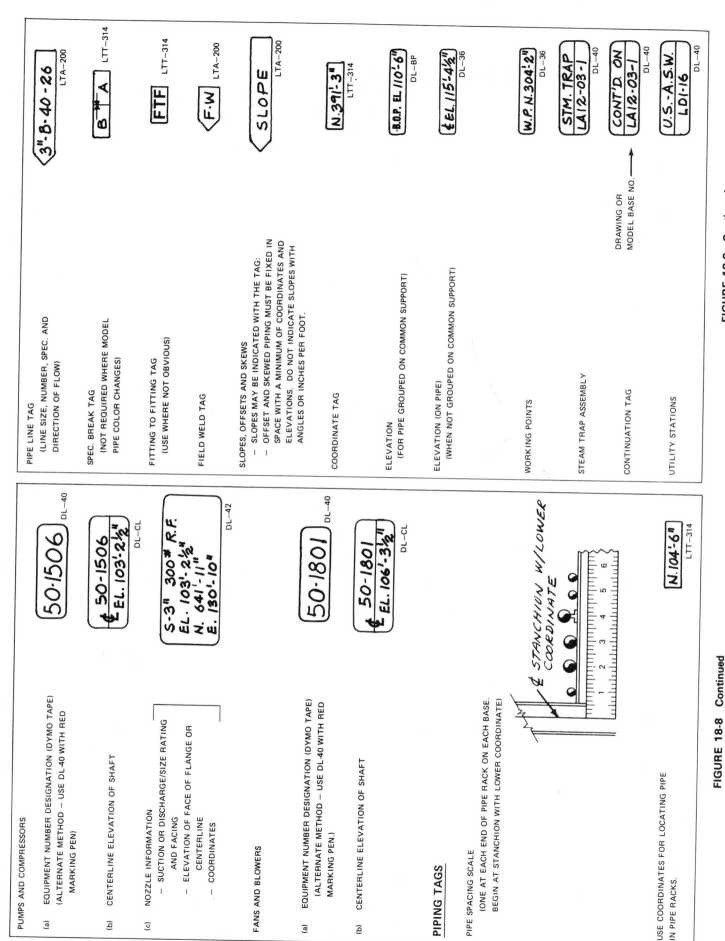

PUMPS AND COMPRESSORS

(a) EQUIPMENT NUMBER DESIGNATION (DYMO TAPE)
    (ALTERNATE METHOD — USE DL-40 WITH RED
    MARKING PEN)

(b) CENTERLINE ELEVATION OF SHAFT

(c) NOZZLE INFORMATION
    — SUCTION OR DISCHARGE/SIZE RATING
      AND FACING
    — ELEVATION OF FACE OF FLANGE OR
      CENTERLINE
    — COORDINATES

FANS AND BLOWERS

(a) EQUIPMENT NUMBER DESIGNATION (DYMO TAPE)
    (ALTERNATE METHOD — USE DL-40 WITH RED
    MARKING PEN.)

(b) CENTERLINE ELEVATION OF SHAFT

PIPING TAGS

PIPE SPACING SCALE
(ONE AT EACH END OF PIPE RACK ON EACH BASE.
BEGIN AT STANCHION WITH LOWER COORDINATE)

USE COORDINATES FOR LOCATING PIPE
IN PIPE RACKS.

PIPE LINE TAG
(LINE SIZE, NUMBER, SPEC. AND
DIRECTION OF FLOW)

SPEC. BREAK TAG
(NOT REQUIRED WHERE MODEL
PIPE COLOR CHANGES)

FITTING TO FITTING TAG
(USE WHERE NOT OBVIOUS)

FIELD WELD TAG

SLOPES, OFFSETS AND SKEWS
— SLOPES MAY BE INDICATED WITH THE TAG:
— OFFSET AND SKEWED PIPING MUST BE FIXED IN
  SPACE WITH A MINIMUM OF COORDINATES AND
  ELEVATIONS. DO NOT INDICATE SLOPES WITH
  ANGLES OR INCHES PER FOOT.

COORDINATE TAG

ELEVATION
(FOR PIPE GROUPED ON COMMON SUPPORT)

ELEVATION (ON PIPE)
(WHEN NOT GROUPED ON COMMON SUPPORT)

WORKING POINTS

STEAM TRAP ASSEMBLY

CONTINUATION TAG

UTILITY STATIONS

FIGURE 18-8   Continued

FIGURE 18-8   Continued

177

ELECTRICAL TAGS

TRAY NO6 — DL-40

ELECTRICAL TRAY NUMBER

TRAY BOT. EL. 115'-0" — DL-40

BOTTOM OF TRAY ELEVATION

MCC NO2 — DL-40

MOTOR CONTROL CENTERS, SWITCHGEARS, TRANSFORMERS, ETC.

IF REQUIRED, THE FOLLOWING ARE INDICATED BY TAG ONLY: (DL-12)

JB — JUNCTION BOX

WR — WELDING RECEPTACLE

REC — RECEPTACLE

PB — PUSHBUTTON

PT — PERMANENT TELEPHONE

TJ — TELEPHONE JACK

INSTRUMENT TAGS

TRAY NO2 — DL-40

INSTRUMENT TRAY OR RACK NUMBER

TRAY BOT. EL. 112'-0" — DL-40

BOTTOM OF TRAY OR RACK ELEVATION

CONT. PANEL NO. 4

INSTRUMENT CONTROL PANELS OR CONSOLES, TRANSMITTERS AND OTHER LARGE INSTRUMENT EQUIPMENT. (DYMO TAPE) (ALTERNATE METHOD — USE DL-42 WITH RED MARKING PEN)

FIGURE 18-8 Continued

TEES AND BRANCH CONNECTIONS:
MODEL USERS SHALL REFER TO JOB SPECIFICATION FOR THE REQUIRED TYPES OF BRANCH CONNECTIONS (i.e. BUTT WELD TEES, WELD NOZZLES, SWEEPOLETS, WELDOLETS, SOCKET WELD TEES, ETC). THESE WILL NOT BE DISTINGUISHED OR TAGGED ON THE MODEL.

FITTING VARIATIONS:
A TAG SHALL BE ADDED FOR SPECIALS SUCH AS SHORT RADIUS ELLS, REDUCING FLANGES, MATERIAL OUT OF SPEC AND OTHER MATERIAL NOT OBVIOUS ON THE MODEL.

SPECIALTY ITEMS:
SUCH ITEMS AS Y STRAINERS AND EXPANSION JOINTS SHALL BE TAGGED WITH THEIR ITEM NUMBER AND FACE TO FACE OR LAYING LENGTH DIMENSIONS (AND RATING AND FACING IF OTHER THAN LINE SPEC).

INSULATION TAGS

EQUIPMENT

INSULATION (WHITE TAPE) DL-12

PIPING (WHITE SLEEVE FOR HOT INSULATION, PURPLE SLEEVE FOR COLD INSULATION)

(a) THICKNESS (ION INSULATION SLEEVE)

(NOTE: SHOW THICKNESS TAG ON PIPE INSULATION ONLY WHEN MORE THAN 4" THICK DL-12)

(b) PERSONNEL PROTECTION — WHITE INSULATION SLEEVE

(c) STEAM TRACING — LIGHT BLUE INSULATION SLEEVE

(d) ELECTRICAL TRACING — GREEN INSULATION SLEEVE

(e) COLD INSULATION (REFRIGERATION) — PURPLE INSULATION SLEEVE

FIGURE 18-8 Continued

IN-LINE INSTRUMENTS

(a) ORIFICE – FLANGES MUST BE SHOWN AND EASILY SCALED. WHEN A MORE CRITICAL LOCATION IS DESIRED, LOCATE WITH A DIMENSION, COORDINATE OR ELEVATION.

FE 321   LTB-120

(b) CONTROL VALVES (APPLY TO VALVE BONNET)

PCV 34   LTB-120

(c) RELIEF VALVES (APPLY TO VALVE BODY)

PSV 442   LTB-120

H.V.A.C. TAGS

DUCTS   18 × 24   DL-36

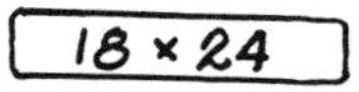

EXPANSION JOINTS   EXP. JT. P-100   DL-36

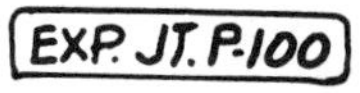

TURNING VANES   TURN. VN. DV-1   DL-36

FANS, BLOWERS AND OTHER H.V.A.C. EQUIPMENT
(SEE EQUIPMENT TAGS – FANS AND BLOWERS)

Listed below are several illustrations of model Tagging:

PIPEWAY TAGGING

A. Both coordinates of each pipeway stanchion

COLUMN N. 201'-0"   COLUMN E. 401'-6"

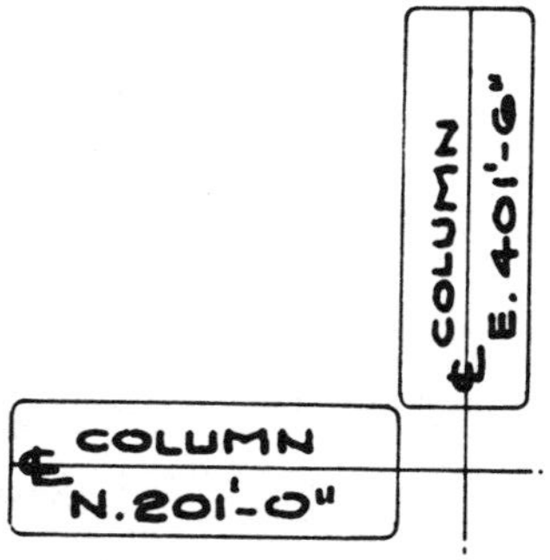

FIGURE 18-8   Continued

B. Number and letter designation of each pipeway stanchion

S-1

C. Elevation of each pipeway level. (Top of steel or top of concrete elevation)

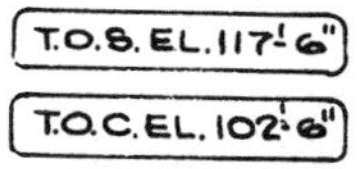

T.O.S. EL. 117'-6"   T.O.C. EL. 102'-6"

D. Pipe spacing scale (one at each end of pipeway on each base at each elevation)

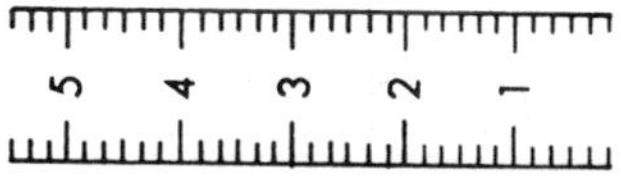

5 4 3 2 1

BASE TAGGING

A. High Point of paving, usually applied near the base North arrow

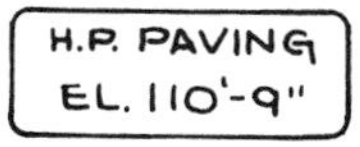

H.P. PAVING EL. 110'-9"

B. Catch basin rim elevation

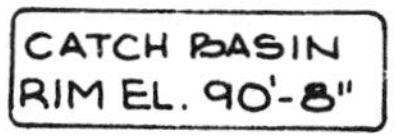

CATCH BASIN RIM EL. 90'-8"

C. Road centerline

ROAD W. 96'-2"

FIGURE 18-8   Continued

SEAM LINE N.133'-0"

K. Horizontal drum seam line (north or west end)

DISCHARGE W.275'-6"

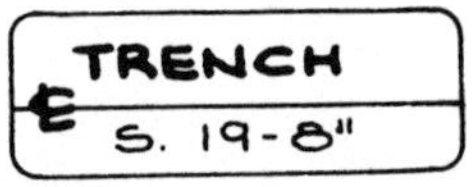

L. Pump discharge or face of foundation

CHANNEL NOZZ. E.127'-6"

M. Exchanger channel nozzle centerline

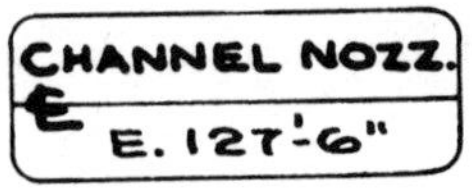

CYLINDER N.251'-0"

N. Compressor cylinder centerline

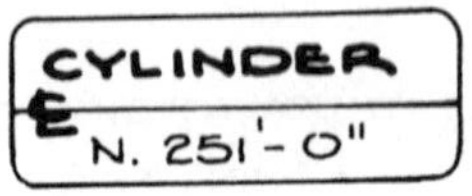

BASE I

O. Base number

P. Base north arrow

FIGURE 18-8 Continued

PLOT LIMIT N.0'-0"

D. Plot area limit

BASE EDGE W.326'-6"

E. Edge of base

TRENCH S.19'-8"

F. Trench centerlines

CURB EDGE N.116'-0"

G. Edge of curb

STRUCTURE W.293'-9"

H. Structure column centerlines

C-202 N.260'-9"

I. Equipment centerline

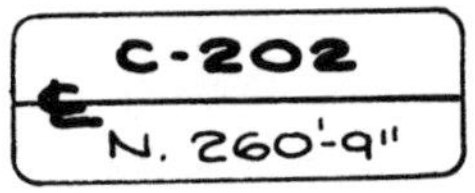

D-301 EL.123'-6"

J. Horizontal drum centerline

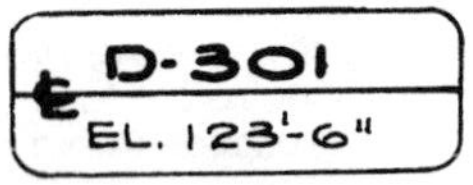

FIGURE 18-8 Continued

Stress relieved vessel (coral colored Tag)

Date to be added by stress analyst when vessel is released

STRESS RELIEVED VESSEL #T-301
LAST CHANGE DATE FOR
PIPING OR ATTACHMENTS
DATE 3-21-76

C.   Couplings and instrument connections, designation only

(K1)

D.   Platforms

1.   Number and elevation (Refer to Structural Tagging, Para. B)

PLATFORM NO.2
T.O.S. EL. 121'-0"

2.   Ladder orientation

LADDER
90°

DRUM TAGGING

A.   Centerline elevation

C-202
EL. 106'-1"

B.   Platform elevation (Refer to Structural Tagging, Para. B)

PLATFORM NO.3
T.O.S. EL. 116'-0"

FIGURE 18-8   Continued

STRUCTURE TAGGING

A.   Top of steel or top of concrete elevation

T.O.C. EL. 120'-0"   T.O.S. EL. 142'-0"

B.   Platform elevation T.O.S. = Top of supporting steel

PLATFORM NO.6
T.O.S. EL. 110'-0"

C.   Equipment centerline where applicable

T-303
E. 210'-6"

COLUMN TAGGING

A.   Nozzles and Manways

Identification
Centerline elevation
Size & Orientation from north
Nozzle projection from vessel centerline
(Manways excluded)

N-3
102'-0"
4"/270°
7'-6"

M-2
142'-6"
18"/90°

B.   Master Tag

Equipment number

T-301

Actual vessel diameter
Model vessel diameter
Nozzle rating and facing

ACTUAL DIA. 1'-6"
MODEL DIA. 1'-8"
300#R.J.

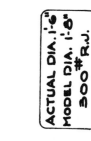

FIGURE 18-8   Continued

C. Nozzles and Manways

Identification
Distance from north or west seam line
Size & centerline elevation or orientation
Nozzle projection from drum centerline (Manways excluded)

N-3
10'-6"
6"/101'-3"
2'-10"
M-3
3'-0"
18"
106'-3"

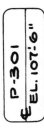

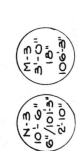

D. Master Tag

Actual diameter
Model diameter
Nozzle rating and facing

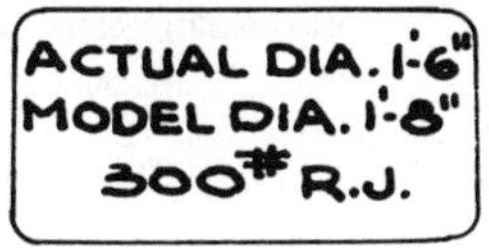
ACTUAL DIA. 1'-6"
MODEL DIA. 1'-8"
300# R.J.

E. Slope

1. Slope Tag

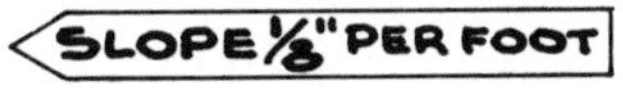
SLOPE 1/8" PER FOOT

2. Work point elevation

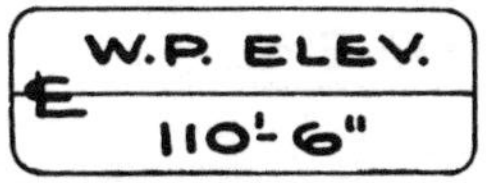
W.P. ELEV.
℄
110'-6"

F. Couplings and instrument connections, designation only

K1

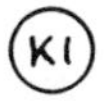

EXCHANGER TAGGING

Centerline elevation

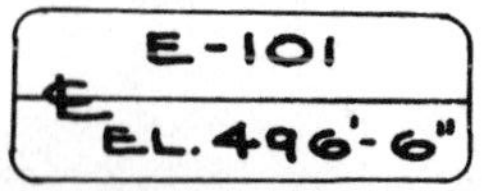
E-101
℄
EL. 496'-6"

FIGURE 18-8 Continued

PUMPS, TURBINE DRIVES AND COMPRESSOR TAGGING

Centerline elevation of shaft

P-301
℄
EL. 107'-6"

PIPE TAGGING

Each pipe in pipeway should be Tagged; normally, Tagging one end of the pipeway is sufficient. Tagging should be sufficient for isometrics and checking. See examples in this instruction for line Tagging guide.

A. Line description

Direction of flow
Line number
Size
Specification

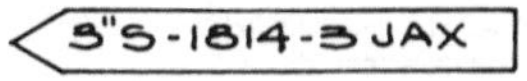
3"S-1814-3 JAX

B. Pipeway spacing — distance from reference stanchion centerline

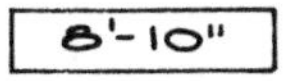
8'-10"

C. Coordinate where line enters or leaves pipeway

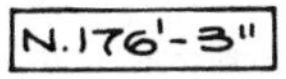
N.176'-3"

D. Centerline elevations where they are not at normal pipeway elevations

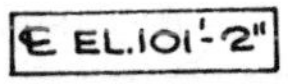
℄ EL.101'-2"

FIGURE 18-8 Continued

INSTRUMENT TAGGING

A. Instrument tray or rack number

TRAY №6

B. Bottom of tray or rack elevation

TRAY BOT. EL. 114'-0"

C. Instrument control panels or consoles. Transmitters and other large instrument equipment.

CONT. PANEL №4

ELECTRICAL TAGGING

A. Electrical tray number

TRAY №2

B. Bottom of tray elevation

TRAY BOT. EL. 110'-0"

C. Motor control centers, switchgears, transformers, etc.

MCC №3

D. If required, the following are indicated by Tag only:

(a) Junction Box

(b) Welding Receptacle

(c) Receptacle

(d) Pushbutton

(e) Permanent Telephone

(f) Telephone Jack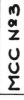

FIGURE 18-8   Continued

E. Vertical lines at columns

1. Coordinates

S.291'-0"

2. Orientation, if not directly connected to Tagged nozzle

 47°

F. Coordinate of legs of control manifolds

N.260'-6"

G. Coordinate of underground lines and stub-ups

E.260'-5"

H. Coordinate of vertical runs with the exception of predetermined vertical drops from pipeway.

E.167'-4"

I. Control valves. Use 3/8" round Tag applied to model base or platform below valve.

 PCV 51

INSULATION

No insulation to be indicated on equipment. White insulation sleeve to show hot insulated lines. Steam tracing insulation shall be shown by a piece of red 1/16" model piping about 1/2" long glued on an appropriate insulation sleeve. Purple insulation sleeve to show cold insulation. Electrical tracing shall be shown by a piece of green 1/16" model piping about 1/2" long glued on an appropriate insulation sleeve. Personnel protection insulation shall be a white sleeve tag with "P" attached.

FIGURE 18-8   Continued

The student should look closely at the photographs provided in the book to get an idea of tagging procedures that are used throughout industry. The photographs were contributed by a variety of petrochemical, nuclear, and other engineering firms, all which have their own preferences as to tagging procedures, but do follow similar specifications.

Note that items that are not tagged on equipment will appear on the model equipment data sheet as shown in Figs. 18-9 to 18-11.

Labeling should be done on the base of the model first, establishing the base number, north arrow orientation, high point of paving, edge of base, plot limit, road centerline, or column designations and coordinates.

For equipment coordinates, tagging should be done for vertical equipment and for horizontal equipment such as knock-out drums; nozzle locations; platforms, including number and elevation;

and ladder orientation. For horizontal vessels, the vessel number, actual diameter, model diameter, and nozzle rating and facing are given; nozzle locations in manways are identified; and centerline and platform elevations given. For pumps and compressors, equipment number designation; centerline elevation of shaft; all nozzle information, including centerline and suction or discharge rating; and elevation of face or flanged centerline are given. For fans and blowers, equipment number designation, centerline elevation of shaft piping tags, and a pipe spacing scale should be provided. These should be established at each end of the pipe rack on each base, beginning at the stanchion with the lower coordinates. Other piping tags that are necessary include coordinates for locating pipe on pipe racks, and general pipeline tags, which should appear on all lines and include their line size number, specification, and direction of flow. A spec break tag may be required, fitting-to-fitting

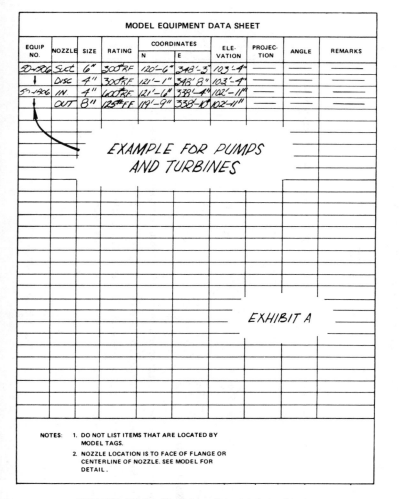

FIGURE 18-9 Model equipment data sheet.

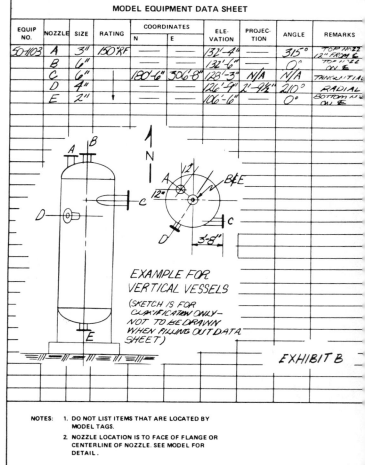

FIGURE 18-10 Model equipment data sheet.

tag, elevation tag, working point tagging, steam trap assembly tagging, continuous tag, and utility station tag.

Many modelers also tag the tees and branch connections, fitting variations, and specialty items, such as strainers and expansion joints.

Insulation tagging is also important and should be provided for with insulation sleeves. A white sleeve is used for hot insulation and a purple sleeve for cold insulation. The thickness tag should appear on pipe insulation only when more than 4″ thick. Personnel protection, modeled as white insulation sleeve, should be tagged. Steam tracing is a light blue insulation sleeve and should receive appropriate tagging, as should electrical tracing (green insulation sleeve).

Electrical tags include electrical tray number, bottom of tray elevation, motor control centers, switch gears, and transformers. Also, a variety of equipment is shown with the position of the tag only, including junction boxes, welding receptacles, pushbuttons, and permanent telephone jacks.

Instrumentation tags include instrument or tray rack number, bottom of tray or rack elevation, instrument control panel or console number and location, transmitters, and other large instrument equipment. Also, in-line instruments should be shown, such as orifice location, control valve, relief valve, pressure safety valve, pressure instruments, pressure/temperature alarm, level alarm, and level recorder. All instrumentation should be tagged where appropriate.

Heating, ventilation, and air conditioning should also be tagged accurately, including ducts, expansion joints, fans, blowers, and other HVAC equipment.

For ductwork, tagging should include:

- Elevation to TOD (top of duct) or BOD (bottom of duct), depending on which will become the controlling factor. For round or oval ducts, the centerline elevation should be used.
- When tagging ducts with size specifications, give the size on the side of the tag first, then the hidden size (example: 36″ × 18″). (*Note:* This also applies to square ducts.)
- Reducing areas of ducts should give the size at both ends of change for each size of duct.
- Give the major/minor axis dimensions for eliptical and flat oval ducting.
- Give the diameter of round ducts.
- Support equipment for duct work must be tagged.
- Doors, grills, handles, and accessways must be tagged.
- Give the centerline of duct floor penetrations from the coordinates or column centerlines.

Tagging must include all structural items, such as column centerlines, bottom of steel or top of steel, floor elevations, and truss elevations.

Placing a north arrow tag on every floor is also common practice for multilevel projects, usually to the high point of the floor (HPOF).

The following is a typical company specification for tagging the design model.

- Accurate complete tagging is essential for isometric take-offs, equipment ordering and placement, computer take-offs, and all associated engineering drawings (pipe supports, etc.).
- Essential tagging procedures:
  —Pipe designer, model maker, and appro-

MODEL EQUIPMENT DATA SHEET

EQUIP NO.	NOZZLE	SIZE	RATING	N	E	ELEVATION	PROJECTION	ANGLE	REMARKS
				COORDINATES					
?-1202	A	3″	150#RF	200'-0″	323'-4″	108'-9″	—	—	
	B	1″		200'-3″	324'-6″	108'-9″	—	—	
	C	1″		190'-1″	328'-6″	110'-3″	—	—	TANGENTIAL
	D	3″		192'-10″	—	—	4'-1″	315°	
	E	6″		191'-6″	324'-6″	—	4'-3″	0°	

EXAMPLE FOR HORIZONTAL VESSELS

(SKETCH IS FOR CLARIFICATION ONLY — NOT TO BE DRAWN WHEN FILLING OUT DATA SHEET)

EXHIBIT C

NOTES:
1. DO NOT LIST ITEMS THAT ARE LOCATED BY MODEL TAGS.
2. NOZZLE LOCATION IS TO FACE OF FLANGE OR CENTERLINE OF NOZZLE. SEE MODEL FOR DETAIL.

FIGURE 18-11 Model equipment data sheet.

FIGURE 18-12 Plan view of tagging on design model.

priate electrical, HVAC, etc., designers will aid in isometric preparation and computer ordering from final model.
—Tagging should be as complete as possible (prior to delivery to design floor) by the model shop.
—Tag piping, equipment, HVAC, etc., after fabrication and as soon as installed on model (in some cases before).
—Place tags to read from north or west where possible.
—Project dimensions must be established from calculations, then tagged on the model (do not scale model for elevations or coordinates).
—Give centerline elevations for pipe, round ducting, and electrical conduit when applicable B.O.L. can be used (if necessary).
• Structural and equipment:

—Give steel shape dimensions with tagging.
—Give T.O.S. for platform elevations.
—Tag all nozzles for elevation and identification.
—Show suction and discharge (S or D) for pumps.
• Pipeline tags:
—Give line number, flow direction, and identification on each line (in general after each change of pipe direction and elevation change); also include size and specification.
—Typical line number:
3"S—1814—3 JAX
3" size
S Material or System I.D.
1814 Line Number
3 Code/Pressure, etc.
JAX Insulation/Jacketing

QUIZ

18-1. Why is tagging necessary for models?

18-2. Name six types of equipment that need tagging.

18-3. Is vertical or horizontal lettering more common on models?

18-4. What are model equipment data sheets, and what information is usually shown on them?

18-5. Who usually tags the model?

18-6. What tagging is done in the model shop?

18-7. List five specifications for tagging the model.

18-8. Is insulation tagged on a normal model?

18-9. What information should be contained on duct tagging?

18-10. Are all structural items tagged?

18-11. What is a pipeline tag, and what information does it usually give?

19

Checking the Model

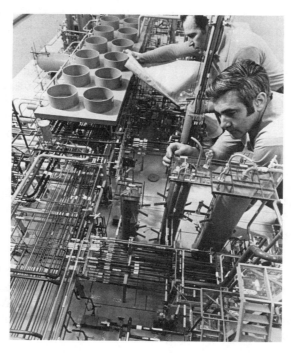

FIGURE 19-1

This chapter discusses the different types of checking that occur on a model project.

INFORMAL CHECKING METHODS

Two checking methods, which have developed hand in hand with modeling, can best be described as "informal." These informal types of checking, which evolve from the three-dimensional reality of the model, are known as continuous checking and spontaneous checking. Both types have proven themselves to be direct benefits of modeling.

Continuous checking occurs on a drafted project, but to a negligible extent compared to a model project. On a drafted project, the designer and drafters will continuously recheck as a natural function of responsibility. On the other hand, their immediate supervisors rarely check. On a model, however, the people who have direct responsibility can check any aspect of the model, from overall progress to individual configurations, simply by walking by or looking at it from a few yards away.

The second type of informal checking, indigenous almost exclusively to models, is spontaneous checking. Because of the physical reality of the model, almost everyone who walks by, regardless of their true responsibilities, will have comments or suggestions. Care must be taken to channel such suggestions so that the designer will not be needlessly disturbed and yet allow for meaningful ideas to be incorporated. Consideration should also be given to the point at which to "freeze" the design so that the changes in striving for sheer "perfection" can be minimized.

FORMAL CHECKING

"Formal" checking also occurs on a model project, and it is this type of checking that parallels the classic method applied to a drafted project. That is, every piece of information must be checked against control documents and specifications, and every item must be checked as to the physical accuracy of configuration and location. Model procedures themselves are also checked, such as correct color coding and tagging.

The physical procedure of model checking is simple. The most widely used method is to use a yellow highlight (transparent) felt-tipped pen. As a tag is determined to be correct, it is marked with the pen. The yellow marker only takes care of the correct tags. Notes must be kept on the incorrect ones, indicating their location, exactly what is wrong with them, and how to correct it. If the notes are numbered, the incorrect items can be "flagged" with that number, making them easier to locate for correction and also requiring less locating information on the notes themselves.

Following is the order in which the different phases of formal model checking should proceed.

Checking of Basic Model Layout

Using the latest issue of the model index drawings or a marked-up plot plan drawing which defines the size and location of each model table top, the first step after completion of the layout of all major structures and equipment is to perform a checking operation. This check should be performed by a person other than the one who actually laid out the table top. The following items should be checked at this stage:

- All coordinates that have been established for the laying out of lines.
- All coordinates that have been established for equipment limits.
- All coordinates that have been laid out for structural centerlines.

- All coordinates for the layout of all the main structural columns.
- Identification of the table base.
- Presence of the north arrow.
- Location and layout of roads and other civil-related items.
- Location and layout of architecturals, such as building walls.

All tagging with the above-mentioned coordinates should be checked.

Completion of Basic Model Check

The next level of checking occurs after completion of the basic model. As mentioned previously, the basic model level of completion will vary a great deal depending upon such items as availability of equipment, scheduling, and information flow. It is probably a rarity that a basic model would be 100 percent complete by the time it is turned over to the design floor to install piping. However, it must be noted that the release to the design floor at less than 100 percent of completion must be done only with the approval of the project engineer. In the event that a model is not complete, a formal record of incomplete items must be given to the basic model checker prior to the start of checking. A copy of this list should also be given to the project engineer.

The accuracy of the model at this point is critical. All the design effort to follow is dependent on the information conveyed on this basic model. Resist the tendency to begin immediately with piping design. Check the basic model.

- All tags must be checked using a plot plan, equipment drawings, and structural sketches or drawings. All tags must be checked for accuracy and completeness as well as just being present.
- Not only must all information on tags be checked, but the actual physical location of what the tags are referring to must be checked by measuring. A tag could be correct but the equipment mounted incorrectly or a nozzle oriented incorrectly.
- Use vendor prints or equipment drawings to check equipment.
- Structures and pipeways are checked for actual configuration and approximate member sizes as well as location and elevations.

The person doing the checking should not change any tags or other items deemed to be incorrect. Any corrections should be performed by the personnel who fabricated the model. Those items which were found to be incorrect should be checked again after they have been corrected on the model. After this check, piping design can begin.

At various stages, reviews will take place. The next formal check will occur at approximately 90 percent of completion of a base or a related area, and after a formal review. This is the check that precedes isometric drafting. A thorough, full-blown check is necessary at this point to assure fast and accurate production of issuable isometrics. The advantages directly attributable to a checked model are reduced checking and correcting time on isometrics (they require only a simple mathematical verification against the checked model and a visual verification of completeness and configuration), faster issue of "isos" to the fabricators, less questions from the field, and, probably most important, reduced "lost time" in the field caused by conflicting information or actual mistakes requiring changes.

Checking after Completion of Piping

The checking function that occurs at this stage of the design model in most cases is considered to be only a spot check for major errors. The critical check for the completed model comes during the checking of the isometrics. However, in the event that isometrics will not be drawn, the complete checking procedure as described in the next section occurs at this level. The checking that normally occurs at this level is stated below.

- Check for the presence of all tags and equipment markings.
- Check all major and/or alloy lines against the P&ID.
- Check all safety items for proper tagging.
- Check the model against the flow sheet to assure complete agreement.
- Check the electrical conduit drawings to ensure proper tag information of model conduits and all other electrical items.

Checking of Piping Isometric Drawings

At this stage of the design model program, a complete and thorough checking procedure must be carried out to maintain and assure an accurate model. Special attention must be given to heavy-wall, large-diameter alloy stress-relieved piping, and piping to stress relieved vessels. The following items should be checked at this level.

- Check isometric drawings for conformance with piping and instrument diagrams for the following:
  —Line number, size, line specification, insulation, steam tracing, and direction of flow
  —Equipment numbers
  —Instrument connections and numbers
  —Valve size and type
- Check for compliance with piping, instrumentation, and all other applicable specifications and/or standard drawings.
- Check the model against equipment drawings and data sheets for correct nozzle sizes and ratings.
- Check for correct arrangement of connections of special equipment, control valves, and multiport valves.
- Check for correct nozzle orientation, accessibility, interferences, and proper clearances.
- Check that the necessary vents, drains, and traps are indicated on the model.
- Check that required coordinates and essential dimensions are correct, utilizing the model coordinate tags and simultaneously checking against the model.
- Check the material list of the isometrics against the model.
- Check the model against the flow sheets and assure complete agreement.
- Check the electrical conduit drawings to ensure proper tag information of model conduits.

Any errors found by the checker should be pointed out to the individual originating the isometric. Should a model change be required, it must be done by the piping designer rather than by the checker or the person producing the isometrics. In the event that designer and checker disagree on design, disagreements will be resolved by the project engineer. This procedure creates a system of checks and balances in addition to developing the person making the isometrics together with the piping designer and checker. In the event that a model change is made, the isometric must be redrawn from the model and run through another check by the checker.

When the final check is complete, the checker will mark the predetermined color code on each line number tag and other data tags that have been checked on isometrics. The checker must sign the tracings and return them to the lead designer for review and official approval.

Some companies that utilize computer-generated isometric systems have minimized their checking both at the "before-isometric" and "after-isometric" checking stages. They are relying very heavily on the computer's ability to make sure that all the inputs from all the isometrics fit together to establish a complete process.

Following is a list of items that also need to be checked on all modeled projects:

- Model should be checked in relationship to the process flow diagram (line number, identification).
- Check that all lines are correctly numbered and tagged (review line list).
- Check model in relationship to vendor-supplied drawings for equipment configuration, size, and identification number.
- All electrical items should be checked in accordance with the electrical drawings provided.
- Electrical conduit schedule, size, and number should be compared to the model procedures and tagging.

- All HVAC information must be checked on both the drawings and model (duct dimensioning, configuration).
- All equipment should be checked with regard to the placement, location, and proper configuration.
- All instrumentation should be checked in accordance with the P&ID and instrumentation drawings (numbers, codes, etc.).
- Models should be checked in relation to the pipe design drawings that have been completed.
- Models should be checked for proper tagging.
- Lighting (when shown on model) must be checked with lighting layout drawings.
- Any relevant architectural and civil design information should be checked with modeled aspects.
- The flow sheet should be checked to see if insulation has been properly represented.
- Check all miscellaneous drawings for the project (structural platforms, penetration details, major pipe supports, ducting, special equipment).

QUIZ

19-1. Who usually checks the model?

19-2. At which stages is the model usually checked?

19-3. Name five considerations in the checking of the piping.

19-4. Why is it necessary to check the piping isometric?

19-5. Name six items that must be checked on a typical model.

20

Model Photography

FIGURE 20-1 Catalytic reformer and hydrofiner unit—aerial view.

The use of photography in engineering modeling is probably one of the most underdeveloped techniques or tools that is presently being used in the engineering model industry. Model photographs, when properly planned, can be a powerful aid both in construction planning and recording of alternative and final equipment and piping arrangements.

Engineering model photographs are commonly used for:

- Sales
- Evaluation of alternative preliminary equipment arrangements
- Construction planning
- Model progress evaluation
- Record of plan view (Fig. 20-1)
- Record of elevation views
- Record of congested areas (Fig. 20-9)
- Record of overall view (Fig. 20-4)

Currently, both Polaroid and professional-quality photographs are being used as an engineering tool or for design recording of engineering modeling projects.

Probably the most common use of photography in modeling is to record alternative equipment arrangements on a preliminary model.

Polaroid shots are totally adequate for this purpose. Using a Polaroid, these "record drawings" can be produced for well under $2 per copy for all labor and material. You cannot purchase much of a sketch or drawing for $2. It is good practice to obtain a professional photographer for record photographs of completed preliminary models. Good photographs are also an excellent aid in communication to the client for prepreliminary model review meetings and/or proposals.

One use of modeling that is just starting to receive wide attention is construction planning. When used for construction planning, the model is fabricated in the same sequence that actual construction will occur. Scale cranes are often used to work out sequence of installation and the movement of large equipment items. Photographs are made of the model at various construction stages. Several photographs are often made from different angles of congested areas. These photographs, together with appropriate written instructions, serve as a construction planning guide to the field construction personnel and become part of the engineering definition. Professional-quality photographs rather than Polaroids are recommended for this purpose.

Another use of photographs is to record job progress. Although photographs cannot completely define job status, they act as a good supplementary tool.

Photographs are frequently used to record

field changes. Where an existing plant is to be expanded or altered, photographs can be taken, blown up, dimensioned, and used as background information from which to build an "as-built" model. The new expansion can now be modeled as an extension or part of the as-built model.

Engineering model critics probably speak loudest about the lack of a permanent record of final engineering design on totally modeled projects. This is where photography can play an important role. Using proper lighting techniques and a professional photographer, high-quality plan, elevation, and overall photographic records can be achieved. Color photographs are excellent to depict the various color-coded piping systems.

One of the difficulties of photography, particularly in attempting to achieve good plan views, is parallax. This is the running together of planes caused by the short focal length between the lens and the model (see Figs. 20-1 and 20-2). Several approaches have been made (some with a good degree of success) to overcome this problem, but they have all been very sophisticated and expensive. Until a breakthrough is made in this area, most companies will continue to ignore the problem.

If photographic techniques are going to be employed as a means of providing permanent records of engineering design information, tags should be located to permit easy photographic recognition. Also, sections of a model can be made

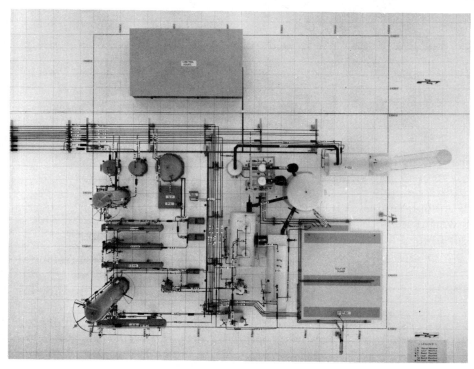

FIGURE 20-2 Gas treating and sulphur recovery unit—aerial view. Plan view of centerline piping model. Notice that this photograph looks more like a drawing and is easier to read than full-bore piping photographs.

removable in order to photograph piping and/or equipment arrangements in congested areas. Scale men should be placed at appropriate locations about the model to demonstrate head clearances, accessibility of valves and safety equipment, and to indicate proportions. Where possible, a backdrop should be used to eliminate unrequired background and also to improve the photographic lighting conditions. With the use of white plexiglass model bases, backlighting can be employed to improve contrast and detail.

Once acceptable plan-view photographs are obtained, reproductions can be made and handled very much like regular drawings.

Although removable or folding-model base table legs are highly recommended for all model base tables, they are mandatory for model base tables that are going to be photographed in order to obtain acceptable plan-view photographs with minimum camera rigging.

Some work has been done in making isometrics through photographic techniques directly from the model.

For black-and-white photographs, orthochromatic film should be used to achieve maximum color differentiation. Filters will improve color contrast and allow selective differentiation. Highlights can be eliminated with the use of dulling spray. Some key factors to remember before taking photographs are:

- Have a purpose for the photograph and denote that purpose to the photographer.
- Determine the quality of the photograph (Polaroid or professional).
- Decide whether to use color or black-and-white film.
- Determine the extent of model detail to be shown.
- Always have north indicated and unique model table or area identification in each photograph.
- Maintain a record of the photographs.

As mentioned earlier, model photography is in its infancy; however, it is gathering momentum and is becoming a powerful engineering tool.

PHOTOGRAPHY FOR CLASS PROJECTS

Model photography is an extremely important aspect of total modeling education. By use of color coding and labeling, the model presents itself as a pictorial drawing that can be recorded through the use of photographs. Pipelines, insulation, instrumentation, HVAC equipment, and so on, all have

FIGURE 20-3 Photograph of an architectural model. (Photo courtesy of Peter Xiques, Mill Valley, CA.)

FIGURE 20-4 Design model.

FIGURE 20-5 Color coding with dark colors helps heighten contrast.

separate color codes. This color coding serves to clarify the model and facilitates accurate interpretation of the fabrication procedures.

A project that should be considered for a model student or class after the construction of a model should be to take appropriate color photographs of various portions of the model to experience the use of photography with models. A variety of views can be taken, including shots of the total model in plan view or at a 45° angle.

During construction of the model, each section or subassembly can also be photographed, including photographs of the model base and major equipment placement.

Detailed views can be shot of various piping configuration areas in either black and white or color. Using the photographs provided in this text, the student should get an idea of the many perspectives that are possible for shooting photographs of the model configuration.

FIGURE 20-7 Small model units are easier to photograph. (Courtesy of The Scale Model Makers, Cleveland, Tennessee.)

In general, a 35mm camera would be the best camera to use, although this is not necessary for a classroom situation. The overall size and proportions of the model should be established by the use of a student or scale in the photograph. For detailed views, scale men should be provided at advantageous points to show the relationship of the worker to the installation, as is done in a variety of photographs provided in the text.

Views, lighting, positions of the camera, color versus black and white, lighting, scale, view, and type of film and camera must all be taken into account when photographing the model.

The student and instructor must be aware of the three most important variables in model photography:

- Background
- Equipment
- Lighting

A dull, off-white background paper or cloth can be used in most cases with excellent results. The model should be positioned so that no clutter or other objects are recorded on the film. For the best possible photographs with a minimum of distortion, an 8 × 10 view camera is suggested, especially where enlargements are necessary. For

FIGURE 20-6 This photograph demonstrates the problems with shadows encountered when photographing models.

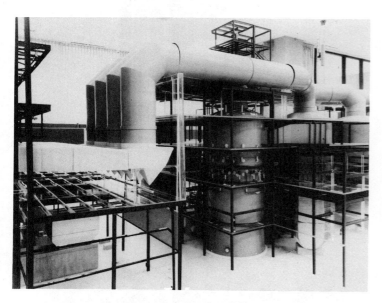

FIGURE 20-8   Photograph of large power plant.

the classroom, a Polaroid or 35mm camera is quite sufficient. A short-focal-length lens will give more perspective than will a long-focal-length lens. For plan views, it is usually preferred to have less perspective, as with most engineering model photographs, although space may make a wide angle (short focal length) essential. A high-contrast black and white or color film such as Plus-X or Tri-X 400, or Kodacolor ASA-400 will allow shooting in soft, low-level lighting, thereby eliminating the need for flash equipment.

An attempt to eliminate shadows by use of multiple light sources, white backgrounds, and floodlights bounded off white cards will give the best all-around photographs.

Because of the maze of piping, equipment,

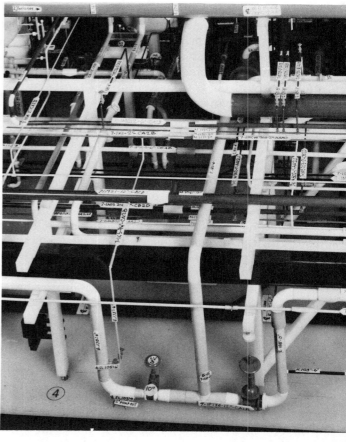

FIGURE 20-9   Closeup photograph of model.

and structural items on the typical model, it is extremely hard to photograph without getting unwanted shadows.

Adequate lighting, backdrops, and the right equipment in combination can achieve professional results.

QUIZ

20-1.   What are model photographs most commonly used for when using the model method?

20-2.   What types of cameras are used for recording the model?

20-3.   Are model photographs usually done in black and white or color?

20-4.   What types of photographs are usually taken of preliminary models?

20-5.   Why is it difficult to obtain good plan views of models in photographs?

20-6.   Why is it important to use removable or folding-model base legs for models that are to be photographed?

21

Model Finalization Crating and Shipping

FIGURE 21-1 Design model ready to be crated. (Courtesy of Design Specialities, Pittsburgh, Pennsylvania.)

FINALIZATION

Finalization of the model reflects the last step of the program before crating or shipping. Finalization means exactly what the word implies. Every item on the model is squared up, correctly oriented or adequately braced, then permanently bonded. Damaged or smeared tags are replaced and "yellowed out."

The model is cleaned as well as possible within practical limits, as follows:

- Dust should be blown off. In this connection, a reversed vacuum cleaner has the approxi-

mate maximum pressure that should be used to achieve blow-off without causing damage.
- Dirt and smudges on the base tops are removed with rags and home-type cleaning liquid.
- Solvent scars on acrylic are sanded smooth and those on ABS materials are dulled with a rubber eraser.

Incidentally, photography precedes finalization. The reason is simple. There may be removable sections that must be removed for photographic clarity. After finalization, these sections will no longer be removable. Figure 21-1 is an example of a petrochemical model after finalization and before splitting in order to crate.

The model is now ready to be released by the design department for crating and/or shipping. Figures 21-2 and 21-3 are examples of models that are small enough not to require splitting.

It should be noted that prior to this point, all personnel not heavily involved in the wrap-up of this project should have been reassigned. Actually, this is the last occasion on the design floor that the project manager has to seriously consider manpower allocation and other human factors. Generally, the best course is to have the model moved to the crating area or shipping after working hours. This will minimize lost time from people still assigned to the project.

Naturally, model finalization represents the climax of a cooperative project involving hard but challenging work. For all of those involved, it is a time of well-deserved satisfaction and inevitably kindles a spirit of celebration.

FIGURE 21-3 Small model ready for shipping. (Courtesy of The Scale Model Makers, Cleveland, Tennessee.)

CRATING AND SHIPPING

If the sections of this book were arranged in order of importance, this section would not be the last section. The material currently used to fabricate models is almost exclusively plastic. The raw materials selected to be molded and extruded into the various components were chosen for their required characteristics of strength, cementing capability, and ability to absorb shock. The finished model, properly assembled, is not delicate; however, extensive damage can easily occur to a model if sufficient shipping and crating arrangements are not made. This chapter describes some of the crating and shipping alternatives for engineering models. For purposes of this discussion, a model should be considered a fragile item. This has long been considered a big disadvantage for modeling. However, with the proper precautions, engineering models can be safely shipped. One point to remember is that a model cannot be totally protected against damage through crating and/or packing. Other stipulations and shipping precautions must be exercised.

A total evaluation of the shipping environment or environments must be made to map out an adequate shipping plan. The best approach is to simply list the temperature and weather conditions that the model will experience during transit, together with potential physical handling.

Without special precautions a model could be exposed to rain, snow, and temperature variations of up to 70° to 80° during shipments of only a few

FIGURE 21-2 Typical component assembly. This type of small unit is easy to crate compared to large design models. (Courtesy of The Scale Model Makers, Cleveland, Tennessee.)

hundred miles. In addition to possible detrimental effects of these conditions, handling damage can also occur. With the increase in distance that a model must be transported, the chances for damage due to both environment and handling increase accordingly.

Knowing the maximum environmental and handling conditions that a model can be exposed to, the best crating and shipping procedures can be designed to minimize the effects of the adverse conditions.

Preparation of Model for Shipping

Every joint between plastic model components and between model components and model base should be rebonded with the appropriate solvent or glue to ensure ultimate joint strength. Clear plastic supports may be required on large structures to minimize vibration. This is the finalization procedure covered in the preceding section.

Filament tape may be required to construct guys on tall and/or fragile equipment. Multilevel structures should be supported with tape also. When taping structures or bents, always tape along the column line or bent. Care should be taken to avoid twist or excessive stress by the application of tape.

The upper sections of a tall vessel which were planned to separate for shipping should be placed on saddles and strapped to the base. If there is not sufficient room on the base to accommodate this equipment, another crate should be provided.

Shock Test

If rough handling is anticipated, a series of shock tests should be performed on the uncrated model after the filament tape has been attached. Rough handling should be expected any time that a model is shipped on commercial carriers in the crated condition. The shock-test procedure is outlined below.

- Elevate one end of table 2″ to 3″ off the floor and drop. Observe for excessive vibrations and loose connections.
- Carry out this procedure a sufficient number of times on each end of model table to ensure that all loose connections and/or potential weak spots are located.
- Between each drop test, make necessary repairs to model. This includes the addition of solvent, bodied glue, clear plastic supports, and/or filament tape.

- Repeat drop tests as described above, except elevate to 4″ to 6″ before dropping. After repairs or reinforcements are completed, the model is ready for crating.

Crating

In the event that it is determined that crating is required to protect the model during shipment, the following crating procedure offers maximum protection in situations containing the highest expected incidence of adverse conditions. See-through openings covered with heavy wire mesh and polyethelene film should be located in two opposing sides or ends of the crate so that anyone handling or transporting it can see the apparently fragile contents (see Fig. 21-4).

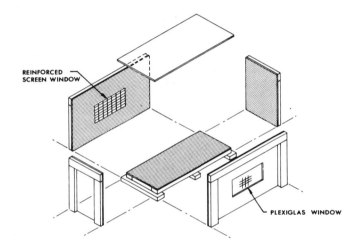

FIGURE 21-4 Model shipping crate.

Crate dimensions

- Inside dimensions shall be 2″ clear from all points of model. This will determine bottom panel dimensions.
- All panels are 3/8″ plywood sheathing.
  —Bottom panel is completely framed with 2″ × 4″ lumber, nailed together.
  —Bottom should have two or three skids, depending on crate length, extending 1-1/8″ beyond the sides and ends. These are to facilitate handling with a fork lift and are of 2″ × 4″ lumber.
  —Assemble bottom panel with 4d and 16d nails.
- End panels are framed with 1″ × 4″ stock lumber on top and sides, and are the width of the bottom panel.
- Side panels are framed with 1″ × 4″ stock

lumber on top and sides, and are the length of the bottom plus both ends.

- Side and end panels are assembled with 4d nails, with nail penetrations crimped.
- Top panel is to maximum dimensions of crate and is unframed.

Crate assembly details

- Assemble the end panels to the bottom with nails, resting the bottom edge of the ends against the skid extension.
- Screw the sides and top onto the ends and bottom, using #10 1-1/2" round-head wood screws and a flat steel washer with each screw. All screws securing these three panels will be daubed with red paint to facilitate uncrating. All screw holes should be pilot-drilled to prevent splitting.
- Handles should be provided on the ends of crates approximately 2" to 4" above the bottom of the crate. Install on crates with 1/4-20 stove bolts and flat steel washers.

Securing and packing model

- Model should be cushioned on 3" rolls of single-faced corrugated cardboard or squares of 3" high-density foam rubber. These cushions are placed in the bottoms of cases to contact sleepers and corners of the model base. The length of the model base will determine the number of cushions to be used. Cushions should be spaced not more than 2' apart at the most.
- Additional protection can be accomplished by the application of packing "worms" after the model has been secured to the crate. If "worms" are used, sift them into the crate so that maximum contact to the model is achieved. Fill to within 1" of crate top. A disadvantage of "worms" is that they are troublesome to remove when uncrating.
- Securing blocks (model securing block, Fig. 21-5) should then be screwed into place.
- Blocks should have cushions between them and the model base. Calculate the height of

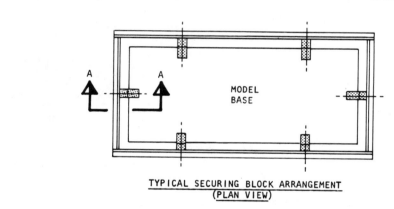

TYPICAL SECURING BLOCK ARRANGEMENT
(PLAN VIEW)

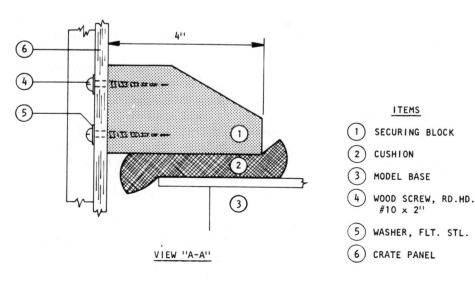

VIEW "A-A"

ITEMS

1. SECURING BLOCK
2. CUSHION
3. MODEL BASE
4. WOOD SCREW, RD.HD. #10 x 2"
5. WASHER, FLT. STL.
6. CRATE PANEL

FIGURE 21-5 Model securing block.

the block to ensure foam compression of one-half its thickness.

- Blocks and crates should be marked for easy replacement of blocks in the event reshipment is necessary.

Crate marking and identification

Crates shall be marked in large letters "THIS SIDE UP," "FRAGILE," and "DO NOT DROP," together with the name and address of shipper and receiver. "TIP (N) TELL" arrows should be attached on the four vertical surfaces of the crate. This is a unique mechanism that makes a permanent record if the crate is excessively tipped.

"TIP (N) TELL"   Index Packages, Inc.
    Supplier: 5048 Ridge Road
                Horseheads, New York 14845
                Phone (607) 739-4276

Uncrating procedure

- First, open the small crate or cardboard carton of supplies. It will normally contain:
  —Model base legs (for tables other than the metal with folding legs). The attaching hardware is with the model bases. The legs are adjustable and therefore are interchangeable.
  —A photograph or base index drawing, showing the model base divisions as a guide to assembly.
  —A parts kit, including plastic solvent and applicator, pointers, scale men, scale rules —butt ended, parts and paint kit if requested, and line and instrument tags.
- Remaining crates are to be opened by removal of red painted screws only.
  —Remove the crate tops first by taking out the red painted screws; there are no nails to remove in uncrating.
  —Remove the sides in the same manner.
  —Remove the model base hold-down blocks.
  —Remove the model base and bolt on the legs —consult photograph if available.
- Remove "worms" that are stuck in model by carefully dislodging them with a pointer or pencil. Use care not to knock loose tagging. After clearing the model of "worms," blow off loose packing and dust.

Should the model be set up in a field office, a fence is desirable to protect the model. The fence should be high enough and strong enough to lean on and provide access for people using the model.

Selecting the Mode of Transportation

Present modes of transportation and their frequency of use are listed below:

Mode of transportation	Order of frequency used
Covered truck/van	1
Air freight	2
Railroad	3
Ship	4

When evaluating the modes of transportation for shipping, getting the model to a predetermined destination on schedule ranks high above cost of shipping and other considerations. Models should be insured, if possible. However, some difficulty has been experienced in negotiating insurance policies that are meaningful.

Regardless of the mode of transportation, it is highly desirable for a company representative to accompany the model, or at least be present when it arrives on the site. Preferably, this person should have sufficient model experience to know how much handling a model can withstand without being damaged. They should also be capable of assisting in setting up the model at its destination and making any repairs.

The type or configuration of a model should be a consideration in determining the mode of transportation. For example, a preliminary model can normally be shipped as safely by rail, air, or van with proper packing and/or crating. However, a model with tall towers and/or structures, being more susceptible to damage, should be shipped by van, if possible. Obviously, van shipment cannot be made to overseas destinations. Air would be the next alternative, and ocean-going vessels the last.

Very frequently, when a model is to be shipped a relatively short distance (1000 miles or less), crates are not used. The models are set on folded moving pads on the floor of an air-cushion suspension van and strapped in place to prevent shifting. Utilization of van shipping minimizes handling and exposure of models to adverse weather conditions. Generally, van shipment is more costly than air freight and takes more time. For long distances or overseas shipping, the use of crates is necessary.

In the event that rail or even ocean vessel

shipment is required, sufficient additional precautions must be made to minimize shipping damage.

Rail shipping can be planned for by increasing the clearance inside the crate, using more and thicker foam shock absorbers, and using thicker plywood and $2'' \times 4''$ bracing. This method of shipping is not recommended unless special handling is assured.

Ocean shipping should only be considered if crates are not to be handled as general cargo, and only if special accommodations such as a cabin or stateroom are provided.

QUIZ

21-1. Name four steps in the finalization of the model.

21-2. Why is it important for models to be adequately crated?

21-3. How does temperature affect models, and why should this be taken into account when crating and shipping?

21-4. How should joints be prepared before crating the model?

21-5. What is a shock test, and why is it used?

21-6. Give four specifications for a typical model crate.

21-7. Why does the type of transportation method and distance affect the crating procedure?

22

Model Reviews

FIGURE 22-1   Closeup view of design model.

This section is meant primarily for industry, but it will also help the student see the process of industrial modeling from a company perspective. It is not necessary to include this section in a model course.

This section deals with the overall purpose of and procedures for planning and carrying out model review meetings.

The main purpose of a model review meeting is to perform an in-depth evaluation of the model and process design progress. There are two basic types of review meetings: in-house and client.

IN-HOUSE REVIEW MEETINGS

Without exception, each client review must be preceded by an in-house review. It is imperative that all in-house differences be resolved and the best solution be presented to the client with a "unified design team approach." A wide participation must be included on each in-house review to achieve the best design approach. Therefore, all engineering disciplines, construction, estimating, management, and other applicable groups must be represented at the in-house reviews.

Scheduling of in-house reviews should allow for adequate time for a follow-up in-house review meeting or meetings to settle differences that surface in the initial in-house review prior to the client review.

CLIENT REVIEW MEETINGS

Like the model itself, the client review meeting serves as a medium or tool for optimum communication. When planning for client review meetings, client satisfaction should be kept foremost. Clients, in general, are most interested in seeing what they are getting for their money. This should be broken down to percentage job completion versus job dollars expended. Along the same line, a complete design status must be presented. Review meetings serve as an excellent time to formalize, document, and resolve points of conflict and/or design proposals to the client. However, review meetings cannot and must not be substituted for the day-to-day and week-to-week communication with the client. A good rule of thumb to remember is that the client, like you, does not like to be hit with surprises. Again, it must be emphasized: don't save potential problems for the review meetings. Sample agendas for client review meetings are included in this section.

FORMALITY OF REVIEW MEETINGS

A wide range of formality is practiced for both in-house and client review meetings. Obviously, in-house meetings are less formal than client meetings. It is recommended that a degree of formality be established for each meeting that will appropriately communicate job status. The degree of formality will vary somewhat depending on the client's wishes. For example, some clients attending a meeting and seeing a large group of engineers and management can only think of the money that the meeting is costing them. On the other hand, some clients like to hear firsthand reports from the various engineering disciplines and project groups.

The following degree of formality is considered necessary in planning for both in-house and client review meetings:

- Published meeting invitation (at least two weeks in advance)
- Published meeting agenda
- Predetermined note keeper

FREQUENCY OF REVIEW MEETINGS

The proper frequency of review meetings is subject to varied opinions. Accepted practice dictates a minimum of two client review meetings. It then follows that there would be a minimum of two in-house review meetings. Scheduling for these two meetings are as follows:

- Preliminary model review
- Piping design model review

However, there is no set number of reviews. The frequency of reviews is dependent on plant size, complexity, type, use of model, desirability of separate discipline reviews, and client/design company relationship, together with project engineer and client wishes.

Plant size: Obviously, large plant projects require more frequent reviews, simply from the standpoint of increased liaison and coordination.

Plant complexity: A very complex, tightly arranged piping system will take more coordination and client consultation than will a straightforward, uncongested area. For example, a tank farm portion of a project takes very little review and coordination as compared to a complex chemical plant with large amounts of alloy and/or heavy wall pipe, which must be reviewed and approved early.

Plant type: The uniqueness of the process that is being modeled dictates the frequency of review. Proven process designs require fewer reviews than those that are new and/or just being developed.

Use of model: Models that require client approval at early design stages require additional reviews. For example, models that are utilized for construction planning and scheduling require several client reviews.

Desirability of separate discipline reviews: On very large complex plants it is often beneficial to set up separate reviews for such functions as civil, electrical, lighting, safety, and maintenance.

Client/design company relationship: Such

traits as personalities and design philosophies will often dictate the quantity of reviews. Where a long-established mode of operation and trust has been built up between the client and customer, fewer reviews are required.

Project engineer and client wishes: Based on all of the above, the project engineer and client should determine during the bidding stage of each project the number of reviews and an approximate review schedule.

PRELIMINARY MODEL REVIEW

In-House Review

The main purpose of a preliminary model is to determine the ultimate equipment arrangement and the location for major and/or critical lines. Equipment, related facilities, operational requirements, safety, flow sheet data, and other design criteria are all involved in the development of a preliminary model.

Only after several arrangements have been evaluated and recorded with appropriate Polaroid photographs and the optimum arrangement is reconstructed on the model should the in-house preliminary model review be scheduled.

The importance of this in-house review cannot be overemphasized. This meeting is scheduled and carried out by the project engineer. Management, process, design, construction, startup, safety, maintenance, and other groups that can provide valuable input to the overall plant design, construction, and operations should be involved.

After all comments and questions from the in-house preliminary design review have been fully evaluated and the preliminary design is optimized, the client preliminary design review is ready to be scheduled. Sufficient time should be allotted between in-house and client preliminary design reviews to resolve any major questions and make any necessary changes to the preliminary design model. Documentation of all discussion, proposed changes, and decisions reached, along with a list of those attending, must be typed and distributed to the meeting attendees. The meeting minutes should be distributed at least one week prior to the client review. The purpose of this is to ensure that all attendees have a clear understanding of the design that will be presented at the client preliminary model review meeting.

Client Review

It is difficult to determine which portion of any project is the most important. The client preliminary model design review may not be the most important; however, it must run a close second or third in that the major project design effort goes into motion immediately after client approval is given to the preliminary model.

Preliminary Model Review Agenda

The sample agenda on page 206 along with the items listed below provide a guide for preparing an agenda for the client's review of the preliminary model.

- Polaroid shots of alternative arrangements
- Professional photographs of proposed preliminary model
- Preliminary model reconstructed to final in-house approved design
- Set of flow diagrams

Objectives of Meeting

To present the ultimate equipment arrangement and the location of major and/or critical lines. Several equipment arrangements have been evaluated for such factors as process optimization, construction, operational requirements, safety, maintenance, and overall economy. This evaluation was conducted in three dimensions using the design model approach rather than study drawings. The selected layout has been reconstructed in preliminary model form along with record photographs. Polaroid photographs are available of some of the alternate considerations.

To secure client comments and written approval of the proposed equipment arrangement and location of major and/or critical lines.

Note: To accomplish these objectives, the agenda has been arranged to provide ample time for the client attendees to meet privately after the initial presentation.

Preliminary Model Conventions

As the name implies, the preliminary model is indeed a preliminary or temporary model. Therefore, materials utilized are very economical and of a less substantial nature than those of the design model.

Sample agenda

Client Preliminary Model Review Agenda Information

Scheduled Meeting Date _____

Project Description:

    Client's Name _____

    Project Title _____

Client's Chief Liaison:

    Name _____

    Title _____

    Mailing Address _____

    _____

Meeting Coordinator:

    Name _____

    Title _____

    Mailing Address _____

    _____

Personnel Scheduled to Attend:

Client	Design Company
_____	_____
_____	_____
_____	_____
_____	_____
_____	_____
_____	_____

Preliminary Model Dimensions

- Scale: 1/4″ = 1′0″.
- Structural: Centerline columns and beams and top of steel are accurate to within 1/8″ actual.
- Equipment: Equipment shapes and locations are accurate to within 6 scale inches overall and are constructed from foam-to-foam recognizable shapes and/or blocked foam with identification tape.
- Civil and architectural: Plot limits, roads, and major building walls are outlined with 1/16″ black tape.
- Underground: Any underground features are shown in colored 1/16″ tape.
- Structural: All primary columns and beams are modeled with preliminary model structural components. Since structural design is not critical at the preliminary model design level, all structures, whether bare steel, fire-protected, or reinforced concrete, will be depicted by the steel preliminary model structural components.

Presentations and Discussions

- Present the optimum equipment arrangement together with sufficient discussion of alternate arrangements. Include in the discussion some of the thought processes that led to the final arrangement. Include such items as:
  —Process efficiency
  —Ease of construction
  —Economy of pipe runs
  —Maintenance considerations
  —Safety
  NOTE: If at all possible, questions and/or comments should be held until after the presentation is completed. Provide material for taking notes.
- Reserve time for client questions and/or comments.
- All questions and/or controversial items should be discussed until they are resolved and the decision is recorded.
- Reserve time for client delegation to privately discuss status and resolve any questions that they may have internally.
- Secure written approval of the preliminary model design.
  Note: The atmosphere of the meeting must be such that the client will feel free to ask questions regarding any phase of the design about which he or she is the least bit apprehensive.

FINAL MODEL REVIEW

As mentioned previously, there could and probably should be intermediate reviews with the client between the preliminary model review and the final model review.

The project would be in serious financial trouble if significant design changes were required at the final model level because of poor client/design company communication. Probably 95 percent of the project funds are expended when the final model review occurs. The ultimate would be to have the model 100 percent complete and ready for isometrics at the time of client final model review. This is normally not practical, in that there are often delays in vendor information and the constant threat of design changes. Therefore, a completion level of 85 percent plus is acceptable for client final model review.

The main purpose of the in-house final model review is to ensure that all the appropriate persons have evaluated and approved the final plant design as developed on the model. Should revisions to the model result from this meeting, a follow-up meeting should be scheduled to evaluate the changed model.

The main purpose of the client's final model review is to obtain the client's comments and approval for the final plant design.

Final Model Review Agenda

The following items provide a guide for preparation of an agenda (shown on page 208) for the client's review of the final model:

- Professional-quality record photographs of the final model, including multiple-angle photographs of congested areas
- Professional-quality record photographs of approved preliminary model
- Plot plans
- Flow diagrams
- Complete model specifications

Objectives of Meeting

To present the final plant design as developed on the engineering model. Starting with the client-approved preliminary model, equipment arrangements and civil/structural coordinates were transferred to the basic model. After all equipment and structures were in place, all piping was designed and installed directly on the model, except for a minimum of study sketches. All equipment, piping, instrumentation, and electricals have been placed on the model together with sufficient tags to ready the model. Any exceptions to a completed model will be covered by the meeting coordinator.

To secure client comments and written approval of the proposed final plant design.
  Note: To accomplish these objectives, the agenda has been arranged to provide ample time for the client attendees to meet privately after the initial presentation.

Presentations and Discussions

- Present the overall project status. The following shall be included:
  —Percent complete
  —Percent budget funds expended
  —Estimated completion dates
  —Estimated funds to be expended
  —Restraints that hinder timely completion of model

Sample agenda

Client Final Model Review Agenda Information

Scheduled Meeting Date _____

Project Description:

    Client's Name _____

    Project Title _____

Client's Chief Liaison:

    Name _____

    Title _____

    Mailing Address _____

    _____

Meeting Coordinator:

    Name _____

    Title _____

    Mailing Address _____

    _____

Personnel Scheduled to Attend:

Client	Design Company
_____	_____
_____	_____
_____	_____
_____	_____
_____	_____
_____	_____

- Present the overall equipment and plant layout. Trace the thought process that was utilized to get from the preliminary model to the final model. This would be handled as a transfer of information, not a justification of the design. Review the model specifications. The following items should be included:
  —Process efficiency
  —Ease of construction
  —Economy of pipe runs
  —Maintenance considerations
  —Safety
  —Operation
  —Structural layout
  —Electrical layout
  —HVAC layout
  —Private meeting
- The highlights of the process should be traced through the plant from major equipment item to major equipment item.
  Note: If at all possible, questions or comments should be held until after the

presentation is complete or until a line-by-line review of the model is held.

- Reserve time for client questions and/or comments.
- Reserve time for the client delegation to privately discuss status and resolve any questions that they may have internally.

- Secure written approval of the final model design.

  Note: The atmosphere of the meeting must be such that the client will feel free to ask questions about any phase of the design of which there is the least bit of apprehension.

QUIZ

22-1. What is a preliminary model review, and why is it necessary?

22-2. What is the difference between a client and an in-house review?

22-3. What are the primary objectives of a preliminary model review?

22-4. What are the primary objectives of a final model review?

22-5. When reviewing the model for specifications, what items should be taken into account?

23

Estimating

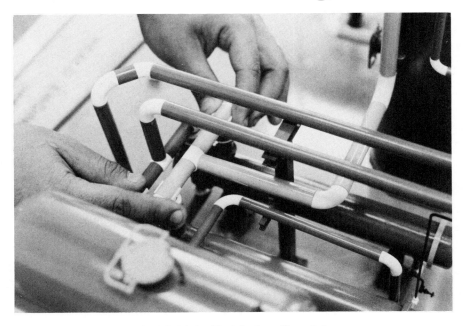

FIGURE 23-1   Modeler installing piping.

This section deals with the factors involved in estimating the cost for design and fabrication of an industry model. There are probably as many varied procedures for estimating the cost of a model as there are companies involved with models. As always, estimating the cost of a given project is of prime importance. The cost of modeling, like the cost of drafting, is dependent upon the industry and the particular type of model that is being fabricated. Even in a given industry, there are wide variations. Each company has developed its own system or procedures for creating a design concept for a plant. Needless to say, each company will try to create a design that works best for that particular company. Some companies may find that it is totally inappropriate for their purposes to produce any detail drawings as part of their basic bid package. Nevertheless, many other companies will spend hundreds of worker-hours for this purpose.

When it comes to modeling, some firms will include such detail as piping, valves, and instrumentation, which are part of a commercially available equipment package; whereas other companies will be satisfied with blocking out the commercially available equipment package and only running major lines to that equipment package. These different procedures obviously have an impact on the design cost. It does not necessarily follow that one is better than the other. In the final analysis, the overall construction costs may be more economical for a company that puts more effort into the design. Widely different types of plants and facilities, as well as the varied procedures for evolving an engineering or design definition, require that each company develop its own estimating process. This section will provide several different procedures for estimating. These procedures are provided as guides to setting up or evaluating one's own estimating system.

PRELIMINARY MODEL

The preliminary model is essentially a temporary tool. Therefore, it is usually fabricated from relatively inexpensive materials in block form. The equipment detail is of little importance, in that the emphasis is on the approximate location rather than on precision modeling. Reusable components and scrap can often be utilized on preliminary models. The relatively low cost of preliminary model materials does not normally justify rigorous cost-control techniques and/or a recording of data. For a more detailed definition of a preliminary model, see Section 13.

FINAL MODEL

For estimating purposes, the final model can be separated into two parts:

- Basic model cost
- General assembly and piping design cost

Both of these should be evaluated and/or estimated in worker-hours and materials. It is always best to reduce as many labor costs as possible back to a base of worker-hours. This will greatly facilitate the buildup of a meaningful history of comparative modeling labor costs, and provide a common base for labor cost studies within other organizations and/or companies in the modeling industry.

Basic Model

The basic model includes all model bases or tables, structures, and all equipment with nozzles and tagging in place ready for the piping to be installed. Roads, trenches, drains, and known under-

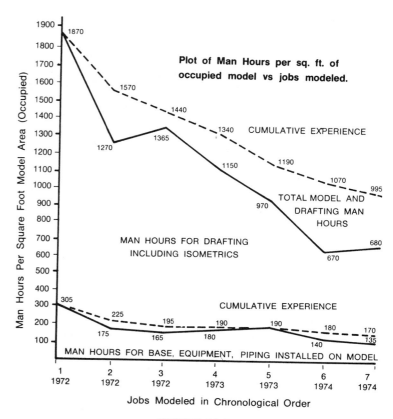

FIGURE 23-2

ground piping should be indicated on the base (with either tape or paint) whenever possible as part of the basic model.

Companies often subcontract certain portions of the basic model. This varies from a model table all the way to a completed basic model ready for piping. Care must be taken to segregate the cost of procured labor from in-house labor. For example, a company may obtain a model table with the equipment installed from a model supplier. This cost is very definitely a part of the basic model; however, it should not be included with either labor or material. It should be carried as a separate category. The main purpose of this segregation is to maintain accurate cost accounting.

As a result of late receipt of equipment information or other slow design information, structures, along with platforms, stairs, ladders, and bracing, must often be added after piping design has begun. In addition, some smaller vessels and pumps will need to be added in the design office. Occasionally, equipment must be located by the piping designer. The labor costs incurred for these additions are very difficult to identify since this work is normally performed by piping designers as part of their design effort. This increment of work is small compared to the overall total, so it can be lumped with the piping design effort. However, for

211

accurate estimating and cost accounting, it is best to break it out and include it with the basic model cost if it can be accomplished without unnecessary labor effort. The key to good estimating is good records of past model costs. On the other hand, record keeping must be tempered to ensure that the effort required is justified by the additional information.

Estimating the cost for the basic model elements, tables, equipment, and structures, is relatively straightforward, and the model shop should be required to build up statistics to cover these elements. Once a table design is chosen (or even multiple designs), costs can be determined. This cost information can easily be charted for various-size tables and design configurations. Unlike the rest of the modeling effort, material is a significant cost of the table. Even though the table material and labor is insignificant as compared to the overall cost, detailed cost control must be maintained on all elements in order to create accurate estimates and perform within those estimates.

Structures, steel interconnections, stairs, railing, and platforms can all be calculated by a count of connections and running feet based on worker-hours per connection and per running foot. This can be further refined after some experience to a "per bay of structure" cost.

The use of standard equipment drawings is mandatory if an accurate record of time and material cost is to be accomplished. In addition, standard drawings eliminate unnecessary detail and enhance uniform equipment. Another advantage is the elimination of unnecessary communication between the model shop and the design floor.

Typical ratios have been developed between the basic model cost (BMC) and the complete model cost (CMC).

Typical figures are

$$\frac{\text{BMC}}{\text{CMC}} = \text{12-1/2\% or 1:8 for refinery units and 20\% or 1:5 for chemical plants}$$

These ratios can be helpful in estimating complete model cost either from the estimated basic model cost or from the actual basic model cost. Obviously, the accuracy of these estimates is only as good as the cost accounting practices that are used on the basic model.

Assuming than an estimated basic model cost (BMC) is $2500, the final model cost can be estimated as follows:

Final model cost—chemical unit
$$= 2500 \times 5 = \$12,500$$

Final model cost—refinery unit
$$= 2500 \times 8 = \$20,000$$

It must be emphasized that these ratios can only be considered estimating guides. Wide variances can occur depending on the accuracy of basic information, changes that occur after the estimate, compactness of plant layout, and type of layout.

Piping Design and Assembly

Typically, piping and final assembly are accomplished in the same area, namely the design office. All work necessary to complete the model through the basic model stage (previously discussed) is considered piping design and assembly.

Although much of the model work performed during the final model stage is piping design, considerable worker-hours are required in other areas. Other areas may include completion of structures, location of platforms, stairs, and ladders, tagging or piping, equipment and structures, taping of underground, and periodic reviews.

Isometric Drafting

The production of piping isometrics is generally not included as a part of the cost of the model.

METHODS OF ESTIMATING COSTS

The first estimating procedure discussed applies to heavy chemical, petrochemical, and refinery-type models. The second, third, and fourth procedures deal primarily with the lighter chemical, soap, and food-processing plants. The fifth procedure is more versatile and could probably be adapted to any of the fields of design modeling.

First Method of Line-Count Estimating

This method of estimating is based on the line count from P&ID's. The line count multiplied by the worker-hours per line yields the worker-hours needed to accomplish this task. A contingency is normally included.

For purposes of establishing a line count, the following definition has been established for a line:

- A line, running from one joint to another joint (a joint means a nozzle or a tee).
- A line, running from a joint to a base split or from a base split to a joint.
- A circular line.

- A header or part of a header, running to a base split.
- A safety line with free end.
- An undivided level gauge.
- Drains and vents are counted as half a line, with the exception of those drains and vents running into a header; then it is one line. This is also the case when a drain disappears into the ground.
- Pressure and temperature connections are not counted as lines.

Based on the above-established definitions, assume a line count of 37 and 8 half lines.

$$37 \times 1 = 37$$
$$8 \times 1/2 = \underline{4}$$
$$41 \text{ lines}$$

Another way of determining a line count is to count the joints and divide by 2. Assume 82 joints from the example given above.

$$\text{Number of joints} = 82$$
$$\text{Number of lines} \quad \frac{82}{2} = 41 \text{ lines}$$

Contingency factors can include an almost endless list of uncertainties. Consideration should be given to the following when establishing contingency factors:

- Stage of P&ID
- Predicted changes in process design
- Level of difficulty expected from client
- Experience of design staff
- Experience of model design staff
- Amount of nonpiping work, such as lighting, cable trays, and structural support additions

The worker-hours per line factor is an "estimate" including two parts: the time required to design and install a line on the model, together with the final model assembly work. However, this number is more than a mere "estimate." It should be based on actual data accumulated by the company or project group that will actually design and install the piping and perform finished assembly work.

Example:

Line count from firm P&ID's	3200
Contingency for P&ID's not available	600
Contingency for process and other changes 25%	950
Total lines	4750

Assume that the factor is 2.6 hours/line from past history

Total hours for piping design on the model and general completion would be

$$4750 \times 2.6 = 12{,}350 \text{ hours}$$

Using the estimated dollars for the piping and final design work, the cost of the basic model could be estimated using the previously given ratio of BMC/CMC = 1:8 for a refinery and 1:5 for a chemical model. This could be used as a check on a basic model cost estimate that was determined by other means.

Other methods for establishing line count

One alternative is based on the assumption that there is a direct relationship between the total number of plant items and the total number of model lines. Assume that modeling experience on a certain type of plant indicates these data:

Model lines per pump	= 4
Model lines per exchanger shell and tube	= 6
Model lines per exchanger air flow	= 6
Model lines per column	= 14
Model lines per drum	= 12
Model lines per compressor	= 26
	68

$$\text{Model lines per plant item (average)} = \frac{68}{6} = 11$$

Assuming 245 equipment items, the total model lines can be estimated at

$$11 \times 245 = 2695 \text{ lines}$$

A further breakdown in this approach requires that the quantity of each plant equipment item be known.

Typical unit	Model	Lines/item	Total lines
Number of columns	12	14	168
Number of drums	20	12	240
Number of pumps	30	4	120
Number of compressors	5	26	130
Number of exchangers, shell and tube	20	6	120
Number of exchangers, air flow	10	6	60
Number of filters	5	20	100
Total model lines = 938	102		938

Over and above the worker-hours per line and contingency factors, additional worker-hours should be included for photography, crating, preparation of model for shipping, and shipping.

Second Method

One very quick method used to arrive at a rough preliminary estimate for an engineering piping model is to take 1 percent of the overall construction cost exclusive of engineering. A preliminary estimate of worker-hours may then be determined by dividing the current engineering worker-hour cost for model designers into the estimated model cost figure.

A sample listing of the approximate breakdown of worker-hours is shown for the different disciplines. It must be remembered that each organization or company must build its own data bank for each type of plant in order to generate accurate estimates.

Piping	40%
Equipment	16%
Structural	11%

Piping	= 225 lines × 2.5 hr/line	= 562.5 hours
Equipment*	= 93 pieces × 3 hr/item	= 279.0 hours
Structure	= 50 × 100 ft × .025 hr/ft²	= 125.0 hours
Ducts of chutes	= 10 ducts × 4 hr/duct	= 40.0 hours
Electrical	= 30 conduits × .9 hr/conduit	= 27.0 hours
Instrument	= 10% of piping, equipment, structures	= 97.0 hours
Code and tag	= 10% of piping, equipment, structures	= 97.0 hours
Lighting	= 50 × 100 ft × .004 hr/ft²	= 20.0 hours
Miscellaneous and unlisted	= 10% of piping, equipment, structures	= 97.0 hours
	Total	1344.5 hours

*Large equipment must be estimated separately.

Code and tag	10%
Electrical	9%
Instruments	9%
Miscellaneous	5%

Third Method

Like any estimate, the accuracy can only be as good as the accuracy of the input data. Therefore, a further refinement in estimating beyond the second method described above can be made if the following information is known:

- Piping—number of piping lines

- Equipment—number of pieces of equipment
- Structure—square footage of plant to be modeled
- Ducts or chutes—number of ducts or chutes
- Electrical—number of conduits

The information can be obtained from piping, instrument, equipment arrangement, and structural drawings.

The general formula for this estimating procedure is shown in the following list:

- Piping—2.5 hr/line
- Equipment—3 hr/piece of equipment (large equipment must be estimated separately)
- Structure—.025 hr/ft² of modeled plant size
- Ducts or chutes—4 hr/duct
- Electrical—.9 hr/conduit
- Instrument—10% of piping, equipment, and structures
- Code and tag—10% of piping, equipment, and structures
- Lighting—.004 hr/ft² (plant size)

Shown below is an example of a 50′ × 100′ plant expansion project.

Fourth Method

A fourth method of estimating involves a more detailed breakdown. This is not to imply that this fourth method is a superior method. It must be kept in mind that the accuracy of a given estimate depends on the accuracy of the input data and the application of the estimating procedure to the actual workings of the engineering group building and designing the model. This fourth procedure is offered simply as another means of estimating.

The following is a list of the unit costs for estimating worker-hours:

- Base or table—5 hr/table up to 8 ft² plus .25 hour/ft² over 8 ft²

- Structural steel and concrete—1 min/ft² per floor (scale size)
- Rectangular ductwork and conduit banks—2 min/line ft (scale size)
- Pumps—1 hr each
- Tanks—3 hr each (including nozzle orientation)
- Miscellaneous equipment—2 hr each
- Large or complicated equipment—estimate individually
- Setting equipment—15 min each
- Piping—1 hr/line from orthographic drawings
- Underground piping—1 hr/line (taped on base)
- Miscellaneous work—2 hr/ft² (actual size)
- Lights—15 sec/ft² per floor (scale size)
- Add 50% of total of above for checking, changes, unknown, etc.

Fifth Method

The fifth method is only useful to a company that has accumulated sufficient experience and data in their modeling background to plot a history of their trends and experience on how many worker-hours it takes to create design models. This procedure works best for industries that produce rather consistent types of models. For example, a company that is primarily involved with refineries could adopt this method quite effectively. However, a firm that deals with a wide variety of models, such as soap plants, food processing, chemicals, and refineries, would be required to develop a set of estimating data for each model category. Using the history from past model jobs, the worker-hours per square foot of occupied model base can be approximated. This information should come from several projects in order to establish an average for projects that had good information flow along with those where the information flow was troublesome; and projects that underwent several changes after the design had started along with projects that had few, if any, changes during the design. Using this factor of worker-hours per square foot of model base, one can then translate this information into square foot of plant and determine the overall model labor cost and/or drafting labor cost for a given project. All data should be normalized to the occupied model area rather than just to the model table area.

There are several approaches to presenting these data for best utilization. Figure 23-2 depicts the data mentioned earlier from Company XYZ. Although the actual numbers may be quite different from any other company's model program, the general shape of the curve should be similar if data from the very first model endeavors are utilized together with data from those projects where basic learning was achieved. "Cumulative experience" curves should always be plotted to account for the accumulation of the total modeling experience. This is even true for companies with established programs and trained personnel. One should always be alert to the pitfalls of estimating from any given set of curves or data. For example, job 7 on Chart V-1 shows a cumulative experience of 170 hr/ft² to build the base and equipment, and install piping on the model, while the actual figure for job 7 is 135 hr/ft². One could interpret these data to estimate the next model job at 135 hr/ft². On the other hand, a conservative approach would be to estimate at 170 hr/ft².

To make an accurate estimate, it is best to look at the total shape of the curve and relate the job under consideration to other jobs, trying to find a similar one. For example, even if the job under consideration is similar in design requirements to job 7, it must be remembered that client review and information flow was ideal and that it probably will not be as good for the next job. Therefore, 170 hr/ft² would probably be more accurate than 135 hr/ft².

A further step that could be taken on this approach is to maintain separate cumulative experience curves for equipment and piping installation. Cost to either build or procure bases should be very easy to establish once a base design is established.

MATERIAL COSTS

On most modeling projects, the cost of the model materials is almost insignificant compared to the labor costs. Therefore, material estimating accuracy is not required. One method that is commonly used is to factor the model worker-hours per square foot by $1.25 to determine the estimated material costs. This factor only holds true where normal model detail is required. Some projects may require twice the labor cost as a similar project and use essentially the same amount of materials. For example, on a 10-ft² model base, assume an approximate design time of 500 hr. The material cost for this project would be about $625. This cost does not include the cost of materials for the model base. Carrying this example a little further, assume that the labor costs for the above-mentioned example were $14 per hour at 500 hours. The cost of the model design effort would be $7000 while the material cost was only $625. Another rule of thumb is that a normal table of 2½′ × 5′ would normally consume between $500 and $750 in material. A further extension of this rule would be that all modeling materials, plus the labor and materials for the model base, cost approximately $1000 in today's market.

Some of the projects in this text will require the maker to prepare a complete list of components and materials to be ordered. As the price of everything rises daily, the student or group should consider estimating the total cost in order to stay within the school or student economic limits.

24

Personnel/Job Opportunities

FIGURE 24-1 Model before piping.

BASIC JOB CLASSIFICATIONS

Basically, there are three different job classifications involved in the design and building of engineering models. A discussion and description of these three different job categories is provided below.

Model Technician

A model technician, frequently referred to in the United States as a model maker, is normally a craftsman familiar with power tools and the vari-

ous wood and plastic materials with which engineering models are built. The technician must have a knowledge of blueprint reading (including piping drawings) and be trained in the judgment required for minimizing model detail. Usually, the model technician works from completed drawings or sketches, but in some cases may work from field measurements to construct as-built models. Technicians normally work in the model shop building tables, vessels, equipment pieces, and structures. They are capable of attaching, altering, or changing any of the model pieces either in the shop or in the design area, and are also capable of installing piping on the model under the direction of a model or piping designer.

Model technicians, because of their exposure to the overall project, particularly the piping aspects, usually develop quite rapidly to model designers.

Model Designer

Model designers should be familiar with piping specifications, pipe fittings, and hardware, vessel and equipment functions, and have a knowledge of the considerations for expansion, insulation, and supporting of piping. The designers should have sufficient design experience to be able to design on the model, or, in other words, to think on the model. They should be able to lay out and route pipe runs directly on the model from flow sheets and piping and instrument diagrams (P&ID's). Most of the current model designers gained their experience on the drafting board, having gone through the traditional training of printroom, piping diagrams, and piping drawings. An ever-increasing number of talented new model designers are from the ranks of model technicians, where the exposure and training is concentrated and accelerated. Because of the need for piping drawings, which will probably never be entirely eliminated, the value of a designer who can work either on the model or the drafting board is obvious.

Model Consultant

Model consultants are generally expert model technicians and designers who also have administrative and teaching skills. They are normally engaged by a firm seeking either to introduce an efficient model program or to update and improve an existing program. Their functions are to advise management on the selection of a program to best suit their requirements, to advise middle management on how best to integrate the program, and to establish training procedures for both model technicians and model designers. They frequently have the responsibility of recruiting or selecting key people to continue the established programs after the completion of their assignment.

ACQUISITION OF QUALIFIED PERSONNEL

Included below is a discussion of several alternatives for obtaining modeling expertise that are open to any company.

Hire Direct—Already Trained Personnel

This approach is often difficult to achieve when the company has an on-going design drafting program and then tries to staff up with a totally new group of outsiders. Model engineering is such a rapidly growing field that there are not nearly enough trained personnel to staff all current jobs at any given time. The effect of the simple law of "supply and demand" could generate some inequities and resentment among existing staff personnel.

The direct-hiring approach can be successful by the employment of a thoroughly experienced model shop supervisor together with a core of trained model designers who could train additional staff. Several junior colleges and technical schools are now teaching model design courses, and thus more skilled people will be available in the future. A company considering an effective ongoing model program must seriously consider the quality of the model supervision.

Hire Contact People ("Job Shoppers")

One approach to staffing for a model program is to hire contract personnel. These people are supplied from a technical services company. The technical service company provides their experienced model technicians and model designers in exactly the same manner as they provide people for other engineering disciplines. These people can be placed in the client's facility for any period of time that the client specifies or agrees to through consultation.

Utilization of contract people as model technicians and model designers can take the peaks out of an overall workload without having to hire and lay off direct personnel. The cost savings of using contract personnel reach far into the various divisions of a given company. For example, all the fringe benefits, such as profit sharing, retirement funds, and so on, are not required for contract people. Also, savings accrue as a result of less timekeeping, bookkeeping, and payroll demands.

The dismissal of contract people leaves no animosities on the part of the contract persons or direct-hire employees, because a contract person knows that he or she is only there for a given period of time and does not expect to stay any longer than the original assignment. There is essentially no "dead weight" when contract personnel are used. They are hired for a specific task and are not carried over during slack times. Obviously, one cannot staff a whole operation with contract people, but there is certainly economy to be gained in their use. A disadvantage of using contract model technicians, designers, and draftsmen is their mobility. However, this can be offset by competitive pay rates and overtime.

Again, with this approach, the quality of the model supervisor is critical to the success of the program.

Train Existing Personnel

The most effective approach for obtaining and developing model expertise is to train your own people. For a model program being newly instituted, or for an existing one being updated, the best approach is to employ the services of a model consultant. Depending on the size of the company and its projects, a consultant with one or two assistants can organize a total in-house modeling program and, in addition, train some of the key engineering staff and the drafting personnel to design on the model. Again, depending on the company and project magnitude, the training can be accomplished over the duration of one or two projects.

There are several advantages to using an outside consultant to train your personnel. Perhaps the greatest benefit lies in the fact that the program will not develop by "trial and error," nor will there be useless and wasted labor-hours "reinventing the wheel." The consultant will have the background of several varied programs and can help you select the features most advantageous for your operation.

Bear in mind that no two companies have identical operating procedures. Some producing companies do their own engineering and thus they are their own "client"; some engineering companies do their own construction, others may not; and there are many other variations of responsibility and client relationships.

Thus, model program requirements differ and your program should be tailored to satisfy your needs.

Continued in-house training is also a valuable investment. It should be noted that training a junior draftsperson on the model will produce a better drafter and eventually a better designer in a far shorter period of time. Some companies strive to hire personnel directly out of high school and run them through their various in-house training programs. This has been true in drafting and also in model building. However, many companies who have hired and trained people directly from high school, and also have hired people with a two-year

technical or junior college background, have experienced a lower turnover rate among the latter. They attributed this to the fact that these older students have invested more in themselves through their additional education.

Once a company decides to establish a model program, the method of acquiring trained model designers will vary among companies. The most feasible approach depends upon the size of the company and its commitment to models. If a company is only going to build one model on a given project because, for instance, the client requires it, it would be economically unwise to hire consultants and direct personnel to establish an ongoing model program. The best approach would be to hire a consultant and several contract people to get the job completed and then disband the group at the end of the project. However, if a company is going to set up an ongoing model program, it is probably best to hire a consultant to train the key personnel. Again, depending upon the size of the company, an ongoing model program requires an ongoing training program for its new personnel. To finish out the complement of designers and model technicians in a given program, it is best to hire sufficient contract personnel to absorb an overload situation, as opposed to the direct hiring of persons with the prospect of laying them off when the job is complete.

The practice of laying off directly hired personnel can adversely affect a company by reputation among design personnel as being a "layoff-of-direct-hands" company. This may soon affect the company's ability to hire the best-qualified persons and may eventually leave only junior or inexperienced people available for hire.

Although it may sound obvious and trite, it is worth repeating that the quality of a model program and its personnel is tied directly to its supervision. Capable, experienced supervisors are essential.

EMPLOYMENT OPPORTUNITIES

The industrial modeling field has greatly expanded in the last 10 years. There are many opportunities for both piping drafter/designers and model builders throughout the country. Because of the energy shortage, industrial projects concerning petrochemical, nuclear power, solar power, fossil-fuel power, and so on, have become extremely important, and as most of these projects need to be modeled, the need for model builders has grown daily, with a great shortage at the present time. Beginning salaries (1979) range from $900 to $1100 per month for the starting modeler (with an A.A. degree). In many cases, modelers with only two to four years of working experience are employed at salary levels ranging from $1800 to $2200 per month. Presently, most model builders and pipe designers come from in-company training programs and from junior college vocational technical programs. The use of modeling in high schools is in its relative infancy, with only two or three existing programs.

With the design model now generally viewed as a prerequisite for fine engineering, schools are supplying an increasing number of the trained model-building technicians industry needs.

The typical two-year A.A. degree modeling program as outlined in Section 5 adequately prepares students to enter industry as model builders, either in independent model shops or in the model departments of large firms.

Because of industry's enthusiasm about this type of program, 99 percent of all graduates have found quick employment. A well-prepared graduate of a typical program permits firms to concentrate on client services, instead of taking time out for training.

Working for technical service firms as "job shoppers" is also on the increase for graduates with a year or more of on-the-job experience. Job shopping is an excellent way of expanding one's knowledge of modeling, seeing the country, and making future employment contacts.

FINAL REVIEW QUIZ

1. When is a model called for in the production of a piping project?
2. Define an industrial model.
3. How can the use of a model save construction time?
4. How is a model a communications tool?
5. Name four advantages to the use of a model.
6. What are five common types of models?
7. How is a check model used?
8. What is the name of the model society?
9. Why are models color-coded? Name three advantages.
10. How is a plot plan model used?
11. A design model is used for a variety of reasons. Name four and explain.
12. How can a model help reduce interferences?
13. Do models always reduce the design cost? Why?
14. How can the use of a design model influence the type, amount, and production of drawings on a project?
15. How are models used after the project is finished and beginning to operate?
16. Name 10 areas in which a model can reduce overall costs of a project.
17. What portion of a project's total construction cost comes from the use of a model?
18. Explain the differences between a model builder and a pipe designer.
19. What are the similarities between the two?
20. At what stage of a model is it possible to start drawing isometrics?
21. What are the first procedures for the construction of a design model?
22. At what stage of completion is the model when the piping designer begins work on it?
23. What is the most common scale used on a process petrochemical?
24. What is the usual scale for power-generation models?
25. How is the scale determined?
26. What are the factors affecting the selection of a scale for a model?
27. What is a preliminary model used for?
28. Name three uses of architectural models.
29. What is the difference between tools used by and in the model shop and tools used by the pipe designer?
30. Name 10 different tools used by both the designer and modeler.
31. Name some uses of clamps in the construction of models.
32. Name five common power tools used in model construction.
33. Why are safety regulations so important in model building?
34. Name some of the fire hazards found in model building.
35. How can air contamination be avoided in the model shop?
36. Model components are manufactured to scale for what reason?
37. Why are different types of glue, cement, and adhesives used in the construction of a model?
38. In what capacity is wood used for the construction of a model?
39. Name five different kinds of plastics used on models.

40. Complete the color code for the following materials:

HVAC   _____

Electrical   _____

Concrete   _____

Instrumentation   _____

Roads   _____

Hot insulation   _____

Equipment   _____

41. What colors are preferred for pipe fittings?
42. Name three uses for design sketches in the planning stages of a model.
43. Describe a method to measure the circumference of a model vessel.
44. How are chalk lines used in modeling measurements?
45. What is the maximum size of a base used in the construction of a model?
46. How are doors shown on a model?
47. All ladders and stairs are shown to _____.
48. Equipment should be accurate within _____ of an inch.
49. All piping must be at the _____ elevation.
50. What is the suggested model tolerance for model piping?
51. How is underground piping shown?
52. Name five types of electrical equipment shown on the model.
53. Name three types of HVAC shown on the model.
54. Do not drill holes in excess of _____ in vessels.
55. Name some uses of block shapes in modeling.
56. How is insulation shown on a model?
57. What is the difference between centerline piping and full-scale piping on models? Name three uses of each.
58. When is full-scale piping always used?
59. What is a bending board?
60. When is bending used in model construction?
61. Define the common steps for bending small-diameter pipe.
62. Name the reasons for model tagging.
63. What are coordinate tags?
64. What is usually shown on pipeline tags?
65. How are vessels tagged?
66. Name three differences in the construction and use of power-generation models in comparison to chemical process models.
67. Why are isometrics needed when a model is used?
68. Describe the procedure for the construction of computer-made isometrics from models.
69. How can photography be utilized when models are used?
70. Name five types of photographs used in relation to models.
71. Why is color preferred to black and white for model photographs?
72. Name 10 things to check on a model at the completion of a job.
73. When does the client's review of the model take place?
74. What is a preliminary review?

25

EMA's
Design Training Model

FIGURE 25-1 EMA Design Training Manual KIT-02.

PETROCHEMICAL MODELS

Because of the energy shortage and the concern that has been generated within the last 10 years for a comprehensive energy policy, oil and its associated products have become an extremely important industry. The number of jobs generated in this area for drafters/modelers, piping designers, and engineers has multiplied rapidly and will continue to do so for the foreseeable future. The scarcity and diminishing supplies of natural gas and the many uses of petrochemical products will make this area of employment extremely im-

portant for the rest of this century, as the demand for oil and its associated products becomes greater than the supply.

Process petrochemical plants or refineries are piping systems and associated equipment which use raw crude oil as the primary component in the processing and production of a multitude of end and by-products that are utilized by society and industry. Crude oil is to be considered the primary feed or charge that is used throughout the refinery in the production of its many products, all of which are based on hydrocarbon compounds.

In general, the most important products that

are obtained from these processes are different forms of gases, oils, and subproducts. Light ends, which are a form of hydrocarbon compound, include the various pure and mixed hydrocarbon products: fuel gas, ethane, propane, butane, and liquid petroleum gas.

The heavier compounds can be grouped together under oils and include diesel fuel, fuel oil, lubricating oil, gasoline, and kerosene. The heaviest hydrocarbon compounds associated with the petrochemical refining process are asphalt, grease, and wax. Other products are manufactured with hydrocarbons as one of their primary ingredients, such as synthetic rubber, chemicals, medicines, drugs, and plastics.

The refining of crude oil and petroleum involves many processes, including the simple separation of hydrocarbons into lighter and heavy compounds by the use of fractional distillation and cracking. All hydrocarbons are composed of a molecular structure containing hydrogen and carbon; such compounds are found in naturally occurring petroleum.

Since crude oil comes in consistencies of very thin to almost solid, it is necessary to refine or fractionate the stock or feed to produce the required products for society's needs. Gasoline and some of the lighter end products are in far greater demand than the heavier hydrocarbon products. Processes have been developed to separate the lighter and heavier compounds.

Hydrocarbon compounds that are composed of more hydrogen than carbon are lighter compounds and are the lighter end products. Unfortunately, a majority of the products that can be obtained by simple fractionization or distillation (separation of lower and higher hydrogen compounds) are heavy end products. Thus, fractional distillation or separation of the higher and lower (lighter and heavier) compounds does not meet the heavy demand for the lighter end products. Therefore, many refining procedures and techniques have been created to crack or hydrogenate the heavier hydrocarbons in order to produce from them the amount of light hydrocarbon compounds required. Catalytic cracking, hydrogenation, thermal cracking, and other types of reactions are used to produce more light and end products from the original crude stock. It is now possible to utilize crude oil in such a way as to create the more important light end products in far more abundance than was formerly possible.

Because of this ability to create the desired quantity of light or heavy end products (depending on the needs of society), it is possible to plan and alter the amount of end products according to the season or other economic factors.

Besides the primary end products that are available through fractional distillation, thermal and catalytic cracking, hydrogenation, and other processes, the refinery also produces certain amounts of by-products, depending on the type of plant or facility in question. Light gases that can be used in the refinery, petroleum coke, acid sludge, and many types of waste gases are just a few of the lower-quantity by-products that are obtained by the general processes associated with petrochemical refining.

Hydrocarbon compounds are to be considered the primary feed or stock in all the processes that are going on in the various types of equipment and piping systems. The typical petrochemical complex or refinery consists of a maze of piping for transportation or movement of hydrocarbons and for utilities and backup systems, and vessels and associated equipment needed to move and process the raw material (crude oil and hydrocarbon compounds).

There are many types of processing units or plants associated with petrochemical refining. Among them are chemical, gasoline, and ammonia plants. In a majority of cases, more than one type of plant or process will take place at the same site or refinery. A typical petrochemical refinery with all its associated plants or process sections may cover many square miles and include not only many types of plant and processing units, but also storage facilities and a vast array of piping that is associated with the transportation and movement of the raw material and the end products.

Petrochemical sites or refineries are constructed to use many types and consistencies of hydrocarbon products in their crude form. The nature of the material determines the type of processing units that will be constructed and utilized in a particular area. Installations that have access to natural gas along with crude oils from the many different crude-oil-exporting nations of the world will have a wider variety of types of plants and processing units at the same site, all adapted to meet the needs and abilities of the particular crude oils to produce the many products that are associated with petrochemical refining.

Some types of crude oil have a higher sulfur content than others and are also in a semisolid state. Therefore, the type of equipment and transportation piping must meet the processing requirements of this type of raw material. Refineries that must utilize high-sulfur-content crude oil must construct and design process units that can separate the sulfur from the oil. Therefore, in this type of refinery, sulfur becomes a by-product. The thicker, almost solid types of crude oil require extensive heating before they can be pumped and moved through pipelines from the tanker or other shipping equipment to the refinery site. It is necessary to heat-trace these pipelines.

As can be seen, the typical petrochemical installation is composed of more than just the piping and equipment necessary for the production of gas and oil. Among the additional kinds of plants that may be present at a refinery site or at their own separate installations are chemical plants which, in general, take hydrocarbon compounds that have been refined or semirefined, then mix, blend, change, and convert the actual chemical/molecular structure of the hydrocarbons along with various additives to produce the wide variety of chemicals that are available to both industry and society at large, including medicines, plastics, drugs, fertilizers, insecticides, and food additives. Another type of plant that is associated with petrochemical installations is the gasoline plant, which uses natural gas or liquid natural gas (LNG) as a charge instead of the heavier hydrocarbons that are associated with crude oil to produce gasoline, propane, butane, methane, olefins, and so on.

The products that are associated with the use of the heavier hydrocarbon compounds, which have a larger quantity of carbon atoms, are not manufactured in a gasoline plant. Therefore, motor oils, asphalt, wax, grease, lubricating oil, and diesel fuel are usually not associated with the gasoline plant's material and products. The production and discovery of oil is usually accompanied by the presence of a quantity of natural gas. Unfortunately, it is impossible at times to transfer the natural gas to a processing area because of the inaccessibility of the oil field, as in the case of the Alaska fields. Natural gas is also found in areas that do not have any or substantial oil discoveries, such as coal fields. Natural gases, although used sometimes in gasoline plants, have been primarily used as heating fuel for housing and buildings, especially in areas where they are in abundance.

In the early stages of the petrochemical and oil industry, natural gas was considered almost a nuisance, making it harder and more dangerous to drill and pipe the oil from the oil fields. Now the natural gas is considered to be almost as important as oil, depending on the area of the world where it is located.

Ammonia plants and other types of processing units are also associated with the refinery site or are located separately. The typical petrochemical installation will also have separate plants for the production of waxes, asphalt, tar, and many of the other products that are associated with the use of hydrocarbons as the primary charge or feedstock. This has been only an introduction to the four petrochemical model projects offered in this book. *Piping Systems Drafting and Design* covers this area in great depth and should be consulted for essential data, theory, specifications, and so on, for petrochemical design and modeling.

Sections 25 to 28 are projects involving petrochemical units.

EMA TRAINING MODEL

The Basic Model

The basic stage of the design model is usually accomplished in the model shop from drawings. The basic model for training will be constructed in this class to give the students a general knowledge of how various tasks are accomplished and the time required for each operation. Also, tagging the basic model will introduce the student to the tagging procedures. Information applied to the basic model will be that which is required for the purpose of designing piping later.

Each step in basic model layout and construction in this section is explained in detail with accompanying photographs for reference. Materials and tools required are listed for each operation. Other sections do not detail modeling steps as in this project.

Basic model construction can be simplified for the purpose of keeping lab costs to a minimum. An example of this is that equipment tubing pieces, when using the kit, are cut to exact lengths rather than having standard lengths of material, resulting in waste. Other shortcuts are explained in the text.

Base for Training Model

Drawings required:

- Sketch 1, plot plan
- Sketch 2, equipment location plan
- Sketch 3, paving and underground piping layout (see SK-1, SK-2, and SK-3).

FIGURE 25-2   Closeup view of pump station and pipe rack.

FIGURE 25-4   EMA design training model.

FIGURE 25-3   Closeup view of training model.

Bill of material:

- Model base 20″ × 24″ (actual inches)

Materials and tools required:

- Straightedge
- 3/8″ scale rule
- Pocket scribe
- Fine-point pen or hard lead pencil
- Centerline tape for underground piping (Chart-Pak TL362A)

Steps to be taken:

- Check plot plan for north orientation and apply north arrow tag.
- Establish and mark reference work edge at south and west sides of base. Each individual measurement should be made from either of these edges to avoid an accumulation of er-

rors and to act as a check on other measurements.
- Lay out major structures first (i.e., pipeway and equipment structure).
- Locate and mark centerlines of equipment on base using a black film marker. In the case of pumps, mark centerline in N-S direction and centerline of discharge in the E-W direction.
- Tag layout with proper coordinates as you proceed. Also, tag equipment locations (vessels, pumps, etc.). (See Section 18.)
- Lay out underground utilities, piping, and drains using black centerline tape.
  Note: Normally underground piping has not been designed at the time of basic model construction, but for the purposes of the training it is installed before structures and equipment to make installation most convenient.
- Use SK-1, SK-2, and SK-3 to complete this portion of the assignment.

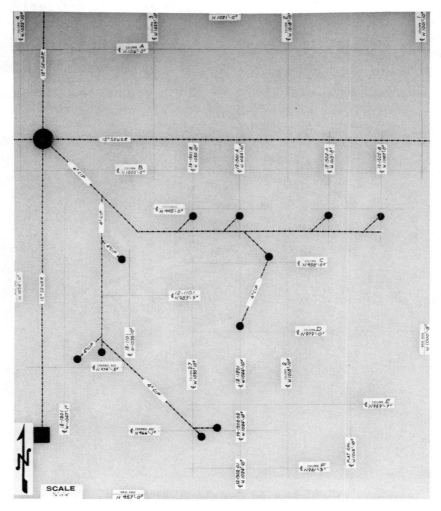

FIGURE 25-5 Base for KIT-02 model.

Construction of Pipeway and Equipment Structure

Drawings required:

- Sketch 4, pipeway isometric (SK-4)
- Sketch 5, equipment structure isometric (SK-5)

Bill of materials—pipeway structure:

- 6 columns 12" × 12" × 21'0" (FPH-12)
- 2 columns 12" × 12" × 23'6" (FPH-12)
- 6 beams 8" × 10" × 16'6" (FPB-10)
- 8 beams 8" × 10" × 15'0" (FPB-10)
- 5 beams (outriggers) 8" × 10" × 3'6" (FPB-10)

Bill of materials—equipment structure:

- 8 columns 12" × 12" × 26'0" (FPH-12)
- 8 beams 8" × 12" × 11'0" (FPB-12)
- 4 beams 8" × 10" × 7'4" (FPB-10)
- 4 beams 8" × 10" × 8'0" (FPB-10)
- 4 beams 8" × 10" × 8'5" (FPB-10)
- 1 column 8" × 8" × 16'0" (PSH-8)
- 1 channel for stair platforms (PSC-8)
- 2 stairs (ST-14)
- Scraps of beam stock (FPB-10) for structure continuation

Materials and tools required:

- Solvent, PPC-2
- Right-angle blocks
- Double-sided adhesive tape
- 1" strips of 3/4" plywood
- Formica-surfaced work area
- Scraps of P-3 (pipe)

Steps to be taken:

- A jig is constructed to assemble pipeway and structure bents. Attach a straight-edged strip to the lower portion of your work board with double-sided tape. This strip will represent the base elevation or elevation 100'0" (Fig. 25-6).
- From this reference plan, lay out at 90° the centerlines of the columns and parallel top-of-steel elevations. This will look like an east-west section through the pipeway and a north-south section through the structure.
- Attach two small pieces of double-sided tape to the layout on either the right or left side of each column centerline. Locate them about one-third and two-thirds of the distance from the reference plan to the top-of-steel (Fig. 25-7).

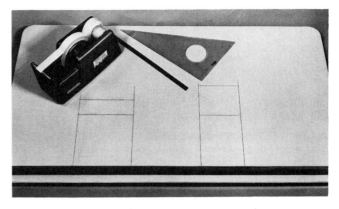

FIGURE 25-6

FIGURE 25-7

- Lay appropriate columns on the tape while aligning one edge against the pencil line (Fig. 25-8).
- Fit beams at top-of-steel elevations using shims of scrap plastic or pipe to raise them to the column centerline (Fig. 25-9).
- Apply solvent to the jigged column joints and allow ample time for the solvent to set before removing the bent from its jig.
- Repeating the steps above, construct enough bents to complete structure of the pipeway.

FIGURE 25-8

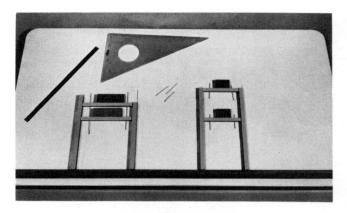

FIGURE 25-9

- Bond one end bent of the pipeway in place using right-angle blocks for vertical alignment. These blocks are held in place with double-sided tape (Fig. 25-10).
- Repeat the preceding step with the next bent and add interconnecting beams. The beams can be held at the proper elevation with an elevation block cut to the bottom of the beam elevation.
- Add all additional bents in the same manner and proceed with the structure until complete (Figs. 25-11 and 25-12).

FIGURE 25-10

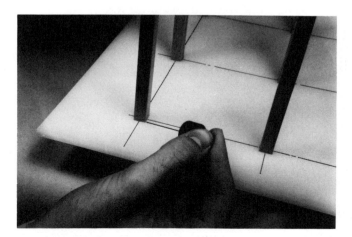

FIGURE 25-11

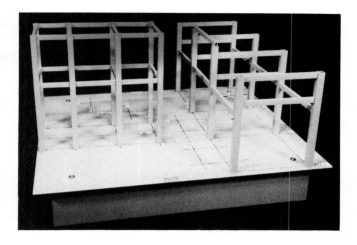

FIGURE 25-12

Note: The bonding of the structural members to the base is for the purpose of this training and may not be practiced by individual companies using models. Column blocks are often inserted into the base of fireproofed or concrete columns and are secured to the base with self-tapping screws from below. Base pins are used to secure structural steel columns to the base (Figs. 25-11 and 25-12).

- When the structure is in place, add the members required for the stair platforms. Proceed with installation of the stairs (Fig. 25-13).
- Add small pieces of plastic screen (cut to right angles with a dodged section across the hypotenuse) to the corners of the platforms to represent grating. These pieces are about 1 1/4″ on the straight sides (Fig. 25-14).
- Indicate the limits of the grating on the operating levels of the structures by showing the corners in the same manner as the platforms in the preceding step. In places where

FIGURE 25-13

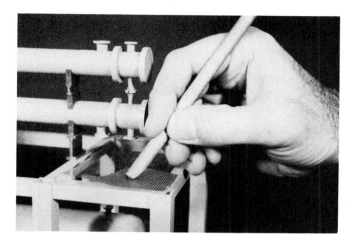

FIGURE 25-14

no support exists for the plastic screen, bond it to a scrap of platform material of the same shape and attach with a small amount of solvent.

- When the pipeway is in place, add the outriggers for support of the flare header.
- Tag structure top-of-steel elevations.

**Construction of Vertical Vessel
(12-1101 Stabilizer Column)**

Drawings required:

- Sketch 6, stabilizer drawing (SK-6)
- Sketch 6A, B, C, D, and E, vessel orientations (SK6A, B, C, D, and E)
- Sketch 8, level gauges and controllers (SK-8)

Bill of materials:

- 1 tube 4′8″ dia. × 46′1″ long (VT-175)
- 1 tube 3′4″ dia. × 25′8″ long (VT-40)
- 1 transition
- 1 elliptical head 3′4″ dia. (VHE-40)
- 3 18″ manways (VMH-18)
- Nozzles
  —7 2″ (VN-2)
  —2 4″ (VN-4)
  —1 6″ (VN-6)
  —1 8″ (VN-8)
  —1 10″ (VN-10)
- Platform stock, 1 piece 4″ × 12″ (VP-40)
- 8 platform brackets (VPB-12C)
- 3 ladders (KL-12)
- 9 ladder clips (KLC-12)
- 2 Davit supports (PS-4C)
- 1 octagon base (VO6-243)

Materials and tools required:

- Solvent, PPC-2
- Pin vise with 1/8″, #43, and #51 drill bits

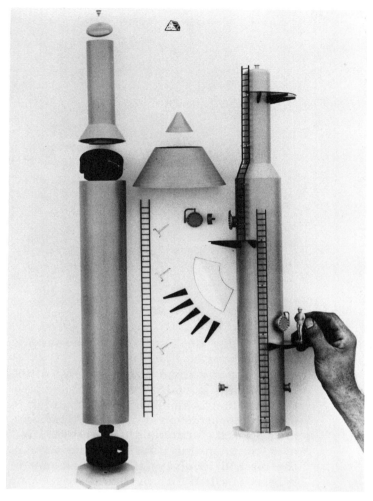

FIGURE 25-15 This photograph depicts materials and methods of construction for vertical vessels.

- Diagonal cutters
- Pocket scribe
- 3/8″ scale rule
- Scrap 4″ pipe (P-4)

Steps to be taken:

- Select the materials, listed in the bill of materials (Fig. 25-16). (The vessel tubing for the stabilizer column and other equipment pieces are cut to length for the convenience of this training.) (Fig. 25-16.)
- As the first step, locate the bottom tangent line on the larger tube and scribe a line around the circumference. This can be done by using a scrap block of wood or plastic cut to length and used as a gauge or by using a strip cut from heavy paper such as a manila folder. When using the strip-of-paper method, be sure that one edge is perfectly straight. Wrap the paper around the tube at the point to be scribed and line up the overlapping

229

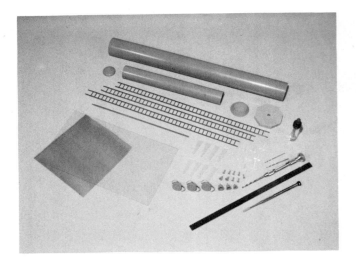

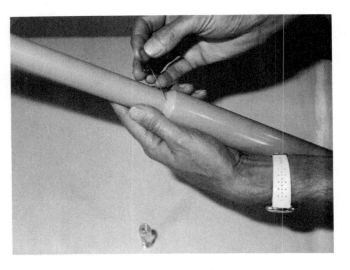

FIGURE 25-16

FIGURE 25-18

straight edge. Use a scribe along the paper to mark the tangent line (Fig. 25-17).

- Attach the transition piece to the top of the larger tube (Fig. 25-18). (*Note:* The solid plastic transition is supplied in this training to expedite construction of this vessel and minimize the cost of materials for the lab kit. However, to make this transition from scratch, the method involving the least amount of time is to cut the piece from a vessel cone VC-60. Instructions for cutting cones are given in the EMA catalog with the description of cones.) (See Fig. 25-18.)
- Attach the smaller tube to the transition, being careful to line up the vertical scribe lines.

- Attach the top head (Fig. 25-19).
- Select one vertical scribe line to represent north and mark it 0°. This is a reference for locating all attachments.
- Locate all nozzles and manways and drill a 1/8" hole for each regardless of nozzle sizes. Do not attach nozzles at this time.
- Locate elevations of all platforms (elevations on orientation sketches) and mark a horizontal line around the vessel at these points. A method of making a guide for the purpose of marking a horizontal line around a tube is to take a 1/2" strip of paper with at least one straight edge and wrap it around until the paper overlaps and the straight edge lines up,

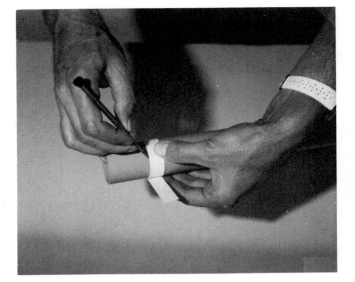

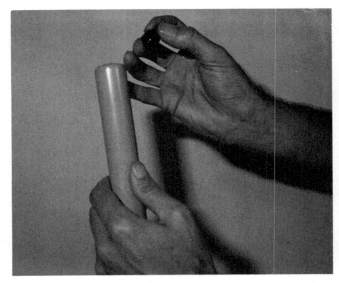

FIGURE 25-17

FIGURE 25-19

as was done to scribe the bottom tangent line. Do not attach platforms or brackets at this time.

- Locate the vertical centerline of the ladders and mark with a light pencil line. Drill holes to receive ladder clips using a #43 drill. The elevations of the holes are not critical but should be about one-fourth of the distance from both the bottom and the top of the ladder. Do not attach ladder clips at this time.
- Locate the davit (refer to orientation SK-6D) with a short vertical line near the top of the vessel. Mark and drill two #51 holes on this line for pipe clips to hold the davit. One hole is at the base of the davit, 4′3″ below the tangent line and the other hole is about 9″ below the tangent line.
- The stabilizer is now ready for all attachments. Attach clear platform brackets 1/16″ below the horizontal lines previously made on the vessel. The radical location of these will not be critical since the actual location is not established on the training model. If the actual location were known, the brackets would be installed using steel gray pieces. The general location can be determined from the vessel orientation sketches. Use two brackets for the smallest platform and three for each of the others (Fig. 25-20).

- To cut the platforms, lay the clear butyrate material over the orientation sketch, which is to scale and trace the outline with a scribe (dividers can be used for the arcs). Deep scoring will permit the plastic to be broken at the scribe lines (Fig. 25-21).
- Attach platforms to the brackets with a very small amount of solvent at the edges only. Add plastic screen material to represent grating as was done for the structure, and clip off excess lengths of platform brackets with diagonal cutters (Fig. 25-22).
- Center the vessel on the octagon base, making sure north on the vessel lines up with the "N" on the octagon and that all other vertical

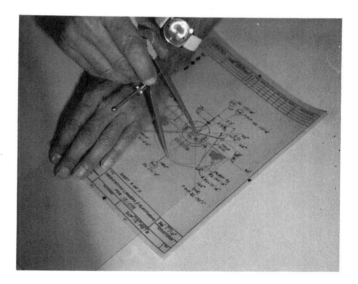

FIGURE 25-21

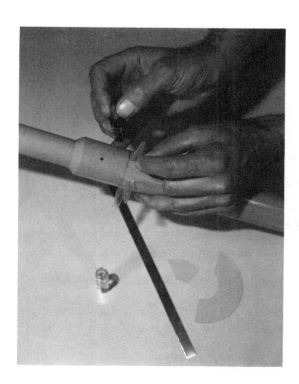

FIGURE 25-20

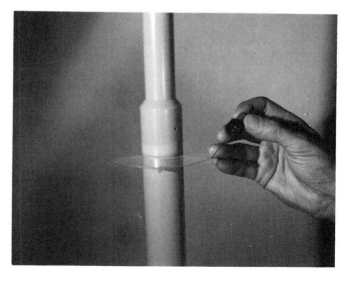

FIGURE 25-22

scribe lines match. Cement these together (Fig. 25-23).

Note: Common practice when making base supports for vertical vessels is to provide a screw hold-down for removal to make piping the vessel more convenient. This is done using an EMA mounting ring and nut inside the bottom of the vessel and using a 1/4" #20 bolt through the model base and octagon for attaching. This operation is deleted in favor of expediency and lower cost for training purposes.

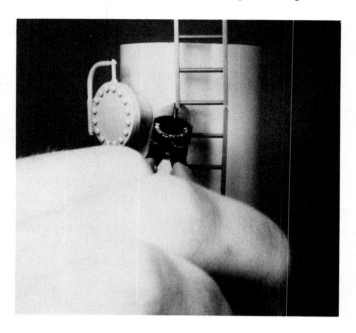

FIGURE 25-24

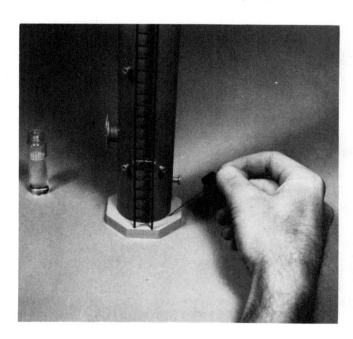

FIGURE 25-23

- Attach ladder clips so that the ladder will be the proper distance from the vessel shell, and bond in place (refer to orientation sketches). Snap on ladders and clip off excess about 3'6" above the platforms with diagonal cutters (Fig. 25-24).
- Plug nozzles and manways in their appropriate locations, adding a very small amount of solvent to tack them in place.
- Attach the two pipe clips to hold the davit so that the center of the davit will be 8" from the vessel shell.
- Bend a piece of 4" pipe around a 16" (1/2" actual) tube to form a 5-diameter bend. Cut one leg 2'5" center to end and the other leg 11'6" center to end. Paint the equipment and snap into pipe clips (Fig. 25-25).

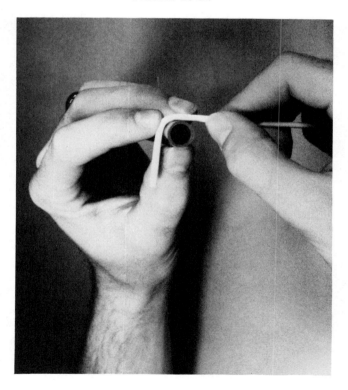

FIGURE 25-25

- Select the appropriate material from piping components, and install level gauges and controllers (see SK-7).
- Refer to tagging procedures and tag all nozzles, platforms, and ladders with the appropriate information (Fig. 25-26).

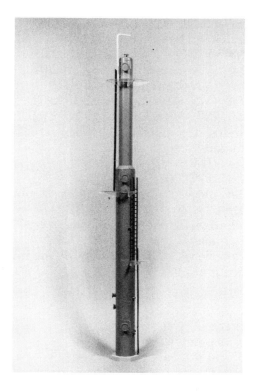

FIGURE 25-26

Construction of Horizontal Vessel 12-1201 Stabilizer Reflux Drum

Drawings required:

- Sketch 7, level gauges and controllers (SK-7)
- Sketch 8, stabilizer reflux drum drawing (SK-8)

Bill of materials:

- 1 tube 4'9" dia. × 15'9" long (VT-175)
- 2 elliptical heads 4'8" dia. (VHE-175)
- 2 saddles 4'8" (VS-175)
- 1 18" manway (VMH-18)
- Nozzles
  —4 2" (VN-2)
  —2 3" (VN-3)
  —1 4" (VN-4)
- 2 drum supports 8" × 48" × 17" plexiglass

Materials and tools required:

- Solvent, PPC-2
- Pin vise with 1/8" drill bit
- 3/8" = 1'0" scale rule

Steps to be taken:

- Select the materials, listed in the bill of materials (Fig. 25-27).

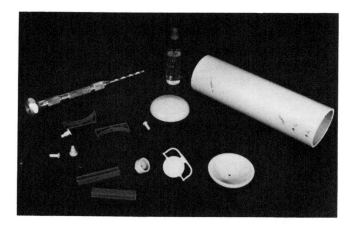

FIGURE 25-27

- Locate with a pencil mark only the center of the N4 and N5 nozzles. This is a reference point for locating saddles.
- Mark the location of both saddles. Use a small amount of solvent to bond one saddle in place, being careful to have it straddle one of the scribe lines.
- Set the reflux drum on the saddles on a flat surface before bonding the second saddle in place. Cement the heads in place.
- Locate and drill 1/8"-diameter holes for all nozzles, using a pencil mark for reference (Fig. 25-28).

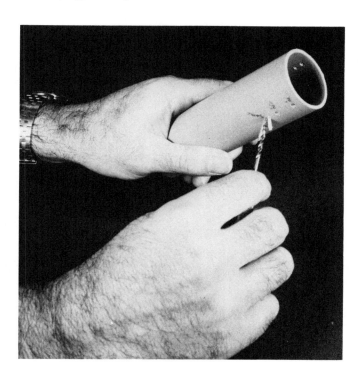

FIGURE 25-28

- Attach the nozzles (Fig. 25-29).
- Select appropriate material from piping components, and install level gauges and controllers (SK-7).
- Refer to tagging procedures and tag all nozzles.

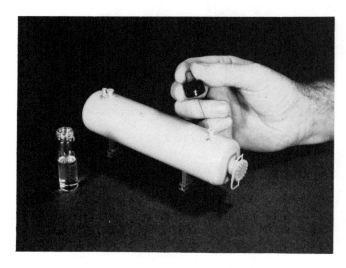

FIGURE 25-29

Construction of Heat Exchangers Stabilizer Reflux Condensers and Reboiler

Drawings required:

- Sketch 9, stabilizer reboiler (SK-9)
- Sketch 10, stabilizer reflux condenser (lower) (SK-10)
- Sketch 11, stabilizer reflux condenser (upper) (SK-11)

Bill of materials—stabilizer reboiler:

- 1 tube 32" dia. × 11'0" (VT-32)
- 2 32" exchanger flanges (VX-32)
- 1 32" elliptical head (VHE-32)
- 1 32" flanged head (VHF-32)
- 2 32" saddles (VS-32)
- Nozzles
  —2 4" (VN-4)
  —3 8" (VN-8)
- Exchanger supports, 2 blocks 8" × 28" × 36" plexiglass

Bill of materials—stabilizer reflux condensers:

- 2 tubes 18" dia. × 18'9" (VT-18)
- 4 18" exchanger flanges (VX-18)
- 2 18" elliptical heads (VHE-18)
- 2 18" flanged heads (VHF-18)

- 6 18" saddles (VS-18)
- Nozzles
  —1 3" (VN-3) exchanger 12-1302-01
  —2 4" (VN-4) exchanger 12-1302-01
  —1 6" (VN-6) exchanger 12-1302-01
  —2 4" (VN-4) exchanger 12-1302-02
  —2 6" (VN-6) exchanger 12-1302-02
- Flanges for nozzles between stacked exchangers
  —1 4" (F-VG-4)
  —1 6" (F-VG-6)
- Filler pieces between saddles, 2 pieces 6" beam 6" × 3" × 16" long (PSB-6)
- Exchanger supports, 2 block 8" × 20" × 21" plexiglass
- Scrap pieces of 4" and 6" pipe for interconnecting nozzles

Materials and tools required:

- Solvent, PPC-2
- Pin vise and 1/8" drill bit
- 3/8" = 1'0" scale rule
- Scrap 4" and 6" pipe (P-4 and P-6)

Steps to be taken:

- Select the materials, listed in the bill of materials (Fig. 25-30).
- Slip on exchanger flanges and flanged caps and "tack" in place. Locate with pencil mark only the center of the channel nozzles. This is the reference point for locating saddles.
- Mark the location of both saddles. Use a small amount of solvent to bond one saddle in place, being careful to have it straddle one of the scribe lines (Fig. 25-31).
- Set the exchanger on the saddles on a flat surface before bonding the second saddle in place. Cement the head in place.
- Locate and drill 1/8" holes for all nozzles, using the channel nozzle for reference (Fig. 25-32).
- Before attaching nozzles, make a filler piece for the saddles on the stacked exchangers, using short lengths of PSB-6 supplied in the kit.
- Attach the filler pieces to the saddles on one exchanger and to these add another set of saddles inverted (Fig. 25-33).
- Before attaching stacked exchangers, attention must be given to the interconnecting nozzles. In this instance, if scale-model nozzles were used, the nozzle flanges would not provide the proper distance between the ex-

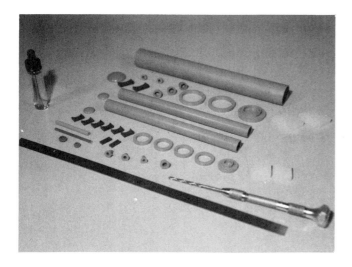

FIGURE 25-30

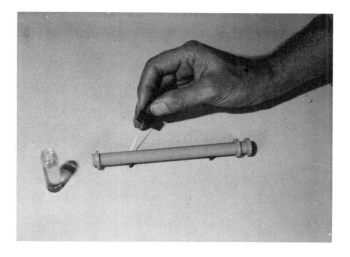

FIGURE 25-31

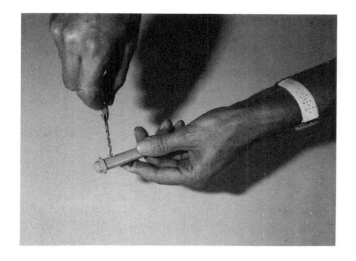

FIGURE 25-32

FIGURE 25-33

changers. The technique in this case is to use small pieces of pipe between the exchangers with weld neck flanges placed to represent nozzle flanges bolted together. These pieces of pipe are put in place before stacking the exchangers and bonding at the saddles.

- To stack the exchangers, place the lower one on a flat surface and line up the upper one using a small square or triangle. Bond the connecting saddles (Fig. 25-34).
- Add all other nozzles.
- Attach the piers to the lower exchanger's saddle to make it the proper height (Fig. 25-35).
- Refer to the tagging procedures and tag all nozzles (Fig. 25-36).

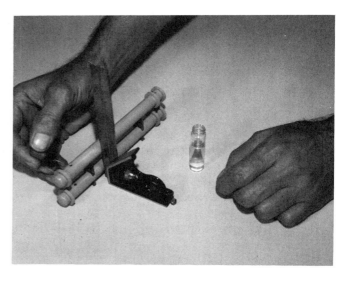

FIGURE 25-34

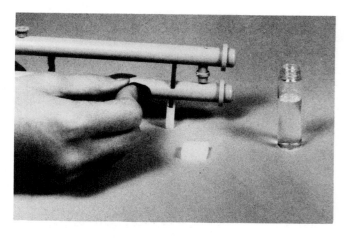

FIGURE 25-35

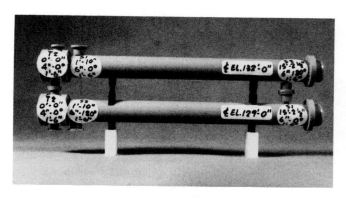

FIGURE 25-36

Assembly of Pumps with Drivers
10-1501 A and B and 10-1502 A and B

Drawings required:

- Sketch 12 10-1501 A and B, stabilizer reflux pumps
- Sketch 13 10-1502 A, overhead product pump
- Sketch 14 10-1502 B, overhead product pump

Bill of materials:

Pumps, stabilizer reflux and overhead product

- 2 PCM-7 (stabilizer reflux pump)
- 1 PCM-40 (overhead product pump with motor)
- 1 PCM-40 (overhead product pump with turbine)
- Turbine (PSH-8 cut to 3/4" plus FPB-16 cut to 3/4"
- Nozzles
  —4 VN-2
  —1 VN-3

—4 VN-4
—1 VN-6
- Pump pads (2 blocks plexiglass cut to 12" × 26" × 60" plus 2 blocks cut to 12" × 36" × 72")

Materials and tools required:

- Solvent, PPC-2
- Pin vise with 1/8" and #51 drill bits
- 3/8" scale rule

Steps to be taken—end suction pumps (SK-12)

- Select the materials, listed in the bill of materials (Fig. 25-37).

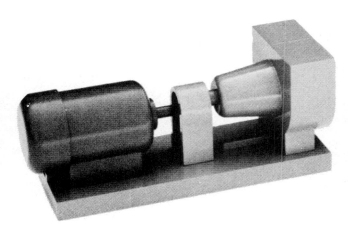

FIGURE 25-37 Pump and motor asembly.

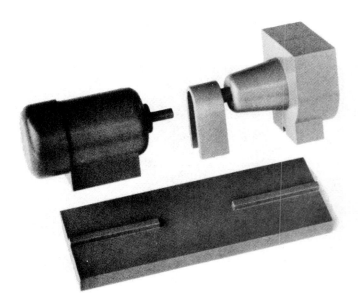

FIGURE 25-38 Pump and motor asembly.

- To assemble pumps, first locate the discharge, since this is the reference to the pump's location on the base plate. To locate the discharge, work from the face of the flange of the suction, which is represented by the face of the plastic part. This dimension is 6″.
- Attach the pumps to the base plate, using the drawing to find the dimension from the face of the base plate to the centerline of the discharge.
- Attach the motor so that the dimension between the face of the suction nozzle (face of plastic block) and the end of motor will be correct.
- Locate the discharge centerline from the centerline of the pumps and drill a nozzle-size hole (1/8″).
- Locate the suction centerlines and drill a nozzle-size hole (1/8″).

Steps to be taken—top suction pumps (SK-13):

- Select the materials, listed in the bill of materials (Fig. 25-39).
- Locate and mark the centerlines of the suction and discharge nozzles.
- Attach the pumps to the plates, using the drawing to find the dimension from the face of the plate to the centerline of the discharge (Fig. 25-40).
- Drill 1/8″ holes for both suction and discharge on both pumps. Attach the nozzles.
- Attach the motor on one base plate so that the dimension from the end of the pump to the end of the motor will be correct (dimension HC + P).

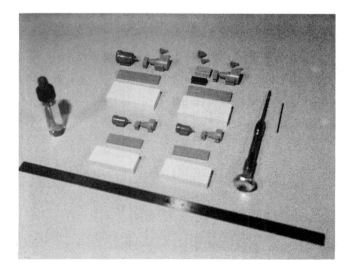

FIGURE 25-39

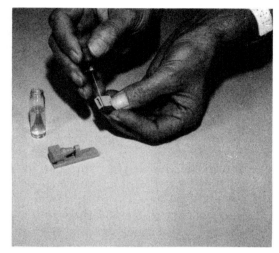

FIGURE 25-40

- Attach the block that represents the turbine (PSH-8 and FPB-16 bonded together) to the base plate so that the dimension from the end of the pump to the end of the turbine will be correct (dimensions HC + P) (SK-14).
- Locate and drill 1/8″ holes for the inlet and outlet nozzles of the turbine.
- Attach the nozzles to the turbine.
- Attach the pumps to the blocks representing concrete pads.
- Refer to the tagging procedures and make tags for nozzles.

Locating Equipment Components

Materials and tools required:

- Fabricated equipment components
- Solvent, PPC-2
- 3/8″ scale rule
- Equipment location drawing, SK #2

Steps to be taken:

- Stabilizer reflux drum—Find the center of the equipment structure in the east-west direction at elevation 116′0″. Mark the center of the beams. Locate the drum supports in the exact center of the beams, being careful to keep the fixed saddle on column line "D". Bond the supports to the beams with a very small amount of solvent at the sides of the support. Always consider that the equipment in the model may have to be removed to facilitate piping. Check the location of the south tangent line from column "D."
- Stabilizer reflux condensers—Repeat the pre-

ceding step at elevation 126'0". Again apply only a small drop of solvent when located. Check the location of the channel nozzles from column line "D."

- Stabilizer reboiler—The centerline of the reboiler as well as the centerline of the channel nozzles have been located on the model base during the previous operation of the base layout. To locate the centerline of the piers, refer to the stabilizer reboiler drawing (SK-8) and use the dimensions given for pier location from the channel nozzle. Mark these locations on the base and center the exchanger piers on the marks. Bond lightly to the base.
- Stabilizer—Center the octagon pad on the previously marked centerlines on the base. Pay particular attention to orient the vessel north with the base north. Apply a small amount of solvent to hold in place.
- Pumps—The centerlines of discharges have been located on the base as well as the centerlines of pumps. Attach each pump with a small amount of solvent. Attach to the base the tags made for pump nozzle information.

Installation of Piping

The information supplied in this text is similar to that which is available to the model designer for the purpose of designing piping and using the model on an actual project. Design information developed for this stage of the project is represented by the drawings used to construct the basic model and the drawings, sketches, and line summary listed below and supplied on the following pages.

At this point in the training, as on an actual project, the model has been tagged with dimensional and other information sufficient for the designer to install the piping.

The starting procedure for detail piping is performed in a logical order based on priorities. The alloy, exotic, or heavy wall piping is installed first for various reasons. The pipes are usually the most critical and the most expensive, so they are given the "right of way," and fabrication and delivery time is longer so that ordering (purchasing) must be done early enough to have the fabricated pipe at the job site on schedule. Piping design that would affect the location of nozzles on equipment requiring a long delivery time would also be of high priority regardless of material or size, so that the equipment piece could be specified and purchased.

The design and installation of the large-diameter pipe is accomplished next, usually working down in size. Then the pipe not requiring shop fabrication (field-run pipe) is designed. This sequence generally results in fewer unnecessary fittings requiring extra welds on the larger pipes, where it is the most expensive.

The work flow outlined above is simplified and does not take into account the interrelationship of other design disciplines, such as civil, structural, instrumentation, and electrical groups, plus other factors that influence project schedules, such as process changes after design has begun. It does, however, provide the student with a practical knowledge of how to proceed with the piping on a model.

Drawing list for piping design:

Sketch 15, isometric drawing
Sketch 16, isometric drawing
Sketch 17, flow-sheet symbols
Sketch 18, process piping and instrument diagram
Sketch 19, utility piping and instrument diagram
Sketch 20, routing diagram
Sketch 21, line summary
Sketch 22, piping drawings
Sketch 23, piping drawings
Sketch 24, piping drawings (SK24 A and SK-24 B)

Bill of materials:

Quantity	Code	Description
1	P-O-2	Pipe
1	P-O-3	Pipe
3	P-O-4	Pipe
9	P-B-2	Pipe
2	P-B-3	Pipe
4	P-B-4	Pipe
2	P-B-6	Pipe
1	P-B-8	Pipe
1	P-B-12	Pipe
9	P-Y-2	Pipe
3	P-Y-3	Pipe
4	P-Y-4	Pipe
4	P-Y-6	Pipe
1	P-Y-8	Pipe
1	P-Y-10	Pipe
1	P-P-2	Pipe
1	P-P-3	Pipe
7	BRO-47	Inserts
11	BRO-60	Inserts
12	E-Y-4	90° elbows

Quantity	Code	Description
14	E-Y-6	90° elbows
5	E-Y-8	90° elbows
1	E-Y-10	90° elbows
2	A-Y-6	45° elbows
1	A-Y-8	45° elbows
2	EF-Y-6	90° female elbows
50	TF-C-2	Snap-on tees
25	TF-C-3	Snap-on tees
25	TF-C-4	Snap-on tees
1	TS-Y-6	Tees
1	TS-Y-10	Tees
36	CS-2	Sleeves
10	CS-3	Sleeves
20	CS-4	Sleeves
1	F-P-2	Flanges
1	F-P-3	Flanges
1	F-Y-3	Flanges
2	F-P-4	Flanges
1	F-VG-4	Flanges
2	F-B-4	Flanges
1	F-O-4	Flanges
35	SX-2C	Support flanges
10	SX-3C	Support flanges
5	SX-4C	Support flanges
2	W-B-6	Weld caps
1	W-B-8	Weld caps
1	W-B-12	Weld caps
3	R-Y-4	Reducers
2	R-Y-8	Reducers
35	PS-2C	Pipe supports
10	PS-3C	Pipe supports
15	PS-4C	Pipe supports
5	PS-6C	Pipe supports
20	GV-1	150# Gate valves
20	GV-2	150# Gate valves
8	GV-3	150# Gate valves
12	GV-4	150# Gate valves
3	GV-6	150# Gate valves
3	GLV-2	Globe valves
3	GLV-4	Globe valves
3	CV-4	Check valves
1	RV-2	Relief valves
1	RV-3	Relief valves
1	RV-4	Relief valves
2	MV-2	Control valves
3	MV-3	Control valves
2	LL-12P	Liquid-level controllers
6	LS-2	Insulation sleeves
6	LS-3	Insulation sleeves
6	LS-4	Insulation sleeves
6	LS-6	Insulation sleeves
3	LS-8	Insulation sleeves
2	LS-10	Insulation sleeves
1	LTB-120	Tags
1	LTT-314	Tags
1	LTA-200	Tags
1	DL-CL	Labels
2	DL-24	Labels
1	DL-42	Labels
1	DL-TS	Labels
1	DL-PN	Labels
1	DL-NA	Labels

Miscellaneous:

- 1-SC-12 3/8" = 1'0" scale
- 1 cement applicator
- 1 ET-26 electrical tray
- 1 pipe support #5 (FPH-8 cut to 4-13/16" and FPH-8 cut to 1-1/8")
- Material for fictitious supports (plexiglass)
- Bending board
- 1 scale figure RF-12

Model color code:

Process	Yellow (see SK-7)
Utility	Blue (see SK-19)
Alloy	Orange (see SK-18)
Instrumentation	Pink

The Bending Board

One of the most valuable tools the model designer will use is the bending board. It will enable the designer to work with maximum speed and accuracy, and the importance of its use cannot be overemphasized. Therefore, each beginning model designer should master all facets of the use of the bending board.

This portion of the training will cover the basic uses of the bending board for:

- Layout of dimensions
- Layout of angles and offsets
- Adding and subtracting
- Checking accuracy of pipe bends
- Checking piping configuration
- Alignment of pipe runs

Practice in the use of the bending board for these tasks will be required during the training sessions. Further practice when fabricating piping for the training model should point out the speed and accuracy attainable.

Simplified piping isometrics are supplied for use as a guide during the practice of bending pipe for this training. Select appropriate material and bend 4" B-12-1 and assemble 6" A-10-57-1 and install on the model. It must be noted that during actual work on the model, isometrics are not used to fabricate piping; they are, however, made after piping has been installed and checked.

At this point, using the drawing provided, the student is to "pipe up the model." See Section 16 for bending information.

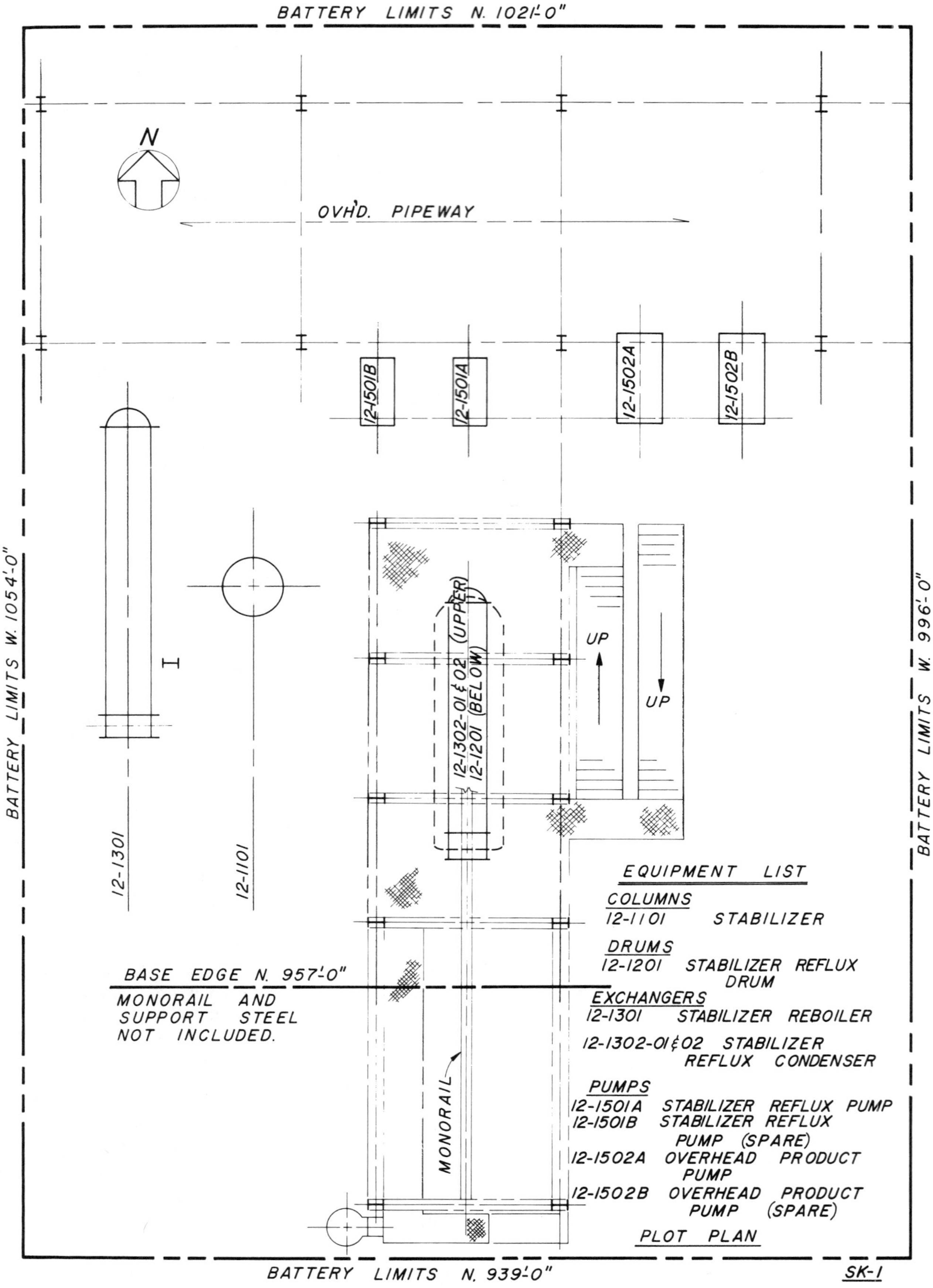

BATTERY LIMITS N. 1021'-0"

N

OVH'D. PIPEWAY

BATTERY LIMITS W. 1054'-0"

BATTERY LIMITS W. 996'-0"

12-1501B
12-1501A
12-1502A
12-1502B

12-1301

12-1101

12-1302-01&02 (UPPER)
12-1201 (BELOW)

UP

UP

EQUIPMENT LIST

COLUMNS
12-1101   STABILIZER

DRUMS
12-1201   STABILIZER REFLUX
                DRUM

EXCHANGERS
12-1301   STABILIZER REBOILER

12-1302-01&02 STABILIZER
                REFLUX CONDENSER

BASE EDGE N. 957'-0"

MONORAIL   AND
SUPPORT   STEEL
NOT INCLUDED.

MONORAIL

PUMPS
12-1501A   STABILIZER REFLUX PUMP
12-1501B   STABILIZER REFLUX
                PUMP (SPARE)
12-1502A OVERHEAD   PRODUCT
                PUMP
12-1502B OVERHEAD   PRODUCT
                PUMP (SPARE)

PLOT PLAN

BATTERY LIMITS N. 939'-0"

SK-1

240

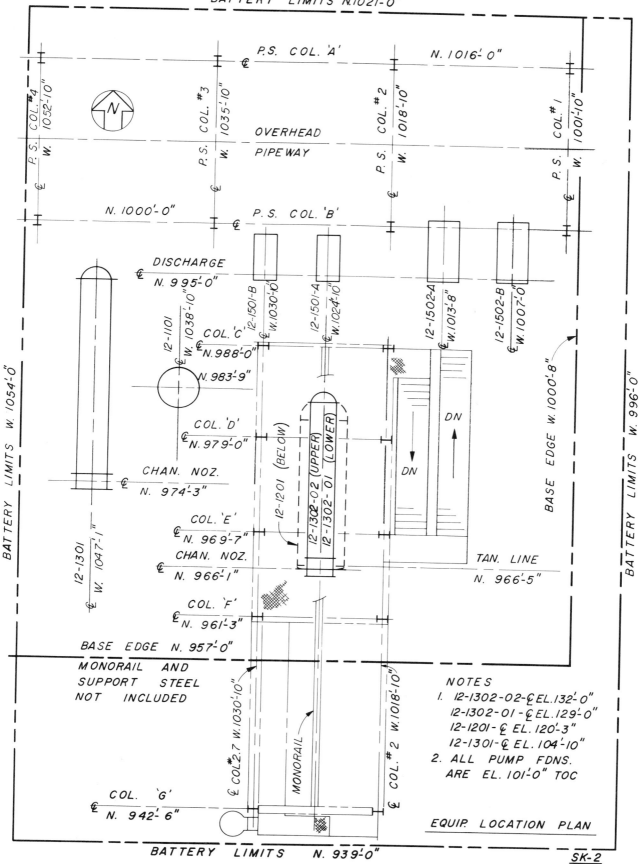

BATTERY LIMITS N.1021'-0"

P.S. COL. 'A' N. 1016'-0"

OVERHEAD
PIPEWAY

N. 1000'-0" P.S. COL. 'B'

DISCHARGE
N. 995'-0"

COL. 'C'
N. 988'-0"

N. 983'-9"

COL. 'D'
N. 979'-0"

CHAN. NOZ.
N. 974'-3"

COL. 'E'
N. 969'-7"
CHAN. NOZ.
N. 966'-1"

COL. 'F'
N. 961'-3"

BASE EDGE N. 957'-0"

MONORAIL AND
SUPPORT STEEL
NOT INCLUDED

COL. 'G'
N. 942'-6"

BATTERY LIMITS N. 939'-0"

DN

DN

TAN. LINE
N. 966'-5"

BASE EDGE W.1000'-8"

NOTES
1. 12-1302-02-₵ EL.132'-0"
   12-1302-01-₵ EL.129'-0"
   12-1201-₵ EL. 120'-3"
   12-1301-₵ EL. 104'-10"
2. ALL PUMP FDNS.
   ARE EL. 101'-0" TOC

EQUIP. LOCATION PLAN

SK-2

241

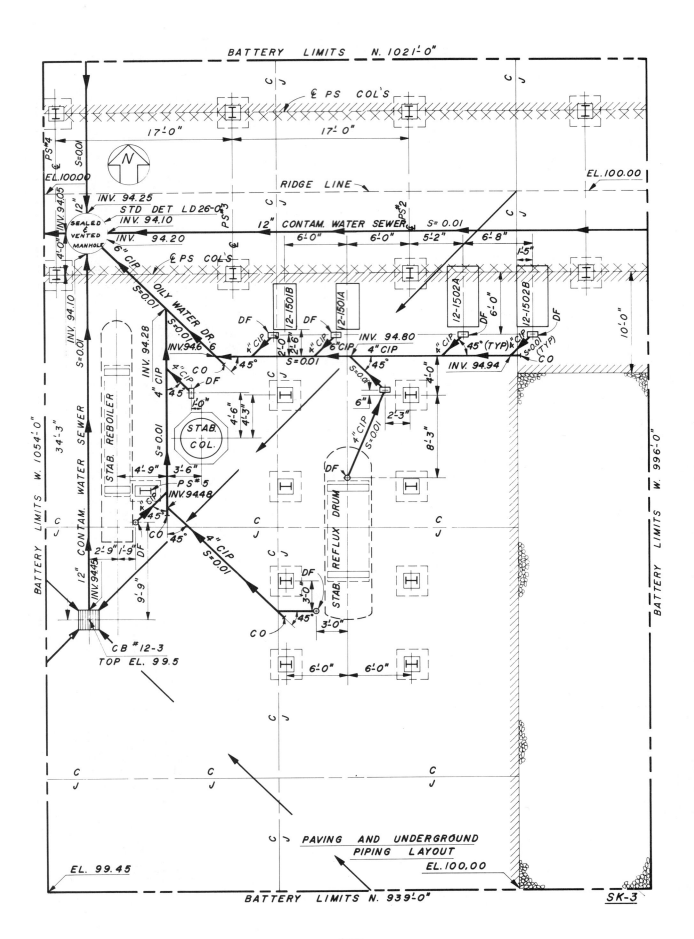

SK-3

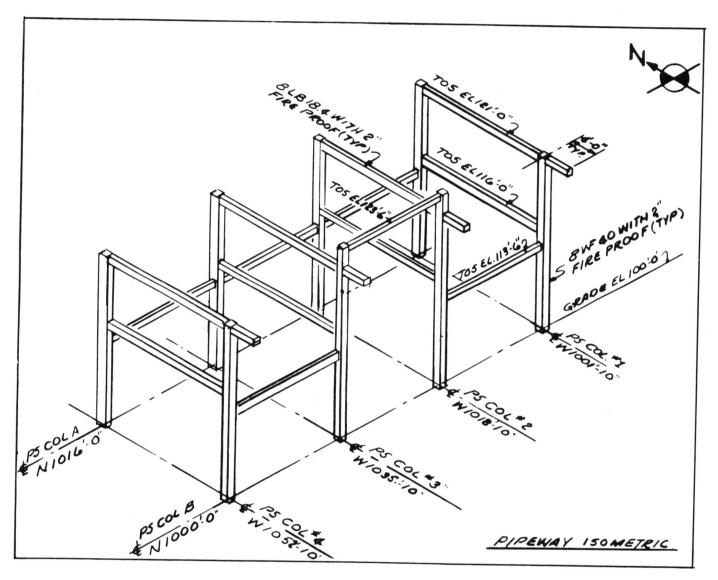

N

8 LB 18.4 WITH 2"
FIRE PROOF (TYP)

TOS EL 121'-0"

TOS EL 116'-0"

TOS EL 113'-6"

TOS EL 113'-6"

8 WF 40 WITH 2"
FIRE PROOF (TYP)

EL 121'-0"
WT

GRADE EL 100'-0"

PS COL A
℄ N 1016'-0"

PS COL B
℄ N 1000'-0"

PS COL #1
℄ W 1001'-0"

PS COL #2
℄ W 1018'-0"

PS COL #3
℄ W 1035'-0"

PS COL #4
℄ W 1052'-0"

PIPEWAY ISOMETRIC

SK-4

243

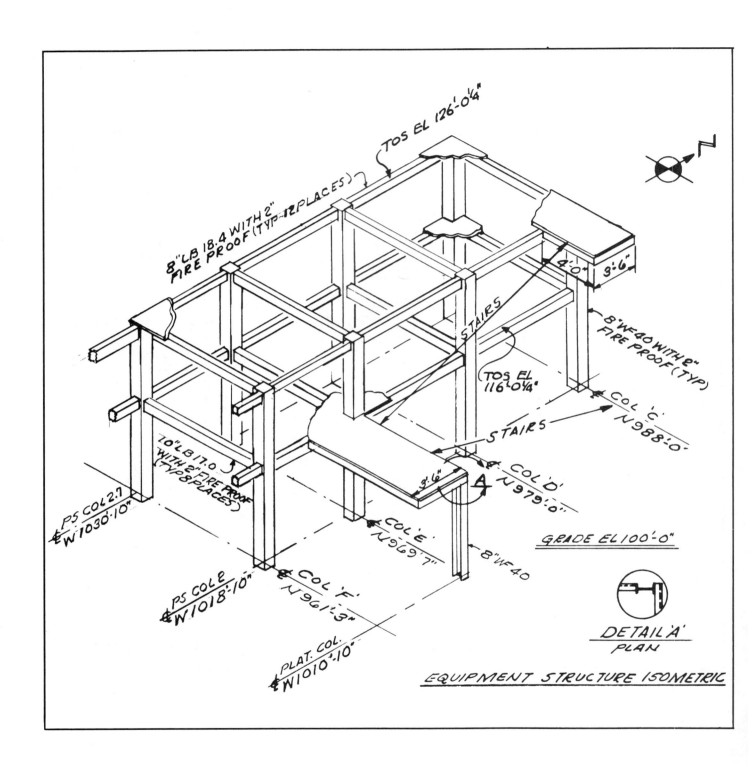

TOS EL 126'-0¼"

8"LB 18.4 WITH 2"
FIRE PROOF (TYP-12 PLACES)

4'-0"   3'-6"

8"WF 40 WITH 2"
FIRE PROOF (TYP)

STAIRS

TOS EL 116'-0¼"

COL 'C'
N 988'-0"

STAIRS

10"LB 17.0
WITH 2" FIRE PROOF
(TYP 8 PLACES)

COL 'D'
N 979'-0"

3'-6"

A

PS COL 2.7
W 1030'-10"

COL 'E'
N 969'-7"

GRADE EL 100'-0"

8"WF 40

PS COL 2
W 1018'-10"

COL 'F'
N 961'-3"

DETAIL 'A'
PLAN

PLAT. COL.
W 1010'-10"

EQUIPMENT STRUCTURE ISOMETRIC

SK-5

244

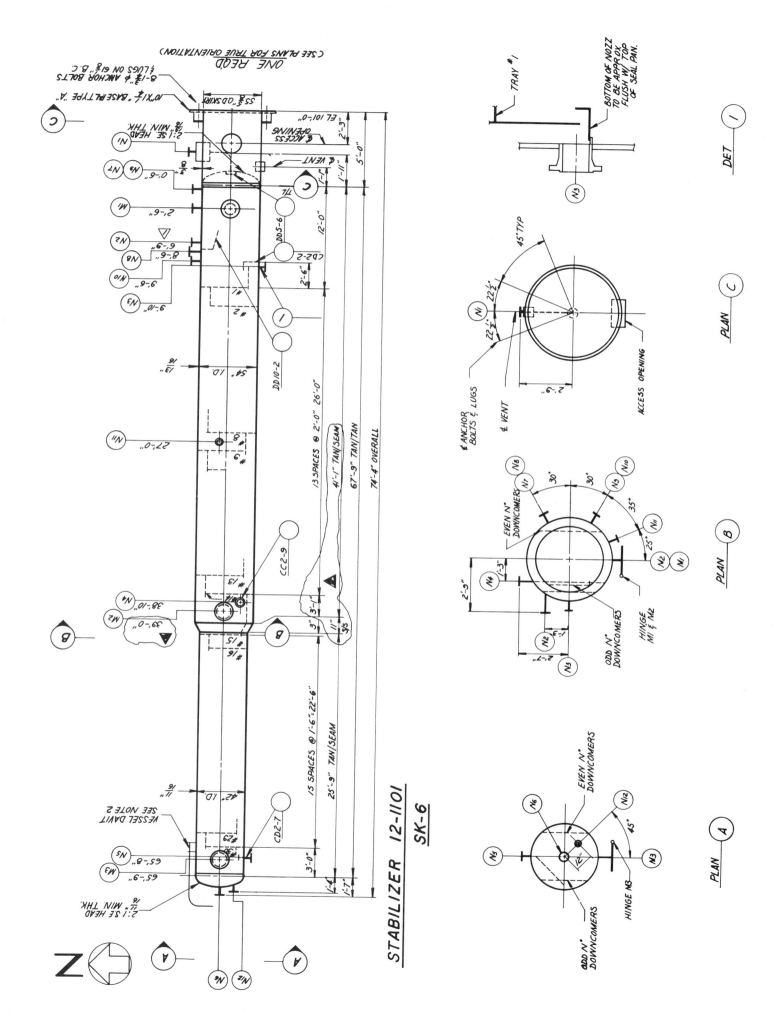

STABILIZER 12-1101

SK-6

NOTES

1. TRAYS ARE FURNISHED BY TRAY FABRICATOR AND SHOP INSTALLED BY VESSEL FABRICATOR.

2. VESSEL FABRICATOR SHALL FURNISH AND INSTALL VESSEL DAVIT COMPLETE.

ITEM	NO. REQ'D	SIZE	RATING	FACING	SERVICE
N12	1	2″	300.	RF	VENT
N11	1	1½″	300.	RF	TIC
N9,N10	2	2″	300.	RF	L.G. CONN.
N7,N8	2	2″	300.	RF	LIC CONN.
N6	1	6″	300.	RF	VAPOR OUT
N5	1	2″	300.	RF	REFLUX
N4	1	4″	300.	RF	FEED
N3	1	8″	300.	RF	REBLR DRAW
N2	1	10″	300.	RF	REBLR RETURN
N1	1	4″	300.	RF	BOTTOMS OUT
M1,M2,M3	3	18″10	300.	RF	MANHOLES 1 FIG. 1

NOZZLES AND COUPLINGS

RADIAL NOZZLE AND MANHOLE PROJECTIONS FROM O.D.
OF VESSEL TO EXTREME FACE OF FLANGE;

SIZE	PROJECTION	SIZE	PROJECTION
THRU 4″	6″	6″,8″ AND 10″	8″
12″,14″,16″,18″, AND 20″	10″	24″	12″

EXCEPT FOR INTEGRAL-REINFORCED NOZZLES, OR AS NOTED

DD 5-6	VORTEX BREAKER VESSELS
DD 4-8	1500 # VESSEL DAVITS
DD 1-5	PRESSURE VESSEL TOLERANCES
DC 9-9	SKIRT AND BASE DETAILS
DC 4-7	PIPE SUPPORTS FOR VESSELS
CD 2-7	TOP TRAY DISTRIBUTOR PIPES
CD 2-2	TRAY SEAL PANS
CC 2-9	INTERMEDIATE TRAY DISTRIBUTOR PIPES
RMP STDS	REFERENCE DRAWINGS
ODI	PAINT SPECIFICATION
CDI	TRAY SPECIFICATION
DDI	VESSEL SPECIFICATIONS
1000	
DD 10-2	VAPOR INLET DEFLECTOR BAFFLE
DD 9-4	INSULATION & FIREPROOFING SUPPORTS
DD 8-10	STD. BOLT HOLE ORIENTATION
DD 8-4	MANHOLE COVER HINGE & HANDLE
DD 8-2	MIN. NOZZLE NECKS
RMP. STDS.	REFERENCE DRAWINGS

DESIGN DATA

1. OPERATING PRESSURE AT __466__ F __335__ PSIG
2. DESIGN PRESSURE AT __491__ F __369__ PSIG

3. PRESSURE NEW LTD. BY __CONE__ AT __AMB__ F __435__ PSIG
4. CORROSION ALLOWANCE: SHELL __⅛″__, HEADS __⅛″__
5. CODE __ASME SECT VIII DIV. 1 LATEST EDITION__

6. CODE CERTIFICATES REQ'D __YES__, CODE STAMP __YES__
7. PW HT __NO__, X-RAYED __SPOT__
8. ALL STRESS AT DESIGN TEMP. __17500__ JT. EFF. SHELL __85%__
9. HYDROTEST AT __653__ PSIG (HORIZONTAL) HEADS __85%__
10. MATERIALS:
    SHELL __SA-515-70__
    HEAD __SA-515-70__
    SUPPORT __SA-36__
    TRAYS __SEE TRAY DATA SHT__
    BOLTS (EXTERNAL) __SA-181-1__ NUTS __SA-194-2H__
    FLANGES __SA-181-1__ CPLGS. __SA-105__
    NOZZLE-NECKS __SA-106B__
    GASKETS __1/16″ JM 60 OR EQUAL__
11. CAPACITY __984 CU. FT.__
12. FABRICATION WEIGHT (EXCLUDING TRAYS) __42400 LBS.__
13. TRAYS, CAPS AND RISERS, WEIGHT __4100 LBS.__
14. EMPTY WEIGHT __59500 LBS.__
15. OPERATING WEIGHT __75900 LBS.__
16. TEST WEIGHT __118700 LBS.__
17. PAINT __PER PAINT SPECIFICATION 1000-001__
18. INSULATION __2″__
19. FIREPROOFING __2″ O.S. SKIRT ONLY__
20. ACCESSORIES SUPPLIED & INSTALLED BY FABRICATOR:
    VESSEL DAVIT __YES__ MARK NO. __10__
    LADDER AND PLATFORM CLIPS __YES__
    PIPE SUPPORT AND PIPE GUIDE CLIPS __YES__
    INSULATION SUPPORTS __YES__
    FIREPROOFING SUPPORTS __YES__
21. ALL TRAY ELEVATIONS ARE TO TOP OF TRAY SUPPORT RING.
22. ALL DIMENSIONS ARE FROM BOTTOM HEAD TANGENT LINE EXCEPT AS SHOWN.
23. BOLT HOLES SHALL STRADDLE CENTER LINES EXCEPT AS NOTED
24. NOZZLES, MANHOLES AND TRAYS SHALL HAVE THE SAME DESIGNATION AS SHOWN ON THIS DRAWING.
25. VESSEL SHALL BE THOROUGHLY CLEANED INSIDE AND OUTSIDE, AND FREE FROM RUST, SLAG, SCALE, WELD SPATTER AND FOREIGN MATTER.

SCALE: NONE

STABILIZER 12-1101

REV. NO.	CUST. APP.	DATE	REVISIONS	BY	CHK.	JOB ENGR.	PROJ ENGR.
2			REV'D S/S OF CONE & OTHERS TO SUIT. ELEV. MZ was 44'-0″				
1			DWG. NO. was 1000-CB, ELEV. NOZ. NR was 7'-6″				
0							

SK-6   REV. 2

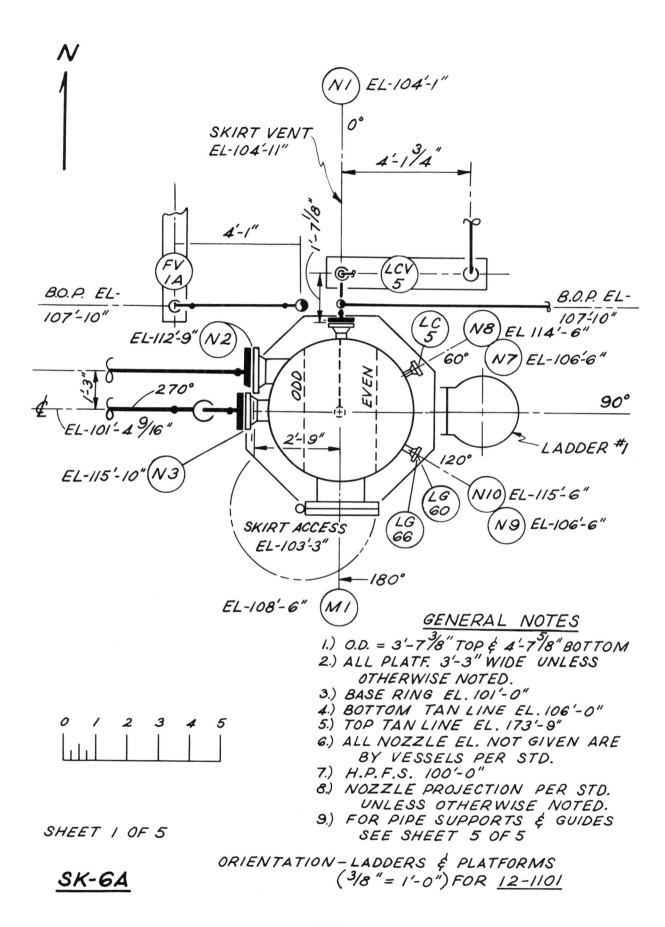

N

N1 EL-104'-1"

0°

SKIRT VENT
EL-104'-11"

4'-1 3/4"

4'-1"

1'-7 1/8"

FV
1A

LCV
5

B.O.P. EL-
107'-10"

B.O.P. EL-
107'-10"

EL-112'-9" N2

LC
5

N8 EL 114'-6"

60°

N7 EL-106'-6"

ODD   EVEN

270°

90°

1'-3"

EL-101'-4 9/16"

LADDER #1

EL-115'-10" N3

2'-9"

120°

LG
60

N10 EL-115'-6"

LG
66

N9 EL-106'-6"

SKIRT ACCESS
EL-103'-3"

180°

EL-108'-6" M1

GENERAL NOTES

1.) O.D. = 3'-7 3/8" TOP & 4'-7 5/8" BOTTOM
2.) ALL PLATF. 3'-3" WIDE UNLESS
    OTHERWISE NOTED.
3.) BASE RING EL.101'-0"
4.) BOTTOM TAN LINE EL.106'-0"
5.) TOP TAN LINE EL.173'-9"
6.) ALL NOZZLE EL. NOT GIVEN ARE
    BY VESSELS PER STD.
7.) H.P.F.S. 100'-0"
8.) NOZZLE PROJECTION PER STD.
    UNLESS OTHERWISE NOTED.
9.) FOR PIPE SUPPORTS & GUIDES
    SEE SHEET 5 OF 5

0 1 2 3 4 5

SHEET 1 OF 5

SK-6A

ORIENTATION—LADDERS & PLATFORMS
(3/8" = 1'-0") FOR 12-1101

247

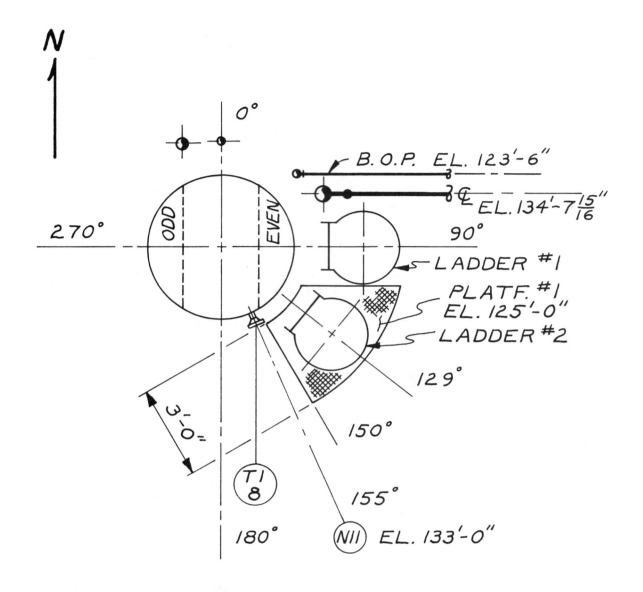

N

0°

B.O.P. EL. 123'-6"

270°

ODD EVEN

90°

C̵ EL. 134'-7 15/16"

LADDER #1

PLATF. #1
EL. 125'-0"

LADDER #2

129°

150°

3'-0"

155°

T1/8

N11 EL. 133'-0"

180°

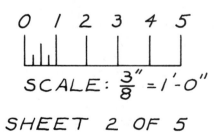

0 1 2 3 4 5

SCALE: 3/8" = 1'-0"

SHEET 2 OF 5

BASE ELEVATION
ORIENTATION - LADDERS & PLATFORMS
_SK-6B_

248

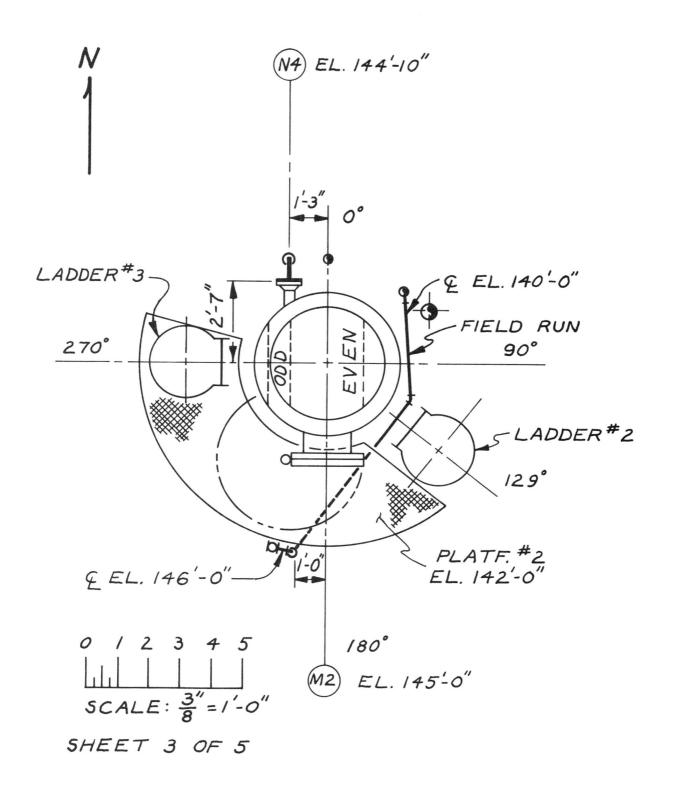

N

N4 EL. 144'-10"

1'-3" 0°

LADDER #3

2'-7"

270°

℄ EL. 140'-0"

FIELD RUN
90°

ODD EVEN

LADDER #2

129°

℄ EL. 146'-0"

1'-0"

PLATF. #2
EL. 142'-0"

180°

M2 EL. 145'-0"

0 1 2 3 4 5

SCALE: $\frac{3''}{8}=1'-0''$

SHEET 3 OF 5

BASE ELEVATION
ORIENTATION – LADDERS & PLATFORMS
FOR 12-1101

SK-6C

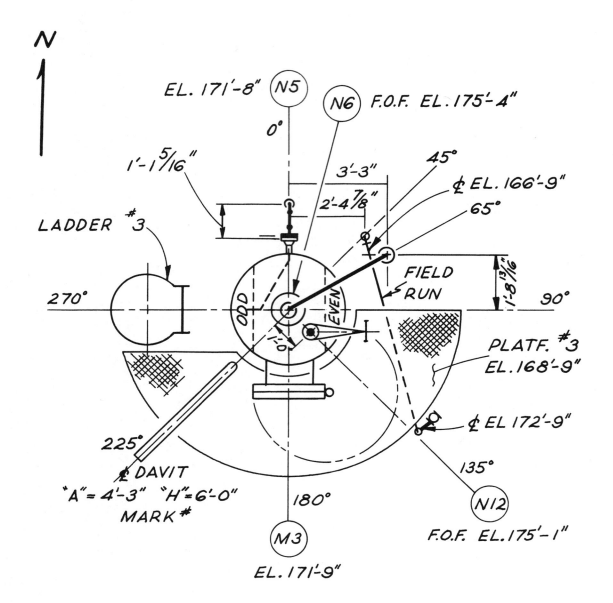

N

LADDER #3

EL. 171'-8" (N5)

(N6) F.O.F. EL. 175'-4"

0°

1'-1 5/16"

45°

℄ EL. 166'-9"

3'-3"

65°

2'-4 7/8"

270°

ODD

EVEN

FIELD RUN

90°

1'-8 13/16"

PLATF. #3
EL. 168'-9"

225°

℄ DAVIT
"A" = 4'-3" "H" = 6'-0"
MARK #

180°

℄ EL. 172'-9"

135°

(N12)

F.O.F. EL. 175'-1"

(M3)

EL. 171'-9"

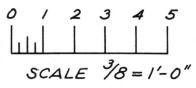

0   1   2   3   4   5

SCALE 3/8 = 1'-0"

SHEET 4 OF 5

BASE ELEVATION
ORIENTATION - LADDERS & PLATFORMS
FOR 12-1101
SK-6D

NOZZLE NO. & SIZE		P.S. STD. DC 4-7			"L" DIM.	P.G. STD. DC 4-6		APPROX. WT. FULL OF WATER
		MK	ORIENT. FR. NORTH (C.W.)	W.L. ELEV.		ORIENT. FR. NORTH	W.L. ELEV.	
NG	6″	PS-2	65°	166′-6″	18⅛″	—	—	
					12″	65°	136′-6″	
N4	4″	PS-1	345°	137′-3″	12″	345°	111′-3″	
N5	2″	PS-1	0°	164′-8″	18⅛″	0°	144′-8″	
					12″	0°	128′-8″	
					12″	0°	18′-8″	
X	1½″	PS-1	45°	160′-6″	12⅛″	45°	144′-8″	
					6″	45°	134′-0″	

SHEET 5 OF 5

	TITLE		SCALE: NONE
MA	PIPE SUPPORTS & GUIDES FOR 12-1101		ACCOUNT NUMBER
	JOB NUMBER	DRAWING NUMBER **SK-6E**	REV.

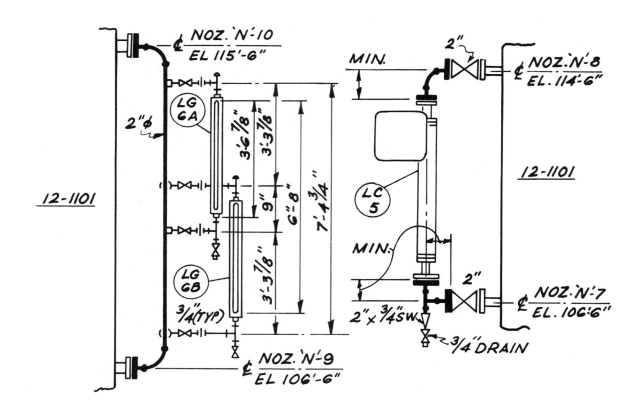

NOZ. `N-10`
EL 115'-6"

LG 6A

NOZ. `N-8`
EL. 114'-6"

2"

2"φ

12-1101

12-1101

3'-6⅞"
3'-3⅜"
9"
6'-8"
7'-4¼"

LG 6B

LC 5

3'-3⅜"

¾"(TYP)

MIN.

MIN.

2"

2" x ¾"SW

¾"DRAIN

NOZ. `N-9`
EL 106'-6"

NOZ. `N-7`
EL. 106'-6"

SK-7

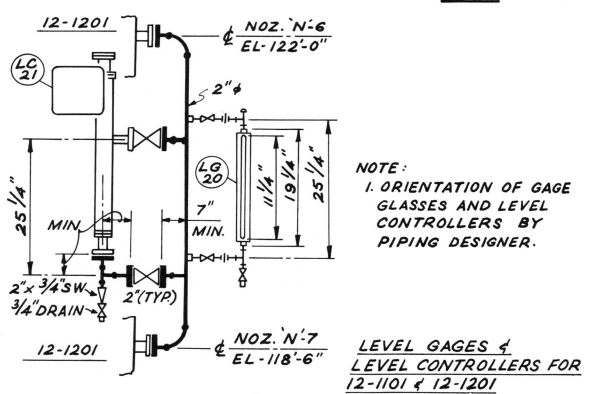

12-1201

NOZ. `N-6`
EL-122'-0"

LC 21

2"φ

LG 20

11¼"
19¼"
25¼"

25¼"

NOTE:
1. ORIENTATION OF GAGE
   GLASSES AND LEVEL
   CONTROLLERS BY
   PIPING DESIGNER.

MIN.

7"
MIN.

2" x ¾"SW
¾"DRAIN

2"(TYP.)

12-1201

NOZ. `N-7`
EL.-118'-6"

LEVEL GAGES &
LEVEL CONTROLLERS FOR
12-1101 & 12-1201

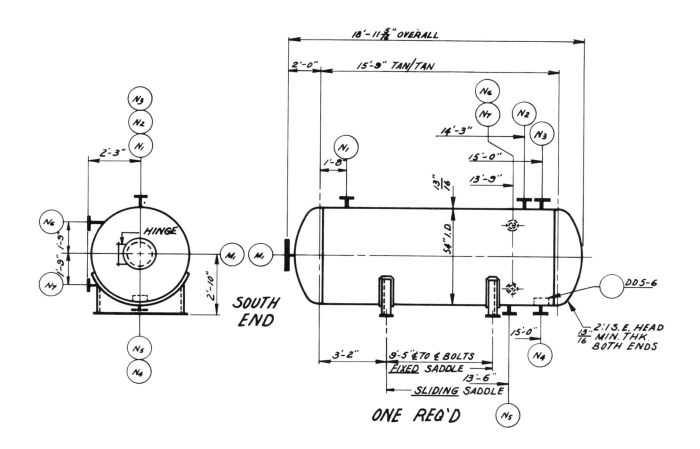

18'-11⅝" OVERALL
15'-9" TAN/TAN
2'-0"
14'-3"
15'-0"
13'-9"
1'-8"
13"/16
54" I.D.
N₃
N₂
N₁
2'-3"
N₆
HINGE
N₇
1'-9" 1'-9"
M₁ M₁
2'-10"
SOUTH END
N₅
N₄
N₆
N₇
N₂
N₃
DD5-6
2:1 S.E. HEAD
13"/16 MIN. THK.
BOTH ENDS
3'-2"
9'-5" ₵ TO ₵ BOLTS
FIXED SADDLE
13'-6"
SLIDING SADDLE
15'-0"
N₄
N₅
ONE REQ'D

STABILIZER REFLUX PUMP
SK-8

253

DESIGN DATA

1. OPERATING PRESSURE AT ___100___ F ___325___ PSIG
2. DESIGN PRESSURE AT ___125___ F ___369___ PSIG
   _____
3. PRESSURE NEW LTD. BY ___SHELL___ AT ___AMB___ F ___439___ PSIG
4. CORROSION ALLOWANCE: SHELL ___1/8″___, HEADS ___1/8″___
5. CODE ___ASME SECT VIII DIV. 1 LATEST EDITION___
   ___SPEC 1000-DD1-1___
6. CODE CERTIFICATES REQ'D ___YES___, CODE STAMP ___YES___
7. PW HT ___NO___, X-RAYED ___SPOT___
8. ALL STRESS AT DESIGN TEMP. ___17500___ JT. EFF. SHELL ___85%___
9. HYDROTEST AT ___658___ PSIG (HORIZONTAL)   HEADS ___85%___
10. MATERIALS:
    SHELL ___SA-515-70___
    HEAD ___SA-515-70___
    SUPPORT ___SA-36___
    TRAYS _____
    BOLTS (EXTERNAL) ___SA-193-B7___ NUTS ___SA-194-2H___
    FLANGES ___SA-181-1___ CPLGS. _____
    NOZZLE-NECKS ___SA-106-B___
    GASKETS ___1/16″ JM 60 OR EQUAL___
11. CAPACITY ___274 CU. FT.___
12. FABRICATION WEIGHT (EXCLUDING TRAYS) ___12000*___
13. TRAYS, CAPS AND RISERS, WEIGHT _____
14. EMPTY WEIGHT ___13300*___
15. OPERATING WEIGHT ___21900*___
16. TEST WEIGHT ___30500*___
17. PAINT ___PER PAINT SPECIFICATION 1000-001___
18. INSULATION ___NO___
19. FIREPROOFING ___NO___
20. ACCESSORIES SUPPLIED & INSTALLED BY FABRICATOR:
    VESSEL DAVIT ___NO___ MARK NO. _____
    LADDER AND PLATFORM CLIPS _____
    PIPE SUPPORT AND PIPE GUIDE CLIPS ___NO___
    INSULATION SUPPORTS ___NO___
    FIREPROOFING SUPPORTS ___NO___
21. ALL TRAY ELEVATIONS ARE TO TOP OF TRAY SUPPORT RING.
22. ALL DIMENSIONS ARE FROM LEFT HEAD TANGENT LINE EXCEPT AS SHOWN.
23. BOLT HOLES SHALL STRADDLE CENTER LINES EXCEPT AS NOTED
24. NOZZLES, MANHOLES AND TRAYS SHALL HAVE THE SAME DESIGNATION AS SHOWN ON THIS DRAWING.
25. VESSEL SHALL BE THOROUGHLY CLEANED INSIDE AND OUTSIDE, AND FREE FROM RUST, SLAG, SCALE, WELD SPATTER AND FOREIGN MATTER.

ITEM	NO. REQ'D	SIZE	RATING	FACING	SERVICE
N6-7	2	2″	300.	RF	LG-LC CONN
N5	1	2″	300.	RF	DRAIN
N4	1	4″	300.	RF	HC LIQUID OUT
N3	1	1 1/2″	300.	RF	VENT
N2	1	3″	300.	RF	VAPOR OUT
N1	1	3″	300.	RF	FEED
M1	1	18″	300.	RF	MANHOLE W7 HINGE FIG 1

NOZZLES AND COUPLINGS

RADIAL NOZZLE AND MANHOLE PROJECTIONS FROM O.D.
OF VESSEL TO EXTREME FACE OF FLANGE;

SIZE	PROJECTION	SIZE	PROJECTION
THRU 4″	6″	6″,8″ AND 10″	8″
12″,14″,16″,18″, AND 20″	10″	24″	12″

EXCEPT FOR INTEGRAL-REINFORCED NOZZLES, OR AS NOTED

DD 1-5	PRESSURE VESSEL TOLERANCES
DD 8-10	STANDARD BOLT HOLE ORIENTATION
DD 8-2	MIN NOZZLE NECK THICKNESS
DD 8-4	MANHOLE COVER WITH HINGE & HANDLE
DD 5-6	VORTEX BREAKER VESSELS
DC 9-8	WELDED SADDLES FOR VESSELS
RMP STD	REFERENCE DRAWINGS

OD 1	PAINT SPECIFICATION
DD 1-1	PRESSURE VESSEL SPECIFICATION
1000	REFERENCE DRAWINGS

SCALE ___NONE___

STABILIZER REFLUX DRUM

SK—8   REV. 0

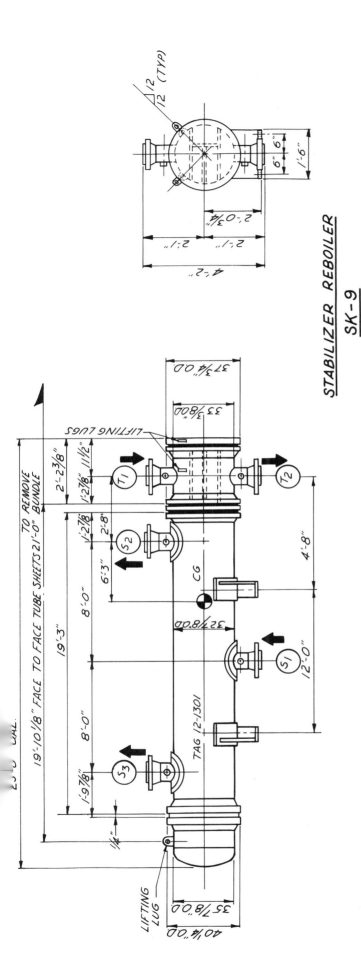

STABILIZER REBOILER
SK-9

EST. WEIGHTS	
DRY	18,400 #
WET	25,800 #
BUNDLE	10,800 #

NOZZLES		
T_1	4"	150# RF-WN
T_2	4"	150# RF-WN
S_1	8"	300# RF-WN
S_2	8"	300# RF-WN
S_3	8"	300# RF-WN

	SHELL	CHAN	MATERIALS
DESIGN PRESS PSI	375	85	ALL MATERIAL
TEST PRESS PSI	562#	128#	CARBON
DESIGN TEMP °F	510	691	STEEL
CORR. ALLOW	1/8"	1/8"	
NO. PASSES	DIV	8	
X-RAY	SPOT	SPOT	
HEAT TREAT			

TUBES 534 3/4"OD x14 BWG (MIN) x20'-0" LG
TUBE PITCH 1"□
ALL BOLT HOLES TO STRADDLE ℄'S.
1"(NS) 6000# CPLG. IN EA. NOZZLE
PAINT SSPC-SP6 GREEN,GRAY INORGANIC ZINC, MOBIL
ZINC 7 COMPOUND,TO 2.5 TO 3.0 MILS.(MIN)DRY FILM
THICKNESS ON 1.0 TO 1.5 MILS MAX. SURFACE PROFILE
GASKETS 1/8"THK SOLID ARMCO IRON
(1-SET SPARE GASKETS REQ'D)
TEMA "R" ASME CODE (SECTION VIII DIVISION I) ℰ
SO STAMPED.

ASSEMBLY & SPECIFICATIONS
FOR STABILIZER REBOILER
SK-9

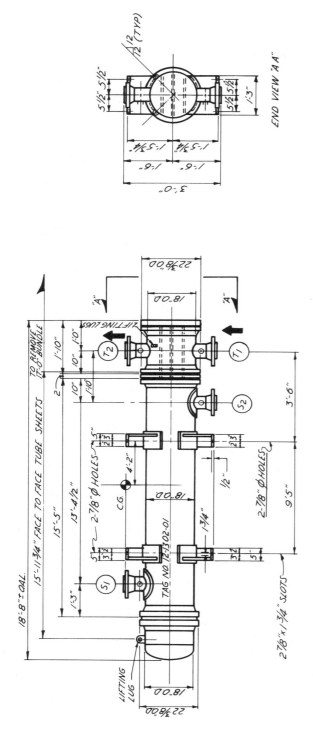

END VIEW "A-A"

	SHELL	CHAN	MATERIALS
DESIGN PRESS A.S.D.	369	75	ALL MATERIAL
TEST PRESS P.S.I.	554	113	CARBON STEEL
DESIGN TEMP. °F	189	160	
CORR. ALLOW.	1/8"	1/8"	
NO. PASSES	1	6	
X-RAY	SPOT	SPOT	
HEAT TREAT	NO	YES	

TUBES: 100 - 3/4" O.D. x 14 BWG.(MIN.) x 16'-0" LG
TUBE PITCH 1" □
ALL BOLT HOLES TO STRADDLE ℄'s
1"(N.S) 6000# CPLG IN EA. NOZZLE
PAINT: SSPC-SP6 GREEN, GRAY INORGANIC ZINC, MOBIL
ZINC 7 COMPOUND, TO 2.5 TO 3.0 MILS.(MIN.) DRY FILM
THICKNESS ON 1.0 TO 1.5 MILS. MAX. SURFACE PROFILE
GASKETS: 1/8" THK: SOLID ARMCO IRON
(1-SET SPARE GASKETS REQ'D.)

TEMA "R", ASME CODE (SECTION VIII. DIVISION I)
& SO STAMPED.

NOZZLES		EST. WEIGHTS
T1	4"-150# RF-WN	DRY: 5600#
T2	4"-150# RF-WN	WET: 7400#
S1	6"-300# RF-WN	BUNDLE: 2100#
S2	3"-300# RF-WN	

ASSEMBLY & SPECIFICATIONS

FOR STABILIZER REFLUX CONDENSER

SK-10

NOTE:
THIS EXCHANGER
STACKS W/12-J302-02
SEE DWG #74-19-8-1
FOR ARRANGEMENT.

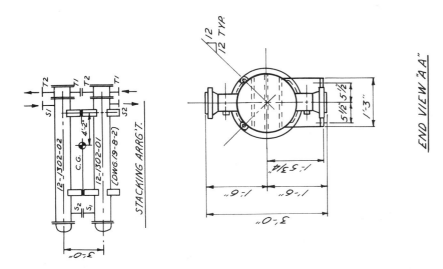

STACKING ARR'G'T.

END VIEW "AA"

NOTE: SAME SPECIFICATIONS AS SK-10

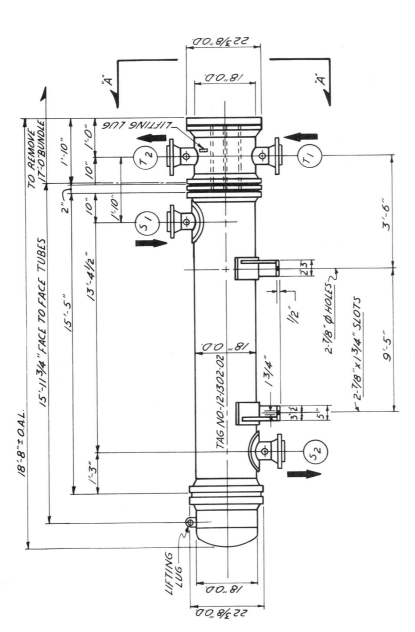

ASSEMBLY & SPECIFICATIONS
FOR STABLIZER REFLUX CONDENSER

SK-11

257

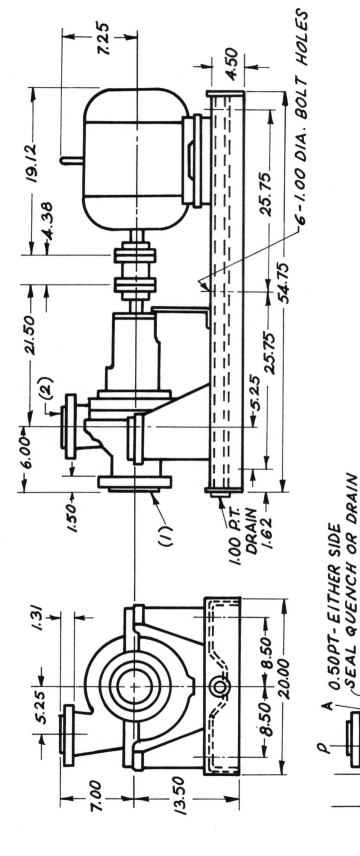

PUMP 150 X 8 AN WT.-270# MOTOR FRAME 213TS   H.P. 7½   RPM 3600   WT. 141#   BED WT   215#

7.25

19.12

4.38

21.50

(2)

6.00

1.50

(1)

4.50

25.75

6 - 1.00 DIA. BOLT HOLES

54.75

25.75

5.25

1.00 P.T. DRAIN

1.62

1.31

5.25

7.00

13.50

8.50

8.50

20.00

A   0.50 PT.- EITHER SIDE
SEAL QUENCH OR DRAIN

P

BN   BD

E   BE   U   Y

G

STABILIZER REFLUX PUMP

SK-12

(1) 4" SUCTION—300# ASA R.F.
(2) 2" DISCHARGE—300# ASA R.F.

A 0.50PT SEAL VENT—INTERNAL CIRCULATION
E 0.75PT BRG BRKT DRAIN-GLAND LEAKAGE
G 0.75PT CASING DRAIN-PLUGGED
P 0.75PT CASING VENT-PLUGGED
U 1.00PT BRG COOLING CARTRIDGE INLET- FAR SIDE-PLUGGED-COOLING NOT FURN.
   1.00PT BRG COOLING CARTRIDGE OUTLET- FAR SIDE-PLUGGED-COOLING NOT FURN.

BN 0.50PT BRG HSG OIL FILL-PLUGGED
BD 0.50PT BRG HSG OIL VENT-PLUGGED
BE 0.75PT BRG HSG DRAIN-PLUGGED

TRICO OILER FURNISHED-LOCATED ON LEFT SIDE OF
BEARING HOUSING WHEN FACING COUPLING END.

COUPLING & GUARD FURN BY VENDOR.

BASEPLATE DRIVER SUPPORTS WILL NOT BE DRILLED
AND TAPPED BY VENDOR'S SHOPS WHEN DRIVER
IS TO BE FIELD MOUNTED.

GENERAL NOTES

ALLOW 25 FOR VARIATION OF DRAINS. CENTERLINE HEIGHT AND FOUNDATION BOLT HOLES FOUNDATION BOLTS SHOULD NOT BE SET RIGIDLY UNTIL RECEIPT OF EQUIPMENT ALLOW 75 UNDER BEDPLATE FOR GROUTING.

PIPING AND FITTINGS NOT REFERENCED ARE TO BE FURNISHED BY CUSTOMER.

DESIGN PIPING SYSTEMS TO MINIMIZE PUMP NOZZLE LOADS.

ALL HOLES IN FLANGES STRADDLE CENTERLINE.

WHEN OPERATING FOR SOME TIME AT REDUCED CAPACITY, MUCH OF THE PUMP HORSEPOWER WILL GO INTO THE LIQUID IN THE FORM OF HEAT. A BY-PASS MUST BE PROVIDED UNDER THESE CONDITIONS TO PREVENT THE LIQUID IN THE PUMP FROM BECOMING HOT ENOUGH TO VAPORIZE.

DAMAGE TO PUMP MAY RESULT FROM PROLONGED OPERATIONS AT CAPACITIES LESS THAN TWENTY FIVE PERCENT OF THE BEST EFFICIENCY POINT.

THIS DRAWING IS NOT TO SCALE WORK FROM DIMENSIONS.

REALIGN UNIT AND READ INSTRUCTION BOOK BEFORE STARTING EQUIPMENT.

CUSTOMER	
CUST. ORD.	CUST IT.
CUST. REQ	
P.O. ORD.	P.O. IT.
LIQUID LIGHT HYDROCARBON	
SERVICE STABILIZER REFLUX	
CERTIFIED REVISION	

STABILIZER REFLUX PUMP

GENERAL ARRANGEMENT

SK-12

REV.

OVERHEAD PRODUCT PUMP

GSJ TOP SUCTION–MOTOR DRIVEN

SK-13

PUMP ROTATION CCW FROM COUPLING END

$\frac{7}{8}$" DIA HOLE – (4) PLACES

$3\frac{1}{2}$" $3\frac{1}{2}$" $\frac{1}{8}$"

AIR COOLED ⊠

CONDUIT HOLE AA

PUMP SIZE / MOTOR FRAME SIZE

Dis-charge	Suc-tion	Im-peller	P	H	M	S	W	X	Z	HT	HR	HD (C)	324TS HC (28⅛)	324TS Base No.	326TS HD (29⅝)	326TS HC	326TS Base No.	364TS HD (30 15/16)	364TS HC	364TS Base No.	405TS HD (31 15/16)	405TS HC	405TS Base No.
1½	3	10½	4¼	7½	2¼	1⅜	28 15/16	10	5¾	4⅜	3¾	21¼	61 7/16	12A	21¼	62 15/16	12A	21¼	64¼	12B	21¼	65¼	12B
2	3	11½	5	8	2½	2	29	10½	6½	5	4¼	21¼	62⅛	12A	21¼	63⅜	12A	21¼	64 15/16	12B	21¼	65 15/16	12B
3	4	11½	5½	9	3¼	2½	30 7/16	11	7½	5	6¼	21¼	63 9/16	12A	21¼	65 1/16	12A	21¼	66⅜	12B	21¼	67⅜	12B
2	4	13	5	8	2⅞	2½	30	12	7½	5	8	21¼	63⅛	12A	21¼	64⅝	12A	21¼	65 15/16	12B	21¼	66 15/16	12B

SK-13

ITEM	SIZE	DESCRIPTION	YES	NO
P-1	4 OZ.	OILER FAR SIDE	X	
P-2		OIL FILLER CUP	X	
P-3	½ P.T.	SEAL RECIRCULATION CASE TAP.	X	
P-4	½ P.T.	OIL DRAIN PLUGGED	X	
P-5	¾ P.T.	DRAIN	X	
P-6	¾ P.T.	CASE DRAIN PLUGGED	X	
P-7	1½ P.T.	BASE PLATE DRAIN	X	
P-8	½ P.T.	PED. COOL WATER IN & OUT		X
P-9	½ P.T.	INLET BRG. WATER JACKET		X
P-10	½ P.T.	OUTLET BRG. WATER JACKET		X
P-11	¼ P.T.	PACKING GLAND QUENCH		X
P-12	½ P.T.	CAGE RING CONN. IN & OUT ON NORI7		
P-13	SEE NOTE 4	STUFF BOX WATER JACKET CLOSURE		
P-14	½ P.T.	SEAL VENT OR QUENCH INLET	X	
P-15	½ P.T.	SEAL QUENCH DRAIN	X	
P-16	½ P.T.	SEAL INJECTION	X	
P-17	¾ P.T.	GAGE CONNECTION		X
P-18	¾ P.T.	VENT CONNECTION		X

NOTES:
1. PUMPS ARE SELF VENTING.
2. SUCT. & DISCH FLGS. = 300 A.S.A. ¼ R.F.
3. THREE 4″ DIA GROUT HOLES (MIN.) ⅜ DIA VENT HOLES—
   AS REQUIRED FOR FULL GROUTING.
4. ½ P T IN & OUT ON VERT. & ALWAYS SUPPLIED WITH OR
   WITHOUT WATER JACKET CLOSURE.
5. BOSSES PROVIDED FOR ADDITION OF TAPS WHEN REQUIRED.
6. BJ STD. COUPLING GUARD MEETS CALIF. SAFETY REQUIREMENTS.

BASEPLATE DIMENSIONS

BASE NO.	HA	HB	HE	HF	HL
12A.B	31	66	14	42	24

MOTOR: MFGR _____
  HP _____ R.P.M. _____
  TYPE _____ FRAME   405 TS
  PHASE _____ CYCLE _____ VOLTS _____

CONDUIT BOX DIMENSIONS

AA	AC	AF	L

WEIGHT: PUMP AND BASE_____
  MOTOR _____ TOTAL _____

REVISIONS

DESCRIPTION	DATE	APPROVED

A. NO PIPING WILL BE SHOWN ON THIS DRAWING.
   SEE DRAWING INFORMATION BELOW.

B. COOL WATER PIPING SUPPLIED BY B.J.   YES ☐   NO ☐
   PER DRAWING _____

C. SEAL RECIRCULATION LINE - FURN BY B.J. YES ☐   NO ☐
   A.P.I. PLAN _____   DRAWING NO. _____

D. COUPLING FASTS. MOD B.J. SIZE   ☐
   OTHER _____

E. COUPLING GUARD B.J. STD. (SEE NOTE 6)   ☐
   OTHER _____

F. PUMP WITH PACKING   YES ☐   NO ☐
   6 RINGS SIZE _____ TYPE _____

G. PUMP WITH MECHANICAL SEAL   YES ☐   NO ☐
   TYPE _____

CUSTOMER: _____
  USER _____
  LOCATION _____
  CUSTOMER ORDER NO. _____
  CUSTOMER ITEM NO. _____

SERVICE: _____ OVERHEAD PRODUCT _____
  B.J. ORDER NO. _____

PUMP:
  SIZE & TYPE   2 X 4 X 131   GSJ _____

APPROVED FOR CONSTRUCTION
  BY _____
  DATE _____

IMPORTANT—APPROVAL DRAWING NOTES

1. PURCHASER'S COMMENTS AND/OR CORRECTIONS WITHIN THE SCOPE OF CONTRACT WILL BE MADE ON THE FIRST COMPLETED CERTIFIED DRAWING SUBSTITUTED BY _____ CORP. AND RETURNED FOR CORRECTION.

2. CORRECTIONS, ALTERATIONS, ADDITIONS, AND/OR MODIFICATIONS OUTSIDE SCOPE OR CONTRATE OR MADE AFTER FIRST SUBMITTAL WILL REQUIRE AN ENGINEERING SERVICE CHARGE AND MAY CHANGE PRICE.

3. ITEMS CONDITIONALLY APPROVED OR NEEDING DEFERRED APPROVAL BY PURCHASER MUST BE SPECIFICALLY STATED. DELIVERY MAY BE AFFECTED.

THIS MATERIAL IS THE PROPERTY OF _____ CORPORATION AND IS FURNISHED ONLY FOR THE PURPOSE INDICATED. ANY AND ALL CONFIDENTIAL PROPRIETARY, PATENT, AND OTHER RIGHTS IN THE SUBJECT MATTER BEING RETAINED INCLUDING ANY INCLUSIVE RIGHT OF USE AND/OR MANUFACTURE AND/OR SALE. POSSESSION OF THIS MATERIAL DOES NOT CONVEY ANY PERMISSION TO REPRODUCE THIS MATERIAL IN WHOLE OR IN PART OR MANUFACTURE THE SUBJECT MATTER SHOWN THEREIN OR USE THE CONFIDENTIAL OR PROPRIETARY INFORMATION THEREON. SUCH PERMISSION TO BE GRANTED ONLY BY SPECIFIC AUTHORIZATION IN WRITING SIGNED BY AN OFFICER OR OTHER AUTHORIZED AGENT OF _____ CORPORATION, ITS DIVISIONS OR SUBSIDIARIES.

OVERHEAD PRODUCT PUMP

DRAWING TITLE:
GSJ   TOP SUCTION—MOTOR DRIVEN

DRAWN BY	DATE	DRAWING NO.
CHECKED BY	DATE	SK13-A

OVERHEAD PRODUCT PUMP
TOP SUCTION – TURBINE DRIVEN
SK-14

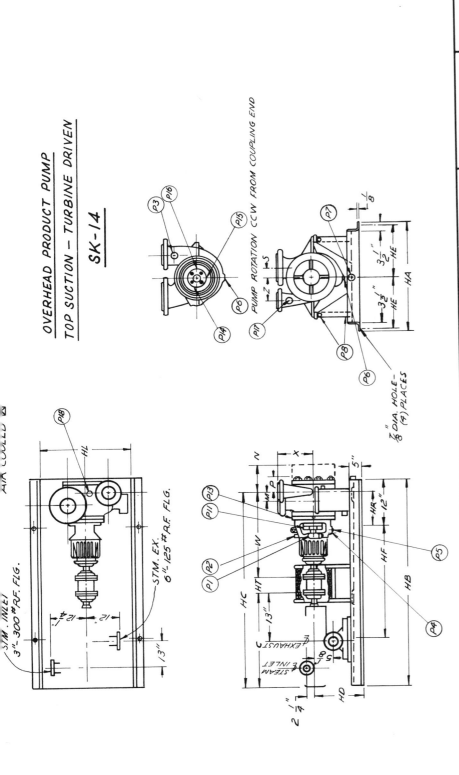

PUMP ROTATION CCW FROM COUPLING END

7/8" DIA. HOLE - (4) PLACES

STM. INLET 3"-300# R.F. FLG.

STM. EX. 6"-125# R.F. FLG.

STEAM INLET

EXHAUST

SK-14

PUMP SIZE													MOTOR FRAME SIZE											
												C	324TS 28 1/8			326TS 29 5/8			364TS 30 15/16			405TS 31 15/16		
Dis-charge	Suc-tion	Im-peller	P	H	M	S	W	X	Z	HT	HR		HD	HC	Base No.	HD	HC	Base No.	HD	HC	Base No.	HD	HC	Base No.
1 1/2	3	10 1/2	4 1/4	7 1/2	2 1/4	1 3/8	28 15/16	10	5 3/4	4 3/8	3 3/4		21 1/4	61 7/16	12A	21 1/4	62 15/16	12A	21 1/4	64 1/4	12B	21 1/4	65 1/4	12B
2	3	11 1/2	5	8	2 1/2	2	29	10 1/2	6 1/2	5	4 1/4		21 1/4	62 1/8	12A	21 1/4	63 5/8	12A	21 1/4	64 15/16	12B	21 1/4	65 15/16	12B
3	4	11 1/2	5 1/2	9	3 1/4	2 1/2	30 7/16	11	7 1/2	5	6 1/4		21 1/4	63 9/16	12A	21 1/4	65 1/16	12A	21 1/4	66 3/8	12B	21 1/4	67 3/8	12B
2	4	13	5	8	2 7/8	2 1/2	30	12	7 1/2	5	8		21 1/4	63 1/8	12A	21 1/4	64 5/8	12A	21 1/4	65 15/16	12B	21 1/4	66 15/16	12B

ITEM	SIZE	DESCRIPTION	YES	NO
P-1	4 OZ.	OILER FAR SIDE	X	
P-2		OIL FILLER CUP	X	
P-3	½ P.T.	SEAL RECIRCULATION CASE TAP.	X	
P-4	½ P.T.	OIL DRAIN PLUGGED	X	
P-5	¾ P.T.	DRAIN	X	
P-6	¾ P.T.	CASE DRAIN PLUGGED	X	
P-7	1 ½ P.T.	BASE PLATE DRAIN	X	
P-8	½ P.T.	PED. COOL WATER IN & OUT		X
P-9	½ P.T.	INLET BRG. WATER JACKET		X
P-10	½ P.T.	OUTLET BRG. WATER JACKET		X
P-11	¼ P.T.	PACKING GLAND QUENCH		X
P-12	½ P.T.	CAGE RING CONN. IN & OUT ON NOR17		
P-13	SEE NOTE 4	STUFF BOX WATER JACKET CLOSURE		
P-14	½ P.T.	SEAL VENT OR QUENCH INLET	X	
P-15	½ P.T.	SEAL QUENCH DRAIN	X	
P-16	½ P.T.	SEAL INJECTION	X	
P-17	¾ P.T.	GAGE CONNECTION		X
P-18	¾ P.T.	VENT CONNECTION		X

NOTES:
1. PUMPS ARE SELF VENTING.
2. SUCT. & DISCH FLGS. = 300 A.S.A. ¼ R.F.
3. THREE 4" DIA GROUT HOLES (MIN.) ⅜ DIA VENT HOLES—
   AS REQUIRED FOR FULL GROUTING.
4. ½ P T IN & OUT ON VERT. & ALWAYS SUPPLIED WITH OR
   WITHOUT WATER JACKET CLOSURE.
5. BOSSES PROVIDED FOR ADDITION OF TAPS WHEN REQUIRED.
6. BJ STD. COUPLING GUARD MEETS CALIF. SAFETY REQUIREMENTS.

BASEPLATE DIMENSIONS					
BASE NO.	HA	HB	HE	HF	HL
12A.B	31	66	14	42	24

MFGR _____
HP _____ R.P.M. _____
TYPE _____ FRAME _____ 405 TS _____
PHASE _____ CYCLE _____ VOLTS _____

WEIGHT: PUMP AND BASE _____
    MOTOR _____ TOTAL _____

REVISIONS		
DESCRIPTION	DATE	APPROVED

A. NO PIPING WILL BE SHOWN ON THIS DRAWING.
   SEE DRAWING INFORMATION BELOW.

B. COOL WATER PIPING SUPPLIED BY B.J.   YES ☐   NO ☐
   PER DRAWING _____

C. SEAL RECIRCULATION LINE - FURN BY B.J. YES ☐   NO ☐
   A.P.I. PLAN _____ DRAWING NO. _____

D. COUPLING FASTS. MOD B.J. SIZE   ☐
   OTHER _____

E. COUPLING GUARD B.J. STD.   (SEE NOTE 6)   ☐
   OTHER _____

F. PUMP WITH PACKING   YES ☐   NO ☐
   6 RINGS SIZE _____ TYPE _____

G. PUMP WITH MECHANICAL SEAL   YES ☐   NO ☐
   TYPE _____

CUSTOMER: _____
    USER _____
    LOCATION _____
    CUSTOMER ORDER NO. _____
    CUSTOMER ITEM NO. _____

SERVICE: _____ OVERHEAD PRODUCT _____
    B.J. ORDER NO. _____

PUMP:
    SIZE & TYPE ____ 2 × 4 × 131 ____ GSJ ____

APPROVED FOR CONSTRUCTION
    BY _____
    DATE _____

IMPORTANT—APPROVAL DRAWING NOTES
1. PURCHASER'S COMMENTS AND/OR CORRECTIONS WITHIN THE SCOPE OF
CONTRACT WILL BE MADE ON THE FIRST COMPLETED CERTIFIED DRAWING
SUBSTITUTED BY   CORP. AND RETURNED FOR CORRECTION.

2. CORRECTIONS, ALTERATIONS, ADDITIONS, AND/OR MODIFICATIONS OUTSIDE
SCOPE OR CONTRATE OR MADE AFTER FIRST SUBMITTAL WILL REQUIRE AN
ENGINEERING SERVICE CHARGE AND MAY CHANGE PRICE.

3. ITEMS CONDITIONALLY APPROVED OR NEEDING DEFERRED APPROVAL BY
PURCHASER MUST BE SPECIFICALLY STATED. DELIVERY MAY BE AFFECTED.

OVERHEAD PRODUCT PUMP

DRAWING TITLE:
GSJ   TOP SUCTION—TURBINE DRIVEN

DRAWN BY	DATE	DRAWING NO.	
CHECKED BY	DATE		SK 14-A

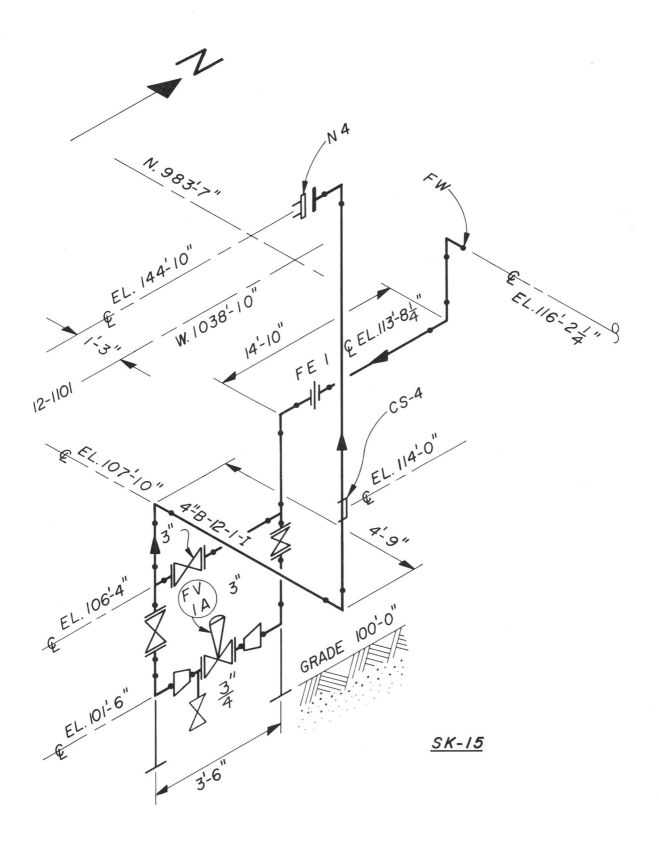

N

N 4

FW

N. 983'-7"

EL. 144'-10"

W. 1038'-10"

1'-3"

12-1101

14'-10"

FE 1

EL. 113'-8¼"

EL. 116'-2¼"

CS-4

EL. 107'-10"

EL. 114'-0"

4"B-12-1-1

3"

4'-9"

FV
1A

3"

EL. 106'-4"

3"
4

EL. 101'-6"

GRADE 100'-0"

SK-15

3'-6"

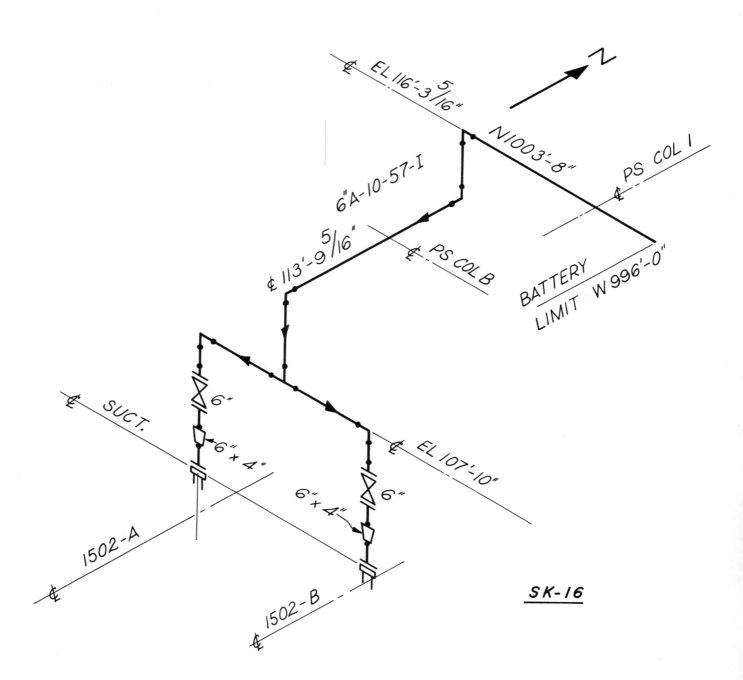

N

EL 116'-3 5/16"

N 1003'-8"

6"A-10-57-I

PS COL I

¢ 113'-9 5/16"

¢ PS COL B

BATTERY
LIMIT W 996'-0"

SUCT.

6"

6" x 4"

6" x 4"

6"

EL 107'-10"

1502-A

1502-B

SK-16

FLOW SHEET SYMBOLS

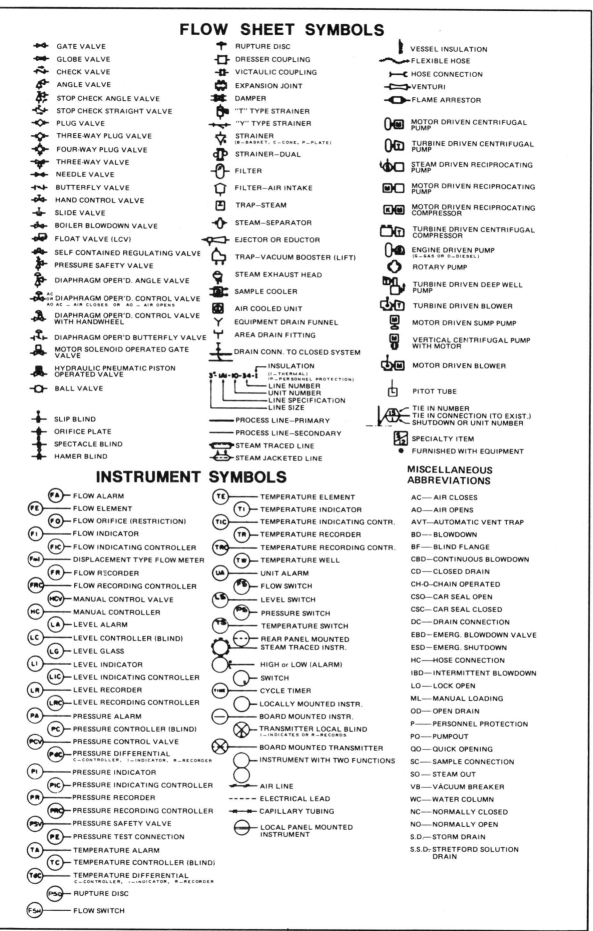

GATE VALVE
GLOBE VALVE
CHECK VALVE
ANGLE VALVE
STOP CHECK ANGLE VALVE
STOP CHECK STRAIGHT VALVE
PLUG VALVE
THREE-WAY PLUG VALVE
FOUR-WAY PLUG VALVE
THREE-WAY VALVE
NEEDLE VALVE
BUTTERFLY VALVE
HAND CONTROL VALVE
SLIDE VALVE
BOILER BLOWDOWN VALVE
FLOAT VALVE (LCV)
SELF CONTAINED REGULATING VALVE
PRESSURE SAFETY VALVE
DIAPHRAGM OPER'D. ANGLE VALVE
DIAPHRAGM OPER'D. CONTROL VALVE
AO AC — AIR CLOSES OR AO — AIR OPENS
DIAPHRAGM OPER'D. CONTROL VALVE WITH HANDWHEEL
DIAPHRAGM OPER'D BUTTERFLY VALVE
MOTOR SOLENOID OPERATED GATE VALVE
HYDRAULIC PNEUMATIC PISTON OPERATED VALVE
BALL VALVE

SLIP BLIND
ORIFICE PLATE
SPECTACLE BLIND
HAMER BLIND

RUPTURE DISC
DRESSER COUPLING
VICTAULIC COUPLING
EXPANSION JOINT
DAMPER
"T" TYPE STRAINER
"Y" TYPE STRAINER
STRAINER (B—BASKET, C—CONE, P—PLATE)
STRAINER–DUAL
FILTER
FILTER–AIR INTAKE
TRAP–STEAM
STEAM–SEPARATOR
EJECTOR OR EDUCTOR
TRAP–VACUUM BOOSTER (LIFT)
STEAM EXHAUST HEAD
SAMPLE COOLER
AIR COOLED UNIT
EQUIPMENT DRAIN FUNNEL
AREA DRAIN FITTING
DRAIN CONN. TO CLOSED SYSTEM

3" LAI-IO-34-I
— INSULATION (I—THERMAL) (P—PERSONNEL PROTECTION)
— LINE NUMBER
— UNIT NUMBER
— LINE SPECIFICATION
— LINE SIZE

PROCESS LINE–PRIMARY
PROCESS LINE–SECONDARY
STEAM TRACED LINE
STEAM JACKETED LINE

VESSEL INSULATION
FLEXIBLE HOSE
HOSE CONNECTION
VENTURI
FLAME ARRESTOR
MOTOR DRIVEN CENTRIFUGAL PUMP
TURBINE DRIVEN CENTRIFUGAL PUMP
STEAM DRIVEN RECIPROCATING PUMP
MOTOR DRIVEN RECIPROCATING PUMP
MOTOR DRIVEN RECIPROCATING COMPRESSOR
TURBINE DRIVEN CENTRIFUGAL COMPRESSOR
ENGINE DRIVEN PUMP (G—GAS OR D—DIESEL)
ROTARY PUMP
TURBINE DRIVEN DEEP WELL PUMP
TURBINE DRIVEN BLOWER
MOTOR DRIVEN SUMP PUMP
VERTICAL CENTRIFUGAL PUMP WITH MOTOR
MOTOR DRIVEN BLOWER

PITOT TUBE

TIE IN NUMBER
TIE IN CONNECTION (TO EXIST.)
SHUTDOWN OR UNIT NUMBER

SPECIALTY ITEM
FURNISHED WITH EQUIPMENT

INSTRUMENT SYMBOLS

FA — FLOW ALARM
FE — FLOW ELEMENT
FO — FLOW ORIFICE (RESTRICTION)
FI — FLOW INDICATOR
FIC — FLOW INDICATING CONTROLLER
Fml — DISPLACEMENT TYPE FLOW METER
FR — FLOW RECORDER
FRC — FLOW RECORDING CONTROLLER
MCV — MANUAL CONTROL VALVE
MC — MANUAL CONTROLLER
LA — LEVEL ALARM
LC — LEVEL CONTROLLER (BLIND)
LG — LEVEL GLASS
LI — LEVEL INDICATOR
LIC — LEVEL INDICATING CONTROLLER
LR — LEVEL RECORDER
LRC — LEVEL RECORDING CONTROLLER
PA — PRESSURE ALARM
PC — PRESSURE CONTROLLER (BLIND)
PCV — PRESSURE CONTROL VALVE
PdC — PRESSURE DIFFERENTIAL C—CONTROLLER, I—INDICATOR, R—RECORDER
PI — PRESSURE INDICATOR
PIC — PRESSURE INDICATING CONTROLLER
PR — PRESSURE RECORDER
PRC — PRESSURE RECORDING CONTROLLER
PSV — PRESSURE SAFETY VALVE
PE — PRESSURE TEST CONNECTION
TA — TEMPERATURE ALARM
TC — TEMPERATURE CONTROLLER (BLIND)
TdC — TEMPERATURE DIFFERENTIAL C—CONTROLLER, I—INDICATOR, R—RECORDER
PSd — RUPTURE DISC
FSw — FLOW SWITCH

TE — TEMPERATURE ELEMENT
TI — TEMPERATURE INDICATOR
TIC — TEMPERATURE INDICATING CONTR.
TR — TEMPERATURE RECORDER
TRC — TEMPERATURE RECORDING CONTR.
TW — TEMPERATURE WELL
UA — UNIT ALARM
FS — FLOW SWITCH
LS — LEVEL SWITCH
PS — PRESSURE SWITCH
TS — TEMPERATURE SWITCH
REAR PANEL MOUNTED STEAM TRACED INSTR.
HIGH or LOW (ALARM)
SWITCH
TIME — CYCLE TIMER
LOCALLY MOUNTED INSTR.
BOARD MOUNTED INSTR.
TRANSMITTER LOCAL BLIND I—INDICATES OR R—RECORDS
BOARD MOUNTED TRANSMITTER
INSTRUMENT WITH TWO FUNCTIONS
AIR LINE
ELECTRICAL LEAD
CAPILLARY TUBING
LOCAL PANEL MOUNTED INSTRUMENT

MISCELLANEOUS ABBREVIATIONS

AC— AIR CLOSES
AO— AIR OPENS
AVT—AUTOMATIC VENT TRAP
BD— BLOWDOWN
BF— BLIND FLANGE
CBD—CONTINUOUS BLOWDOWN
CD— CLOSED DRAIN
CH-O—CHAIN OPERATED
CSO— CAR SEAL OPEN
CSC— CAR SEAL CLOSED
DC— DRAIN CONNECTION
EBD—EMERG. BLOWDOWN VALVE
ESD—EMERG. SHUTDOWN
HC—HOSE CONNECTION
IBD—INTERMITTENT BLOWDOWN
LO—LOCK OPEN
ML—MANUAL LOADING
OD—OPEN DRAIN
P—PERSONNEL PROTECTION
PO—PUMPOUT
QO—QUICK OPENING
SC—SAMPLE CONNECTION
SO—STEAM OUT
VB—VACUUM BREAKER
WC—WATER COLUMN
NC—NORMALLY CLOSED
NO—NORMALLY OPEN
S.D.—STORM DRAIN
S.S.D.—STRETFORD SOLUTION DRAIN

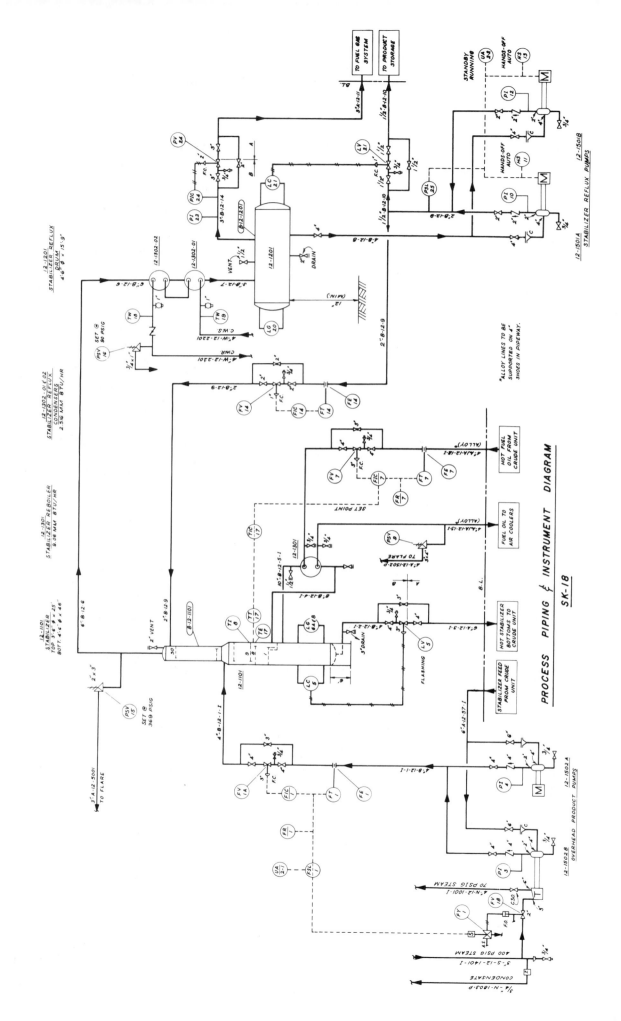

PROCESS PIPING & INSTRUMENT DIAGRAM

SK-18

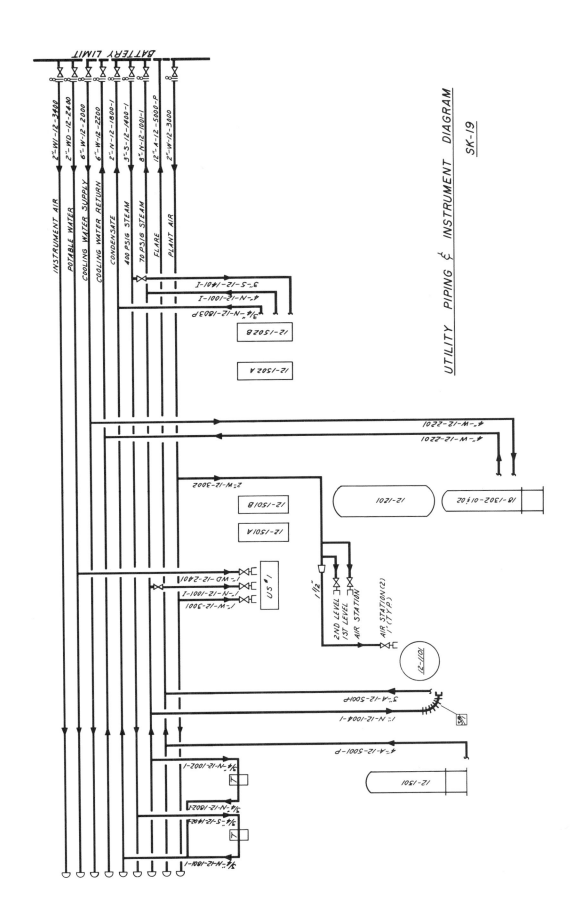

UTILITY PIPING & INSTRUMENT DIAGRAM

SK-19

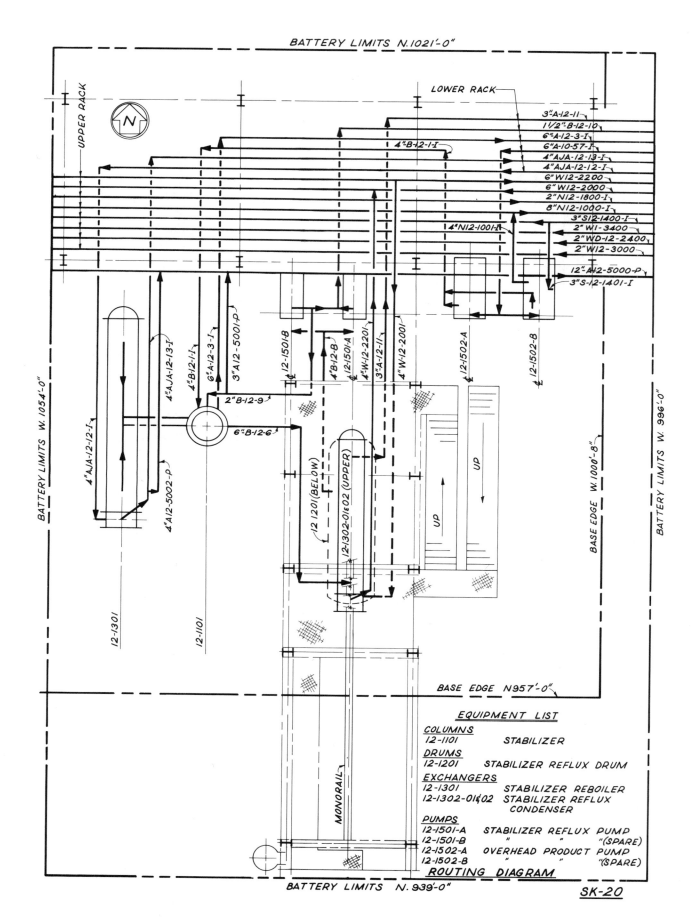

BATTERY LIMITS N.1021'-0"

UPPER RACK

LOWER RACK

3"A-12-11
1 1/2"B-12-10
6"A-12-3-I
6"A-10-57-I
4"B-12-I-I
4"AJA-12-13-I
4"AJA-12-12-I
6"W12-2200
6"W12-2000
2"N12-1800-I
8"N12-1000-I
3"S12-1400-I
4"N12-1001-I
2"WI-3400
2"WD-12-2400
2"W12-3000
12"A12-5000-P
3"S-12-1401-I

BATTERY LIMITS W.1054'-0"

4"AJA-12-12-I
4"AJA-12-13-I
4"B-12-I-I
6"A-12-3-I
3"A12-5001-P

2"B-12-9

6"B-12-6

4"A12-5002-P

12-1501-B
4"B-12-B
4"A12-1501-A
4"W-12-220I
3"A-12-1I
4"W-12-2201
12-1502-A
12-1502-B

12-1201 (BELOW)
12-1302-01&02 (UPPER)

UP

UP

BASE EDGE W.1000'-8"

BATTERY LIMITS W. 996'-0"

12-1301

12-1101

BASE EDGE N957'-0"

MONORAIL

EQUIPMENT LIST

COLUMNS
12-1101   STABILIZER

DRUMS
12-1201   STABILIZER REFLUX DRUM

EXCHANGERS
12-1301   STABILIZER REBOILER
12-1302-01&02 STABILIZER REFLUX
               CONDENSER

PUMPS
12-1501-A   STABILIZER REFLUX PUMP
12-1501-B   "   "   "(SPARE)
12-1502-A   OVERHEAD PRODUCT PUMP
12-1502-B   "   "   "(SPARE)

ROUTING DIAGRAM

SK-20

BATTERY LIMITS N.939'-0"

270

DESCRIPTION						DESIGN CONDITIONS							REMARKS
NOM SIZE (IN.)	PIPE SPEC	LINE NO.	SERVICE	FROM	TO	PRESS (PSIG)	TEMP (°F)	CALC THKNS (IN.)	ACTUAL	MIN TEST (PSIG)	INS THKNS (IN.)	OPR TEMP (°F)	
6″	A	57	LIGHT. HYDRC.	UNIT-10	12-1502	25	200	—	STD	38	1½″	200	
4″	B	1	LIGHT. HYDRC.	12-1502	12-1101	340	200	—	STD	300	1½	200	
4″	B	2	STABILIZER BOTTOMS	12-1101	LN. 3	340	370	—	STD	555	1½	370	
6″	A	3	STABILIZER BOTTOMS	LN 2	OFF PLOT	165	370	—	STD	248	2″	370	
8″	B	4	REBOILER FEED	12-1101	12-1301	340	466	—	30	510	2″	466	
10″	B	5	REBOILER RETURN	12-1301	12-1101	340	466	—	30	510	2″	466	
6″	B	6	COLUMN OVHEAD	12-1101	12-1302	325	139	—	STD	488	—	139	
3″	B	7	CONDENSER OUTLET	12-1302	12-1201	330	100	—	STD	495	—	100	
4″	B	8	REFLUX PUMP SUCT	12-1201	12-1501	330	100	—	STD	495	—	100	
3″	B	9	REFLUX	12-1501	12-1101	340	100	—	STD	510	—	100	
1½″	B	10	PRODUCT	LN 9	OFF PLOT	40	100	—	XS	60	—	100	
3″	A	11	FUEL GAS	LN 14	OFF PLOT	60	100	—	STD	90	—	100	
4″	AJA	12	FUEL OIL	UNIT 10	12-1301	85	666	—	405	129	2½″	600	
4″	AJA	13	REBOILER FUEL OIL	12-1301	UNIT-10	75	500	—	405	113	2″	550	
3″	B	14	FUEL GAS	12-1201	LN-11	325	100	—	STD	488	—	100	

NOTE: ALL LINES OPERATING AT 500° OR HIGHER TO BE SUPPORTED ON 4″ PIPE SHOES.

LINE SUMMARY

SHEET 1 OF 1

JOB NUMBER | DRAWING NUMBER | REV

SK-21

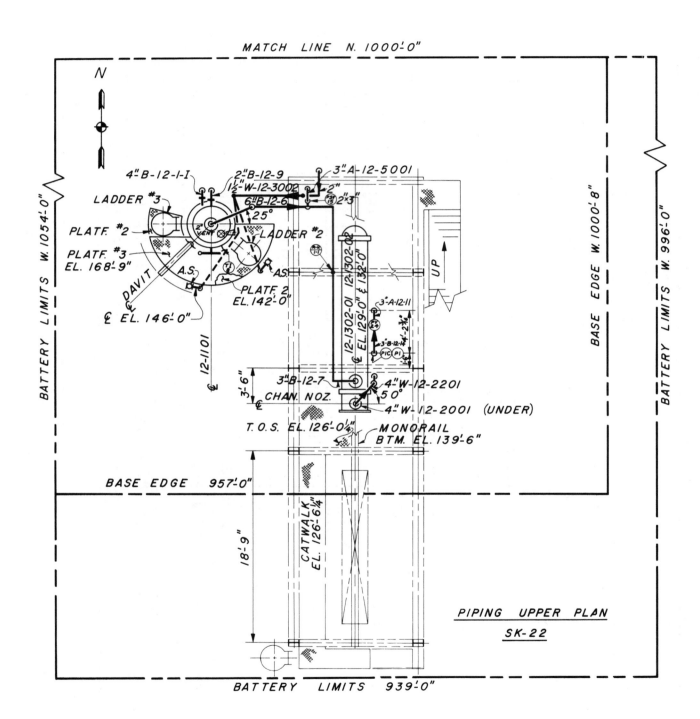

N

4"B-12-1-1

2"B-12-9
1½"W-12-3002

3"A-12-5001

2"

LADDER #3

6"B-12-6

2"3"

PLATF. #2

25°

2" VENT

LADDER #2

PLATF. #3
EL. 168'-9"

A.S.

AS.

DAVIT

PLATF. 2
EL. 142'-0"

12-1302-01 12-1302-02
EL. 129'-0" EL. 132'-0"

3"-A-12-11

3"-B-12-14

PIC PI

UP

₵ EL. 146'-0"

12-1101

BATTERY LIMITS W. 1054'-0"

BASE EDGE W. 1000'-8"

BATTERY LIMITS W. 996'-0"

3'-6"

3"B-12-7

CHAN. NOZ.

4"W-12-2201
50°

4"W-12-2001 (UNDER)

T.O.S. EL. 126'-0¼"

MONORAIL
BTM. EL. 139'-6"

BASE EDGE 957'-0"

18'-9"

CATWALK
EL. 126'-6¼"

PIPING UPPER PLAN

SK-22

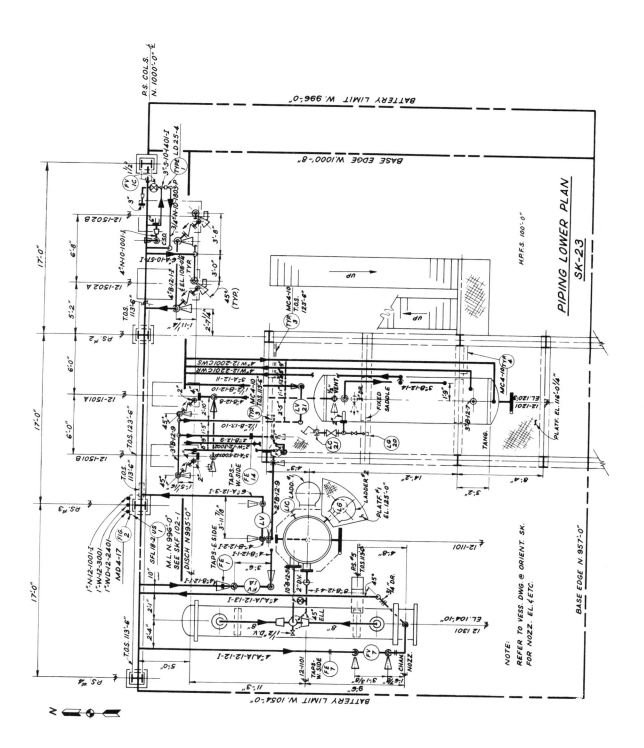

PIPING LOWER PLAN
SK-23

273

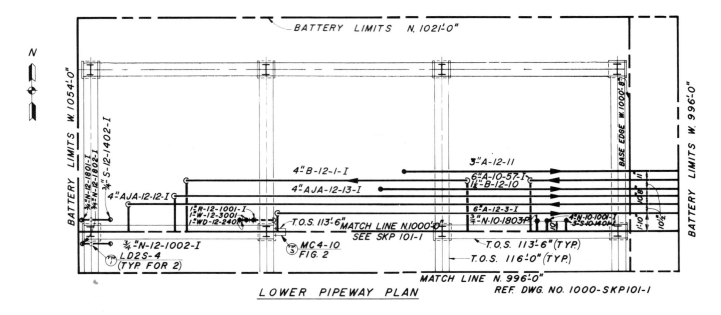

LOWER PIPEWAY PLAN

SK-24A

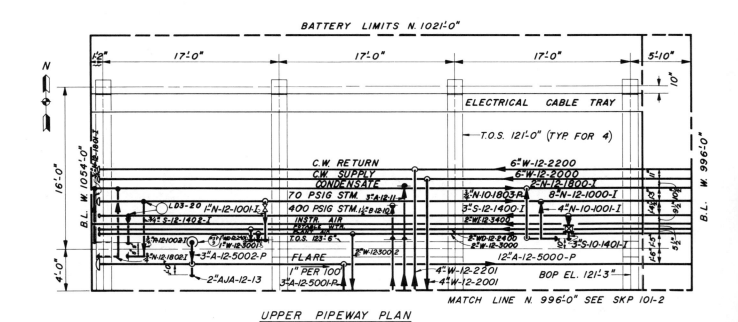

UPPER PIPEWAY PLAN

SK-24B

26

EMA's Introduction to Design Modeling

FIGURE 26-1 EMA's introduction to design modeling project.

This project consists of a very basic, simplified model project that is suitable for junior-high-school and high-school-level beginning modeling courses. Kit-05 consists of the EMA *Introduction to Design Modeling* training manual with a complete set of photographs and instructions and all the necessary model components to build the project.

Figure 26-1 is a photograph of this project and it should be possible to see the level of complexity that this project entails.

Kit-05 is relatively inexpensive compared to other projects described in this text (check EMA for up-to-date prices).

Again, it is suggested that only beginning/basic modeling classes in junior high and high school use this as a project.

27

Fin-Fan Project

FIGURE 27-1 Petrochemical unit with multiple air coolers (fin fans) installed above pipe rack.

Fin fans are a type of cooling unit used on petrochemical units. Figures 27-1, 2-1, and 6-2 show examples of multiple fin fans. Notice that all of these installations have the fin fans installed above the primary pipe rack.

In this project only a small portion of the total complex is shown. Figures 27-2 to 27-6 are a set of photographs showing this project from a variety of angles. This project is somewhat more complex and expensive to model than the projects in Sections 25, 26, and 28; therefore, it is suggested that two or more students work as a group when doing the model. Follow instructions for layout and construction in Sections 15, 16, and 17.

FIGURE 27-2 Plan view of Project 27-8, fin fan, valve station, and pipe rack (see Fig. 27-10).

FIGURE 27-3 Side elevation of V-599 (vessel) (see Fig. 27-13).

FIGURE 27-4 End view (see Fig. 27-16).

FIGURE 27-5 End view showing valve station (see Fig. 27-14).

FIGURE 27-6 Closeup side elevation view of valve station and platform.

FIGURE 27-7 Valve station (see Fig. 27-15).

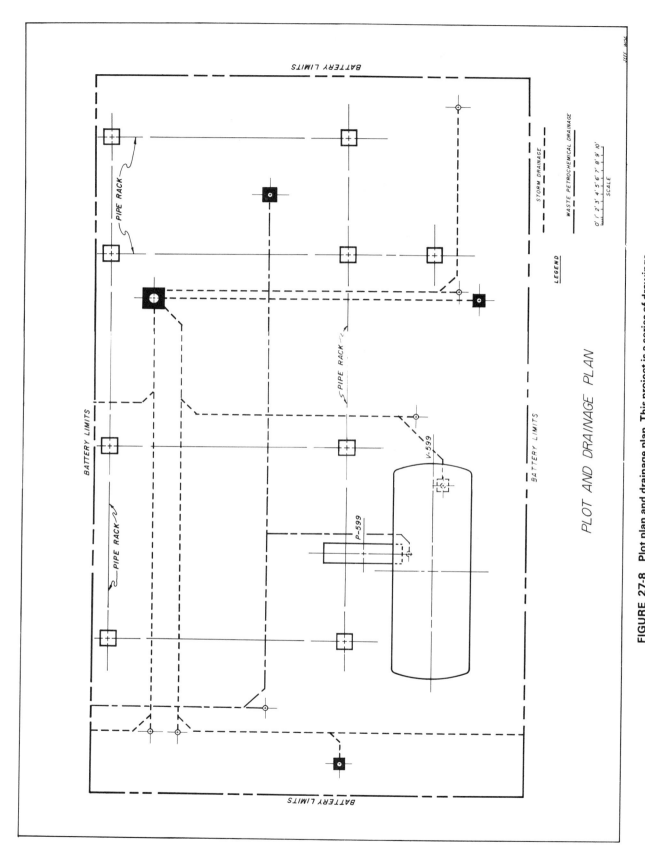

PLOT AND DRAINAGE PLAN

FIGURE 27-8 Plot plan and drainage plan. This project is a series of drawings for a fin-fan tandem cooler mounted on top of a pipe rack and includes a major valve station for the pipe rack.

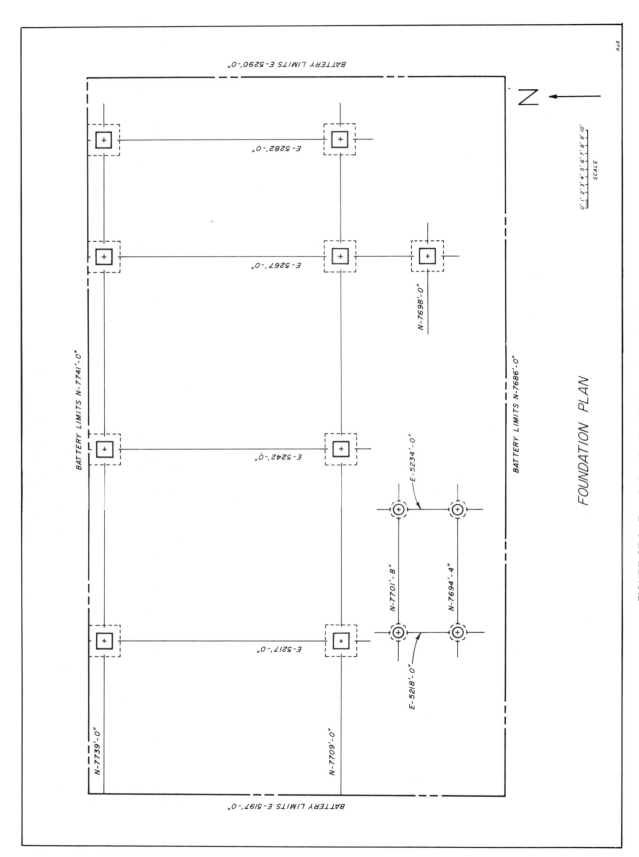

FOUNDATION PLAN

FIGURE 27-9 Foundation plan for fin-fan cooler and rack.

280

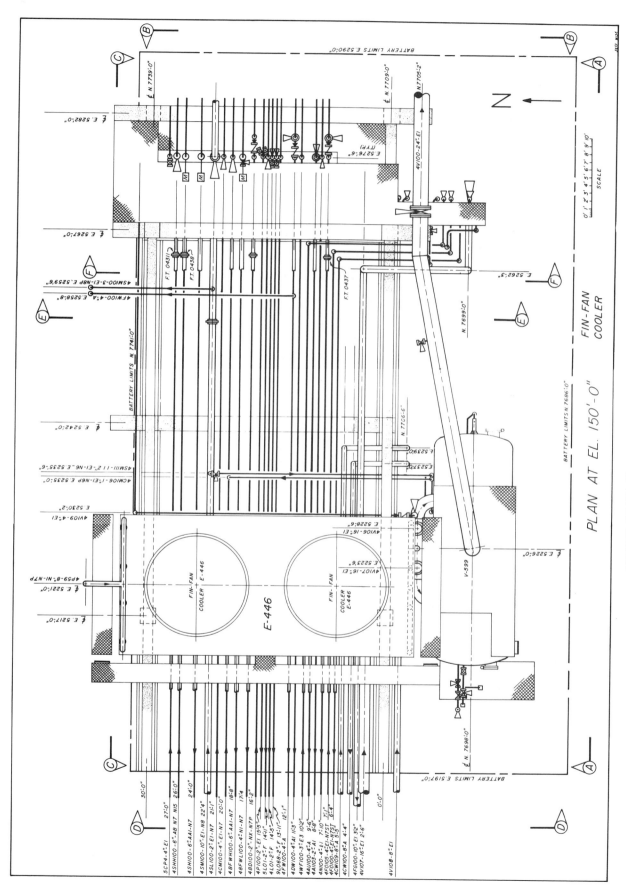

PLAN AT EL. 150'-0"   FIN-FAN COOLER

FIGURE 27-10 Plan at 150' elevation.

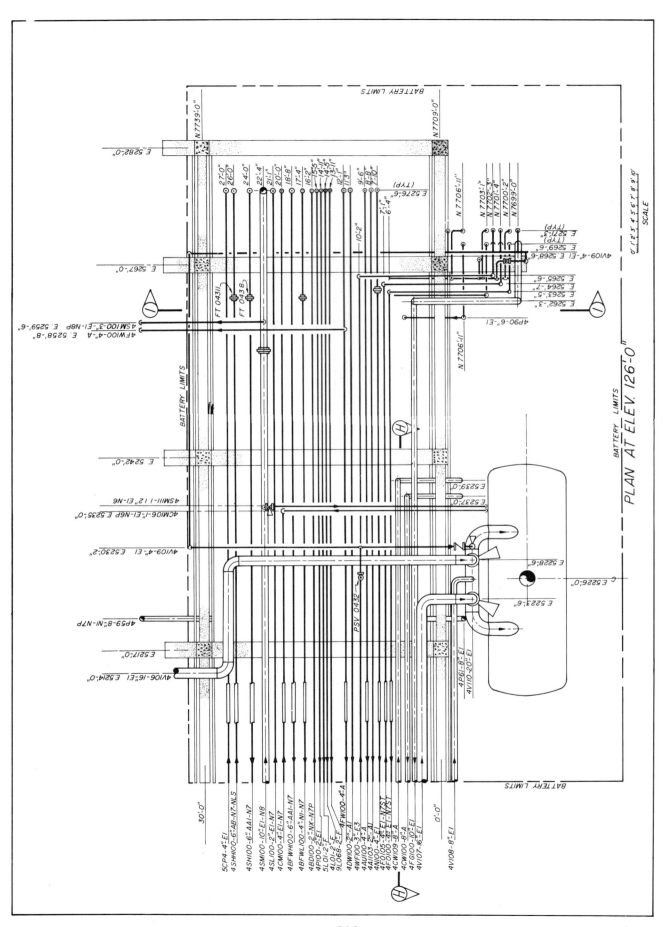

FIGURE 27-11 Plan at 126' elevation.

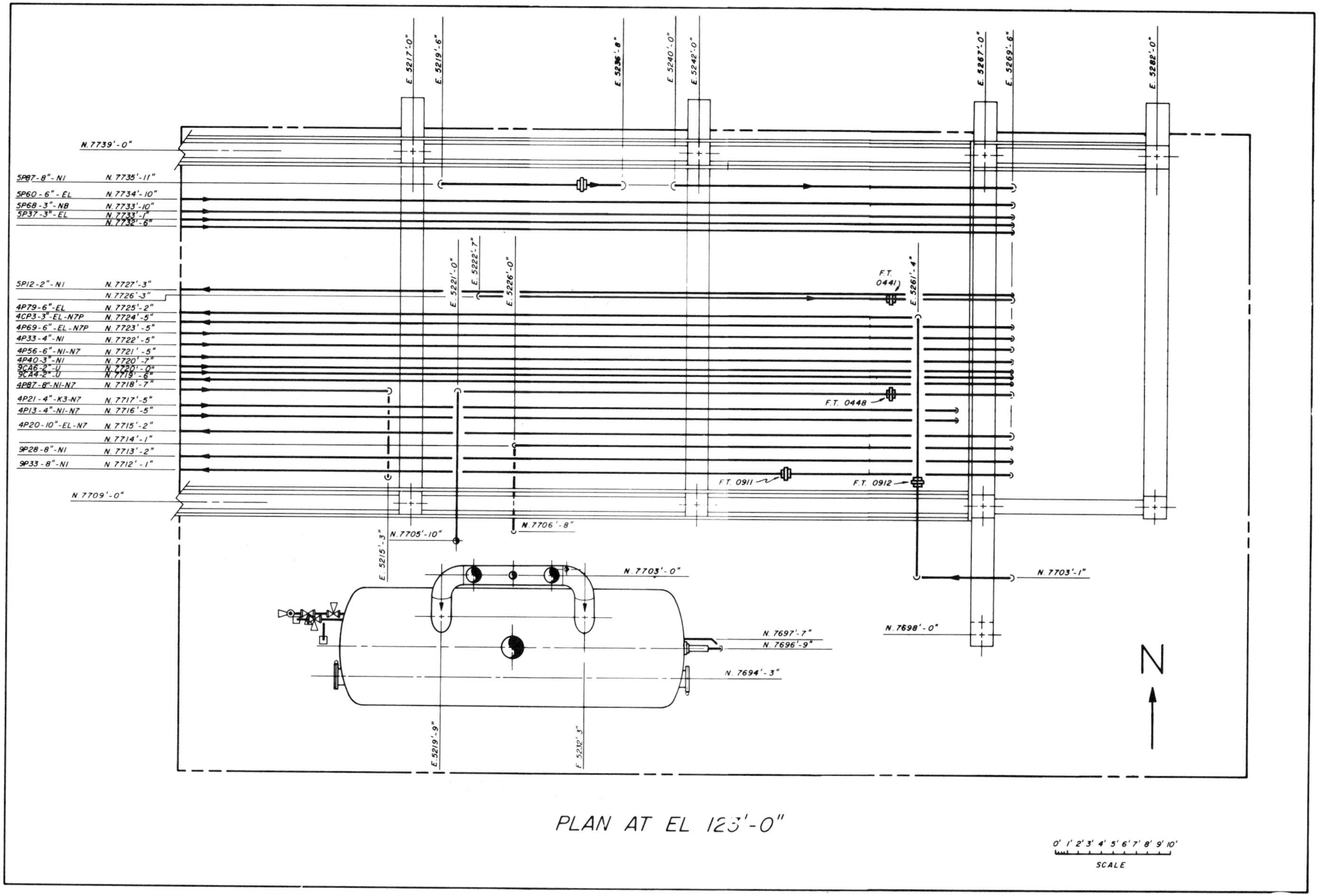

PLAN AT EL 123'-0"

FIGURE 27-12   Plan at 123' elevation.

283

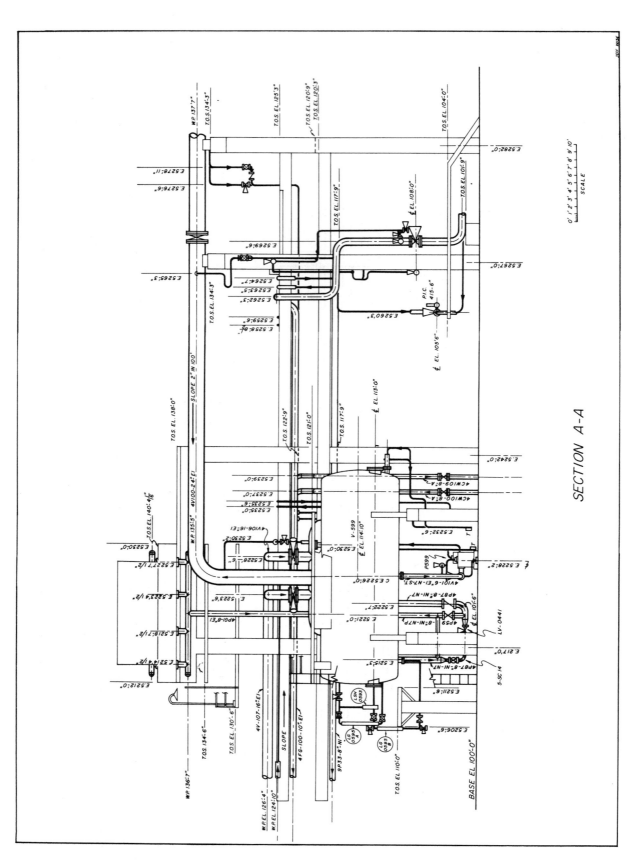

SECTION A-A

FIGURE 27-13 Section A-A.

284

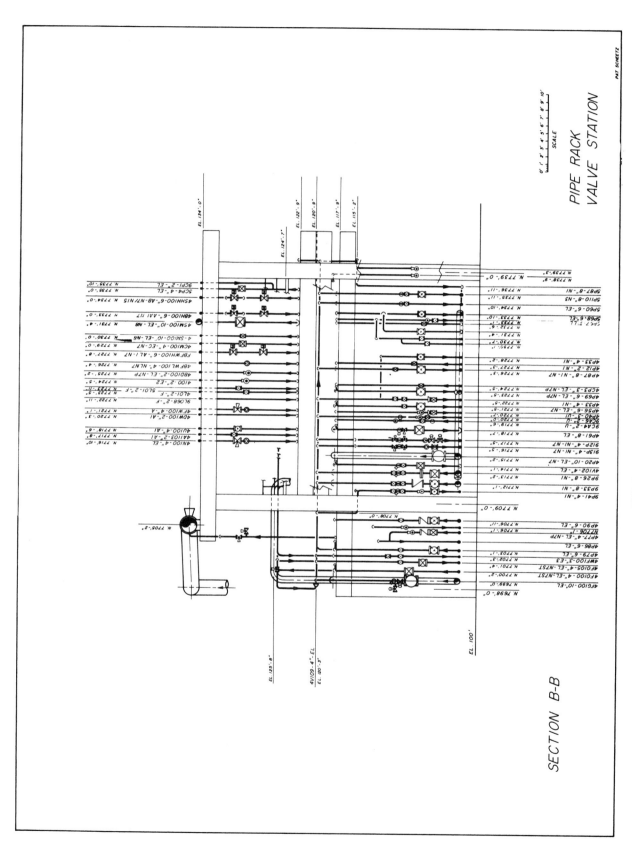

PIPE RACK
VALVE STATION

SECTION B-B

FIGURE 27-14 Section B-B.

285

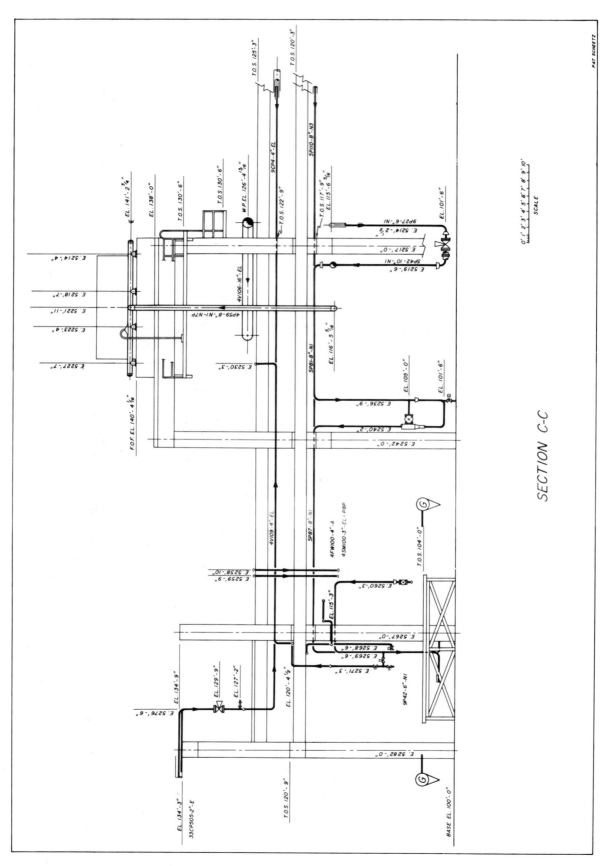

SECTION C-C

FIGURE 27-15 Section C-C.

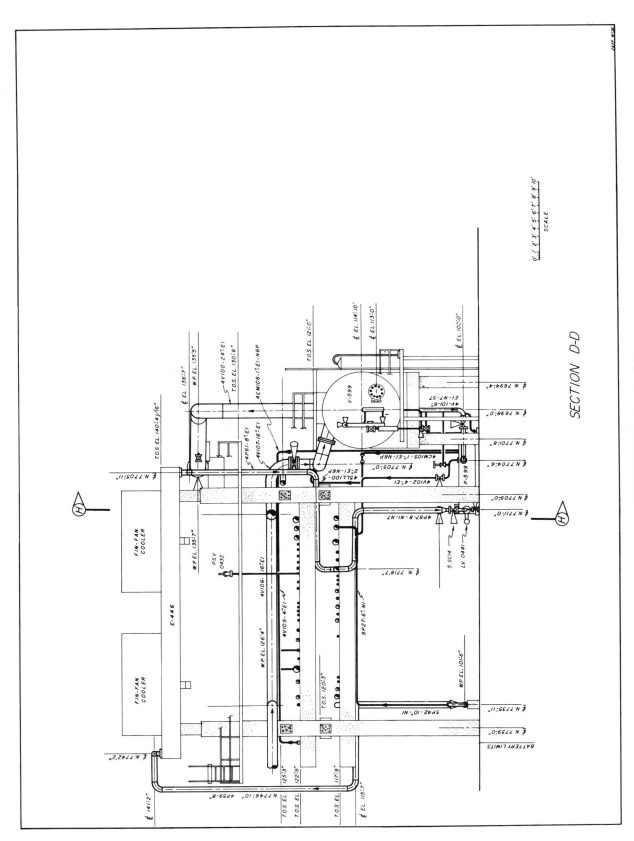

FIGURE 27-16 Section D-D.

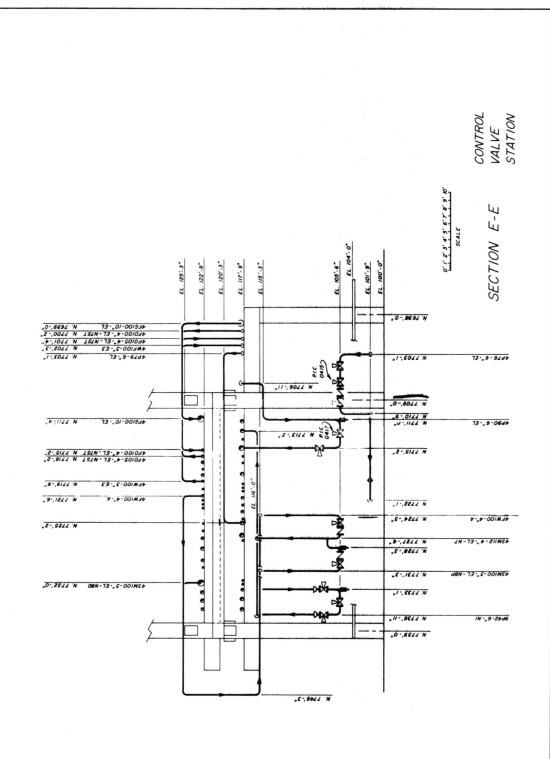

FIGURE 27-17 Section E-E, control valve station.

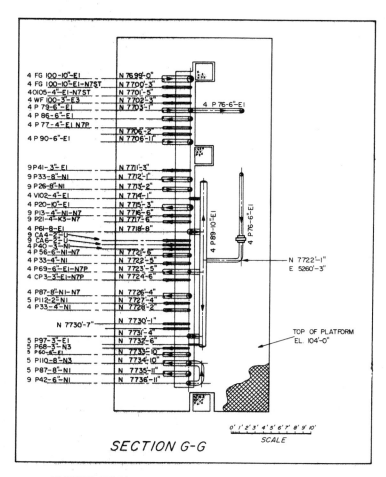

SECTION G-G

FIGURE 27-18 Section G-G, top of platform at 104'.

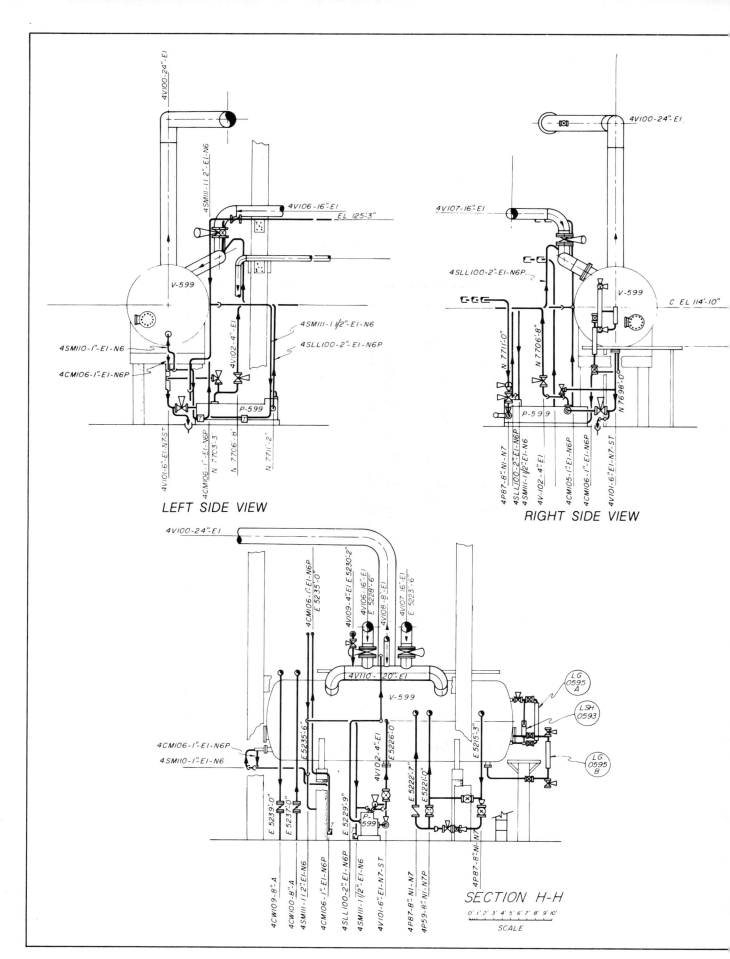

FIGURE 27-19 Section H-H, horizontal vessel, three views.

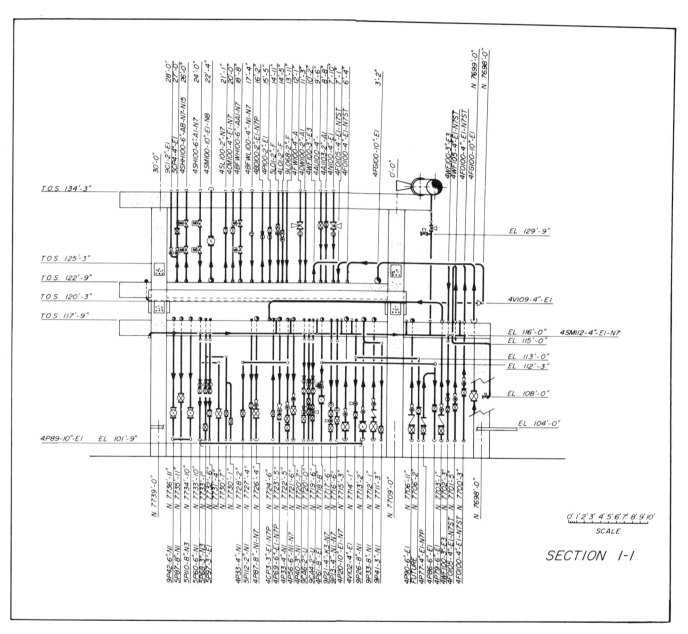

FIGURE 27-20 Section I-I.

28

Water Quench
Blowdown System Project

FIGURE 28-1 Photograph of quench tower project (see Fig. 28-13).

The purpose of the water quench blowdown system is to provide for the sudden cooling of hot material that may be discharged from another processing unit, such as cracking coil. The cooling is done by injecting cooling water directly into the hot oil.

 This section contains a set of plan, elevation, section, and detail views of a small unit in a refinery installation. Figure 28-1 shows a flow diagram of a water quench blowdown system for the disposal of hot liquids. The vertical vessel is equipped with a variety of connections, baffles,

and piping, together with a tall outlet stack which provides for vapor emissions. The hot hydrocarbon material is piped into the blowdown stack above the liquid level. The water flow is actuated by the entrance of the hot liquid into the vessel and additional water from sprays is introduced above the blowdown line. Steam (in some variations) is piped to the top of the stack, providing a spray that helps disperse the vapors. The inside of the vessel is equipped with a series of baffles, which help the cooling process.

FIGURE 28-2 Closeup view of piping. (Note that these photographs should be referred to when piping the model.)

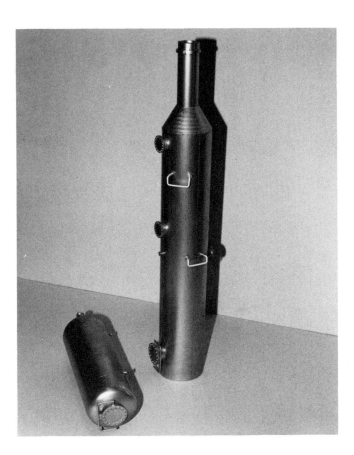

FIGURE 28-4 These vessels have been completely fabricated and painted before attaching to the base (see Figs. 28-18 and 28-19).

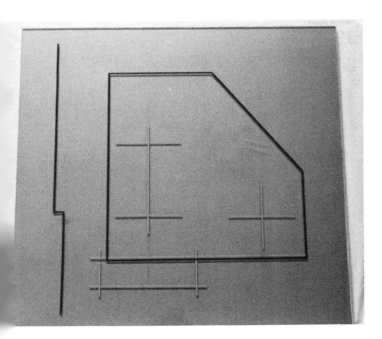

FIGURE 28-3 Base laid out with tape for center-line of vessels, pipe rack, and unit limits (see Fig. 28-12).

FIGURE 28-5 Plan view of project before entering the design (piping) stage.

FIGURE 28-6   Photograph during piping stage, before tagging.

FIGURE 28-8   Pump and control valve station.

FIGURE 28-9   The model completely piped up before final tagging.

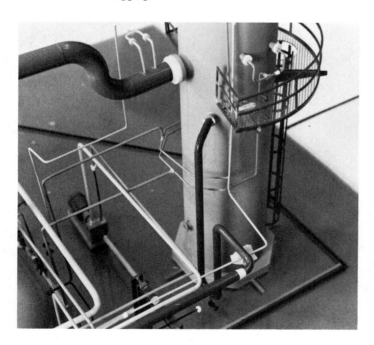

FIGURE 28-7

FIGURE 28-10

294

Cooling water is used for this type of service as it is mixed directly with the hydrocarbon material. A system of drains and siphons that channel the cooled water into the sewer system is also provided.

A blowdown drum usually accompanies this type of unit. The blowdown drum is used to accumulate liquid hydrocarbons that have a low vaporization level. The hydrocarbon mixture is channeled into the horizontal drum. The drum itself contains a series of baffles (Fig. 28-18). The drum helps separate the first stage of hydrocarbons and possible vapors.

Following is a description of the water quench blowdown unit, including the flow diagram (Fig. 28-11), the plan view (Fig. 28-12), section A from elevation view (Fig. 28-16), section C from plan view (Fig. 28-17), the fabrication drawing for the horizontal drum (Fig. 28-18), and the fabrication drawing and detail for the quench tower (Fig. 28-19).

The project shown in this section is an example of a typical petrochemical unit. This series of drawings, including the flow diagram, plan, elevation, section views, and the accompanying details of the drum and stack are examples of a typical set of drawings that might be required of a piping drafter. The student should use 3/8″ = 1′ to model the project.

The general procedure for the construction of such a unit will be that the engineering flow diagram will have already been sketched by the process engineer. This sketch will then be laid out by the piping drafter in a completed form as shown in Fig. 28-11. The P&ID covers all the essential equipment, piping, components, valving, and instrumentation. From this P&ID it should be possible for an experienced pipe drafter/designer to lay out the drawings or construct a model.

As the student completes this project, it will become clear that certain aspects of this design could be improved upon or are incorrect as far as line spacing, labeling, and other aspects that will become obvious as the project progresses. Also, note that certain aspects shown on the flow diagram are not included on the set of drawings, such as the level glass that should be attached to the water quench blowdown stack, a number of missing drains and valves, and instrumentation. By paying strict attention to all the information on the P&ID and comparing it to the drawings, it will be possible to model the missing and incorrect aspects of this project, locating the drains, piping, valves, and so on.

Using the book's drawings, order the necessary components, fabricate the base and structural elements, and construct a complete model of this unit using the model specifications found in the text.

When constructing a model of this project, an adequate-size base would be the first step (Fig. 28-3). Match lines and foundation limits should be shown on the base with pin striping tape (Fig. 28-3). Then the major equipment centerlines for the stack, drum, pump, and pipe racks should be established with color-coded tape. After this, using the drawings provided, the student should fabricate the vessels (Fig. 28-4), assemble the pump, and fabricate the necessary piers and foundations for the stack, pump, and knock-out drum. After major equipment and foundations have been fabricated, they should be accurately located on the model base (Figs. 28-5 and 28-6). At this point, it is possible to start establishing the pipe rack lines and the large-diameter pipelines, such as 19BD062 20″ C and 19BD0601 10″ EE. From here, the student should follow all the details laid out on the drawings that are provided, using established procedures for the construction of models.

The student should not assume that all the procedures, design, layout, and arrangement of this and other projects provided in this book are absolutely correct or the best possible solution as far as economy, placement, arrangement, and procedures are concerned. One of the most important aspects of being a piping designer and modeler is to be able to take the specifications and use them to their utmost, perfecting existing systems, and eventually being able to establish new facilities straight from the P&ID drawings.

The instructor may also wish to have the student draw individual isometric spools of the major pipelines, such as line 19BD0606 10″ EE, which has a confusing configuration. Isometrics of 19BD0621 20″ C and many of the other lines will also help the student.

When ordering and constructing this project, care should be taken to follow the specifications set down in Section 12 on color coding, base preparation in Section 14, construction and piping the model in Sections 15 and 16, and tagging the model in Section 18.

Upon completion, photographs can be taken of the model (see Section 20).

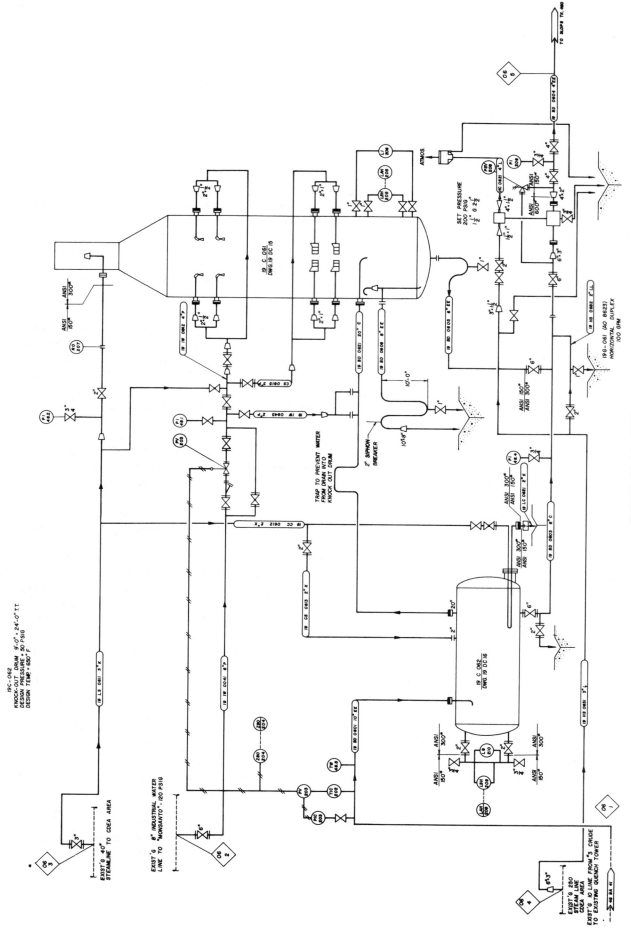

FIGURE 28-11 P&ID.

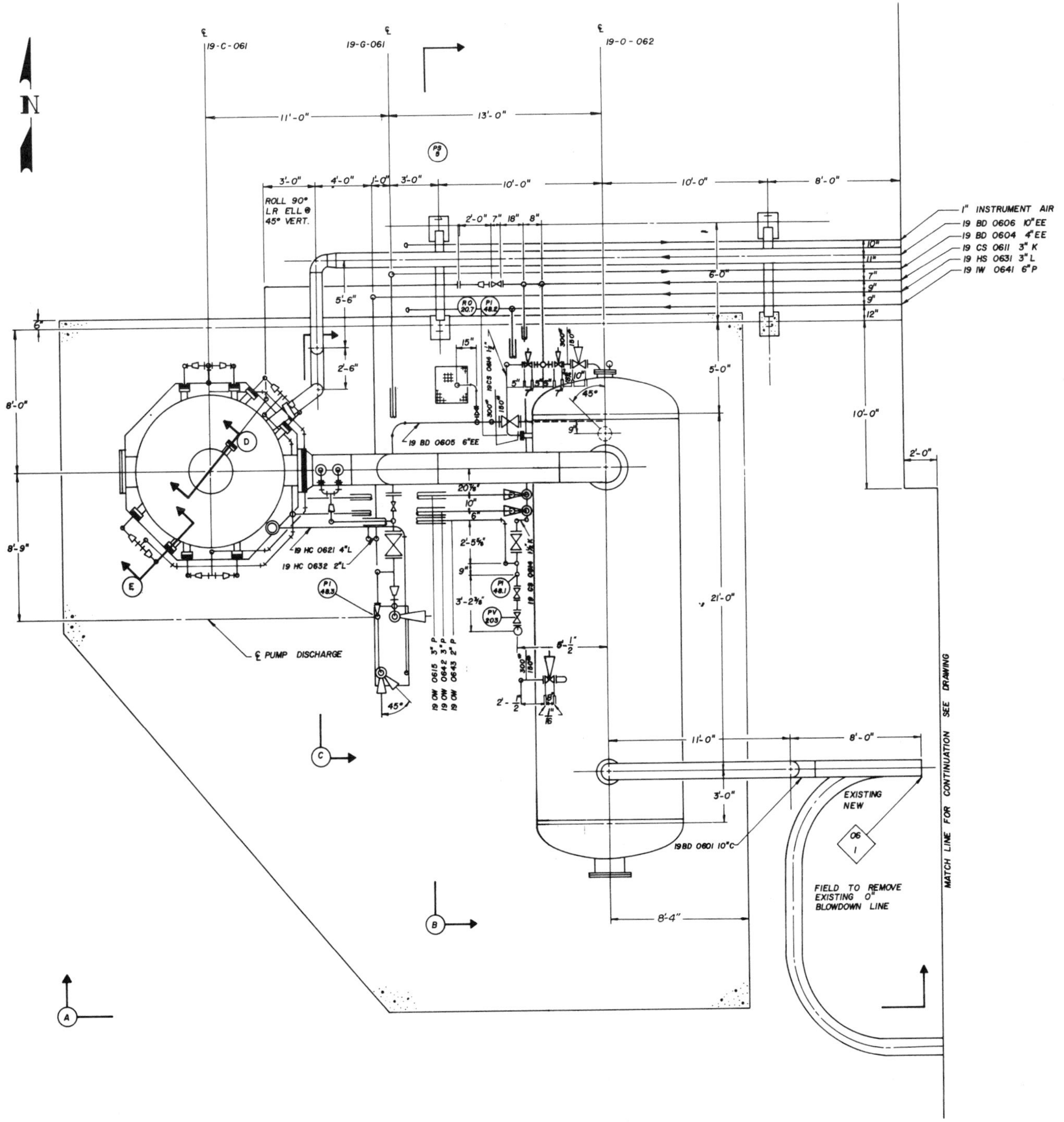

FIGURE 28-12 Plan view.

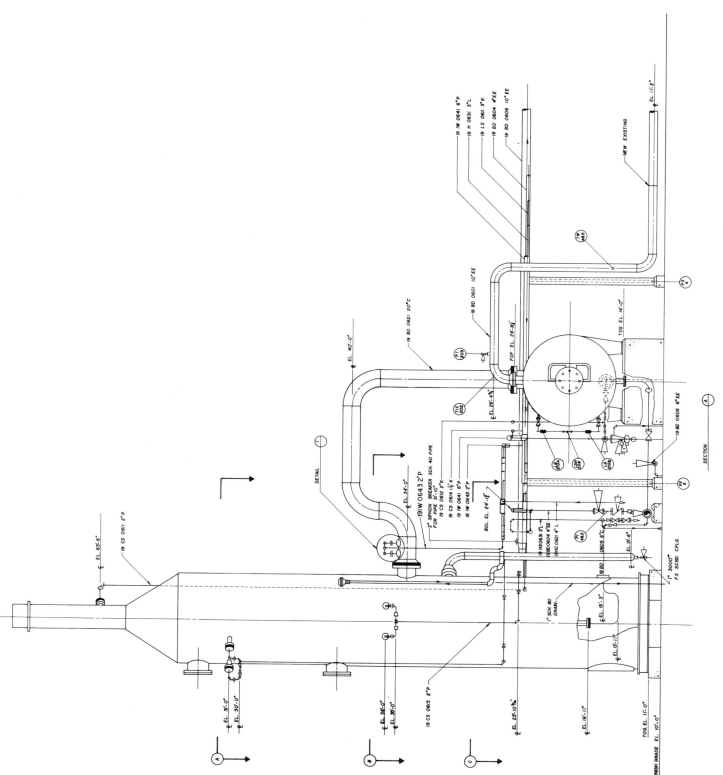

FIGURE 28-13 Section A-A.

298

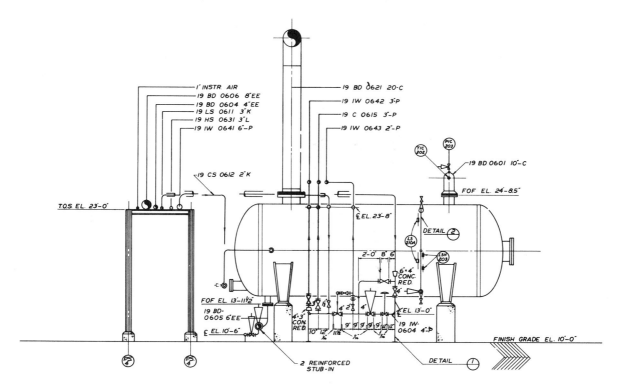

FIGURE 28-14

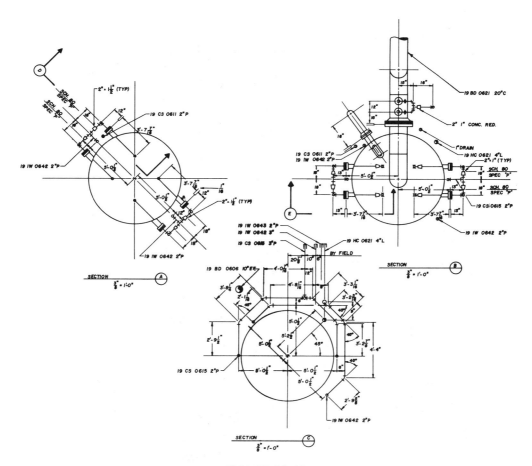

FIGURE 28-15

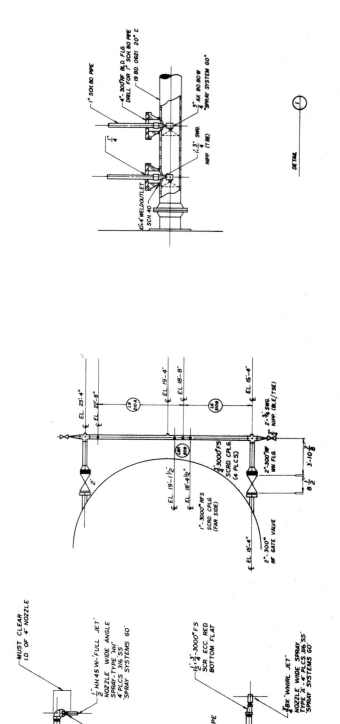

FIGURE 28-16

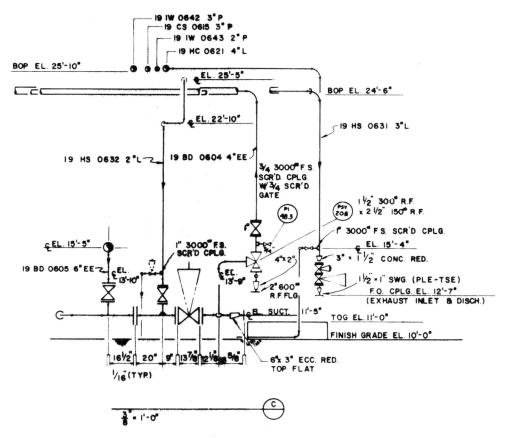

19 IW 0642 3"P
19 CS 0615 3"P
19 IW 0643 2"P
19 HC 0621 4"L

BOP EL. 25'-10"

EL. 25'-5"

BOP EL. 24'-6"

EL. 22'-10"

19 HS 0631 3"L

19 HS 0632 2"L

19 BD 0604 4"EE

¾ 3000# F.S. SCR'D CPLG. W/¾ SCR'D. GATE

PI 483

PSV 208

1½" 300# R.F. x 2½" 150# R.F.

1" 3000# F.S. SCR'D CPLG.

EL. 15'-5"

1" 3000# F.S. SCR'D CPLG.

EL. 15'-4"

19 BD 0605 6"EE

3" x 1½" CONC. RED.

EL. 13'-10"

4"x2"

EL. 13'-9"

1½" x 1" SWG. (PLE-TSE)

2" 600# R.F. FLG.

F.O. CPLG. EL. 12'-7" (EXHAUST INLET & DISCH.)

SUCT. 11'-5"

TOG EL. 11'-0"

FINISH GRADE EL. 10'-0"

16½" 20" 9" 13⅞" 2⅛" 5⅛"

6"x 3" ECC. RED. TOP FLAT

1/16 (TYP.)

C

⅜" = 1'-0"

FIGURE 28-17

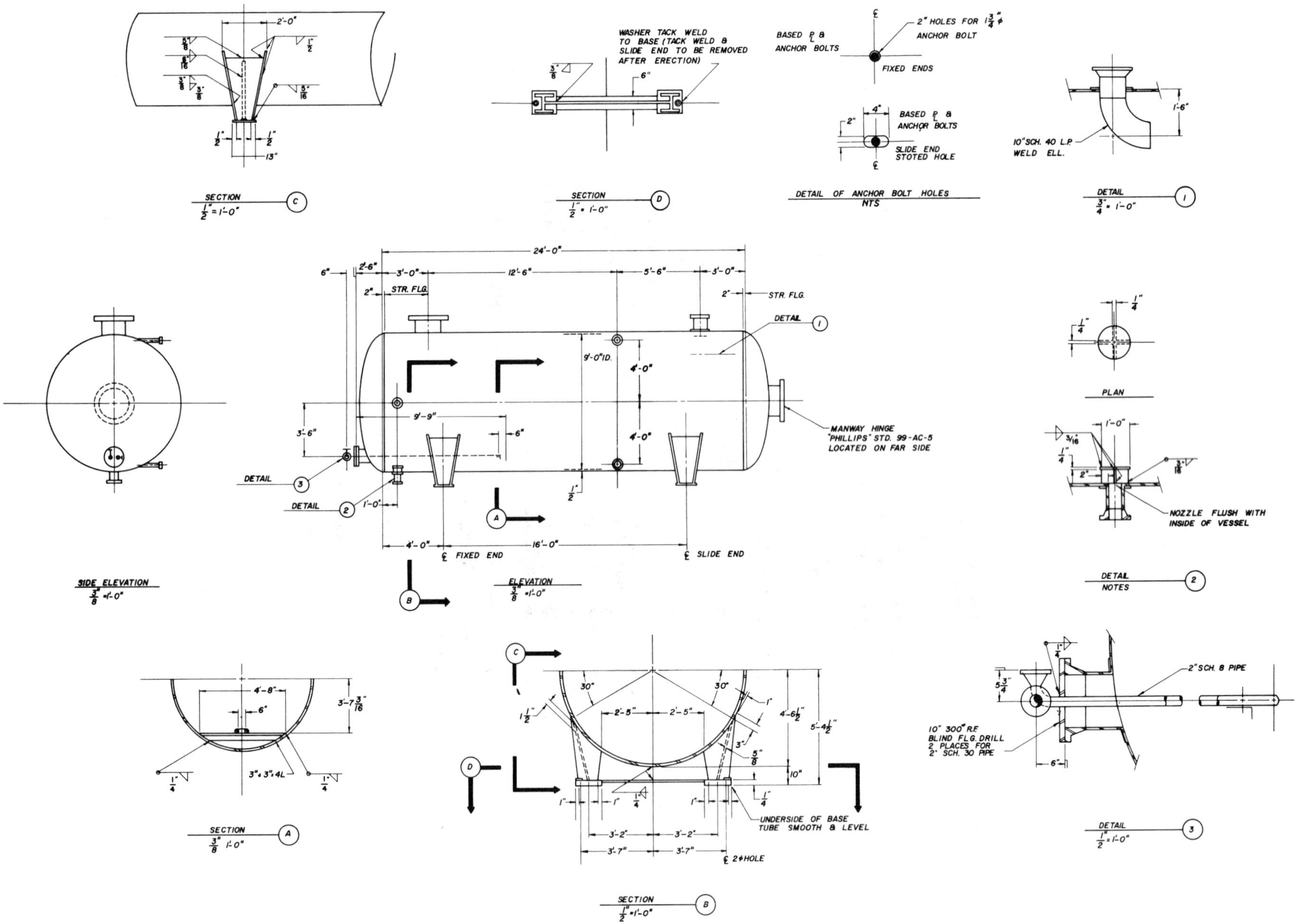

FIGURE 28-18 Vessel detail.

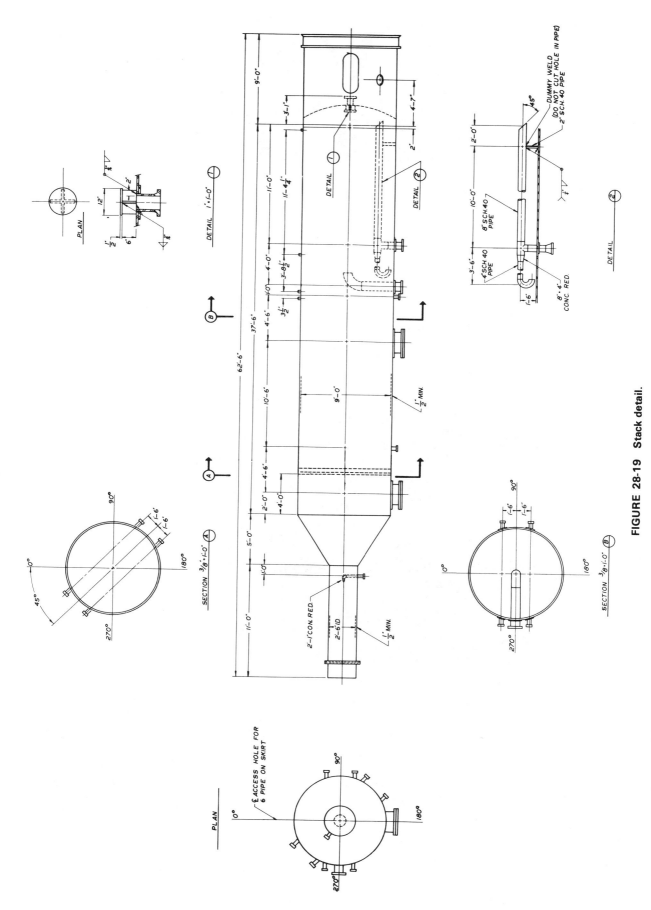

FIGURE 28-19 Stack detail.

303

29

Nuclear Power Project

FIGURE 29-1 Diablo Canyon nuclear power plant.

Nuclear-fission power is seen by most energy specialists as a transitional source of energy. Fossil fuels are rapidly being used, and we have not yet made the technological breakthroughs necessary for large-scale solar and nuclear fusion power capability. Although a great deal of energy is produced by a small amount of fissionable (or fossil) material, these fuels, uranium and plutonium, are quite rare and the supply is definitely limited. In fact, all plutonium is produced from uranium in nuclear plants, so it is mainly uranium deposits that concern us, although we can produce some fossil uranium from natural thorium.

Nuclear fission (the splitting of the nuclei of uranium or plutonium atoms) is a source of heat, as is also the case with fossil fuels and solar energy. As such, it supplies the energy for steam-driven turbines to produce electricity. That is, apart from the nuclear reactor, a nuclear power plant is very much like a conventional power plant. No special turbine or generator designs are needed. The major new considerations are not so much concerned with the generation of power, but with the fact that a tremendous release of nuclear radiation accompanies the power generation, which requires the isolation of the reactor itself and much remote instrumentation, along with heavy and bulky shields. Because the fuel material is not entirely used, the used fuel assemblies must be chemically reprocessed to go into the new assembly and the radioactive waste somehow stored for hundred of years until the radioactivity subsides. All this processing must also be done by remote control, and since it involves the handling of acids and radioactive liquids, much special piping is needed apart from the power plant piping itself.

NUCLEAR POWER AND THE MODEL

The model provides three-dimensional visibility, and therefore the necessary assurance can be established that a variety of licensing requirements for separation of redundant systems (backups), safety-related items, including mechanical, equipment, and electrical, all meet with the various licensing codes and design requirements. The use of the model in nuclear piping design has become almost universally accepted by all power construction firms, because of the ease with which piping can be routed to avoid problems or damage to safety-related equipment in the event of piping breaks and pipe whips. The location of seismic supports, restraints, and other pipe-support locations can be optimized with the use of the model.

FIGURE 29-3 Photograph of modeled containment area (see Fig. 29-4).

FIGURE 29-2 Nuclear power plant in construction stage.

Models allow the designer to plan for the removal and replacement of equipment. With the model, designers can develop detailed equipment locations, removal procedures, plant operation sequences, and construction sequences, besides using the model at later dates for training aides for operators and maintenance crews.

Nuclear-power-plant models, as with all piping models, utilize color coding which is able to highlight safety separations and fire protection provisions; access areas for installation, maintenance, and removal of equipment; and access for in-service inspection. Because of the vast amount of piping and the associated components, fittings, and intricate configurations, especially around the reactor area, the model provides for a much easier three-dimensional visualization in comparison to the multitude of drawings that are associated with a typical nuclear power plant, where there may be thousands of individual overlays, elevations, sections, plans, and developments. Because of the size of the nuclear power plant, models are usually constructed so as to be modular in form, which can be sectioned at obvious breakpoints, providing for easy assembly and access to the interior of the modeled nuclear plant. These sections can be easily separated from the overall model and can allow for easy change in design and rerouting of piping. The areas to be modeled are carefully studied at a variety of elevations and then split horizontally and vertically to increase visibility and access to the modeled plant. This also provides for the installation and design of piping hangers and related equipment in the later stages of the design process. Material take-off and isometric fabrication details are both facilitated by the use of the model.

The typical nuclear power model may encompass one whole floor of an engineering firm's building and cost upward of $1 million in time, materials, and construction. The advantages far outweigh the cost of the process. To be effective for nuclear power industry, models must be begun and in the early stages of the project, to help eliminate redundant, complicated drawings from a variety of fields, such as electrical, HVAC, and orthographic projection pipe design procedures. By utilizing the model in the beginning stages all the way through to the construction of the plant, it is possible to maximize its effectiveness.

Figure 29-4 shows a series of eight drawings at various elevations and sections of a nuclear containment area, showing the major equipment placement and major routing of large-diameter pipe. These drawings provide an excellent opportunity for the user of the book to become more familiar with a nuclear power plant, especially in the containment area, which is the major difference when comparing nuclear to conventional power plants. The turbine building in either the conventional or nuclear power plant works, and is designed somewhat in the same manner. The generation of heat is the primary difference between the two types of power generation. The eight drawings in Fig. 29-4 should be utilized either as a group or large individual drafting project. Before constructing a model of this containment area, the drawings can be done at the same scale as the model so as to make the construction of the model easier. Most dimensions will of necessity be scaled directly from the book drawings. The liner or containment building need not be constructed, although a circular area should be described along the base of the model to show where the containment wall would be. It is possible to use thin acrylic sheets and, by the use of a jig and fixture arrangement, bend plastic sheeting into a designed configuration, usually using two to three thicknesses of 1/16" sheeting. The fixture will provide adequate restraint during the gluing process. One problem with using this method is that large holes (cutouts, dodging) need to be cut out of the containment wall to show the various pieces of equipment and pipe routing of the model. Clear plastic sheeting can be utilized, therefore, eliminating problems. However, it is probably more economical to eliminate the containment building and just provide for 1"- or 2"-high containment walls around the area of the reactor, symbolizing the extent of the containment building, but not actually constructing it in total. The dome shape on top of the containment area should be eliminated in either case. Much of the concrete sections in the lower areas of the plant can be constructed from plastic and be painted gray to provide for a simulated concrete representation. In this particular power plant, four steam generators must also be fabricated together with the reactor core. Great care must be taken when attempting to construct a model from these drawings, especially when sufficient views may not be available. It may be necessary to reroute piping or place equipment approximately. Figure 29-3 is a photograph of the model containment area of the power plant shown in Fig. 29-1. This photograph can give some idea of the possibilities for this particular model project. Note the use of structural steel and various levels of flooring that are provided.

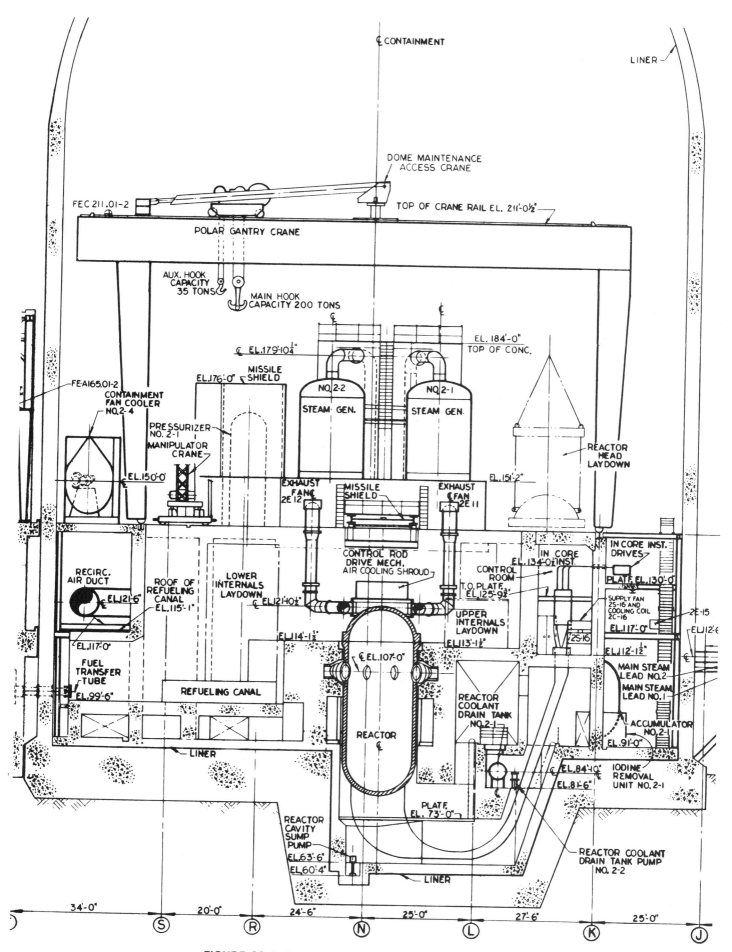

FIGURE 29-4 Nuclear power plant containment area.

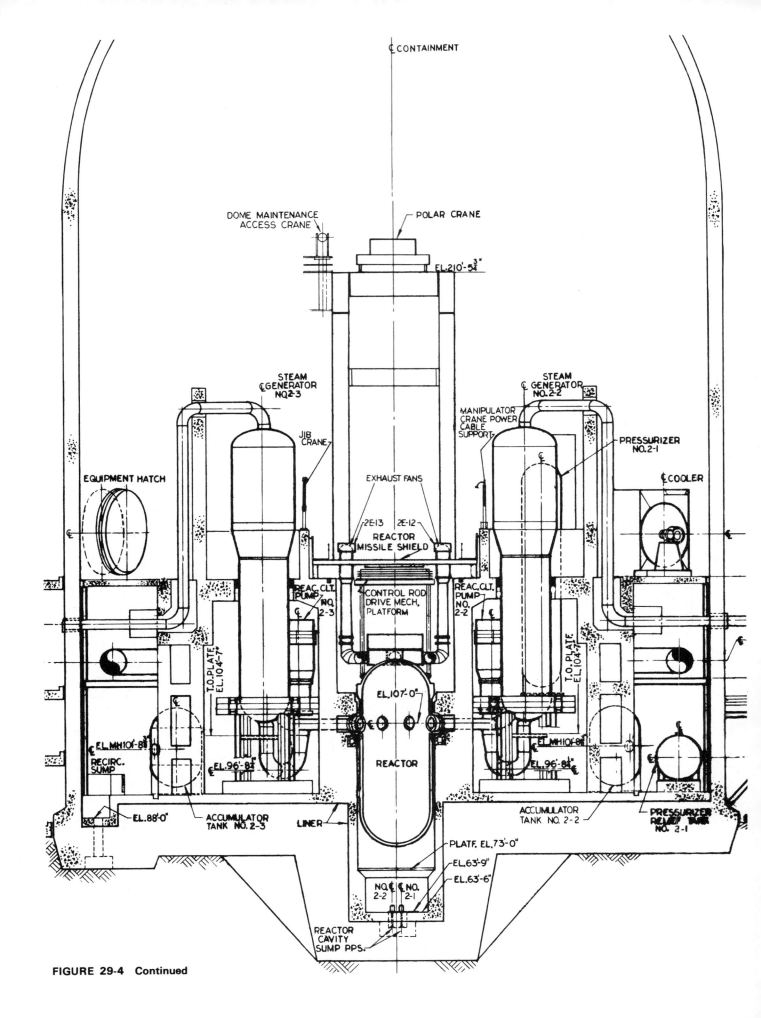

FIGURE 29-4   Continued

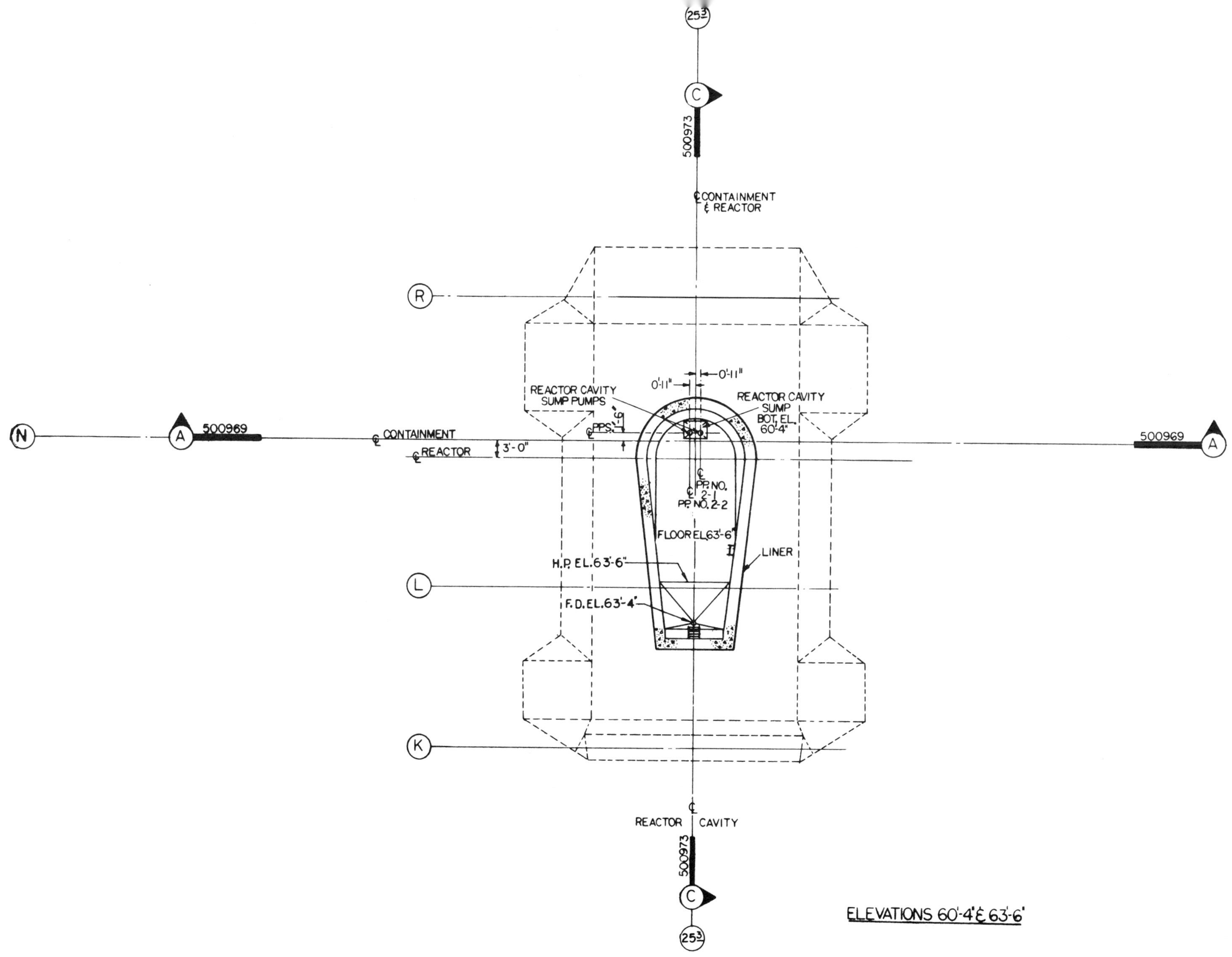

FIGURE 29-4 Continued

ELEVATIONS 60'-4"& 63'-6"

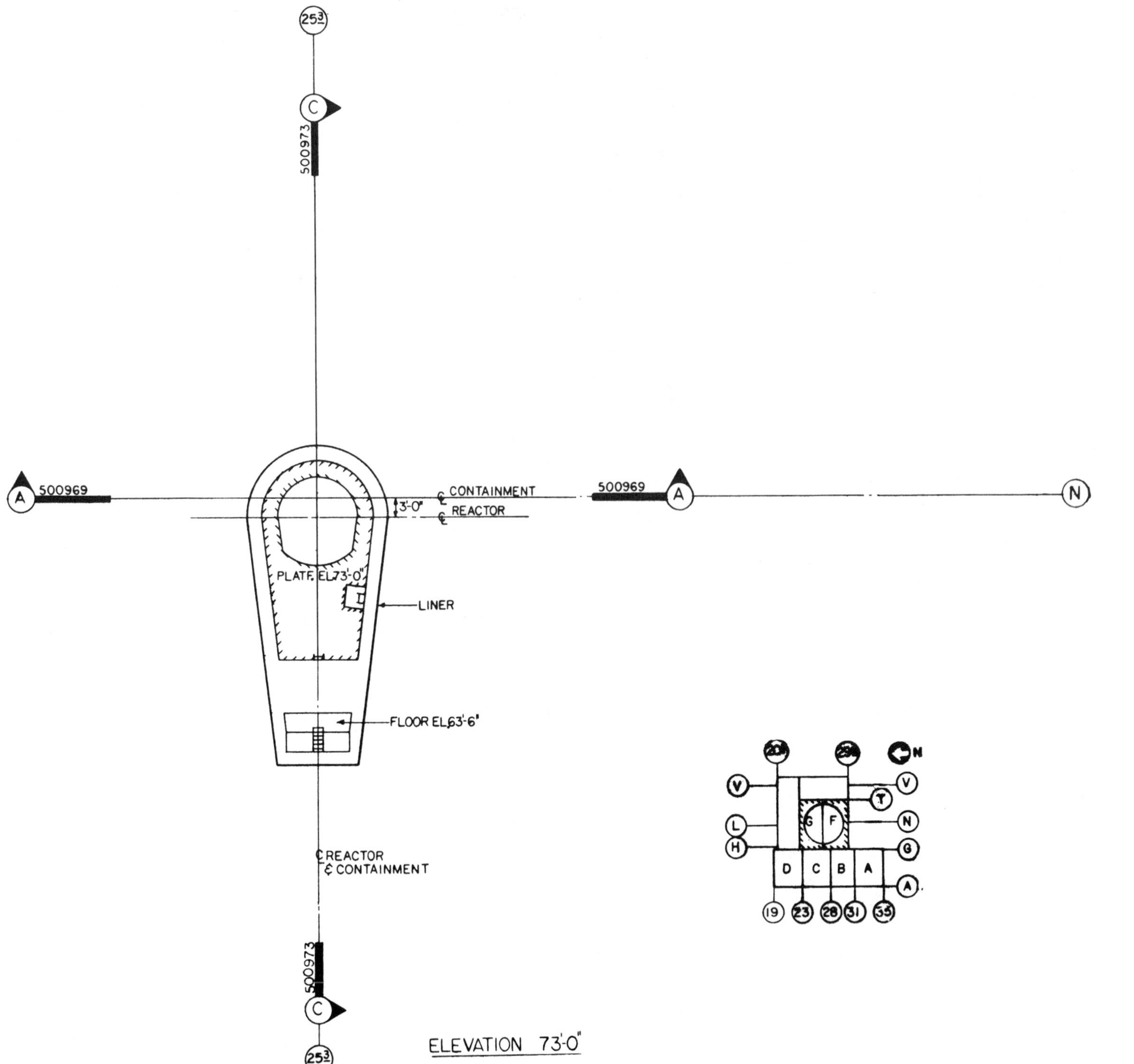

ELEVATION 73'-0"

FIGURE 29-4 Continued

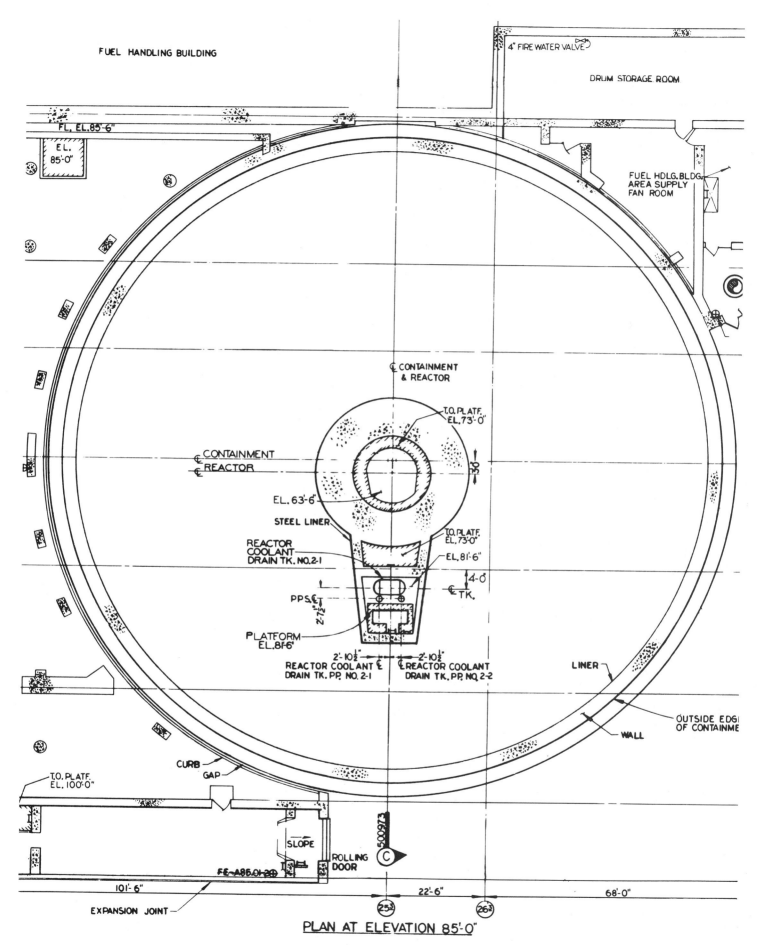

FUEL HANDLING BUILDING

DRUM STORAGE ROOM

4" FIRE WATER VALVE

FUEL HDLG. BLDG.
AREA SUPPLY
FAN ROOM

FL. EL.85'-6"

EL.
85'-0"

CONTAINMENT
& REACTOR

T.O. PLATF.
EL. 73'-0"

CONTAINMENT
REACTOR

EL. 63'-6"

STEEL LINER

REACTOR
COOLANT
DRAIN TK. NO.2-1

T.O. PLATF.
EL. 73'-0"

EL. 81'-6"

4'-0"

TK.

PPS

2'-7½"

PLATFORM
EL. 81'-6"

2'-10½"   2'-10½"

REACTOR COOLANT
DRAIN TK. PP. NO. 2-1

REACTOR COOLANT
DRAIN TK. PP. NO. 2-2

LINER

OUTSIDE EDGE
OF CONTAINME

WALL

T.O. PLATF.
EL. 100'-0"

CURB

GAP

SLOPE

ROLLING
DOOR

500973

C

FE-A85.01-2

101'-6"

22'-6"

68'-0"

EXPANSION JOINT

25⅗   26⅗

PLAN AT ELEVATION 85'-0"

FIGURE 29-4   Continued

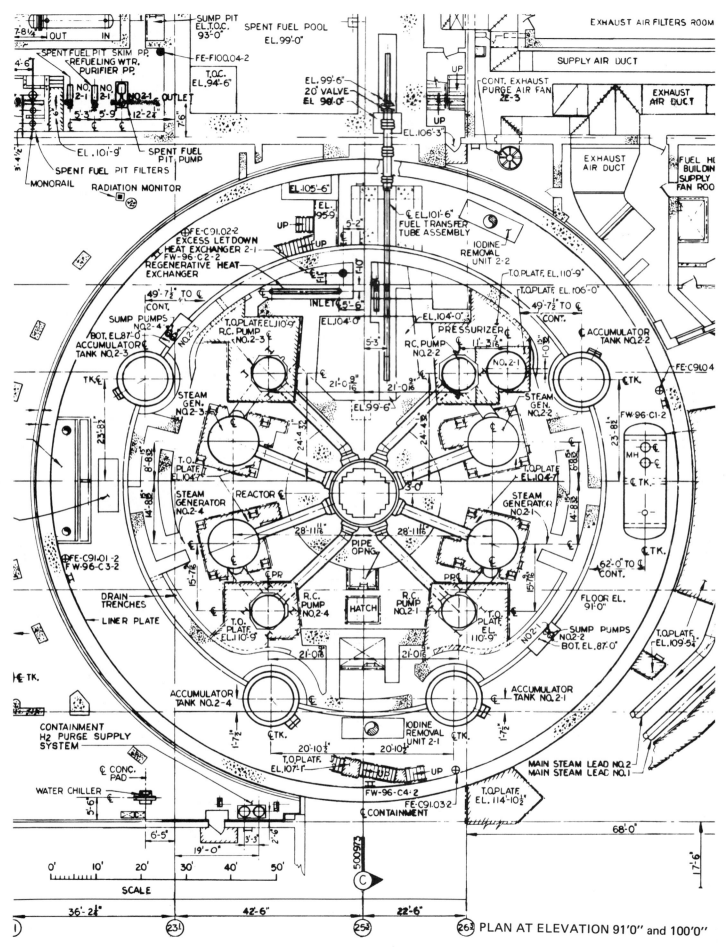

FIGURE 29-4 Continued

PLAN AT ELEVATION 91'0" and 100'0"

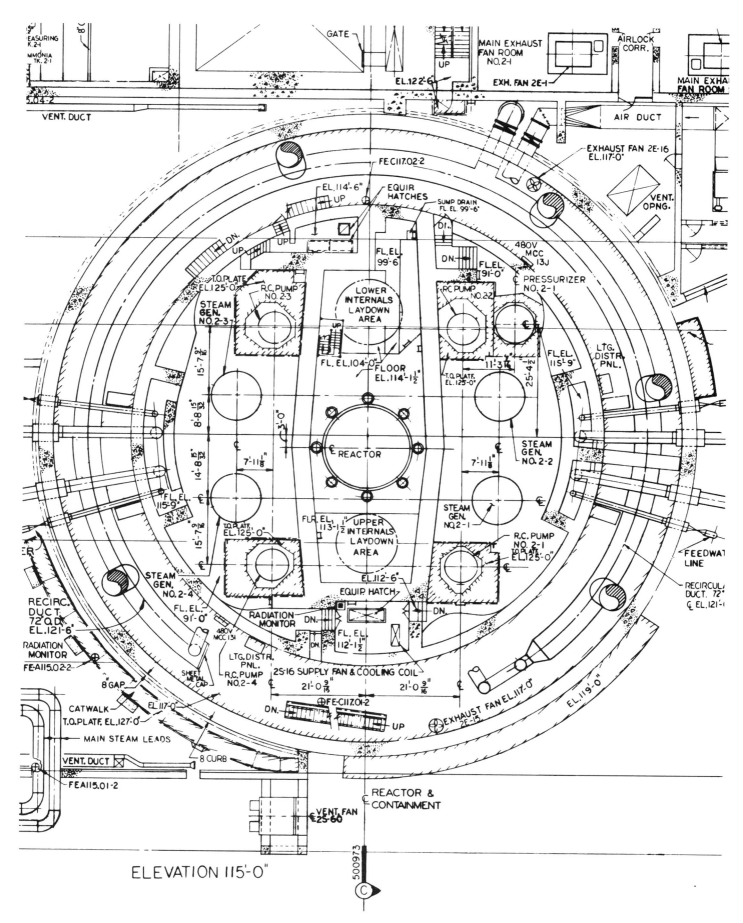

ELEVATION 115'-0"

FIGURE 29-4 Continued

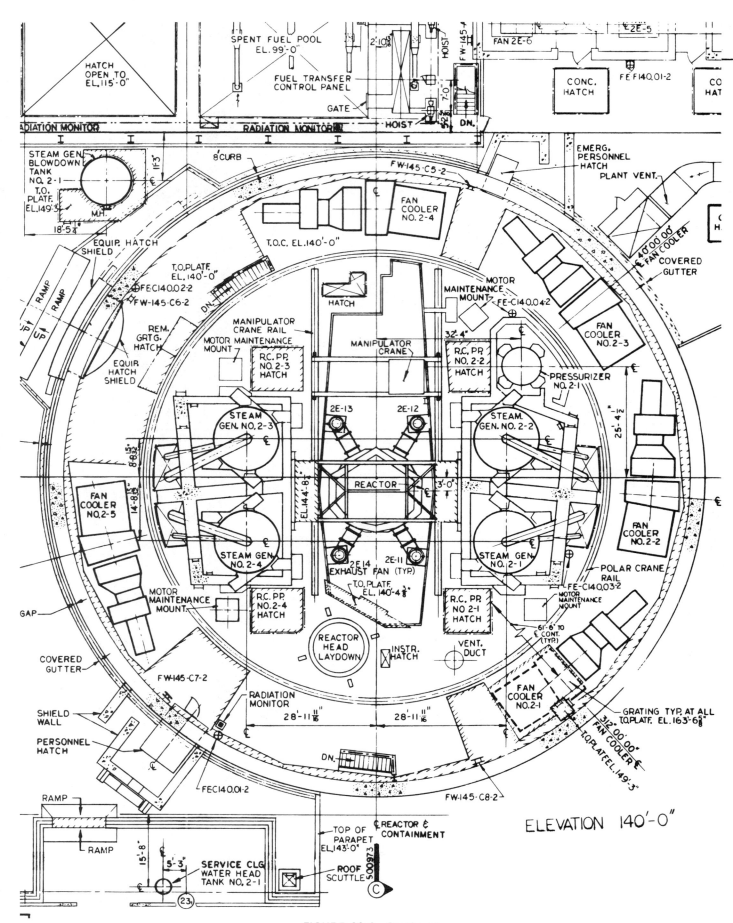

FIGURE 29-4 Continued

30

Fossil-Fuel Power Plant

FIGURE 30-1   Fossil-fuel power plant.

In the past, fossil-fuel and hydroelectric power have been the two main producers of electricity in modern industrial states and developing nations. As the year 2000 approaches, it becomes more apparent that fossil fuels are reaching the end of their usefulness to society because of their high pollution level; the extreme amount of energy required to find, locate, and produce them; their rapidly rising price; and the rapidly diminishing level of known reserves.

Coal is about the only fossil fuel left in great abundance and there will be a short period of time where it is utilized again as it was at the turn of the

last century, but because of the environmental pollution, the use of coal will eventually become obsolete. Conventional power plants using fossil fuels are basically a thing of the past. Already new combustion equipment for clean burning is being produced, but at increased cost, and even then only to extend the time of transition to solar, fusion, and geothermal power.

The uses of steam in industry are numerous. They include heating, food processing, oil refining, and various other chemical processes. In general, most of the design characteristics of steam piping are similar, depending of course on their relative pressure and temperature. In power plants, steam piping is utilized to transfer the energy created by the heating of water and production of steam to the turbine, which, in turn, will produce electricity by turning a generator. In small industrial plants, it is possible when generating process steam to create steam at a higher pressure and install a turbine generator for the creation of in-plant electrical energy, besides the use of the steam for production processes within the building.

In power generation, the use of fossil-fuel steam generation has a long and varied history. The first central station for power production was completed in Philadelphia in 1881, where four Babcock and Wilcox boilers were installed to produce electricity for the Brush Electric Light Company. By the early 1900s, steam pressures rose considerably in the larger central stations that were being constructed throughout the nation, and by 1914, pressures of 150 psi and 500°F (260°C) were considered normal. During the years 1924 and 1925, a large jump in steam pressures for central stations came into being with major changes in the production and the utilization of steam throughout this period. Larger boilers were constructed which produced higher rates of output because of the ability to pulverize coal as fuel. This created the need for the water-cooled furnace. At the present time, temperatures of over 1000°F (537.7°C) with pressures from 2000 to 5000 psig are common throughout the power-generation fields. The feedwater is pumped into the preheater area, where it goes to the boiler, which turns it into steam. From there it is piped to the high-pressure turbine and back out through the boiler through the reheater into the intermediate-pressure turbine. From there, it goes into the low-pressure turbine. The turbine turns the generators to produce electricity. At many points along this cycle, extraction lines remove condensate from the steam after it has been utilized by the turbine and feed it back into the original feedwater. Steam exhausted by the low-pressure turbine is sent to the condensor and converted to feedwater to begin the process again. In this way, the system loses very little of its original water and the process can be cycled over and over again with little waste entailed. The boiler itself can be fueled by coal, oil, natural gas, or a combination of other fossil fuels. In the modern power plant, the turbine will receive steam from the boiler which is created by the burning of fossil fuel. Water from a local source will sometimes be preheated by the flue gases that are saved for recycling from the power plant stack.

Gases from the burning of the fuel pass over the boiler tubes and superheater tubes, and then run out of the boiler to the economizer, where the heat is used to prewarm the feedwater before it enters the boiler. The steam generator itself or the boiler usually has either natural circulation or forced circulation. In the latter case, water is moved through the pipes by use of boiler feed pumps or booster pumps.

Another important item in the power plant is the crane used to move the turbine and generator for replacement installation, periodic inspection, or repair. In the set of drawings provided of the power plant, the crane can be seen in the sectional view along with the control cabin and main hook assembly.

In the modern power plant very few operating personnel are used. The majority of the plant is on automatic controls for everything from the boiler water level to the automatic control of the fuel and air supply. A good percentage of the valves and equipment are motor or cylinder-operated and are controlled from a central instrumentation room, from which the operation of the plant is monitored by a technician.

In this section, a set of drawings is provided showing elevations and equipment locations of a typical single-turbine power plant using conventional fossil fuels. These plans are in no way the complete set of all the various minute piping situations within the plant; they only represent the general layout of major piping and equipment location at various elevations.

This is an excellent group project for a model class. Specifications set down in the previous sections should provide sufficient guidelines to complete this project. All photographs provided in this section are of a similar but somewhat more complicated power plant. The project to be modeled is a single-turbine unit, whereas the photographs exhibit a double-turbine unit. A close examination of the photographs will still be of help when constructing this project. Remember to follow the specifications set down in earlier sections.

The project should be modeled at 1/8″ = 1′, 3/16″ = 1′, or 3/32″ = 1′, depending on the total cost, which may be $300 to $500, depending on scale. A majority of equipment (boiler, stack), ducting, and so on, must be fabricated from plastic sheeting or wood. It would be a good idea to draw this project before modeling, so as to have to scale a set of prints from which to work.

This project offers a wide variety of experimenting with materials and construction techniques for the fabrication of the tower, boiler, ducting, and so on.

The tower shown in the photographs was made by a student out of papier-mâché with considerable time and effort. The steam generator (boiler) was constructed of thin balsa wood, but this project should be done with plastic sheets, as is more common in industry.

FIGURE 30-2

FIGURE 30-5 Ducting made of balsa wood.

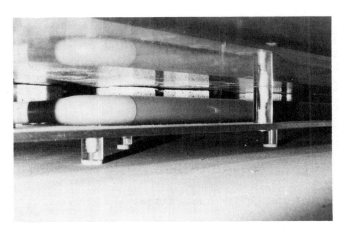

FIGURE 30-3 View of basement piping; notice how clear plastic is used to raise the basement above the wood base.

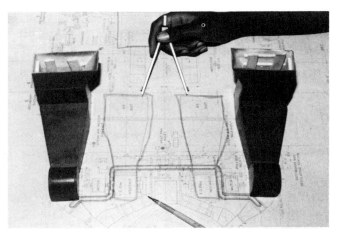

FIGURE 30-6 Air ducts after fabrication.

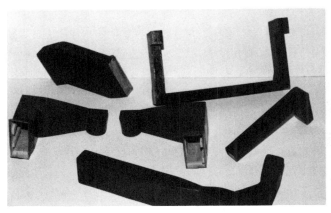

FIGURE 30-4 Prefabricated ducting.

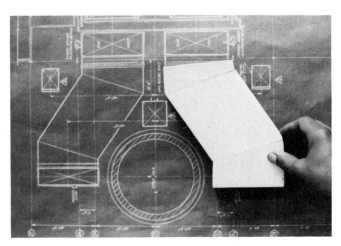

FIGURE 30-7 Gas ducting.

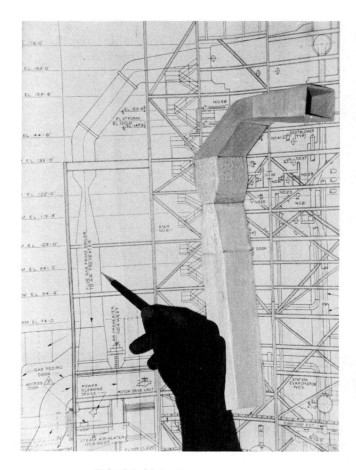

FIGURE 30-8 Flue gas ducting.

FIGURE 30-10 Checking the ducting from generator. (Note that the steam generator will eventually hang from the steel and not be supported from the bottom.)

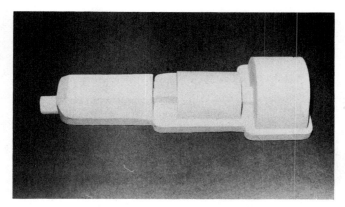

FIGURE 30-11 Turbine and generator fabricated from wood.

FIGURE 30-9 Major ducting, steam generator, and stack placed on model.

FIGURE 30-12 Tandem turbines. (Note that the project in Fig. 30-23 has only single turbine.)

FIGURE 30-13 Elevation view of turbine and crane.

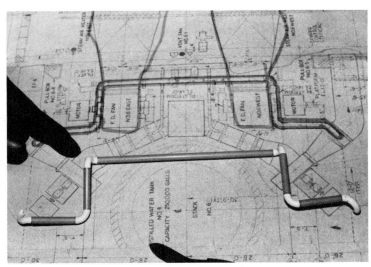

FIGURE 30-14 Piping the model.

FIGURE 30-15 End view showing ducting and stack.

FIGURE 30-16 Whole sections of steel were prefabricated off the model.

FIGURE 30-17 Model during construction stage.

FIGURE 30-18

FIGURE 30-19

320

FIGURE 30-20 Note that only a limited amount
of flooring was shown.

FIGURE 30-21

FIGURE 30-22

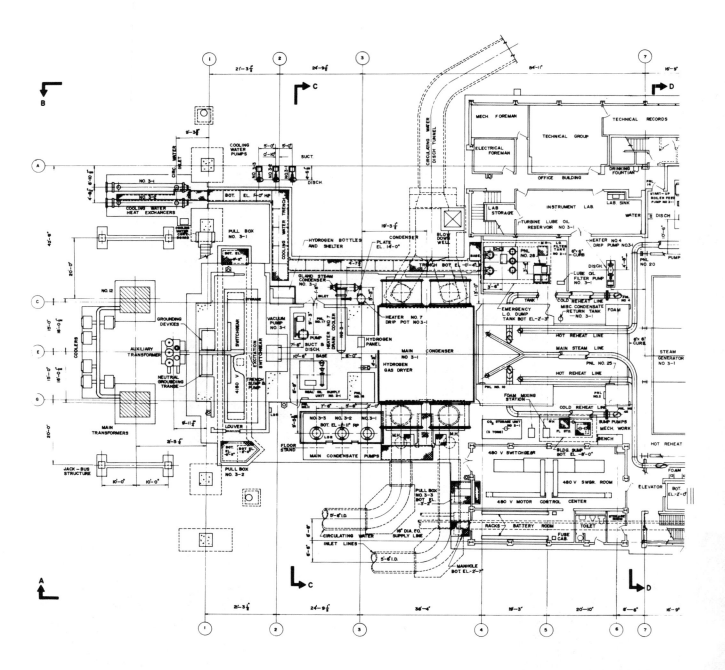

PLAN AT ELEV. 3'-0"

FIGURE 30-23 Power plant drawings.

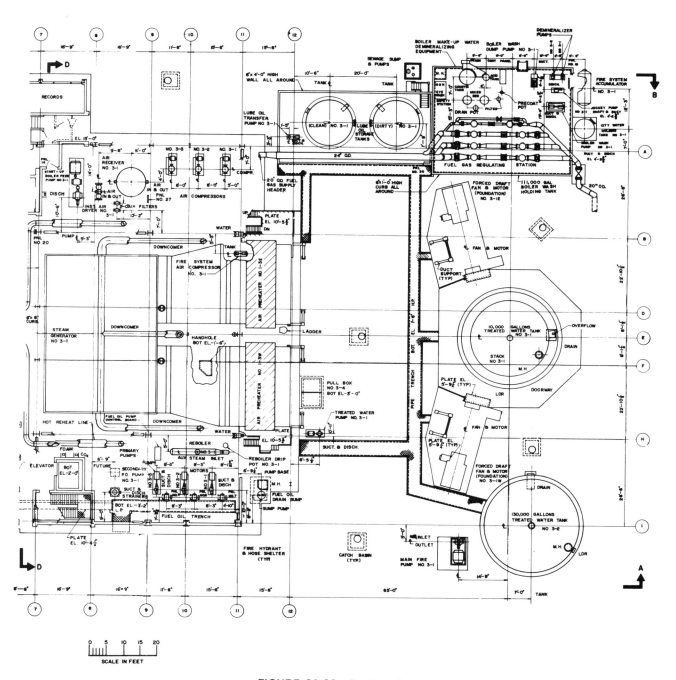

SCALE IN FEET

FIGURE 30-23 Continued

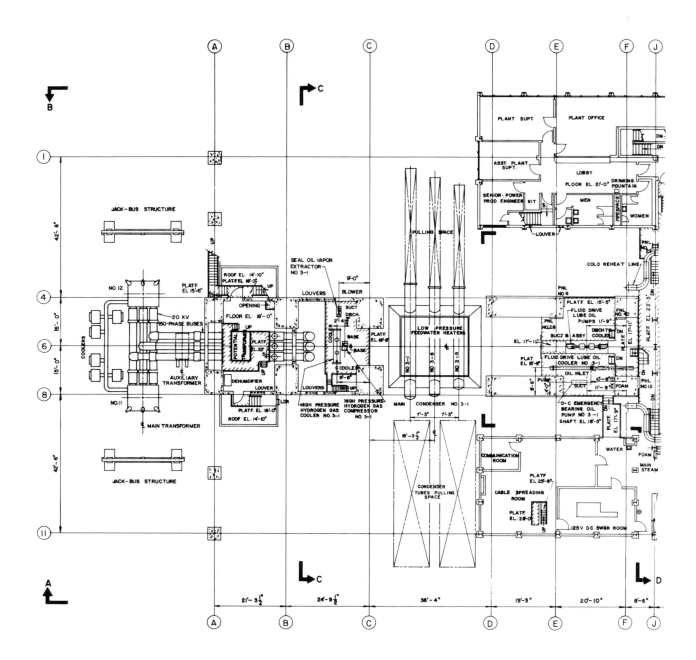

PLAN AT ELEV. 17'-9"

FIGURE 30-23 Continued

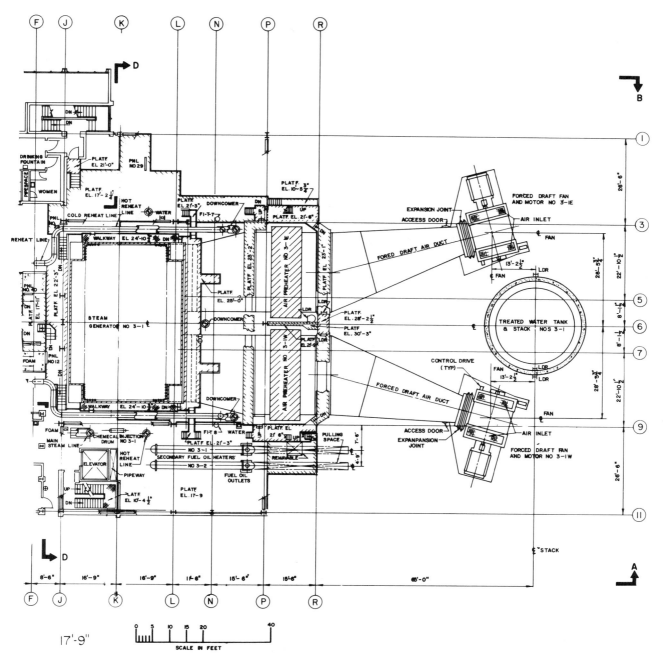

17'-9"

FIGURE 30-23 Continued

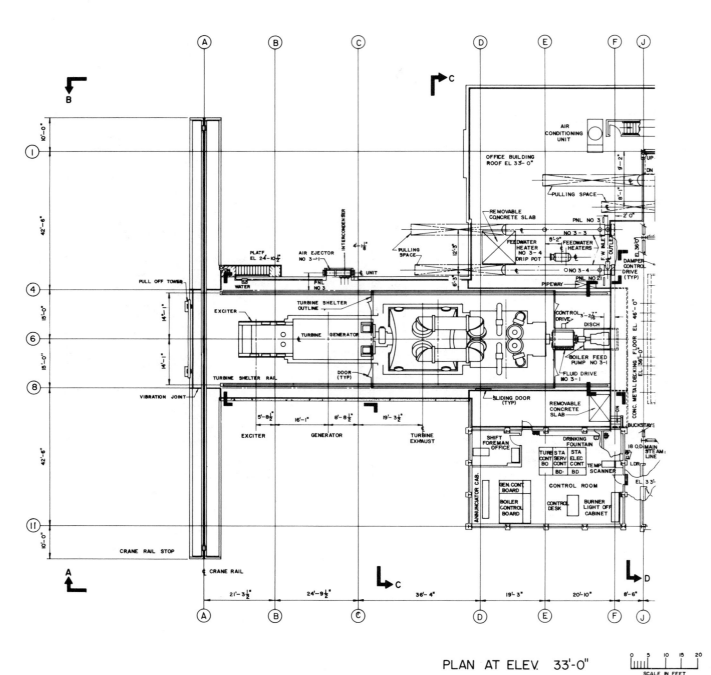

PLAN AT ELEV. 33'-0"

FIGURE 30-23 Continued

326

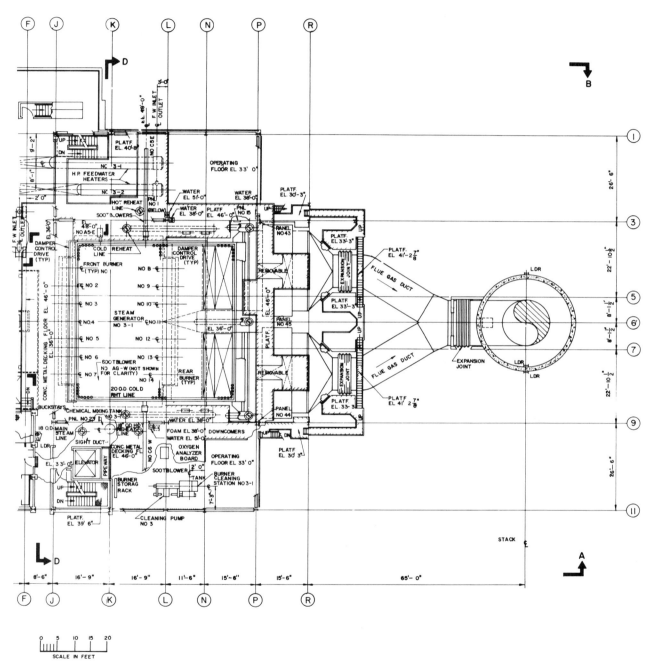

SCALE IN FEET
0 5 10 15 20

FIGURE 30-23 Continued

327

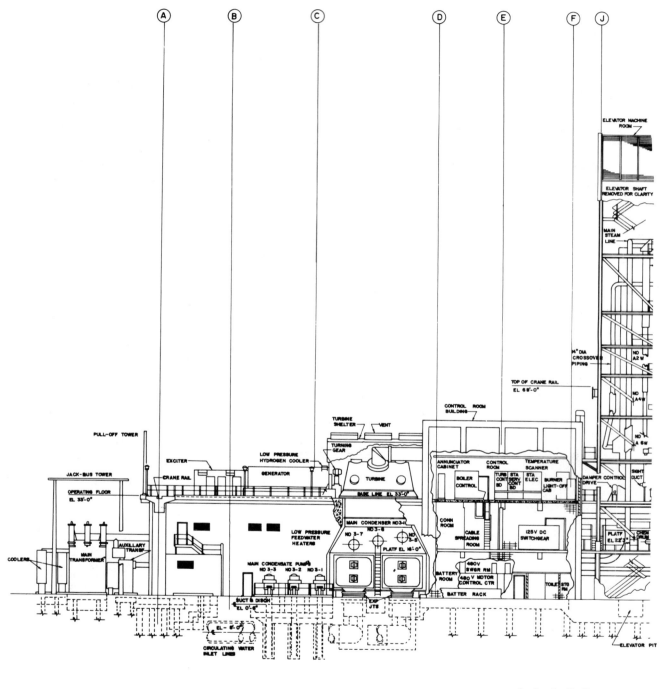

SECTION A-A

SCALE IN FEET

FIGURE 30-23 Continued

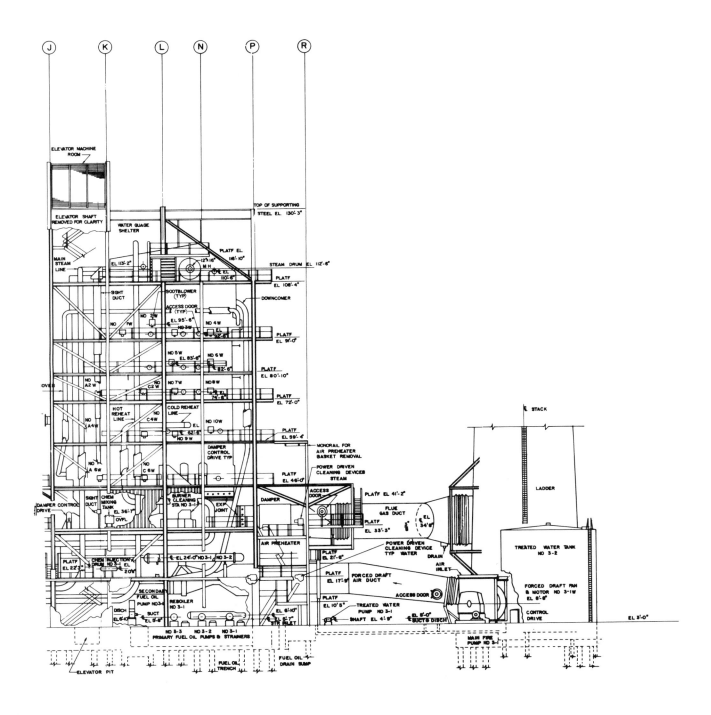

FIGURE 30-23 Continued

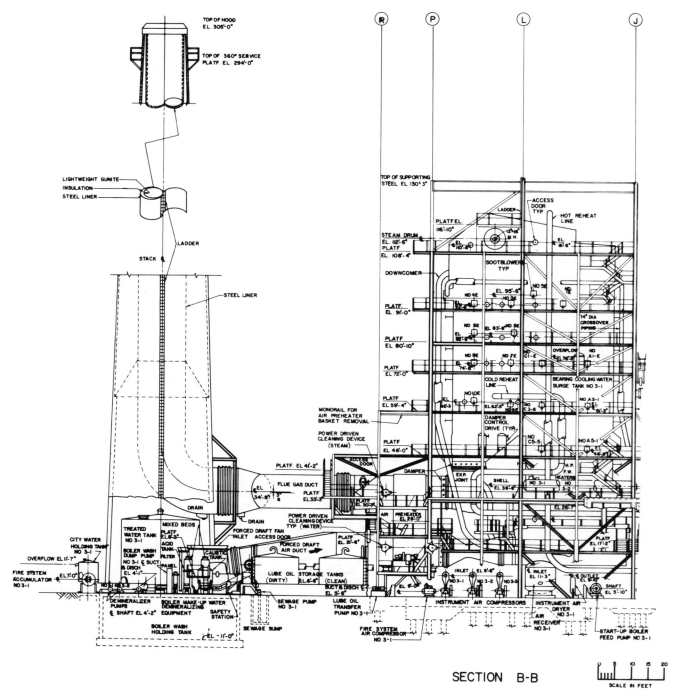

TOP OF HOOD
EL. 305'-0"

TOP OF 360° SERVICE
PLATF. EL. 294'-0"

LIGHTWEIGHT GUNITE
INSULATION
STEEL LINER

LADDER

STACK

STEEL LINER

DRAIN

TREATED
WATER TANK
NO 3-1
CITY WATER
HOLDING TANK
NO 3-1

OVERFLOW EL 11'-7"

FIRE SYSTEM
ACCUMULATOR
NO 3-1

EL 7'-0"

NO 3-1

DEMINERALIZER
PUMPS
€ SHAFT EL 4'-2"

MIXED BEDS
PLATF.
EL. 6'-2"
ACID
TANK
BOILER WASH
DUMP PUMP
NO 3-1 € SUCT
& DISCH
EL. 4'-1"

PANEL

CAUSTIC
TANK

FILTER

BOILER MAKE-UP WATER
DEMINERALIZING
EQUIPMENT

SAFETY
STATION

BOILER WASH
HOLDING TANK

EL.-11'-0"

LUBE OIL STORAGE TANKS
(DIRTY) EL.6'-0"(CLEAN)
SUCT & DISCH
EL. 5'-6"

SEWAGE PUMP
NO 3-1

SEWAGE SUMP

LUBE OIL
TRANSFER
PUMP NO 3-1

DRAIN

FORCED DRAFT FAN
INLET ACCESS DOOR

FORCED DRAFT
AIR DUCT

POWER DRIVEN
CLEANING DEVICE
TYP (WATER)

PLATF. EL 4'-2"

€ EL
34'-8"

FLUE GAS DUCT
PLATF
EL 33'-3"

PLATF
EL 30'-

ACCESS
DOOR

DAMPER

POWER DRIVEN
CLEANING DEVICE
(STEAM)

MONORAIL FOR
AIR PREHEATER
BASKET REMOVAL

AIR PREHEATER
EL 39'-0"

PLATF
EL 21'-8"

PLATF
EL 46'-0"

PLATF
EL 59'-4"

PLATF
EL 72'-0"

PLATF
EL 80'-10"

PLATF
EL 91'-0"

DOWNCOMER

STEAM DRUM
EL. 112'-6"
PLATF
EL. 108'-4"

PLATF EL.
116'-10"

SOOTBLOWER
TYP

NO 4E
NO 5E

NO 6E
NO 8E

EL 62'-3"

NO IDE

EXP
JOINT

SHELL
EL 36'-6"

EL 83'-0"NO 8E

NO 7E   C1-E

NO
C3-5

NO
C5-5

DAMPER
CONTROL
DRIVE (TYP)

COLD REHEAT
LINE

EL 95'-6"   NO 5E

EL
82'-3"

12" H.
M.H.

ACCESS
DOOR
TYP

HOT REHEAT
LINE

LADDER

EL
111'-3"

14" DIA
CROSSOVER
PIPING

OVERFLOW NO
EL 76'-3" A1-E

BEARING COOLING WATER
SURGE TANK NO 3-1

NO A3-1
EL

NO A5-1
EL

TOP OF SUPPORTING
STEEL EL 130'-3"

H.P.
F.W.
HEATER
NO 3-1

EL 28'-7"

NO
3-2

PLATF
EL 17'-2"

€ INLET
EL 11'-3"

€ INLET
EL 9'-6"

NO 3-1   NO 3-2   NO 3-3

INSTRUMENT AIR COMPRESSORS

FIRE SYSTEM
AIR COMPRESSOR
NO 3-1

AIR
RECEIVER
NO 3-1

INSTRUMENT AIR
DRYER
NO 3-1

€ OUTLET
EL 9'-0"

€ SHAFT
EL 5'-10"

START-UP BOILER
FEED PUMP NO 3-1

R   P   L   J

SECTION B-B

SCALE IN FEET
0 5 10 15 20

FIGURE 30-23 Continued

330

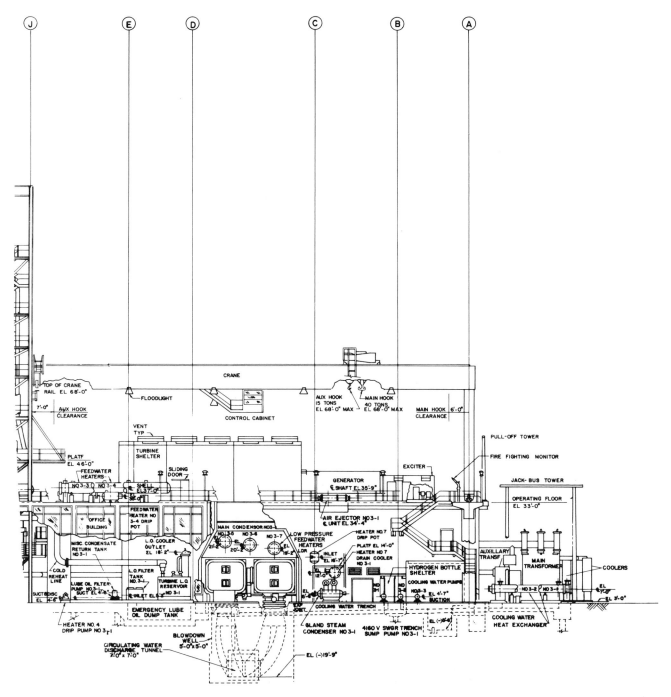

FIGURE 30-23 Continued

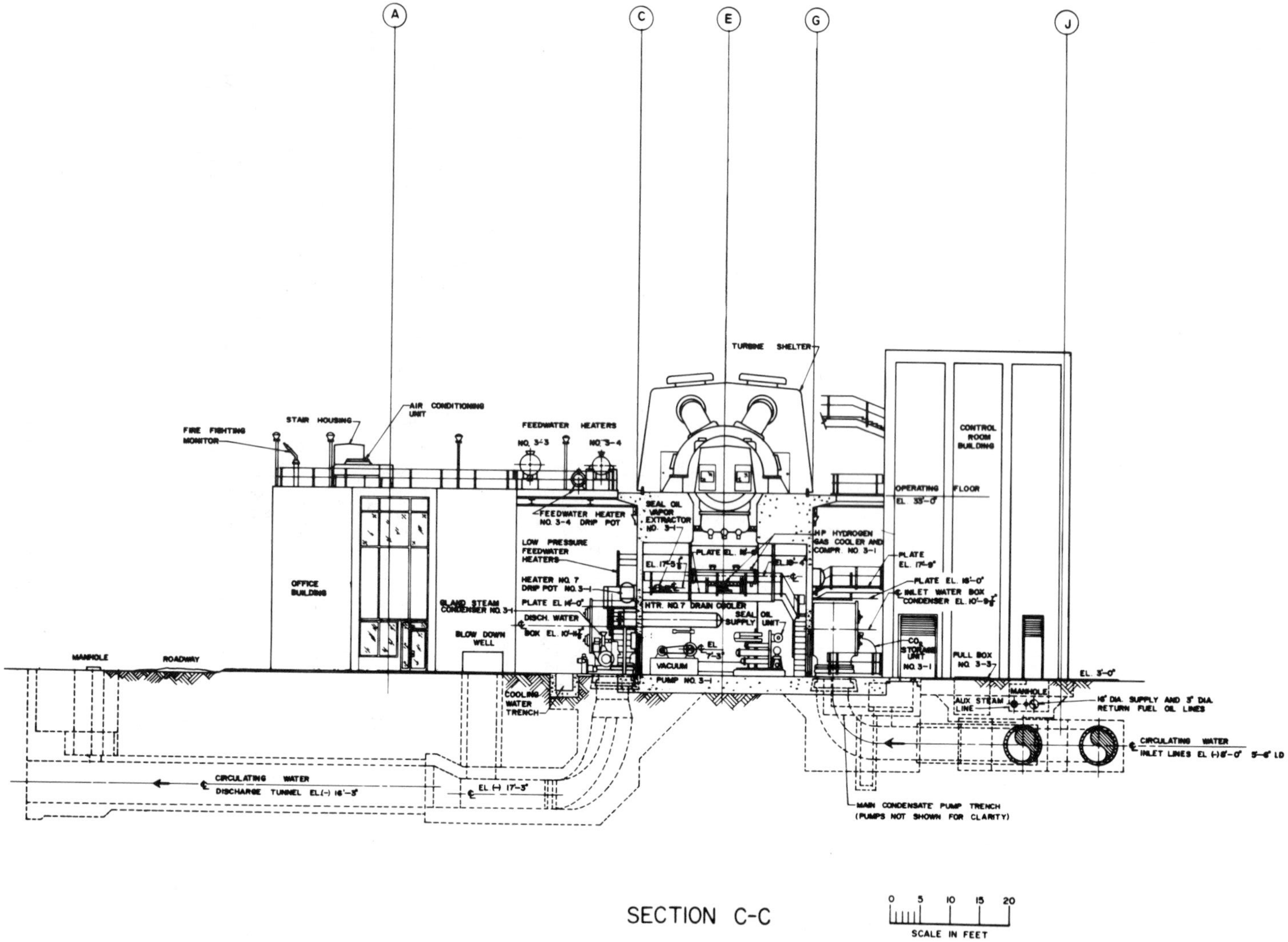

SECTION C-C

FIGURE 30-23 Continued

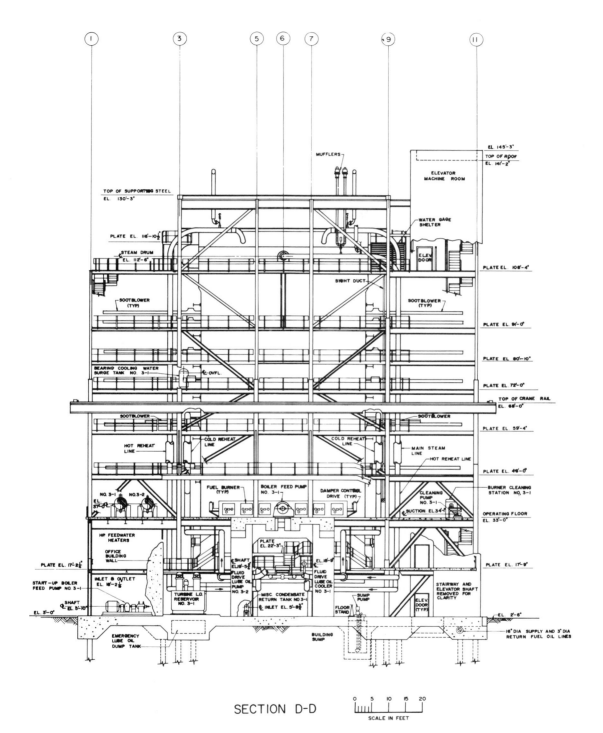

SECTION D-D

SCALE IN FEET
0 5 10 15 20

FIGURE 30-23 Continued

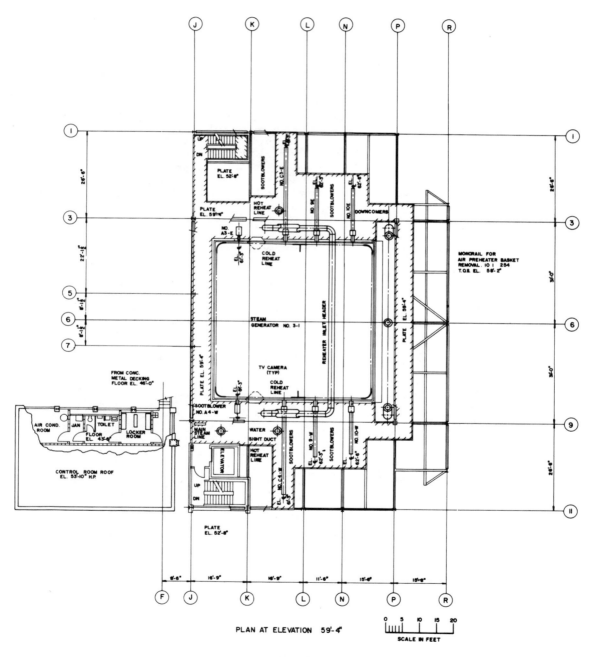

PLAN AT ELEVATION 59'-4"

SCALE IN FEET

FIGURE 30-23 Continued

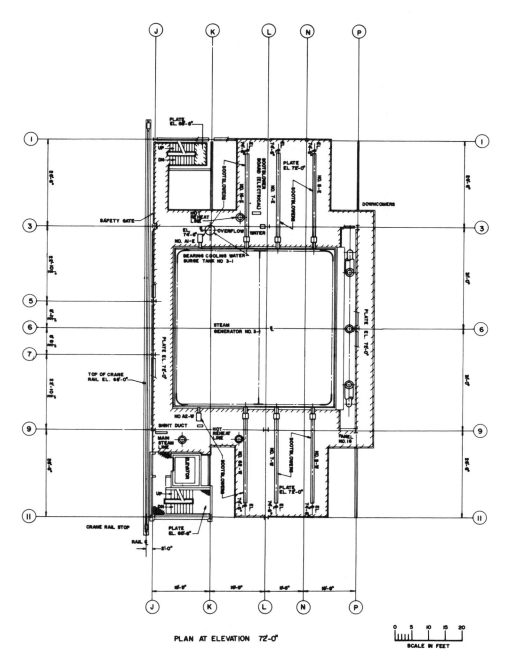

PLAN AT ELEVATION 72'-0"

SCALE IN FEET

FIGURE 30-23 Continued

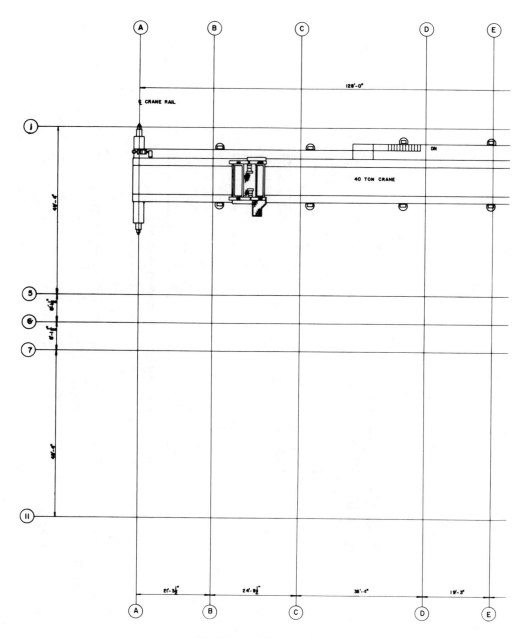

FIGURE 30-23 Continued

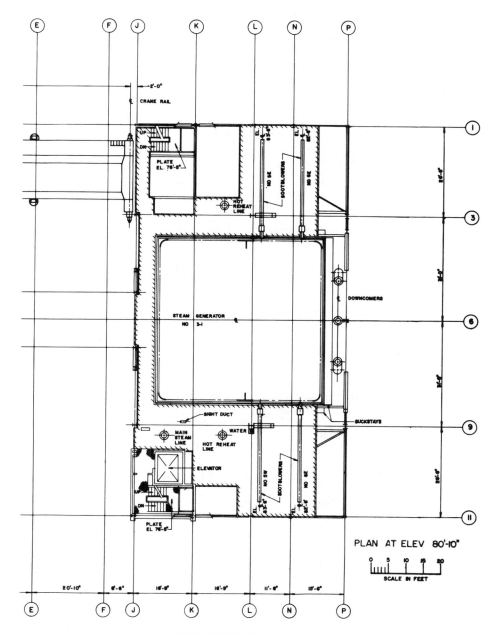

PLAN AT ELEV 80'-10"

SCALE IN FEET

FIGURE 30-23 Continued

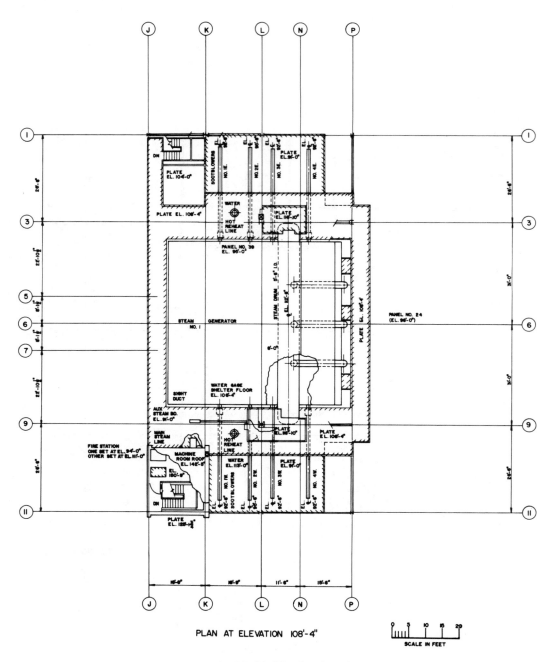

PLAN AT ELEVATION 108'-4"

SCALE IN FEET

FIGURE 30-23 Continued

338

31

Geothermal Power Plant

Geothermal energy, which is underground hot water and steam, has been increasingly viewed as a possibility of alternative energy for the future. A growing number of nations throughout the world have made attempts to harnass this energy in order to spin the turbine generators that make electricity. The project in this section is of the Geysers Power Plant, 90 miles north of San Francisco. It is a project of the Pacific Gas and Electric Company. The Geysers power project is the largest of its kind in the world that uses geothermal steam. The Geysers is really not a geyser but more appropriately a fumarole. The difference between real geysers and fumaroles is that fumaroles emit a constant stream of steam, whereas geysers are primarily intermittent, fountain-like jets of hot water and steam, which come only at intervals. In the Geysers power plants, which are separate units similar to the one in this section, steam is supplied to the turbine at 355°F and 100 to 125 psi. About 2000 pounds of steam per hour is required to operate a 110,000-kW generating unit similar to the one shown in this project. As of now, the Geysers contains 15 separate units, which require 18,000,000 pounds of steam per hour.

One of the first necessities of a geyser plant is

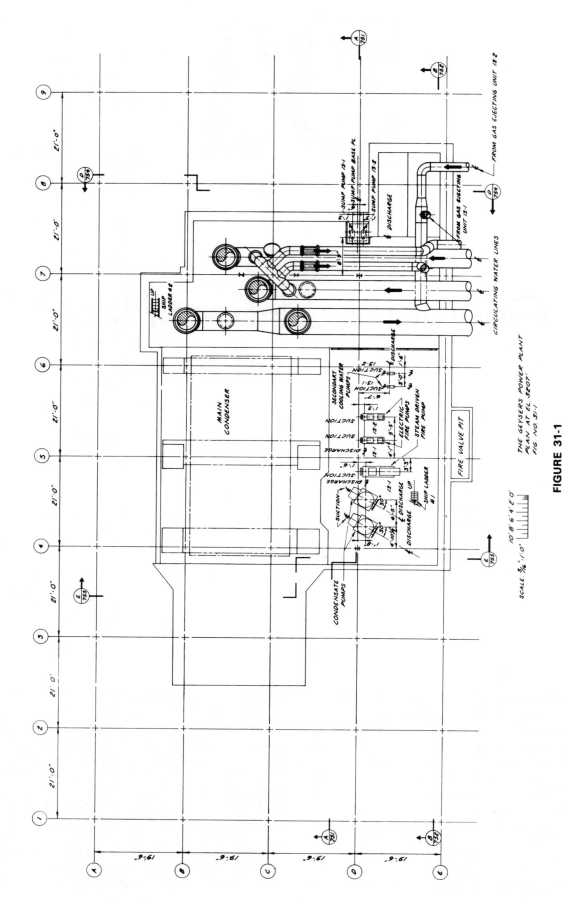

THE GEYSERS POWER PLANT
PLAN AT EL. 3203'
FIG. NO. 31-1

FIGURE 31-1

340

to cleanse the minute fragments of rock by the use of centrifugal separator chambers so as to eliminate these harmful particles, which would damage the turbine blades. Just as in any other power plant, steam is then delivered through insulated pipes to the main building in the power plant, where the turbine is housed. This steam is used to spin the turbine blades, which drive generators and therefore produce electricity. After the steam is spent in the turbine blades, it flows into the condenser, where it is changed into warm water. The warm water is in a partial vacuum, which helps extract 50 percent more energy from the steam than would otherwise be available under normal conditions. This prewarmed water is pumped from the condenser to the cooling tower, where its temperature is reduced by evaporation. The cooling towers are similar to all cooling towers used in power plants, where the water is partially evaporated by flowing over a series of baffles and being exposed to an updraft of air. Excess water, which occurs after the cooling process, is reinjected into the steam-producing reservoir; therefore, no new water is required for the cooling tower because it is supplied by the condensing geothermal steam.

Geothermal power originates deep inside the earth about 20 miles below the crust, where magma or molten mass is in the process of cooling. In places where this magma is close to the surface, say 5 or 10 miles, the heat produced by the magma in conjunction with water that is trapped in fractures in the near surface rocks provides a natural heating unit which produces gases and water vapor, which surface as hot springs and fumaroles. Reservoirs are deep inside the earth; by drilling, the pressure is released, which allows the hot water and steam to flow to the surface where it may be used to generate electricity, as in the case of the Geysers Power Plant.

This type of unit is considerably cleaner than many other types of power sources. The Geysers' clean, superheated dry steam is relatively rare in comparison to other types of geothermal situations. Hot water, because it is filled with more impurities, is less useful and also more common in other geothermal resource areas throughout the world. In Iceland, New Zealand, Mexico, the Phillipines, Nicaragua, Turkey, El Salvadore, Hungary, and other places, there are geothermal plants in production or being studied.

The geothermal power being developed at the Geysers has many environmental advantages, especially over present power sources such as coal, oil, natural gas, and nuclear power. One of the obvious advantages is that there are no combustion products emitted to contribute to our ever-increasing world pollution. Also, the cost of fossil fuels and their diminishing supply make geothermal prospects such as the Geysers more attractive than ever. In comparison to hydroelectric power plants, geothermal plants do not require that pristine rivers be dammed; also, the condensed steam is recycled in the process of cooling and the extra water reinjected underground into the steam reservoir, thereby creating an almost closed, perfect system. The drawbacks of geothermal power are, of course, the relative scarcity of such situations in comparison to the ability to build other types of power plants. Of course, geothermal power is not entirely free of pollution because of the impurities, especially sulfur, which are in the steam and water. The odor of hydrogen sulfide gas associated with geothermal resources has to be reduced as much as possible by installing special equipment at the generating unit. So far, approximately 90 percent of hydrogen sulfide in the steam can be eliminated, although these residues must also be dealt with. PG&E in California believes that by 1990, approximately 10 percent of their total power system could come from the geothermal sources of the Geysers, which will be a welcome addition to the present power plants, such as fossil-fuel-fired or nuclear power plants, which are extremely hazardous to the environment. Included in this project is a set of drawings. These drawings show only the major equipment and primary piping together with the turbine building housing.

This project is an excellent group problem and it may be advantageous to do the drawings before the modeling, although this is not necessary. These drawings can be scaled directly from the book. The housing walls can be constructed by just showing the structural steel aspects, leaving out the outer sheeting. The amount of detail, of course, depends on the emphasis placed on the project by the student and teacher. This project provides students with an example of a major industrial alternative-energy-source model project, which is quite rare.

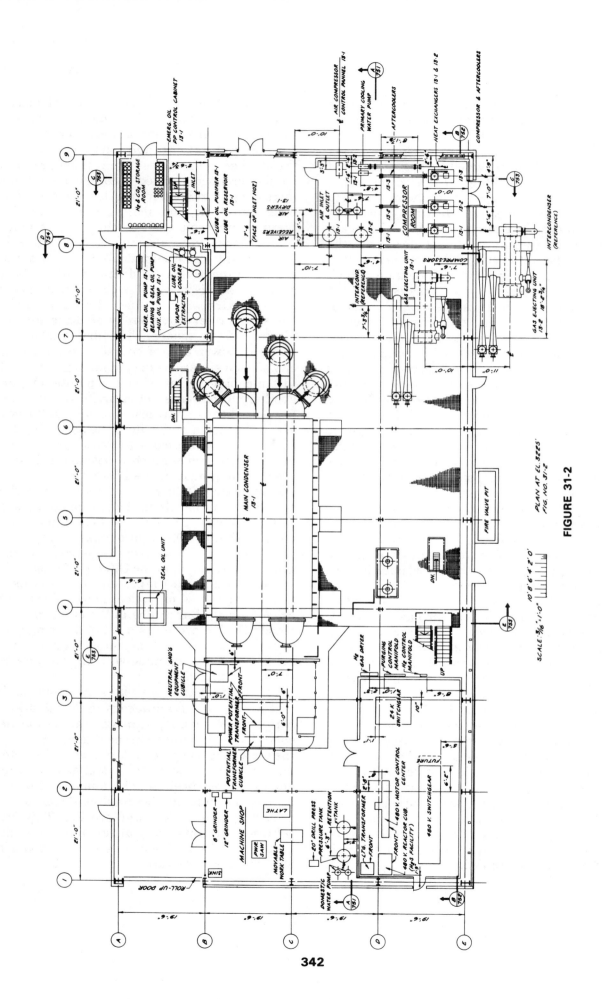

PLAN AT EL. 322'5"
FIG. NO. 31-2

FIGURE 31-2

SCALE: 3/16"=1'-0"

342

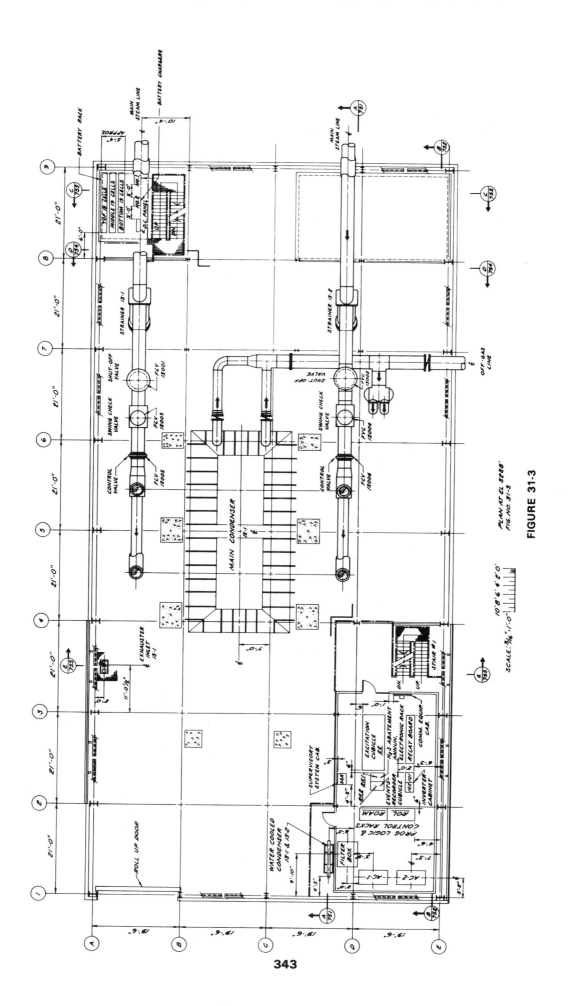

PLAN AT EL 3726'
FIG.NO. 31-3

FIGURE 31-3

SCALE: 3/16"=1'-0"

343

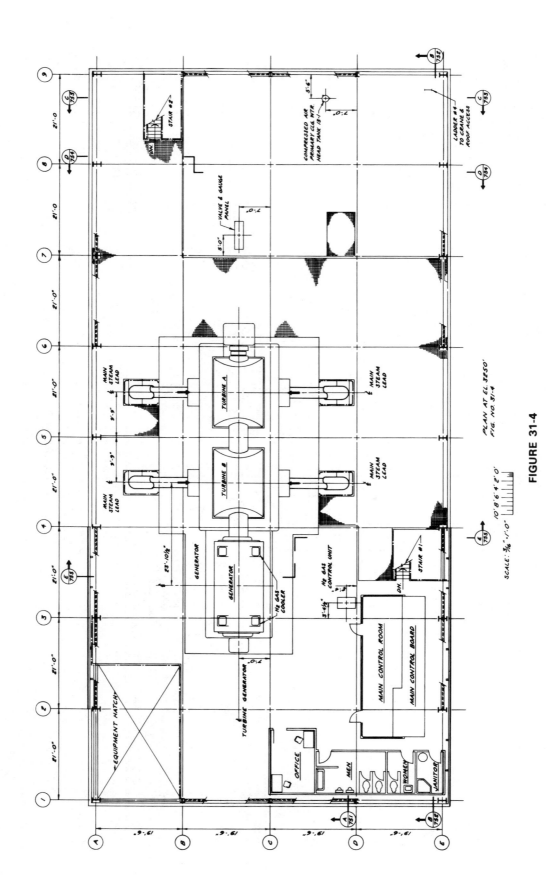

FIGURE 31-4

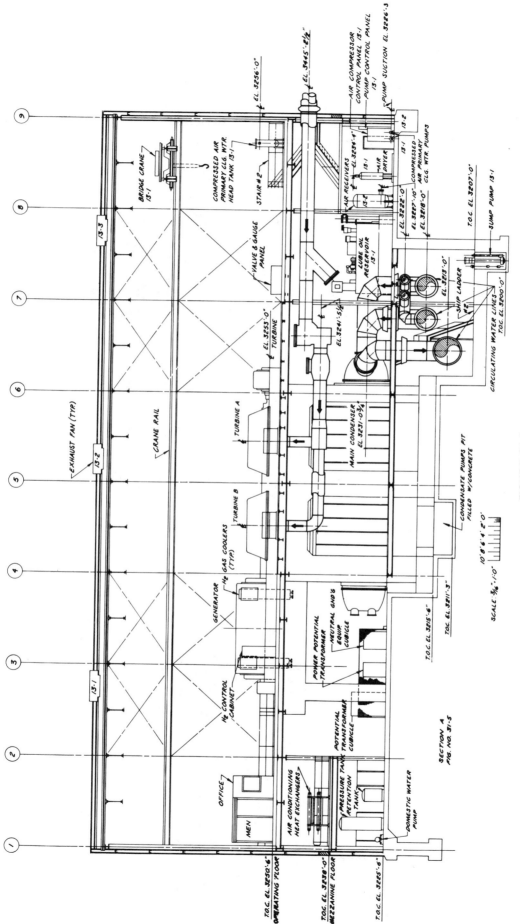

FIGURE 31-5

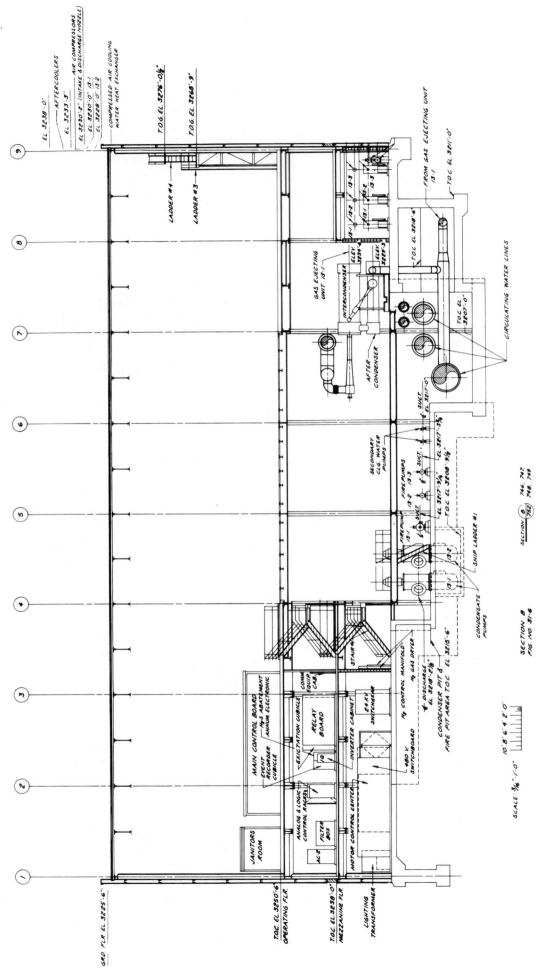

FIGURE 31-6

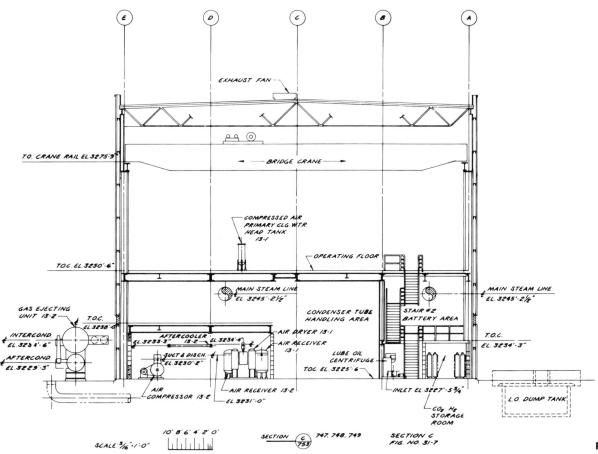

EXHAUST FAN

T.O. CRANE RAIL EL.3275'-9"

BRIDGE CRANE

COMPRESSED AIR
PRIMARY CLG. WTR.
HEAD TANK
13-1

OPERATING FLOOR

T.O.C. EL.3250'-6"

MAIN STEAM LINE
EL.3245'-2½"

MAIN STEAM LINE
EL.3245'-2½"

GAS EJECTING
UNIT 13-2

T.O.C.
EL.3238'-0"

CONDENSER TUBE
HANDLING AREA

STAIR #2
BATTERY AREA

INTERCOND.
EL.3234'-6"

AFTERCOOLER
13-2
EL.3233'-3"

EL.3234'-4"

AIR DRYER 13-1

AIR RECEIVER
13-1

T.O.C.
EL.3234'-3"

SUCT. & DISCH.
EL.3230'-2"

AFTERCOND.
EL.3229'-3"

LUBE OIL
CENTRIFUGE

T.O.C. EL.3225'-6"

INLET EL.3227'-5¾"

L.O. DUMP TANK

AIR
COMPRESSOR 13-2

AIR RECEIVER 13-2

EL.3231'-0"

CO₂ H₂
STORAGE
ROOM

SCALE: ³⁄₁₆"=1'-0"   10' 8' 6' 4' 2' 0'   SECTION C (753) 747, 748, 749   SECTION C
FIG. NO. 31-7

FIGURE 31-7

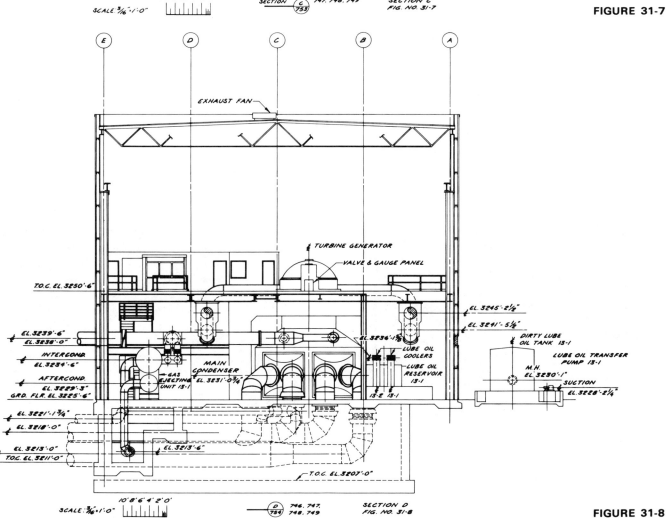

EXHAUST FAN

TURBINE GENERATOR

VALVE & GAUGE PANEL

T.O.C. EL.3250'-6"

EL.3245'-2½"

EL.3241'-5½"

EL.3239'-6"
EL.3238'-0"

DIRTY LUBE
OIL TANK 13-1

LUBE OIL TRANSFER
PUMP 13-1

INTERCOND.
EL.3234'-6"

EL.3236'-1½"

LUBE OIL
COOLERS

M.H.
EL.3230'-1"

SUCTION

AFTERCOND.
EL.3229'-3"
GRD. FLR. EL.3225'-6"

GAS
EJECTING
UNIT 13-1

MAIN
CONDENSER
EL.3231'-0¾"

LUBE OIL
RESERVOIR
13-1

13-2 13-1

EL.3228'-2¼"

EL.3221'-1¾"

EL.3218'-0"

EL.3213'-0"
T.O.C. EL.3211'-0"

EL.3213'-6"

T.O.C. EL.3207'-0"

SCALE: ³⁄₁₆"=1'-0"   10' 8' 6' 4' 2' 0'   D (753) 746, 747, 748, 749   SECTION D
FIG. NO. 31-8

FIGURE 31-8

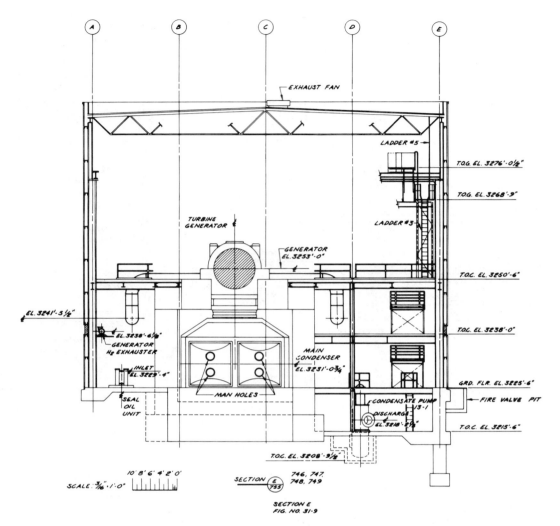

FIGURE 31-9

FIGURE 31-10

FIGURE 31-11

348

FIGURE 31-12

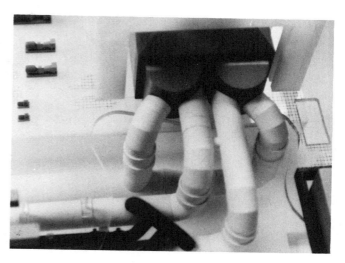

FIGURE 31-15

FIGURE 31-13

FIGURE 31-16

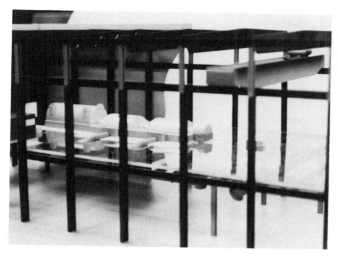

FIGURE 31-14

FIGURE 31-17

32

Solar House

FIGURE 32-1 Solar home.

Solar power represents one of the future alternatives to the energy shortage that has plagued the world in recent years. At present, other forms of energy are of paramount importance to the world at large. Solar power represents a possible alternative which is not as intensive as other forms of power generation and can be designed to fit local domestic energy needs at a favorable cost-effective rate when compared to nuclear and conventional power plants. Solar power at present cannot generate the large quantities of electricity that are needed by an industrial nation, but the systems that are presently available can diminish the dependence of society on fossil and nuclear energy systems. Solar power cannot be compared to the heavy industrial areas of nuclear, petrochemical, and fossil-fuel power generation as far as the type, size, and quality of components, piping, and so on. In general, solar systems deal primarily with 2″- to 3″-diameter piping, usually screwed or soldered fittings, valves, and so on. In solar power we are concerned with many of the same basic items as other systems, such as piping or tubing in many different materials, such as copper, aluminum, and steel; fittings, flanges, and various types of connections, such as welded, soldered, screwed; valves, ranging from control to simple gate, globe, and check valves; instrumentation, including pressure and temperature gauges; pneumatic control devices; and so on. Pumps are also of primary importance to many types of solar energy systems, as are vessels and tanks for heat-exchange units and heat-storage components. Since the temperature/pressure valves of a typical solar-powered unit are low, the solar energy system is classified primarily as a domestic and commercial plumbing system, not as a heavy industrial piping system such as nuclear and petrochemical. However, the future will bring far greater use of solar power and more complicated technically sophisticated systems.

At present, solar energy systems are used primarily for water heating, space heating, and cooling in houses, apartments, and some commercial buildings.

This project is primarily architectural in nature.

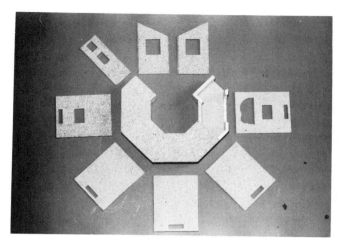

FIGURE 32-3 Walls and floor.

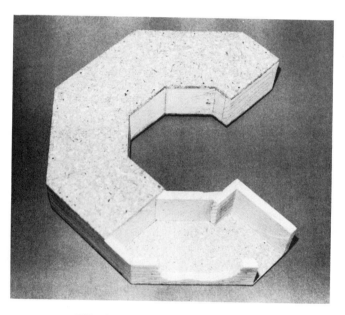

FIGURE 32-4 Floor and basement.

FIGURE 32-2 Walls.

FIGURE 32-5 Interior of house.

FIGURE 32-6 Bath area.

FIGURE 32-7 Top view of hall, bath, kitchen, and bedrooms.

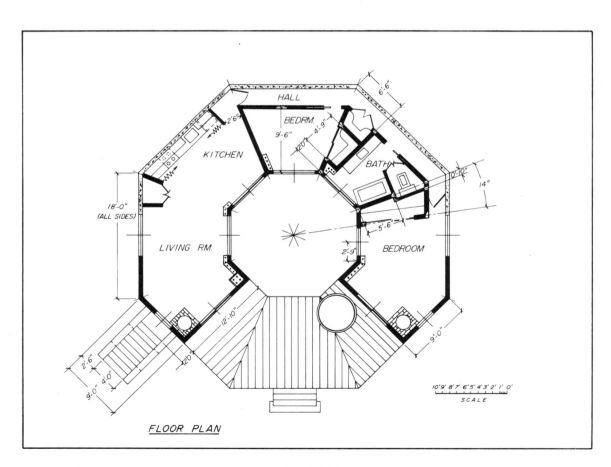

FIGURE 32-8

352

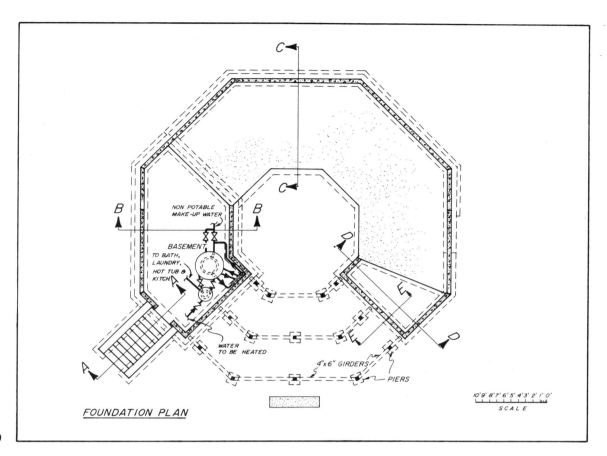

NON POTABLE MAKE-UP WATER

C

B   B

C

D

BASEMENT
TO BATH,
LAUNDRY,
HOT TUB &
KITCH

A

WATER
TO BE HEATED

4"x 6" GIRDERS

PIERS

FOUNDATION PLAN

10' 9' 8' 7' 6' 5' 4' 3' 2' 1' 0'
SCALE

FIGURE 32-9

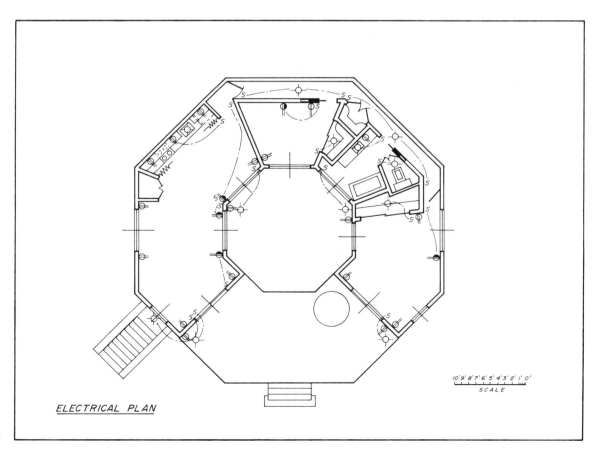

ELECTRICAL PLAN

10' 9' 8' 7' 6' 5' 4' 3' 2' 1' 0'
SCALE

FIGURE 32-10

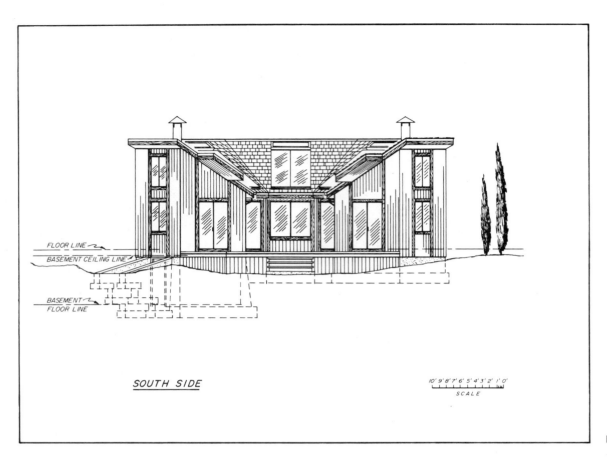

FLOOR LINE

BASEMENT CEILING LINE

BASEMENT
FLOOR LINE

SOUTH SIDE

10' 9' 8' 7' 6' 5' 4' 3' 2' 1' 0'
SCALE

FIGURE 32-11

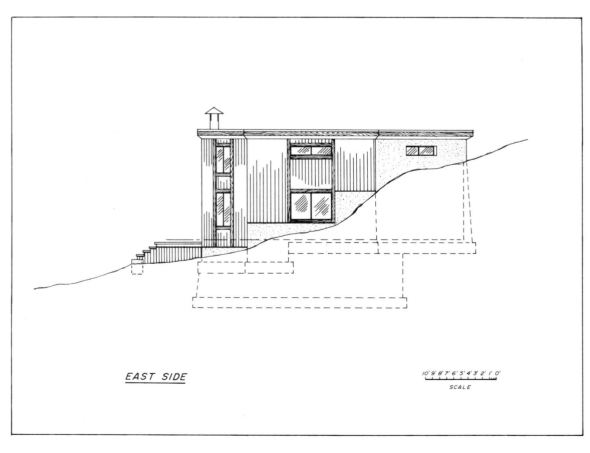

EAST SIDE

10' 9' 8' 7' 6' 5' 4' 3' 2' 1' 0'
SCALE

FIGURE 32-12

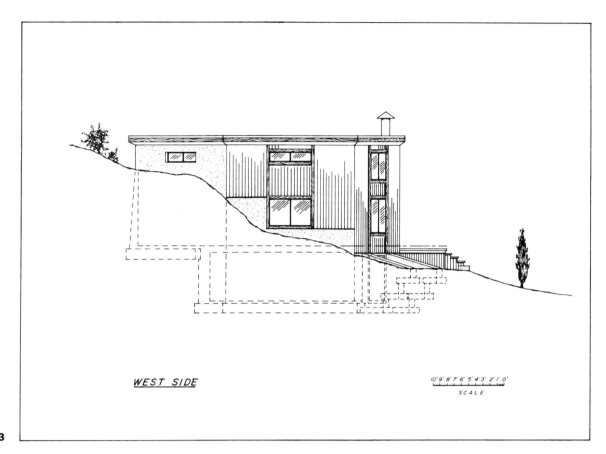

WEST SIDE

10'9' 8'7' 6'5' 4'3' 2' 1' 0'
SCALE

FIGURE 32-13

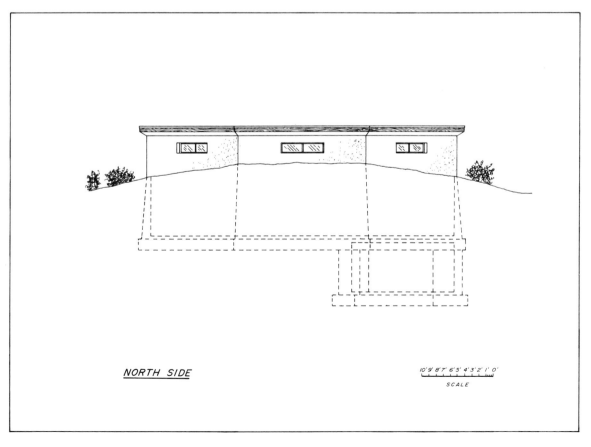

NORTH SIDE

10'9' 8'7' 6'5' 4'3' 2' 1' 0'
SCALE

FIGURE 32-14

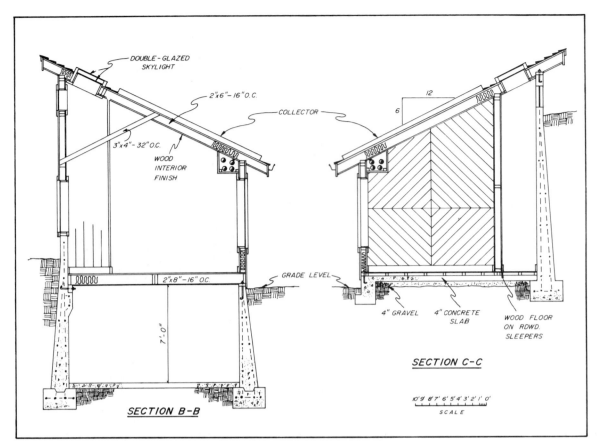

DOUBLE-GLAZED SKYLIGHT

2"x6"-16"O.C.

COLLECTOR

3"x4"-32"O.C.

WOOD INTERIOR FINISH

12
6

GRADE LEVEL

2"x8"-16"O.C.

7'-0"

4" GRAVEL   4" CONCRETE SLAB

WOOD FLOOR ON RDWD. SLEEPERS

SECTION C-C

SECTION B-B

10'9' 8'7' 6'5'4' 3'2' 1' 0'
SCALE

FIGURE 32-15

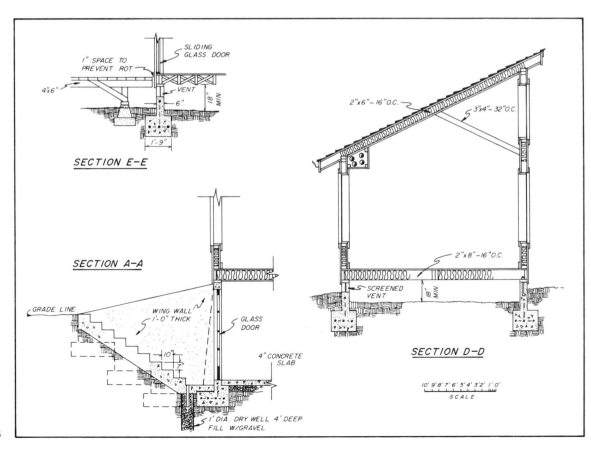

SLIDING GLASS DOOR

1" SPACE TO PREVENT ROT

4"x6"

VENT

6"

18" MIN

1'-9"

SECTION E-E

2"x6"-16"O.C.

3"x4"-32"O.C.

SECTION A-A

GRADE LINE

WING WALL 1'-0" THICK

GLASS DOOR

10"

7"

4" CONCRETE SLAB

2"x8"-16"O.C.

SCREENED VENT

18" MIN

SECTION D-D

1'DIA. DRY WELL 4' DEEP FILL W/GRAVEL

10'9'8'7'6'5'4'3'2' 1' 0'
SCALE

FIGURE 32-16

356

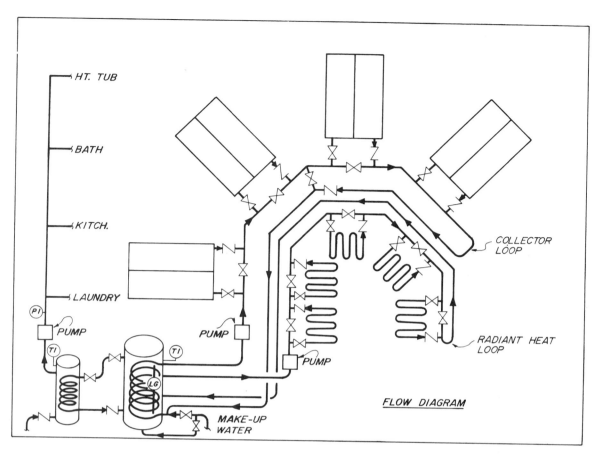

HT. TUB

BATH

KITCH.

LAUNDRY

PI

PUMP

TI

PUMP

TI

LG

PUMP

MAKE-UP
WATER

COLLECTOR
LOOP

RADIANT HEAT
LOOP

FLOW DIAGRAM

FIGURE 32-17

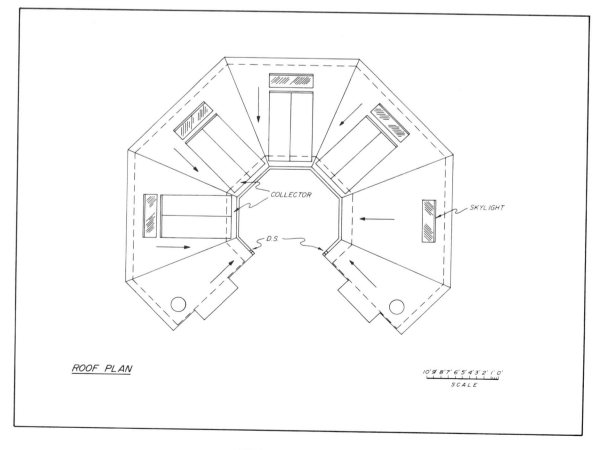

COLLECTOR

SKYLIGHT

D.S.

ROOF PLAN

10'9'8'7'6'5'4'3'2'1'0'
SCALE

FIGURE 32-18

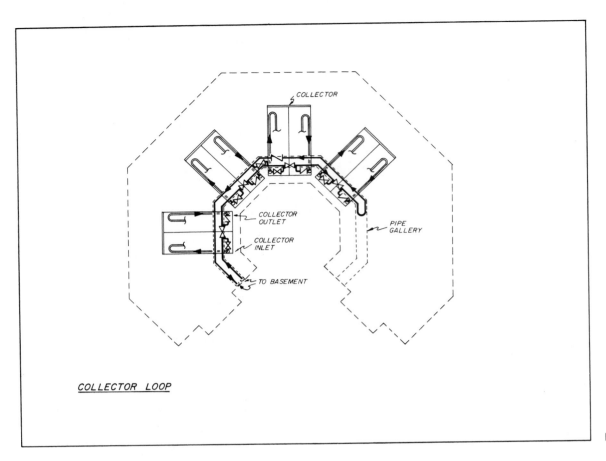

COLLECTOR LOOP

FIGURE 32-19

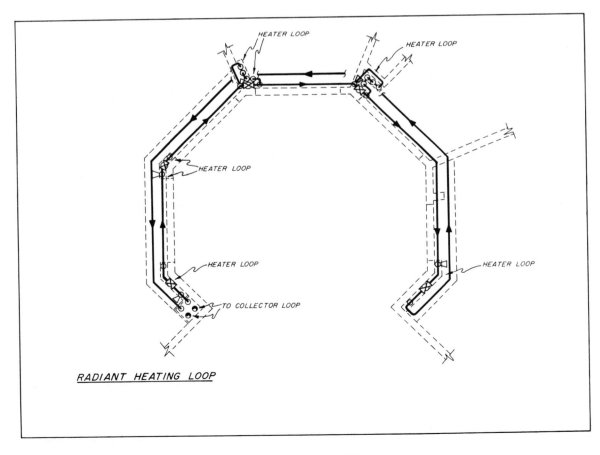

RADIANT HEATING LOOP

FIGURE 32-20

358

Piping Symbols

SYSTEM FLOW DIAGRAM SYMBOLS			
VALVES – FITTINGS – SPECIAL SYMBOLS			
1-F ANGLE VALVE		9-F CHECK VALVE	
2-F AREA DRAIN FITTING		10-F COOLING UNIT 1) AIR	
3-F BALL VALVE	OR	2) SAMPLE	
		11-F CONTROL VALVES 1) BUTTERFLY	
4-F BLINDS 1) HAMER		2) HAND OPERATED	
2) SLIP		3) GLOBE	
3) SPECTACLE		4) DIAPHRAGM	AO ⬀ AC
5-F BOILER BLOW-DOWN VALVE		12-F COUPLINGS 1) DRESSER	
6-F BUTTERFLY VALVE	OR	2) VICTAULIC	
		13-F DAMPER	
7-F CENTRIFUGAL COMPRESSOR (TURBINE DRIVEN)		14-F DIAPHRAGM OPERATED ANGLE VALVE	
8-F CENTRIFUGAL PUMP 1) MOTOR DRIVEN 2) VERTICAL	OR	15-F DIAPHRAGM OPERATED BUTTERFLY	
		16-F EDUCTOR OR EJECTOR	
3) TURBINE DRIVEN		17-F EQUIPMENT DRAIN FUNNEL	

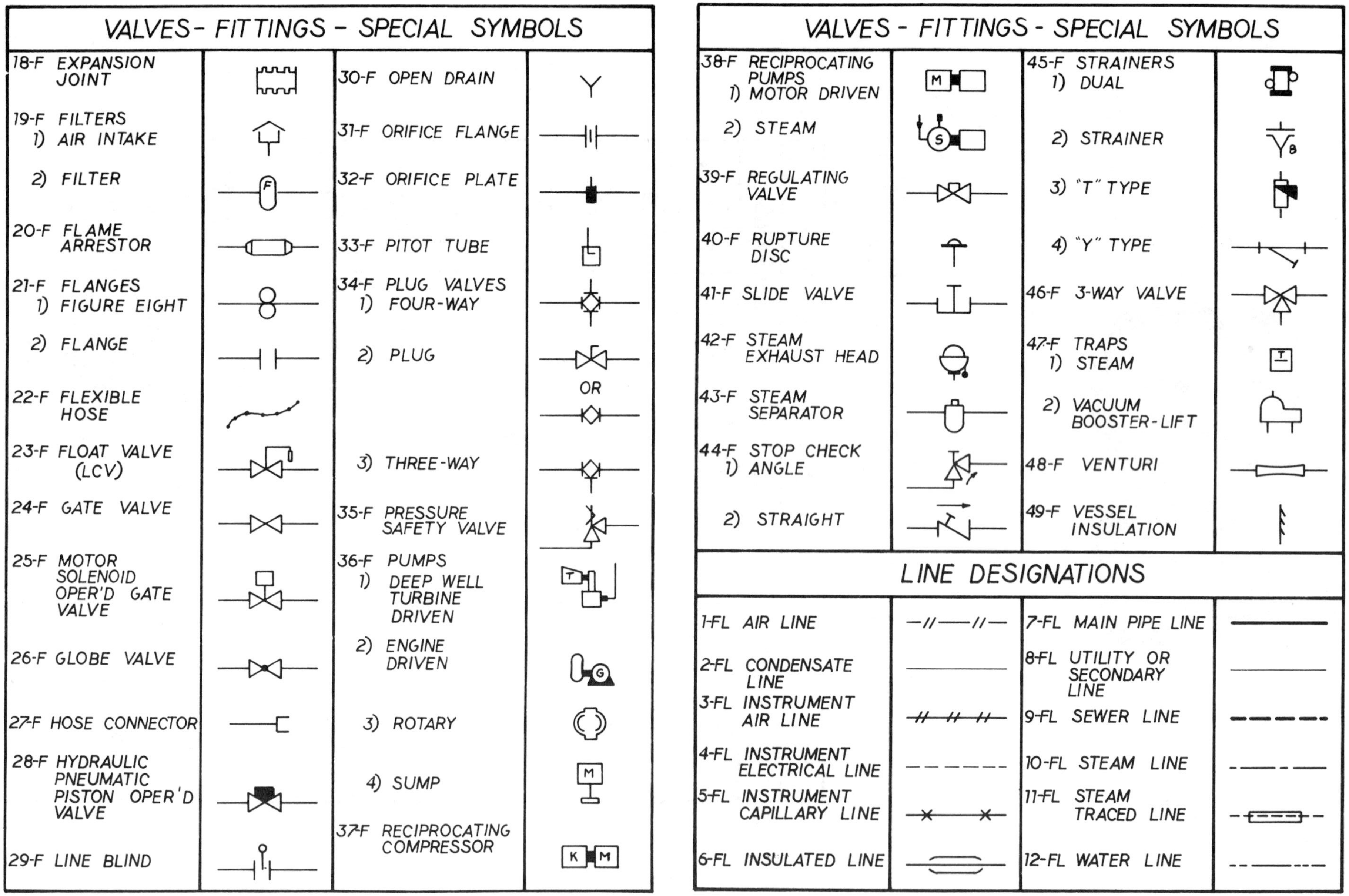

VALVES - FITTINGS - SPECIAL SYMBOLS

18-F	EXPANSION JOINT
19-F	FILTERS 1) AIR INTAKE
	2) FILTER
20-F	FLAME ARRESTOR
21-F	FLANGES 1) FIGURE EIGHT
	2) FLANGE
22-F	FLEXIBLE HOSE
23-F	FLOAT VALVE (LCV)
24-F	GATE VALVE
25-F	MOTOR SOLENOID OPER'D GATE VALVE
26-F	GLOBE VALVE
27-F	HOSE CONNECTOR
28-F	HYDRAULIC PNEUMATIC PISTON OPER'D VALVE
29-F	LINE BLIND
30-F	OPEN DRAIN
31-F	ORIFICE FLANGE
32-F	ORIFICE PLATE
33-F	PITOT TUBE
34-F	PLUG VALVES 1) FOUR-WAY
	2) PLUG
	3) THREE-WAY
35-F	PRESSURE SAFETY VALVE
36-F	PUMPS 1) DEEP WELL TURBINE DRIVEN
	2) ENGINE DRIVEN
	3) ROTARY
	4) SUMP
37-F	RECIPROCATING COMPRESSOR

VALVES - FITTINGS - SPECIAL SYMBOLS

38-F	RECIPROCATING PUMPS 1) MOTOR DRIVEN
	2) STEAM
39-F	REGULATING VALVE
40-F	RUPTURE DISC
41-F	SLIDE VALVE
42-F	STEAM EXHAUST HEAD
43-F	STEAM SEPARATOR
44-F	STOP CHECK 1) ANGLE
	2) STRAIGHT
45-F	STRAINERS 1) DUAL
	2) STRAINER
	3) "T" TYPE
	4) "Y" TYPE
46-F	3-WAY VALVE
47-F	TRAPS 1) STEAM
	2) VACUUM BOOSTER-LIFT
48-F	VENTURI
49-F	VESSEL INSULATION

LINE DESIGNATIONS

1-FL	AIR LINE
2-FL	CONDENSATE LINE
3-FL	INSTRUMENT AIR LINE
4-FL	INSTRUMENT ELECTRICAL LINE
5-FL	INSTRUMENT CAPILLARY LINE
6-FL	INSULATED LINE
7-FL	MAIN PIPE LINE
8-FL	UTILITY OR SECONDARY LINE
9-FL	SEWER LINE
10-FL	STEAM LINE
11-FL	STEAM TRACED LINE
12-FL	WATER LINE

Piping Symbols

360

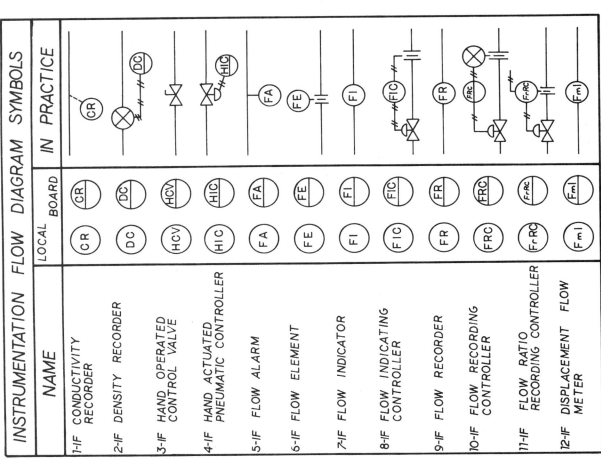

NAME		LOCAL	BOARD	IN PRACTICE
13-IF	LEVEL ALARM	(LA)	(LA)	(LA)
14-IF	LEVEL CONTROLLER	(LC)	(LC)	(LC)
15-IF	LEVEL INDICATOR	(LI)	(LI)	(LI)
16-IF	LEVEL INDICATING CONTROLLER	(LIC)	(LIC)	(LIC)
17-IF	LEVEL GLASS	(LG)	(LG)	(LG)
18-IF	LEVEL RECORDER	(LR)	(LR)	(LR)
19-IF	LEVEL RECORDING CONTROLLER	(LRC)	(LRC)	(LRC)
20-IF	LEVEL SWITCH	(LS)	(LS)	(LS)

INSTRUMENTATION FLOW DIAGRAM SYMBOLS

NAME		LOCAL	BOARD	IN PRACTICE
1-IF	CONDUCTIVITY RECORDER	(CR)	(CR)	(CR)
2-IF	DENSITY RECORDER	(DC)	(DC)	(DC)
3-IF	HAND OPERATED CONTROL VALVE	(HCV)	(HCV)	
4-IF	HAND ACTUATED PNEUMATIC CONTROLLER	(HIC)	(HIC)	(HIC)
5-IF	FLOW ALARM	(FA)	(FA)	(FA)
6-IF	FLOW ELEMENT	(FE)	(FE)	(FE)
7-IF	FLOW INDICATOR	(FI)	(FI)	(FI)
8-IF	FLOW INDICATING CONTROLLER	(FIC)	(FIC)	(FIC)
9-IF	FLOW RECORDER	(FR)	(FR)	(FR)
10-IF	FLOW RECORDING CONTROLLER	(FRC)	(FRC)	(FRC)
11-IF	FLOW RATIO RECORDING CONTROLLER	(FrRC)	(FrRC)	(FrRC)
12-IF	DISPLACEMENT FLOW METER	(Fml)	(Fml)	(Fml)

Piping Symbols

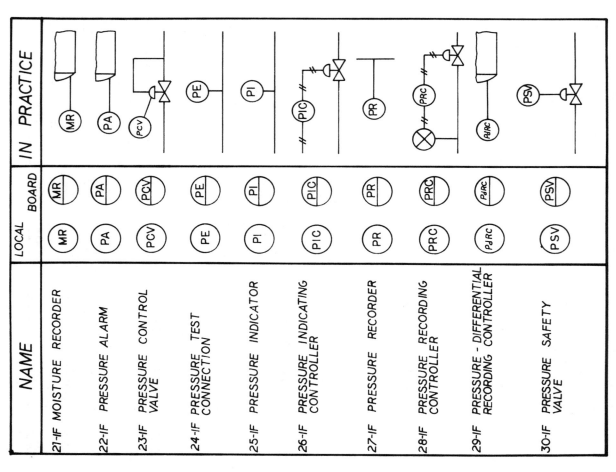

NAME	LOCAL	BOARD	IN PRACTICE
21-IF MOISTURE RECORDER	MR		
22-IF PRESSURE ALARM	PA		
23-IF PRESSURE CONTROL VALVE	PCV		
24-IF PRESSURE TEST CONNECTION	PE		
25-IF PRESSURE INDICATOR	PI		
26-IF PRESSURE INDICATING CONTROLLER	PIC		
27-IF PRESSURE RECORDER	PR		
28-IF PRESSURE RECORDING CONTROLLER	PRC		
29-IF PRESSURE - DIFFERENTIAL RECORDING CONTROLLER	PdRC		
30-IF PRESSURE SAFETY VALVE	PSV		

NAME	LOCAL	BOARD	IN PRACTICE
31-IF SPEED RECORDER	SR		
32-IF STEAM TRAP	T		
33-IF TEMPERATURE ALARM	TA		
34-IF TEMPERATURE CONTROLLER	TC		
35-IF TEMPERATURE INDICATING CONTROLLER	TIC		
36-IF TEMPERATURE ELEMENT	TE		
37-IF TEMPERATURE INDICATOR	TI		
38-IF TEMPERATURE INDICATING CONTROLLER	TIC		
39-IF TEMPERATURE RECORDER	TR		
40-IF TEMPERATURE RECORDING CONTROLLER	TRC		

Piping Symbols

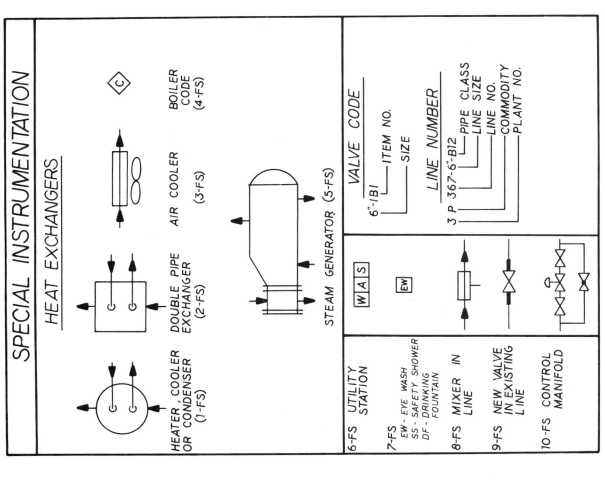

SPECIAL INSTRUMENTATION

HEAT EXCHANGERS

HEATER, COOLER OR CONDENSER (1-FS)

DOUBLE PIPE EXCHANGER (2-FS)

AIR COOLER (3-FS)

BOILER CODE (4-FS)

STEAM GENERATOR (5-FS)

VALVE CODE

6"-1B1
- ITEM NO.
- SIZE

LINE NUMBER

3 P 367-6"-B12
- PIPE CLASS
- LINE SIZE
- LINE NO.
- COMMODITY
- PLANT NO.

6-FS UTILITY STATION

7-FS
EW - EYE WASH
SS - SAFETY SHOWER
DF - DRINKING FOUNTAIN

8-FS MIXER IN LINE

9-FS NEW VALVE IN EXISTING LINE

10-FS CONTROL MANIFOLD

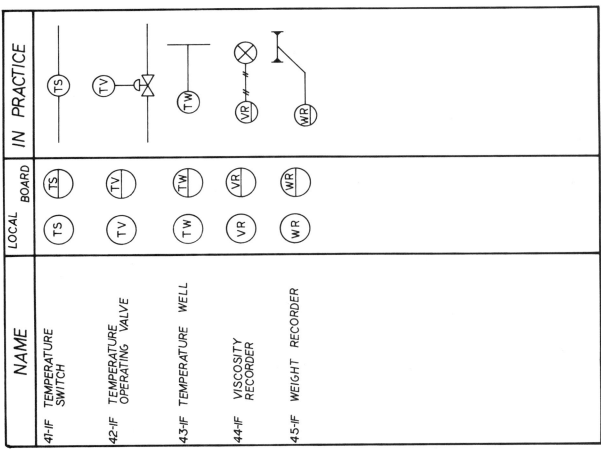

NAME	LOCAL	BOARD	IN PRACTICE
41-IF TEMPERATURE SWITCH	TS	TS	
42-IF TEMPERATURE OPERATING VALVE	TV	TV	
43-IF TEMPERATURE WELL	TW	TW	
44-IF VISCOSITY RECORDER	VR	VR	
45-IF WEIGHT RECORDER	WR	WR	

Piping Symbols

363

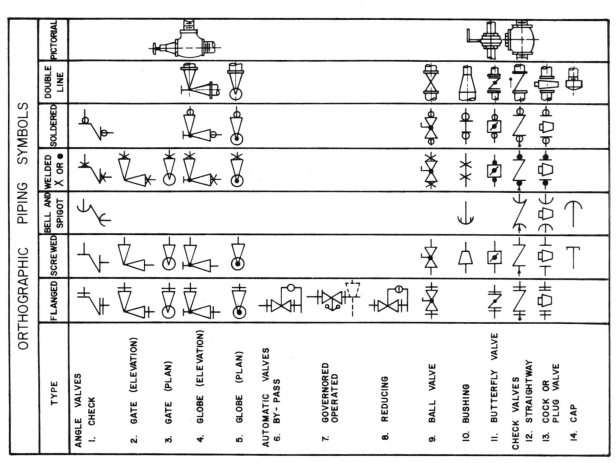

Piping Symbols

ORTHOGRAPHIC PIPING SYMBOLS

TYPE	FLANGED	SCREWED	BELL AND SPIGOT	WELDED X OR ●	SOLDERED	DOUBLE LINE	PICTORIAL
ANGLE VALVES							
1. CHECK							
2. GATE (ELEVATION)							
3. GATE (PLAN)							
4. GLOBE (ELEVATION)							
5. GLOBE (PLAN)							
AUTOMATIC VALVES							
6. BY-PASS							
7. GOVERNORED OPERATED							
8. REDUCING							
9. BALL VALVE							
10. BUSHING							
11. BUTTERFLY VALVE							
CHECK VALVES							
12. STRAIGHTWAY							
13. COCK OR PLUG VALVE							
14. CAP							

TYPE	FLANGED	SCREWED	BELL AND SPIGOT	WELDED X OR ●	SOLDERED	DOUBLE LINE	PICTORIAL
15. COUPLING							
16. CROSS, STRAIGHT							
17. CROSS, REDUCING							
18. CROSS							
19. DIAPHRAGM VALVE							
ELBOWS							
20. 45°							
21. 90°							
22. TURNED DOWN							
23. TURNED UP							
24. BASE							
25. DOUBLE BRANCH							
26. LONG RADIUS							
27. REDUCING							
28. SIDE OUTLET (TURNED DOWN)							
29. SIDE OUTLET (TURNED UP)							
30. ELBOWLET							
FLANGES							
31. BLIND							

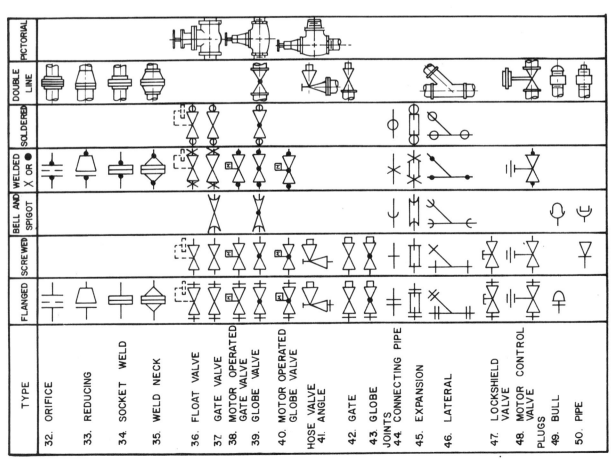

Piping Symbols

Abbreviations

A	Anchor	**APPROX**	Approximate
AC	Air Closes	**ARCH**	Architectural
ACCUM	Accumulator	**ASA**	American Standards Association
AFD	Auxiliary Feedwater	**ASB**	Asbestos
AI	All Iron	**ASME**	American Society of Mechanical Engineers
AISC	American Institute of Steel Construction		
		ASSY	Assembly
AL	All Aluminum	**ASTE**	American Society of Testing Engineers
ALY	Alloy		
ANSI	American National Standards Institute	**ASTM**	American Society for Testing and Materials
AO	Air Opens	**AUT**	Automatic Vent Trap
API	American Petroleum Institute	**AUX**	Auxiliary

AVG	Average
AWS	American Welding Society
AWWA	American Waterworks Association
AZ	Azimuth
B	Beveled
BB	Bolted Bonner
B&B	Bell and Bell
BBE	Bevel Both Ends
BC	Bolted Cap (valves and drilling)
BC	Bolted Circle
BD	Blowdown
BE	Beveled Ends
BF	Blind Flange
BF	Bottom Flat
BHN	Brinell Hardness Number
BLDG	Building
BLE	Bevel Large End
BM	Beam
BM or B/M	Bill of Materials
BOC	Bottom of Concrete
BOP	Bottom of Pipe
BR	Bronze
BRS	Brass
B/S, BOS, or BS	Bottom of Steel
B&S	Bell and Spigot
BSE	Bevel Small End
BTM	Bottom
BTU	British Thermal Unit
BUSH	Bushing
BW	Butt Weld
B/W	Butt-Weld Pipe
BWG	Birmingham Wire Gauge
C	Centerline
C	Channel
°C	Degrees Celsius
CAS	Cast Alloy Steel
CBD	Continuous Blowdown
C to C	Center-to-Center
CCW	Component Cooling Water
CD	Closed Drain
cfm	Cubic Feet per Minute
CHKD	Checked
CH-O (CH.OP)	Chain-Operated
CH OP	Chain-Operated (OR)
CI	Cast Iron
CL (₵)	Centerline
CL	Clearance
CO_2	Carbon Dioxide

CO	Clean Out
CO.	Company
COL	Columns
COMP	Compressor
CONC	Concentric
COND	Condensate
CONN	Connection
CONSTR	Construction
CONT	Continuation (Continued)
CORR.	Corrosion
CORR ALLOW	Corrosion Allowance
CPLG	Coupling
CR	Conductivity Recorder
Cr	Chromium
Cr 13	Type 410 Stainless Steel
CS	Carbon Steel
CS	Cast Steel
CS	Cold Spring
CSC	Car Seal Closed
CSO	Car Seal Opened
CTMT	Containment
CTR	Center
CTRS	Centers
CU	Cubic
Cu	Copper
CVC	Chemical and Volume Control
CWP	Cold Working Pressure
DC	Density Recorder
DC	Drain Connection
DD	Double Disc
(°) Deg.	Degrees
DET	Detail
DF	Drain Funnel
DI	Ductile Iron
DIA (ϕ)	Diameter
DIM	Dimension
DISCH	Discharge
DO	Ditto
DPI	Differential Pressure Indicator
DW	Dummy Weld
DWG	Drawing
DWN	Drawn
DXS	Double Extra Strength
E	East
EA	Each
EBD	Emergency Blowdown Valve
ECC	Eccentric
EF	Electric Furnace
EFW	Electric Fusion Welded
EJ	Ejector

EL	Elevation		FTG or FTTG	Fitting
ELB	Elbowlet		FW	Field Weld
ELEV or EL	Elevation		GA	Gauge, Gage
ELL	Elbow		GAL	Gallon
EMBED	Embedment		GALV	Galvanized
ENGR	Engineer		GEN	General
E-O-L	Elbolet		GEN	Generator
EP	Equipment Piece		GG	Gauge Glass
EQUIP	Equipment		GJ	Ground Joint
ERW	Electric Resistance Welded		GPM	Gallons per Minute
ESD	Emergency Shutdown Valve		gpm	Gallons per Minute
EXCH	Exchanger		GR	Grade
EXH	Exhaust		GRD	Ground
EXIST	Existing		GR. JT.	Ground Joint
F	Furnished by Others		GRV	Groove
F°	Degrees Farenheit		GU	Guide
FA	Flow Alarm		H_2	Hydrogen
FAB	Fabricate		HC	Hose Connection
FCV	Flow Control Valve		HC	Hydrocarbon
FD	Feedwater		HCV	Hand-Operated Control Valve
FE	Flow Element		HDR	Header
FF	Flat Face		HEX	Hexagon
F.F.D.	Flat, Faced, and Drilled		HF	Stellite Face (Hard Face)
FI	Flow Indicator		HGR	Hanger
FIC	Flow-Indicating Controller		HIC	Hand-Actuated Pneumatic Controller
FICV	Flow-Indicating Control Valve			
FIG	Figure Number or Figure		HOR	Horizontal
FL	Floor		HORIZ	Horizontal
FLD	Field		HP	High Point
FLG	Flange		HR	Hanger Rod
FLGD	Flanged		HS	Hanger Spring
Fml	Displacement Flow Meter		HTR	Heater
FO	Flow Orifice		HVAC	Heating, Ventilating, and Air Conditioning
FOB	Flat on Bottom			
FOF	Face of Flange		HVY	Heavy
FOT	Flat on Top		HYD	Hydraulic
FP	Fireproof		I	Iron
FPS	Feet per Second		IBBM	Iron Body Bronze Mounted
FR	Flow Recorder		IBBT	Iron Body Brass Trim
FR	From		IBD	Intermittent Blowdown
FRC	Flow-Recording Controller		ID	Inside Diameter
FRCV	Flow Recorder Control Valve		IDD	Inside Depth of Dish
FrRC	Flow-Ratio-Recording Controller		(") or IN	Inches
			INS (ION)	Insulate
FS	Far Side		INT	Integral
FS	Flow Switch		INV	Invert (inside bottom of pipe)
FS	Forged Steel		IPS	Iron Pipe Size
FSD	Flat Side Down		ISO	Isometric
FSS	Forged Stainless Steel		ISRS	Inside Screw Rising System
FSU	Flat Side Up		JCT	Junction
(') or FT	Foot or Feet		JT	Joint

L	Angle (a structural 4″ angle shape)
LA	Level Alarm
LB	Pound
LBS	Pounds
LC	Level Controller
LC	Lock Closed
LCR	Level Controller Recorder
LCV	Level Control Valve
LG	Length
LG	Level Glass
LI	Level Indicator
LIC	Level-Indicating Controller
LICV	Level-Indicating Control Valve
LLA	Liquid-Level Alarm
LLC	Liquid-Level Controller
LLI	Liquid-Level Indicator
LLR	Liquid-Level Recorder
LO	Lock Opened
LOC	Location
LOL	Latrolet
LP	Low Point
LR	Level Recorder
LR	Long Radius
LRC	Level-Recording Controller
LS	Level Switch
LW (I/W)	Lap Weld
M	Miscellaneous Shapes, Steel
M	Monel Metal
MACH	Machine
MATL	Material
MAX	Maximum
MB	Machine Bolts
MECH	Mechanical
M&F	Male and Female
MFG	Manufacture(ed, ing)
MFR	Manufacture
MI	Malleable Iron
MIN	Minimum
MISC	Miscellaneous
Mo.	Molybdenum
MR	Moisture Recorder
MS	Main Steam
MSS	Manufacturers Standardization Society of Valve and Fittings Industry
MW	Miter Weld
N	Nickel
N	North
NC	Normally Closed
(-) or NEG	Negative
NI	Nickel

NI	Nickel Iron
NICU	Nickel Copper Alloy
NIP	Nipple
NO	Normally Opened
(#) NO	Number
NOM	Nominal
NOZ	Nozzle
NPS	National Pipe Size
NPT	National Pipe Thread PE
NPTF	National Pipe Thread Female
NPTM	National Pipe Thread Male
NRS	Nonrising Stem
NS	Near Side
NTS	Not to Scale
NU	Needle Valve
OA	Overall
OC	On Center
OD	Open Drain
OD	Outside Diameter
OH	Open Hearth
O-O	Out-to-Out
OPER(ING)	Operator
OPP	Opposite
ORIF	Orifice
ORIG	Original
OS&Y	Outside Screw and Yoke
P	Personnel Protection
P	Plain
PA	Pipe Anchor
PA	Pressure Alarm
PC	Pressure Controller
PCMK	Piece Mark
PCV	Pressure Control Valve
PdC	Pressure Differential Controller
PdI	Pressure Differential Indicator
PdRC	Pressure Differential Recording Controller
PE	Plain End (not beveled)
PE	Pressure Test Connection
PERP	Perpendicular
PG	Pipe Guide
PH	Pipe Hanger
PI	Point of Intersection
PI	Pressure Indicator
PIC	Pressure Controller
PICV	Pressure Control Valve
P&ID	Piping and Instrument Diagram
PIM	Pressure-Indicating Manometer
PL (P$_L$)	Plate
PO	Pump Out
(+) or POS	Positive

PP	Personnel Protection	S	Steam Pressure
PP	Pump	SA	Sludge Acid
PPG	Piping	SA	Sulfuric Acid
PR	Pair (two)	SAE	Society of Automotive Engineering
PR	Pressure-Recording Controller	SB	Spectable or Slip Blind
PR	Pressure Regulator	SC	Sample Connection
PRC	Pressure Controller Valve	SC	Screwed Cap
PRESS	Pressure	SCFH	Standard Cubic Feet per Hour
PRI	Primary	SCFM	Standard Cubic Feet per Minute
PRV	Pressure-Reducing Valve	SCH	Schedule
PS	Pipe Strength	SCR	Screwed Ends
PS	Pressure Switch	SCRD	Screwed
PSD	Rupture Disc	SD	Storm Drain
PSI	Pounds per Square Inch	SE	Screwed Ends
psi	Pounds per Square Inch	SECT (SEC)	Section
PSIA	Pounds per Square Inch Absolute	SF	Semifinished
PSIG	Pounds per Square Inch Gauge	SG	Sight Glass
PSV	Pressure Safety Valve	SGA	Special Gravity Alarm
PT	Pipe Tap	SGC	Special Gravity Controller
PT	Point	SGI	Special Gravity Indicator
PVC	Polyvinyl Chloride	SGR	Special Gravity Recorder
QO	Quick Opening	SH	Sheet
QTY	Quantity	SHT	Sheet
QUAD	Quadrant	SI	Safety Injection
R	Radius	SJ	Solder Ends
RB	Reactor Building	SK	Sketch
RC	Reactor Coolant	SLOT	Slotted
RC	Recording Controller	SLV	Sleeve
REAC	Reactor	SMLS	Seamless
RECD	Received	SNUB	Snubber
RED	Reducer	SO	Slip-On
REF	Reference	SO	Steam Out
REINF	Reinforce(ed, ing)	SOL	Sock-O-Let
REQ	Required	SOL	Sweep-O-Let
REQ'D	Required	SP	Steam Pressure
RET	Return	SPEC	Specification
REV	Revision	SPG	Spring
RF	Raised Face	SPI	Special
RFC	Ration Flow Controller	SQ	Square
RFI	Ratio Flow Indicator	SR	Short Radius
RH, H.D.	Round Head	SR	Speed Recorder
RHR	Residual Heat Removal	SS	Seam-to-Seam
RJ	Ring-Type Joint	SS	Shock Suppressor
R/L	Random Length	SS	Stainless Steel
RPM	Revolutions per Minute	S.S.D.	Stretford Solution Drain
RR	Rigid Restraint	SSX	Double Extra Strong
RS	Rising Stem	STD	Standard
RTJ (RJ)	Ring-Type Joint	STIFF	Stiffner
S	South	STL	Steel
S	Standard Beam, (usually called I-beams)	STM	Steam
		STR	Strainer

STR	Structure
STRUCT	Structure
SUCT	Suction
SUPT	Support
SV	Straightening Vanes
SW	Socket Weld
SW	Socket Welding Ends
SWG	Swage
SWP	Standard Working Pressure
SYS	System
T	Steam Trap
T	Threaded
TA	Temperature Alarm
TAN	Tangent
TBE	Threaded Both Ends
TC	Temperature Controller
TC	Test Connection
T&C	Threaded and Coupled
TCV	Temperature Control Valve
TdC	Temperature Differential Controller
TdI	Temperature Differential Indicator
TdR	Temperature Differential Recorder
TE	Threaded End
TECH	Technical
TEF	Teflon
TEMP	Temperature
TEMP	Temporary
TENS	Tension
T&G	Tongue and Groove
THD	Thread(ed)
THRU	Through
TI	Temperature Indicator
TIC	Temperature Controller
TICV	Temperature Control Valve
TLE	Thread Large End
TOC	Top of End
T-O-L	Thread-O-Let
TOP	Top of Pipe
TOS	Top of Steel
TP	Type
TR	Temperature Recorder
TRC	Temperature-Recorder Controller
TS	Temperature Switch
T/S	Top of Steel
TSE	Thread Small End
T-T	Tangent-to-Tangent
TURB	Turbine
TV	Temperature Valve
TW	Temperature Well
TYP	Typical
UB	Union Bonnet

US	Unit Alarm
VA	Valve
VB	Vortex Breaker
VC	Vitrified Clay
VERT	Vertical
VOL	Volume
VR	Viscosity Recorder
W	W Shape (steel)
W	West
W	Width
W/	With
WB	Welded Bonnet
WC	Water Column
WE	Weld End
WF	Welfed Flange
WF	Wide Flange
WH	Weep Hole
WLD	Weld
WN	Weld Neck
WOG	Water, Oil, and Gas Pressure
WOL	Weld-O-Let
WP	Working Point
WP	Working Pressure
WR	Weight Recorder
WSP	Working Steam Pressure
WT	Weight
XH	Extra Heavy
XS	Extra Strong
XXH	Double Extra Heavy

Valve Descriptions

A.I.	All Iron
Al.	Aluminum
BR	Bronze
C.I.	Cast Iron
Cr.	Chromium
Cr. 13	Type 410 Stainless Steel
C.S.	Cast Steel
D.I.	Ductile Iron
F.S.	Forged Steel
HF	Stellite Face (Hard Face)
I.B.B.M.	Iron Body Bronze Mounted
M	Monel Metal
M.I.	Malleable Iron
Mo.	Molybdenum
18-8 Mo.	Type 316 Stainless Steel
N	Nickle
N.I.	Nickel Iron
NICU	Nickle Copper Alloy
PVC	Polyvinyl Chloride
SA	Sludge Acid

SA	Sulfuric Acid		F.E.	Flanged Ends
S.S.	Stainless Steel		FFD	Flanged, Faced, and Drilled
Tef.	Teflon		Flg.	Flanged Ends
			Scr.	Screwed Ends
Operating Mechanism			SE	Screwed Ends
N.R.S.	Nonrising Stem		SJ	Solder Ends
O.S. & Y.	Outside Screw and Yoke		SW	Socket-Welding Ends
R.S.	Rising Stem			

Measurements

Ratings			cfm	Cubic Feet per Minute
C.W.P.	Cold Working Pressure		gpm	Gallons per Minute
S.	Steam Pressure		psi	Pounds per Square Inch
S.P.	Steam Pressure		rpm	Revolutions per Minute
W.O.G.	Water, Oil, and Gas Pressure			
W.P.	Working Pressure		*Societies*	
W.S.P.	Working Steam Pressure		ANSI	American National Standards Institute
			API	American Petroleum Institute
Facings, Disks, and Joints			ASME	American Society of Mechanical Engineers
D.D.	Double Disc		ASTM	American Society of Testing Materials
F.F.	Flat Face			
R.F.	Raised Face		MSS	Manufacturers Standardization Society of the Valve and Fittings Industry
R.T.J.	Ring-Type Joint			
			SAE	Society of Automotive Engineers
End Connections				
B.W.	Butt-Welding Ends			

35

Glossary

MODEL TERMS

AEMS American Engineering Model Society. A society dedicated to dissemination of information on model building, designing techniques, etc., for a wide variety of model types, including piping, architecture, prototype, engineering, check, and design models.

Bending board A device used to bend plastic pipe for a model.

Basic model A model that includes all major structures, all equipment with nozzles and tagging in place ready for the piping to be installed. Included in the basic model is the substructure, or table, with either removable or folding legs.

Check model A model fabricated after all the design work has been completed. It is a three-dimensional representation of the paper design. In some cases, the after-the-fact model is even constructed after the facility has been built (commonly referred to as "as-built model"). No design is performed on the model. After-the-fact models are normally used as a checking mechanism. From an overall cost standpoint, the after-the-fact model is probably the most expensive of all models. Much of the same effort is required on an after-the-fact model and few of the benefits are derived.

Clearasite A solvent-type cement for acrylic materials.

Components, model Standardized model parts and materials manufactured by EMA. Model components can be catalog-ordered.

Design model All of the efforts that go into site models, scope models, and preliminary models culminate in the design model. However, some companies go directly to the design model phase without the benefit of site, scope, or preliminary models. The design model includes all equipment, vessels, piping, valves, fittings, electrical, instrumentation, and HVAC. The main purpose of a design model is to develop the ultimate piping arrangement on the model with a minimum amount of drawings. A design model is constructed in two stages: the basic model stage and the final model stage.

Final model Piping, electrical, and instrumentation can be designed directly on the model with only a minimum of sketches and informal drawings. Design models have also been used for study model purposes, although most of the equipment arrangements are finalized by this stage of the job.

Flag, map A small flag used to indicate interferences on a model, used after a model has been well into construction.

Material take-off from model The use of a model in compiling a complete list of materials, components, standard catalog items, etc., for the ordering of parts used for the construction of an industrial piping project.

Model In the piping industry, a model is an accurately scaled-down replica of a future industrial project, petrochemical plant, power-generation unit, or other type of installation.

Model designer A model designer should be familiar with piping specifications, pipe fittings, and hardware, vessel and equipment functions, and have a knowledge of the considerations for expansion, insulation, and supporting of piping. The designer should have sufficient design experience to be able to design on the model, or, in other words, to think on the model, and should be able to lay out and route pipe runs directly on the model from flow sheets and piping and instrument diagrams (P&ID's). Most current model designers gained their experience on the drafting board, having gone through the traditional training of printroom, piping diagrams, and piping drawings. An ever-increasing number of talented new model designers are from the ranks of model technicians, where exposure and training is concentrated and accelerated. Because the need for piping drawings will probably never be entirely eliminated, the value of a designer who can work either on the model or on the drafting board is obvious.

Model method A piping design method that bypasses much of the traditional drawing procedures by building a scale model of the system in the design stage of a piping project.

Model, preliminary A simplified model used in the beginning stages of the project to experiment with various design, placement, and other variables before the design is started. This model allows for review of the possibilities before actually committing the project to a particular course.

Model technician A model technician, frequently referred to in the United States as a model maker, is normally a craftsman familiar with power tools and the various wood and plastic materials with which engineering models are built. The technician must have a knowledge of blueprint reading (including piping drawings) and be trained in the judgment required for minimizing model detail. Usually, the model technician works from completed drawings or sketches, but in some cases may work from field measurements to construct as-built models. The technician normally works in the model shop building tables, vessels, equipment pieces, and structures for various models. The model technician is capable of attaching, altering, or changing any of the model pieces either in the shop or in the design area, and of installing piping on the model under the direction of a model or piping designer.

OSHA Occupational Safety and Health Administration; a government agency that establishes safety and code regulations concerning work areas and industrial work situations.

Peg, column The model part used to secure a column to the model base. This is a standard part that can be catalog-ordered.

Photography, model The art or science of photographing models for proposals, records, and construction stages and/or details of a particular piping project.

Preliminary model or study model The scope model, which is often considered part of the preliminary model and is not normally considered a separate function. The main purpose of a preliminary model is to determine the ultimate equipment arrangement and the location of major and/or critical lines.

Scale, model Same as a drawing scale. The scale determines the accurately reduced size of a model project, which is usually $3/8'' = 1''$ (1:33 in metric) for petrochemical complexes; $1/2'' = 1''$ (1:24 in metric) for power-generation models.

Scale piping systems The names of the two different piping systems (full-scale piping system and centerline piping system) define the difference between the two piping systems; that is, the full-scale piping system depicts all the pipes, elbows, valves, and other components in the model's full scale, while the centerline piping system utilizes full-scale valving and components with the exception of the pipe runs. The centerline system utilizes 1/16″ plastic coated wire which can easily be formed by hand. Both systems indicate the true centerlines of all piping. This is achieved automatically in the full-scale system and is accomplished in the centerline system by the use of sizing sleeves. Pipe guides, supports, and shoes are represented with equal ease in either system. The centerline system is advantageous where a photo-drawing technique is utilized. The color selection allows for differentiation of coding, and the problem of lines being hidden behind other lines is minimized. Centerline piping can be replaced on the model with full-scale piping with minimum loss of material if the need arises. The process of installing the full-scale piping provides one type of check, because it results in a more accurate representation of the piping on the finished model.

Scope model   Scope models, like site models, are preliminary planning tools. Both the site model and the scope model can be completely eliminated if the project is being constructed in an already existing building or is similar enough to an existing process that has already been constructed. The purposes of the scope model are to evolve the most efficient process and to design the building and/or structures around the process, not to design the process around the structures and/or existing building. The first step in starting on a scope model is to lay out the rough location of all major pieces of equipment. Walls, floors, and bays, together with material storage areas, should be laid out around the process equipment. If more than one floor or level is required in the scope model, the floor levels need to be completely flexible so that they can be moved during evolution of the process. The use of styrofoam is recommended to give the basic shape of all equipment. The scale for scope models should be no larger than 1/4″ = 1′. Common scales for scope models are 1/8″ = 1′ and 1″ = 10′. Before starting a scope model, the following information must be available:

1. List of vessels, towers, exchangers, heaters, compressors, and pumps, together with their approximate sizes.
2. Process flow diagram.
3. Special structure requirements.

All the major equipment and the heating, ventilation, and air conditioning systems should first be located. Pipe racks and motor control centers should be shown on the scope model.

Sections, model   The vertical and horizontal splitting of the model into workable-size proportions and components to facilitate design, layout, and movement of the project.

Site model   After the site for a given project has been selected, the site model can be started. In some cases, the site model or models may be used to evaluate or select sites. The site model requires very little actual engineering information for the new facility or project that is going to be constructed on the site. The main purpose of the site model is to provide a visual concept of the facility to be constructed with its relationship to the surrounding areas. Site models should include the bridges, rail facilities, power rights of way, and utility hookups. In addition to these, any of the major buildings adjacent to the construction site should be shown on the site model. Since site models require very little detail, they should be modeled at a scale of 1″ = 10′. A smaller scale may be chosen to minimize the size of the site model. Site models are used as an engineering tool only in the very early planning stages of a given project. Therefore, the model need only be constructed using temporary materials and in block form rather than using intricate detail parts. It is recommended that this type of model be constructed out of foam and double-sided tape to hold the block forms at their specific location. Colored tape is recommended to outline rails, waterways, bridges, roads, etc.

Tagging   A procedure whereby all lines, coordinates, equipment, valves, etc., are identified on the model by the placement of standard or special tags.

Tags, line   Labels used to identify pipes on a model.

Index